Design of
Dependable
Ada Software

BCS Practitioner Series

Series editor: Ray Welland

BARDEN ET AL Z in practice
BAXTER/LISBURN Reengineering information technology: Success through empowerment
BELINA ET AL SDL with applications from protocol specification
BRAEK/HAUGEN Engineering real time systems
BRINKWORTH Software quality management: A pro-active approach
CRITCHLEY/BATTY Open systems – the reality
EVANS ET AL Client/server: A handbook of modern computer system design
FOLKES/STUBENVOLL Accelerated systems development
GIBSON Managing computer projects: Avoiding the pitfalls
GODART/CHAROY Databases for software engineering
HARRIS-JONES Knowledge based systems methods: A practitioner's guide
HIPPERSON Practical systems analysis: For users, managers and analysts
HORROCKS/MOSS Practical data administration
JEFFCOATE Multimedia in practice: Technology and applications
LEYLAND Electronic data interchange
LOFTUS ET AL Distributed Software Engineering
LOW Writer user documentation: A practical guide for those who want to be read
MACLEAN ET AL Analysing systems: Determining requirements for change and development
MONK ET AL Improving your human–computer interface: A practical technique
O'CONNEL How to run successful projects
THE RAISE LANGUAGE GROUP The RAISE specification language
RICE VMS systems management
TANSLEY/HAYBALL Knowledge based systems analysis and design
THIRLWAY Writing software manuals: A practical guide
VERYARD Information modelling: Practical guidance
WALLMÜLLER Software quality assurance: A practical approach
WELLMAN Software costing

Design of Dependable Ada Software

G. Motet, A. Marpinard and J.C. Geoffroy

 PRENTICE HALL

London New York Toronto Sydney Tokyo Singapore
Madrid Mexico City Munich

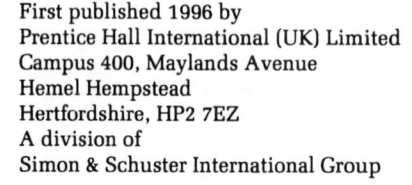

First published 1996 by
Prentice Hall International (UK) Limited
Campus 400, Maylands Avenue
Hemel Hempstead
Hertfordshire, HP2 7EZ
A division of
Simon & Schuster International Group

© Prentice Hall International (UK) Limited 1996

All rights reserved. No part of this publication may be
reproduced, stored in a retrieval system, or transmitted,
in any form, or by any means, electronic, mechanical,
photocopying, recording or otherwise, without prior
permission, in writing, from the publisher.
For permission within the United States of America
contact Prentice Hall Inc., Englewood Cliffs, NJ 07632.

Printed and bound in Great Britain by
Redwood Books, Trowbridge, Wiltshire

Library of Congress Cataloging-in-Publication Data

Motet, G.
    Design of dependable Ada software / G. Motet, A. Marpinard and
J.C. Geoffroy.
       p. cm. – (BCS practitioner series)
   Includes bibliographical references and index.
   ISBN 0-13-204967-8 (pbk. : alk. paper)
   1. Ada (Computer program language) 2. Computer software-
-Development. I. Marpinard. II. Geoffroy, J.C. III. Title.
IV. Series.
   QA76. 73. A35M68   1996
   005. 13'3–dc20   95-39763
                                                                            CIP

British Library Cataloguing-in-Publication Data

A catalogue record for this book is available
from the British Library

ISBN 0-13-204967-8

1 2 3 4 5   00 99 98 97 96

Contents

Figures Xi

Preface Xiii
    1 Objectives Xiii
    2 Background XV
    3 Audience XVi
    4 Acknowledgements XVi

Editorial Preface Xvii

Chapter 1 Introduction 1

1.1 Definitions 1

1.2 Importance of dependability 2

1.3 Reliance measurements 4

1.4 Dependability impairments 6
    1.4.1 Fault, Error, Failure 6
    1.4.2 Why do faults exist? 8

1.5 Means to master faults 14
    1.5.1 Prevent, cure and nurse 14
    1.5.2 Ada language 14
    1.5.3 Exception mechanism 16

1.6 Presentation of the book 18
    1.6.1 Three points of view 18
    1.6.2 Three domains 19
    1.6.3 Four chapters 20
    1.6.4 Several readings 21

Chapter 2 Fault Detection and Correction Techniques   23

2.1 Definition of reliance   23
2.1.1 Contract   23
2.1.2 Formalization of the contract   27
2.1.3 Contract and function   30
2.1.4 Faults and design steps   32
2.1.5 Contents   33

2.2 Fault Avoidance   34
2.2.1 Introduction   34
2.2.2 Requirements analysis   39
2.2.3 Rules   44
2.2.4 F.M.E.A.   51
2.2.5 Gathered Fault Combination Method   54
2.2.6 Fault-Tree Method   56
2.2.7 Petri nets   61
2.2.8 Design review   64
2.2.9 Synthesis   67

2.3 Fault Removal   69
2.3.1 Principles   69
2.3.2 Static analysis: extracting specifications   70
2.3.3 Static analysis: introducing invariant from specification   75
2.3.4 Dynamic analysis: functional testing   78
2.3.5 Dynamic analysis: structural testing   83
2.3.6 Dynamic analysis: structured functional approach   86
2.3.7 Dynamic analysis: introducing invariants   90
2.3.8 Dynamic analysis: execution means dependency   91
2.3.9 Synthesis   92

2.4 Fault Tolerance   95
2.4.1 Principles   96
2.4.2 Backward Recovery technique   101
2.4.3 Recovery blocks   103
2.4.4 Retry mode   107
2.4.5 Termination mode   109
2.4.6 N-version Programming   110
2.4.7 Mixed techniques   112
2.4.8 Synthesis   114

2.5 Integration   115
2.5.1 Introduction   115
2.5.2 Dependability of a system   116
2.5.3 Fault analysis and fault tolerant systems   117
2.5.4 Testability of fault tolerant systems   118
2.5.5 Measurement of performance   120

2.6 Conclusion   121

Chapter 3 Characterization of the Ada exception mechanism 122

3.1 Introduction   122
    3.1.1 Exception, exception mechanism   122
    3.1.2 Designers' points of view   123
    3.1.3 Plan   126

3.2 Nature of an exception   127
    3.2.1 Specification invariant   127
    3.2.2 Standard Domain   130
    3.2.3 Exception Domain   131
    3.2.4 Generalization of the Exception Domain to implementation   134
    3.2.5 Exception Domain and Ada   135
    3.2.6 Exception mechanism   136
    3.2.7 Overview   139

3.3 Expressing an exception   139
    3.3.1 Predefined exceptions   139
    3.3.2 User exception   143

3.4 Association   155
    3.4.1 With what is the exception handler associated?   156
    3.4.2 By what is the exception handler associated?   160
    3.4.3 What is the effect of non-association?   164
    3.4.4 Case of data   165

3.5 Raising   166
    3.5.1 Predefined exceptions   166
    3.5.2 User exceptions   172
    3.5.3 Connection to the exception handler   176

3.6 Handling   178
    3.6.1 Initial state   178
    3.6.2 Handling   181
    3.6.3 Return   183

3.7 Concurrent programming   186
    3.7.1 Predefined exceptions   186
    3.7.2 User exceptions   187
    3.7.3 Handling   191

3.8 Conclusion   192

Chapter 4 Dependable Ada Software 193

4.1 Introduction 193

4.2 Problems associated with some Ada features 194
4.2.1 Unsafe features 195
4.2.2 Hazardous features 196
4.2.3 Impact of an exception on the other features 199

4.3 Fault Avoidance 202
4.3.1 Use of Ada features 203
4.3.2 Failure Modes and Effects Analysis (F.M.E.A.) 207
4.3.3 Fault-Tree Method 209
4.3.4 Petri net 212
4.3.5 Design review 214

4.4 Fault Removal 215
4.4.1 Compilation 215
4.4.2 Test 218
4.4.3 Introducing information stemming from the contract 221

4.5 Fault Tolerance 232
4.5.1 Detection, location, diagnosis, perception 232
4.5.2 Retry 236
4.5.3 Recovery blocks 242
4.5.4 N-version programming 245
4.5.5 Exception Monitor Task 248
4.5.6 Common operation 254
4.5.7 Recovery 255

4.6 Conclusion 259

Chapter 5 Ada Exception Mechanism and Implementation 261

5.1 Introduction 261

5.2 Architecture of the Implementation 262
5.2.1 General view 262
5.2.2 Exception detection 266
5.2.3 Interactions with the R.T.S. involving the E.M.F. 269
5.2.4 Synthetic study of the paths 271
5.2.5 Interface 276

5.3 Implementation of Ada Exceptions 279
5.3.1 Introduction 279
5.3.2 Error detection 280
5.3.3 Raising 281

5.3.4 Identification	283
5.3.5 Selection of the handler	286
5.3.6 Implementation of recovery	289
5.3.7 Implementation in industrial context	292

Chapter 6 Dependability Consequences on Ada Exceptions 301

6.1 Introduction 301

6.2 Hierarchy of errors 302
6.2.1 Requirements	302
6.2.2 Use of the re-raising technique	304
6.2.3 Type Exception	307

6.3 Specification of errors 312

6.4 Relations between an erroneous program and an error handler 314

Chapter 7 Conclusion 318

Appendix A Comparison of exception mechanisms 321

A.1 Aim and contents 321

A.2 Declaration 323
A.2.1 Predefined exceptions	323
A.2.2 User exception declaration	327
A.2.3 Specification	328
A.2.4 Scope and Visibility	331

A.3 Association 334
A.3.1 With what?	334
A.3.2 Where?	336
A.3.3 When?	338
A.3.4 Up to where?	339
A.3.5 And otherwise?	340

A.4 Exception handling 340
A.4.1 Visibility of the objects, authorized statements	341
A.4.2 Parametrizing of exception handlers	343
A.4.3 Common parts of handling	345
A.4.4 Execution conditions	345
A.4.5 Exceptions occurring during exception handling	347

A.5 Relations between exception handling and erroneous treatment 347
A.5.1 Control transfer at raising time	348
A.5.2 Relations during exception handling	349

	A.5.3 Control transfer at end of exception handling	350

A.6 Raising of an exception   353
A.6.1 Implicit raising   353
A.6.2 Explicit raising   354

A.7 Propagation   356
A.7.1 Automatic propagation   356
A.7.2 Explicit propagation   356
A.7.3 Comments   357

A.8 Concurrent programming   358

A.9 Use   359

Appendix B Complete examples   363

B.1 Generic package for stack implementation   363

B.2 Invariant implementation   364
B.2.1 Resource package   364
B.2.2 Assertion definition packages   365
B.2.3 Example of invariant use   368

B.3 Recovery blocks implementation   369
B.3.1 Generic blocks monitor task   369
B.3.2 User program   371
B.3.3 User blocks   372
B.3.4 User Acceptance Test   373

B.4 N-Version Programming implementation   374
B.4.1 Generic versions monitor task   374
B.4.2 User program   376
B.4.3 User versions   378
B.4.4 User voter   379

B.5 Exception Monitor Task   381

B.6 Data Recovery   387
B.6.1 Forward technique   387
B.6.2 Backward technique   388
B.6.3 Systematic backward implementation   389

Bibliography   390

Index   402

Figures

Figure 1.1: MTTF, MDT, MUT, MTBF	5
Figure 1.2: Fault, error, failure	7
Figure 1.3: Design steps	12
Figure 1.4: Book structure	21
Figure 1.5: Book contents	22
Figure 2.1: Software contract elements	26
Figure 2.2: Techniques and production stages	33
Figure 2.3: Structured hierarchy of components	35
Figure 2.4: Component contract	36
Figure 2.5: Verification and Validation	38
Figure 2.6: Relation of cause and effect	51
Figure 2.7: F.M.E.A. worksheet	53
Figure 2.8: Internal gathered failures	55
Figure 2.9: External gathered failures	55
Figure 2.10: Global gathered failures	55
Figure 2.11: Event tree	57
Figure 2.12: Branches removed	58
Figure 2.13: Event removed	59
Figure 2.14: Petri net example	62
Figure 2.15: Deadlock detection	62
Figure 2.16: Definition of an error as a marking	63
Figure 2.17: Synthesis of fault avoidance techniques	68
Figure 2.18: Fault-tree of the if statement	72
Figure 2.19: Fault-tree of the while statement	72
Figure 2.20: Fault-tree of sequence of statements	73
Figure 2.21: Fault-tree of an integer division procedure	74
Figure 2.22: Functional equivalence	78
Figure 2.23: (input, output) test sequence	79
Figure 2.24: Output equivalence	79
Figure 2.25: Sequential specification	80

Figure	Page
Figure 2.26: Control graph	84
Figure 2.27: Time constraints between input and output values	90
Figure 2.28: Synthesis of Fault Removal techniques	94
Figure 2.29: Classification of correction techniques	98
Figure 2.30: First backward recovery implementation	101
Figure 2.31: Second backward recovery implementation	102
Figure 2.32: Frame nesting and recovery points	102
Figure 2.33: Recovery Blocks	103
Figure 2.34: Domino effect	107
Figure 2.35: Retry mode	108
Figure 2.36: Termination mode	109
Figure 2.37: N-version programming	110
Figure 2.38: N-self checking	113
Figure 2.39: Mixing fault tolerance techniques	113
Figure 2.40: Event Tree Method	118
Figure 2.41: A new error	119
Figure 3.1: Abstraction and in and out modes	129
Figure 3.2: Implementation abstraction	134
Figure 3.3: Ada implementation	141
Figure 3.4: Relations between erroneous treatment and exception handling	178
Figure 4.1: Exception and other features relationships	199
Figure 4.2: Exception Underflow cannot be raised	211
Figure 4.3: Petri net and exception	213
Figure 4.4: Normal processing of a cash dispenser	250
Figure 4.5: Error handling of a cash dispenser	251
Figure 5.1: Horizontal and vertical views	263
Figure 5.2: Components of the implementation	264
Figure 5.3: Links between implementation components	265
Figure 5.4: Detection location	269
Figure 5.5: Paths to manage exceptions	274
Figure 5.6: RTS architecture	278
Figure 5.7: First solution for propagation between tasks	282
Figure 5.8: Second solution for propagation between tasks	282
Figure 5.9: Multiple applications	298
Figure 5.10: Multiple Run-Time Systems	300
Figure 6.1: Normal and exceptional controls	303
Figure 6.2: Hierarchy of exceptions	304
Figure 7.1: Influence on the environment	319
Figure 7.2: Influence of the environment	320
Figure A.1: Relations between exception handling and erroneous treatment	348
Figure A.2: Control transfer at end of handling	350
Figure A.3: Control transfer proposal for C++	352

Preface

1   Objectives

The objectives of this book come from the authors' perception that real requirements exist concerning the *design of dependable Ada software*.

Requirements for dependable software

Software technology is more and more used in applications interacting with physical environments which evolve dynamically. Control systems of nuclear power stations or of chemical processes and automatic control systems for planes are examples of such applications. Indeed, the attributes of nuclear or chemical reactions and the altitude of a plane have values changing dynamically because of laws associated with these physical environments (laws of the nuclear or chemical reactions and law of Newton). The software embedded in the control applications aims to take these data evolutions into account and to act on these changing in order to master them. The autonomous evolutions of these environments cannot be suspended, in particular if a failure of the software of the application interacting with such environments occurs. For instance, if the plane control software stops working, it is not possible to wait for a new version to resume the current flight because the Newton law provokes a vertical descent of the plane during this waiting. In the same way the nuclear or chemical reactions evolve even if these reactions are no longer mastered by the software designed to control them. The consequences of the software behaviour interrupt may therefore be tragic. Hazardous behaviours of these software tools are also not acceptable. So, the characteristics of the environments monitored by numerous systems require used software to be dependable.

Even if the effects on human persons are not so tragic, an incorrect behaviour of software tools managing communication nets or banking systems may have important economical effects which are no more acceptable. Lastly the stop or the misfunctionning of the multiple systems embodying software components, used in daily life, are unpleasant for the clients. Moreover they provide a bad image of the companies which built the systems or of the ones which put them at disposal. The dependability of the software systems is therefore a property often essential and frequently very desirable. We will study in this book how to design software applications so that they have such a property.

Ada language

For most of the software applications, their design is completed when a program written in a programming language is available. The following steps, required to obtain an executable program, are mainly done automatically. They concern the program compilation and the linking with a Run-Time Executive which implements for instance the memory management and the input/output functions. The designer possesses just few means to act on these last steps (compilation directives -pragma-, parameters of the linkage order). The dependability of an executable program then depends on:

- the dependability of the work done by the designer whose result is a source code written in a chosen programming language and,
- the dependability of the used Run-Time Environment (compiler, linker and Run-Time Executive) of this programming language.

The choice of a particular programming language is therefore important. So, the fact that we choose Ada must be justified in relation to the two criteria highlighted above, even if the use of Ada language for large dependable applications is growing. For example, Ada was chosen for numerous spatial projects such as the Hermes space shuttle, the Columbus spatial station; it is used for parts of the software tools embedded in Airbus and Boeing aircrafts and in the Rafale fighter aircraft built by Dassault; the French and U.S. Air traffic control systems, the systems of satellite supervision produced by MATRA, CNES (Centre National d'Etudes Spatiales, French space agency), ESA (European Space Agency) with the Infrared Space Observatory satellite are other examples. This language is also used in projects relative to other various domains as for instance patient monitoring systems, the new subway system developed by GEC-Alsthom in Paris and Hong-Kong, etc. (see for instance `http://lglwww.epfl.ch/Ada/Ammo/Success/` on the World Wide Web). The language is also evaluated for a lot of new projects.

The choice of the Ada programming language comes in part from the fact that Ada possesses interesting features for real-time purpose. Most of the project managers also put dependability achievement forward. The benefits of Ada using will be described in this book. In particular we will highlight the potentialities of the exception mechanism. The Ada users are very interested by these capabilities but feel uncomfortable for this mechanism is difficult to master. Other features induce dependable capabilities of the Ada programs: types, parameter modes, etc. Frequently, the Ada application designers are not aware of the blessing of the language they use and then they do not get best benefits from it. One of the goals of this book is to present the specific capabilities of the Ada language to develop dependable software. In particular we will see that the choice of the Ada language as a programming tool has a positive influence on the dependability of the designed software.

Moreover, we signalled that the dependability of a software also depends on the dependability of the Run-Time Environment used (compiler, run-time executive). We must signal the fact that Ada is the unique large-scale distributed language which imposes a certification procedure to the proposed Run-Time Environments. On one hand this guarantees the portability of the programs and, on the other hand, the quality of the available Run-Time Environments. The first aspect also concerns dependability because in the immediate future, software systems will certainly be mainly constructed assembling reusable software components.

2 Background

The authors have experience both the theory and the practice of the presented domain. They work in a research group studying certain theoretical aspects of dependability. The results of these works are confronted with the technology constraints (hardware and software) or studied subjects come from the technology characteristics.

The industrial requirements are considered taking part in industrial research contracts with French companies -French National Centre in Telecommunication Studies (C.N.E.T.), French Atomic Energy Centre (C.E.A.), French National Company for Electricity (E.D.F.)-, as well as international companies (mainly European Projects). In particular, the interests for writing this book are issued from our participation in the European BRITE-EURAM project called IMAGES (Integrated Modular Avionics General Executive Software). This project was attached to studies led for the design of Ada software embedded in planes. The main European aircrafts manufacturers (Aerospatiale, Alenia, British Aerospace, Fokker Aircrafts, MBB) as well as suppliers (Alsys, Captec, CRI, INESC, NLR, SAS, SCYT, Sextant Avionique) and universities (NTUA and INSAT) were involved in this project. Even if our study was situated within the avionics context, the handled problems and the proposed solutions affect the general domain of dependable large scale industrial applications.

3 Audience

At first, this book is addressing persons interested in tackling the dependability domain and in having an illustration of the techniques associated with this domain on the software applications written in Ada. This book then concerns:

- the project managers who need an overview of the dependability requirements and solutions,
- the engineers having to design an Ada dependable application.

This book allows the reader knowledge in the general domain of software dependability to be improved. For this purpose we present the basic methods and techniques used in the software dependability field.

This book is also addressed to the designers of dependable applications having knowledge in dependability domain but who want to judge the potentialities of the Ada language. The use of Ada is presented with a critical point of view and we refer to other languages.

The content of this book is also interesting for beginners or experienced Ada programmers as well. The Ada language possesses a lot of specific features interesting to obtain high quality software. However this potentiality is not well-known. This is particularly the case for exception concept. An extended presentation of the Ada exception mechanism here used to detect and signal the presence of errors is developed. Moreover practical uses illustrate the capabilities and the limits of this mechanism.

Even if they have no dependable software tools to develop immediately, students must receive knowledge in dependability field because, as highlighted in the introduction of this preface, dependability is sometimes a requirement associated with the problem to be solved and is frequently considered as suitable for all software applications. So, the students must acquire fundamental knowledge on this subject. For them we include skeletons of concrete situations but also complete examples. A special effort was done to produce a pedagogical book, including a lot of figures, explaining the origin of the presented techniques, etc.

Moreover, in order to provide a presentation as exhaustive as possible, we tried to synthesize the various knowledges found in the studied domains. So our presentation is based on a large bibliography which is given in this book. Consequently this book is also useful for researchers because it provides them with a basis for further studies.

4 Acknowledgements

Of course the content of this book stems from the authors' thought. However its quality also depends on numerous persons whose names are not written on the cover. These persons read the prototypes of this book and / or gave us pieces of information or advice useful for its writing. We would like to thank Patrick De Bondelli, Michel Gauthier (Limoges University and active member of Ada France group), Jean-Marie Kubek (INSA at Toulouse), Jean-Claude Laprie (LAAS-CNRS at Toulouse), Michel Lemoine (CERT-ONERA at Toulouse), Professor I.C. Pyle (University of Aberystwyth, Wales), Ruurd Sieffers (Philips at Eindhoven), Dr. Satnam Singh (University of Glasgow), Dr. Brian Wichman (National Physics Laboratory at London), for the attention they gave to our works, for their advice and pertinent remarks.

Our research works in dependability domain are conducted in the GERII research group of the LESIA laboratory. This laboratory is located in the Electrical Engineering Department of the National Institute of Applied Sciences (INSA) at Toulouse. Many persons in the laboratory as well as in the department gave various helps to facilitate our work.

The content of this book was also influenced by the teaching done in this domain at INSA. The reactions of the students improved our presentation.

We would also like to give special thanks to:

- Gilbert Roussel from INSA multimedia department for the attention he gave to the realization of the figures and the making up into pages,
- Muriel Baldelli for her help concerning the compilation of parts of our French source text into English target text and Phil Cheetham from Kallitrad at Toulouse for compilation of other parts and for the linkage.

Finally thanks to Helen Martin and Jacqueline Harbor from Prentice Hall and Ray Welland from University of Glasgow, BCS Practitioner Series Editor, for their continuous support during the steps allowing this book to be concluded.

Editorial Preface

This book makes a valuable contribution to the literature on building dependable software. Although primarily targeted at the software developer using Ada, it contains a comprehensive tutorial on fault detection and correction techniques which is of much wider interest. For the Ada specialist, it presents an in-depth description of the exception mechanism and its use in building dependable software, together with examples and an extensive bibliography. This book should be a valuable edition to the bookshelves of all practitioners with an interest in building software for safety-critical systems.

Ray Welland

CHAPTER 1
Introduction

This chapter gives an overview of the dependability domain and then presents the field covered by this book. Our work concentrates on techniques which can be employed to obtain dependable software using the Ada language and highlights the possibilities of the exception mechanism.

We shall first of all define the term *dependability*, then present various points of view associated with this domain and give ours. This will allow us to establish the aims of the book. We shall then describe in this chapter the hurdles which must be overcome to obtain dependable software, fix the sources of the problems to be solved and justify the need to propose solutions. Lastly, we shall overview the means (techniques) which will be used to design dependable programs. These means will be described in detail in this book. In this part, we shall also justify the use of the exception mechanism as a basic tool for implementing some of these techniques. This poorly known mechanism, for which Ada offers specific features, will be frequently used.

We shall conclude this chapter with a general description of the book giving the various subjects dealt with and their correlations. The contents of this book are given in this conclusion allowing the reader to go directly to the information of interest to him.

1.1 Definitions

A client who wants a software tool, either for his or her own use or for other users, calls on a software designer. The **specification** of the software system is defined from the client's **requirements**. This specification describes the **function** that the system must perform, that is, *the purpose of the system*. The **behaviour** of the system produced defines *that which it effectively does*. The equivalence between the function expressed in the specification of a system and the real behaviour of the system produced assesses the *correctness* of this system. Obtaining correctness is one of the basic aims sought by the designer.

Dependability concerns the assessment of a system from the client's point of view and not, initially, from the designers' point of view. Thus, the definition of **dependability** is *the trustworthiness of a computer system such that reliance can justifiably be placed on the service it delivers* (Laprie, 1992). The terms of this phrase call for comments to obtain a precise idea of the motivations behind dependability.

First of all, the **service** provided by a system is defined as being the behaviour of this system *as seen by its users*. This definition implies an *interpretation* of the behaviour of the system by its users in general and initially by the client. This interpretation can be made by means of relations between the system and its users, complemented, if applicable, by data on the structure of the system if the design information is known.

The **reliance** that the client can place in a system will be governed by his or her perception of the system behaviour, that is, in the system capacity to fulfil the specified functions. The need for this reliance is accruing on account of the increasing use of systems in critical fields (avionics, nuclear plants, etc.). Obtaining this reliance is made more difficult due to the increasing complexity of the applications. These aspects will be dealt with in the following section.

The definition of dependability also specifies that this reliance must be **justified**. This implies that the client must have means at his or her disposal to assess this. Much work undertaken in the dependability field concerns the setting up of measurement means. An introduction to these measurements will be given in section 1.3.

However, this book does not deal with this purpose. Our aim is not to provide means to judge systems whose designs are completed but to help the designers to produce dependable systems. Beforehand, the designers must accept that the reasons behind the **client's critical attitude** to their work are well-founded. The client's arguments are presented in section 1.4.

We will then describe three types of **means** proposed to the designers in order to produce dependable systems (section 1.5). These means will be developed in the following chapters.

This book is therefore mainly intended for system designers. Even if the proposed techniques are general, they are applied solely to the software field and illustrated using the Ada language.

1.2 Importance of dependability

In this section, we would like to underscore the importance of dependability by giving a short presentation of its history. This allows the changes in opinion in this field to be better understood.

The dependability field has been intensively studied since the 1950s (Carter, 1987) with the development and the application of computing systems. Initially, these studies mainly concerned the hardware since it made up the main part of the systems. At that time, a few software routines were implemented in these systems and they were used for cyclic processing operations only: reading of sensors, computing of a control law, writing to actuators. The computing was sequential and simple. Consequently few faults were introduced and the proof of the software correctness (no failures) was easy. Moreover, software does not wear out: no new faults are created in the machine code by using it or as time goes by, if software maintenance, i.e. new versions, is not taken into account. So, it seemed pointless to consider software dependability.

The evolution of the systems led to a dramatic **increase in the volume and the complexity** of the software. First, this evolution was due to the growth in the complexity of the controlled process, that is to say, in the requirements for new functionalities (from traffic light control to plane flight control). In addition, the functions needed to be more complex because better performance was required (e.g. smoother control of a plane for better passenger comfort). The increase of the software part (in addition to the hardware part) was also due to the need to obtain easily maintainable systems (it is easier to modify software components than hardware ones). For these reasons numerous studies were therefore required on software dependability.

These studies were all the more important since software was **involved in more and more domains**. We can quote the transport area (trains, planes, subways, cars, space shuttles, etc.), the supervision and control area (air traffic, power stations, automatic manufacturing plants, satellites, etc.). Consequently, dependability became strategic in most of these domains. The examples quoted are from critical applications, in the sense that failures can have dramatic consequences on the human, ecological and economic environments. However, dependability must also be considered as fundamental to all systems as it defines one important criterion of the quality of the systems.

In the past, software production was considered as a craft industry not only because of the way the programs were produced but also because the client was generally the only user of the designed program. Consequently, a program failure affected only his or her own activities and he or she could have it corrected or compensate it himself. Today, the fact that the software tool is sold by the client of the designer to users makes program dependability indispensable. Due to the multiple uses to which the software is put by the users-buyers, the consequences for the client-seller may be far beyond what he or she can imagine. For example, a failure in a software package (compiler, real-time kernel, etc.) used in a system controlling a means of transport can, initially, have an immediate impact on the passengers of this type of transport. The consequences of an accident can however make the client-seller who marketed the software liable and call into question the reliance which can be placed in this software and all the other software that he or she sells. Finally, the same fate may be reserved for the designer of the program and all the programs that he or she designed.

1.3 Reliance measurements

The first way to put the definition of dependability into practice is to offer the client and the users of a system *measurements of the service delivered to justify the reliance* that they can place in the system at their disposal. However, no single measurement for assessing this exists.

Reliance in the software

Dependability can be evaluated from different points of view. Remember that the client and the users judge the *service* delivered and that this notion has been defined as the *perception of the behaviour of a system by its users*. The users can therefore favour any one perception criterion. This could be:

- **availability** defining the capacity of a system to be ready for use,
- **reliability** defining the capacity of a system to provide its service through time (uninterrupted service),
- **safety** defining the capacity of a system not to produce a *catastrophic event*.

The properties given above have a common aim which is the one that will be considered in this book: maintain the expected service or at least prevent the occurrence of undesirable actions by the system (catastrophic failures). These properties, required by the users, assume basically that a designer may have (unintentionally) introduced faults into the system. This possibility will be discussed in the following section.

Once the observation criteria have been established, measurements must be defined in order to **evaluate the reliance**. In the field of dependability, three probability factors are conventionally considered as a function of time:

- *Reliability*: the reliability measurement $R(t)$ is the probability that the system will survive (without failures) in a specified environment until time t, given that it was operational at time 0.
- *Maintainability*: the maintainability measurement $M(t)$ is the probability that the system will be restored at time t, knowing that a failure occurred at time 0. This definition supposes that the system is repairable by external actions (such as human intervention) or internal actions (using the techniques presented in this book).
- *Availability*: the availability measurement $A(t)$ is the probability that the system will be operational at time t. Time 0 defines the start of system operation. It takes into account the reliability and the maintainability: no failures occurred or normal service is available in spite of failures. We obtain the relationship $A(t) \geq R(t)$ because of the repair and the correction processes.

Mean values independent of the time may be deduced from the previous probabilities. Conventionally, these are: MTTF (Mean Time To Failure), MTTR

(Mean Time To Repair), MUT (Mean Up Time: mean operating time without failure after repair), MDT (Mean Down Time: mean time unavailable (between a failure and the resuming of the normal processing)), MTBF (Mean Time Between Failures).

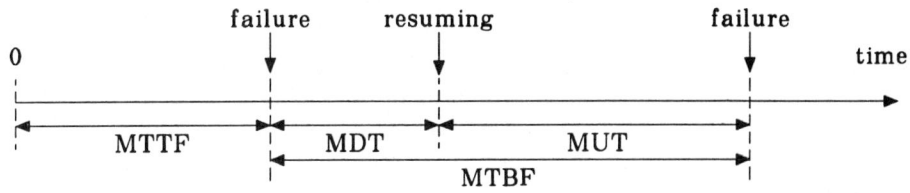

Figure 1.1: MTTF, MDT, MUT, MTBF

These mean times are illustrated in Figure 1.1. They can be obtained from the probability factors, by an integration for time zero to infinity; for instance:

$$\text{MTTF} = \int_0^\infty R(t)dt \qquad \text{MTTR} = \int_0^\infty [1-M(t)]dt$$

R(t), M(t) and A(t) are calculated using a modelling of the system's failures by means of models such as Markov processes (Littlewood, 1975).

The theoretical and practical means for obtaining these measurements will not be developed in this book even though this comprises an important part of the work undertaken in the dependability field. Detailed descriptions on this subject can be found in (Laprie, 1989a-b), (Musa, 1987), (Villemeur, 1991) or (Viswanadham, 1987). Tools such as SURF (Costes, 1981), (Béounes, 1993) have been developed to facilitate the calculations of these measurements.

Reliance in the creation process
If they are available, these various measurements allow the client to evaluate the reliance that he or she may place in the received software system. However, the increasing complexity of software will make it more and more difficult to obtain such measurements. We can therefore think that the reliance placed on software can, in part, be obtained by evaluating the **reliance placed on the software creation process**. This point of view is complementary to the previous one which consisted in obtaining a measurement on the software itself. The judgement of a system evaluating its creation process is frequently used for staple industrial products. The reliance that the client places on a product depends on its *brand image*, that is an overall evaluation of the manufacturer's *know-how* and not simply an evaluation of the purchased product.

Software creation process evaluation requires means to measure the quality of the phases intervening in this process: requirements analysis, specification, design, implementation. These means integrate an evaluation of the tools used such as the numerous design methods. The reliance in the creation process may be also measured on the intermediate results obtained. For instance, at program level, tools exist giving various values on the quality of the programming (the unused variables or subprograms, etc.). They must be extended to the design products for which the quality criteria are more difficult to be defined. Anyway, the problem of designer work quality evaluation is immense and its solutions would not provide a final conclusion. Indeed, even if the *best* design method is chosen and even if criteria on its use are defined, faults may be introduced in the created programs because the rules to be followed to obtain software do not provide *one* unique implementation way and thus *the* correct program but numerous correct and incorrect programs.

Moreover all these measurements judge a posteriori the result of the work (the software) or the way to obtain it (the software creation process) but do not provide advice which must be considered to obtain a priori more dependable software, that is to avoid or to remove or to tolerate faults. So these measurements point out the existence of problems in the design but do not help to avoid them. Our ambition is to provide the designers of Ada programs with techniques allowing them to master faults which may occur when producing software. The use of these means will be one factor increasing the quality of the software production work and so the quality of the software program and will thus justify an increase in the reliance that the users can place on produced software.

1.4 Dependability impairments

Dependability has been defined as the reliance the clients and the users can place in a system. The aim of this section is to justify the reservations that the users have about this reliance. We will discuss the many reasons which can limit the dependability of a software system. This distrust is based on the fact that as software design is totally (or partially) a human activity *faults* can occur. Before replying to the question: 'why do faults exist?', we shall start by specifying terms frequently used in this book.

1.4.1 Fault, Error, Failure

Quite often confusion reigns as to the meaning of the terms 'fault', 'error' and 'failure'. Conventionally (Laprie, 1992) in dependability terminology, distinction is made between these terms by attaching different semantics to them even if they are correlated. We will give the definitions and illustrate them by a first example:

- *Fault*: a fault is a **condition which can prevent a system from delivering** a specified function. For instance, let LP be an POSITIVE variable representing

a left page number in a publishing software tool. This variable must always have an even value. The program statements allowing an uneven value to be assigned represent a fault introduced by the program designer.
- *Error*: an error is the **appearance of a fault through the state of the system**. The state value of a program is a static definition of its execution. For instance, it can be defined depending on the values of the data and the location of the running statement. A state may be a more complicated notion. For instance, a green traffic light for the trains and an open crossing gate for the cars constitute a state of a railway control system. An error is an undesirable state which can be achieved by the system processing. The definition of an error implies that a fault may be the cause of an error. For instance, if the publishing program executes statements producing an uneven value in LP then an error occurs. Faults do not always imply errors as the statements producing the uneven value may never be executed.
- *Failure*: a failure occurs when the system is **unable to perform the required function**. The service provided by the system's behaviour is not equivalent to the function defined in the specification. Failures are due to errors but an error does not always lead to a failure. For instance, if the publishing program assigns an uneven value to LP, then an error exists. However, if the program computes the number of leaves dividing this (normally even) value by two, the result obtained is correct (no failure) if the uneven value follows on from the expected even value. It generates a failure in the other uneven value cases.

The distinction between these terms is explained examining their relations. A **fault** is introduced into a software system during its design (including its programming). It can create an **error** during the execution of the software. If the system cannot compensate for or react properly to this error, this error can provoke a **failure**. The system will be unable to perform its function. The links between the three notions are shown on Figure 1.2 where t expresses the time evolution specifying the relationship of the cause and effect.

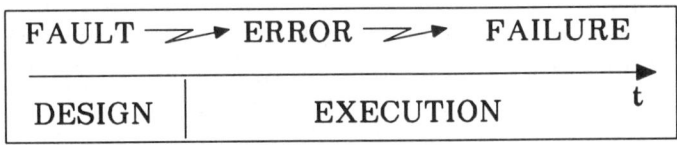

Figure 1.2: Fault, error, failure

In order to highlight the differences between the three notions, consider a procedure which contains the following statement:

```
if A>B then S1;
     else S2;
end if;
```

whereas it was specified:
  'if A > = B then S1 else S2'

The software therefore contains a fault (> instead of >=). The utilization conditions (initial data or parameters) or the computation of the previous statements may never generate the situation where the value of A is equal to the value of B. In this case, this fault will not produce an error. However, the condition 'A is equal to B' can be true (perhaps after multiple executions of the test statement) and the wrong statements (S2 instead of S1) executed. An error occurs under these circumstances. Note that, at this time, the error exists but is not detected by the software processing. Moreover, consider the case where a particular value of A is equal to the value of B. The error does not generate a failure if the execution of the block of statements associated with the `else` branch (S2) and the one associated with the `then` branch (S1) provide the same results.

Let us now assume that a procedure P including this `if` statement gives results R1 and R2 (`out` parameters) as a function of A and B (`in` parameters).

```
procedure P(A, B: in integer; R1, R2: out integer) is
begin
   ...
   if A>B then S1;
          else S2;
   end if;
   ...
end P;
```

Suppose also that if A and B have the same values, the obtained value R1 is correct but the value R2 is not. In this case, the procedure fails. If the calling procedure only uses parameter R1, i.e. if the wrong value is not used, there is a failure of the called procedure and an error in the calling one which does not lead to a failure.

The used design methods produce programs which are structured as a hierarchy of components (for instance as a hierarchy of sub-programs). The example given shows that the fault, error and failure **notions are relative to a component of a given level of the design product** and that a **propagation phenomenon** exists between the components of one level and between the hierarchical levels obtained from design.

1.4.2 Why do faults exist?

The purpose of this book is the mastering of faults to obtain dependable programs. Therefore, we must begin by explaining why faults can potentially exist in most software. Proof that there are no faults would give the users total reliance, completely justified, in the software and the use of fault-mastering techniques by the designer would lose their interest. For this, we shall first of all point out the limits of the formal methods not with the aim of demoting their interest but to show that generally and practically they do not provide a solution sufficient to meet all the requirements of dependability. We shall then establish that faults can be introduced during the conventional software production steps.

Formal approach limitations
The ideal approach for using formal methods consists in having:

- a client supplying, by means of a language, a formal expression (that is an executable one) of the specifications of the problem that he or she wishes to solve and,
- dependable means for implementing this language.

In this case, the behaviour obtained will be, by definition, the one expected. This ideal scenario runs into two major difficulties that we will deal with: the production of formal specifications and their execution.

Expressing the formal specifications of a problem is difficult first of all because of the **gap between the user's real-world concepts and the abstract-world concepts** of the specification model. The client and the designer have two abstractions (points of view) implying two languages to express the system. Generally, the real-world features are very complex and the formal specifications produced are often only an approximation of this world (Wing, 1990). On the one hand, the approximation concerns the objects to be treated. For instance, the evolution of the real (physical) environment may be continuous whereas it must be discretized to be handled by a computer. On the other hand, the approximation is due to a reduction in the number of features used to express the problem. Multiple notions arise in the real world whereas formal methods are generally associated with particular families of concepts: algebraic abstract types (Liskov, 1974) to express types of data, Calculus Communicating Systems (Milner, 1989) to express communicating sequential processes and also Petri nets (Murata, 1989), temporal logic (Emerson, 1990), etc. Consequently, formal specifications often only express a partial point of view of the declared problem. Certain specification languages do, admittedly, integrate several families of concepts but generally they do not allow all the *non-functional constraints*, such as those imposed by the environment (reaction times, user interface ergonomics, memory space, etc.), or by the client (for example, obtained from reliability requirements) to be translated.

Let us now suppose that a complete formal specification is available. In certain cases, the declaration made in the **specification** language **cannot be considered as the program to be executed**. This case arises if, in spite of the possibility of processing the specifications, their execution on the target machine does not meet the time constraints (which are part of the specifications) imposed on the final system. Another case occurs when the model allows user concepts, which are not primitive to the language, to be expressed. This means that the behaviour of these concepts must be specified later. Under these circumstances, the declaration of the specification must be translated into another language, either automatically (transformation of languages conserving the semantics of the declaration and this in a demonstrated manner) or manually, for example, by a design *refinement step*. In the latter but frequent case, a tool must mandatorily demonstrate the behavioural equivalence between the two declarations: the initial specification of the problem and the one obtained by design.

Even if executable specifications can be obtained, **dependability implies a critical attitude towards the execution means**. For example, the use of a Prolog interpreter to execute the specifications can be prohibited as the indeterminism possibility can be considered as too great a risk. Also, constraints exist on the execution means due to the technology used (software and hardware) which must be taken into consideration. An illustrative example is described in (Corbato, 1991). Let us consider function f, dependent on variable t, defined by:

```
         f(t) = k + g(t) * h(t)
   where g(t) = exp(at)
   and   h(t) = exp(-bt)
```

where a and b are strictly positive constants and k any constant.

The client wants a program to calculate f from t=0 to t=t1. To obtain it, a language can be chosen as specification means if the necessary concepts (numerical features) are included in this language. The specification of f is expressed immediately as a function with t as in mode parameter. However, the computation of this continuous function provides a discontinuity: the function suddenly takes the value k from a value t0 of t. This failure is caused by a fault made by the designer who did not take into account the accuracy limits of the microprocessor which identifies small real values as value 0.0 (underflow). More generally, this phenomenon comes from the fact that the specification execution means give an approximation of the real world. The implementation discretized the real numbers (accuracy) whereas in the mathematical world there is continuity (an infinite number of real values between two real numbers). Thus, even if a single language is used by the client and by the software engineer, the semantics of this language is different in their two worlds.

To conclude, formal approaches have to be used effectively as an assistance which is unfortunately partial. On account of this, they must be used for design in conjunction with conventional approaches which can cause numerous faults as we will show in a following paragraph. Even if formal specifications are written, we have also shown that there may be faults due to the execution means which also justifies the use of the techniques presented in this book. Another difficulty in expressing formal specifications may result from the inexperience of the designer to formally specify a problem. The way to search for a solution to a problem is mainly taught in school but the way to formulate problems is not sufficiently dealt with.

Ada as specification language

The use of the Ada language as a specification executable language is an attractive idea, the possibilities and limits of which must be examined. The language is suitable for expressing certain specification models such as abstract objects (using packages) or possibly for communicating systems (using tasks) (Goldsack, 1985). However, this language does not allow axiomatic definitions or properties to be declared. We cannot express, for example, that the succession of push then pop actions on a stack does not change its state (other than by proposing the implementation of these procedures). Also, it is not possible to write rules on synchronizations between communicating tasks. Only the specification of the individual behaviour of the tasks can be expressed in task bodies. For example, it is impossible to declare, using Ada, that a rendezvous must be accepted by one task before another rendezvous can be accepted by another task. We must signal that extensions of the language such as ANNA (Luckham, 1990) and TSL (Helmbold, 1985) were proposed to overcome these drawbacks. However, Ada seems suitable for expressing specifications during the detailed design but not for writing abstractions of high levels.

Even if a tool is completely specified in Ada, faults due to the means used for execution must be considered. For instance, constraints coming from the physical memory size of the computer used to run the program, are managed by the Ada language implementer and may influence the Ada program behaviour. For example, the raising of a STORAGE_ERROR exception depends on the memory size, the run-time size and also the compiler capabilities to optimize the executable code. Moreover, the semantics of the features described in the Ada standard (ARM, 1983) (Ada95, 1995) may be perceived as different for the designer of the Ada program and for the designer of the Ada run-time environment. Such variations correspond to two semantics associated with the features of one language. It is a problem previously quoted. For example, the Ada run-time environment is implemented, in general, using a microprocessor and a real-time kernel to extend the microprocessor's features (with tasking, exceptions, etc.). Various definitions of the task scheduler can be considered for the implementation of the parallelism on a single processor (Wichman, 1990) (Motet, 1995). These solutions consist of an approximation of the initial model (real parallelism). Therefore, the run-time behaviour of a program can vary depending on the *Ada Run-Time Environment* implementation on which the application runs and certain behaviours may not be expected (failure).

The possibilities and the limits of the Ada language concerning dependability will be examined in this book. The purpose of this paragraph was however to highlight that the choice of this good programming tool does not suppress the potentiality for faults in programs.

Faults in conventional approaches

The limits of the formal approaches lead to the use of conventional approaches whose steps (life cycle) are described in most of the books on software design. For these approaches, faults can be introduced during each step in software creation (see Figure 1.3). Six levels are distinguished:

- we said that it is often impossible to obtain from the client the correct formal specifications of the required system. So the first task of a designer is to analyse the client's requirements ((1) on Figure 1.3) from the client's explanations which are generally produced in natural languages. Therefore, any **misunderstanding** may induce faults.
- the requirements must then be translated in functional specifications. This may be the occasion of faults due to an erroneous translation ((2) on Figure 1.3).
- at each stage in the top-down refinement process used during the design, the expression of functions of components must be semantically interpreted by the designer (3) because at the next step he or she has to translate the component semantics involved at this stage. Faults may be introduced by **incorrect interpretation**.
- moreover, even if formal expressions of each function are used at each stage in the design, the **translation** is not done automatically (hand-made) and the behaviour of the solution may not be in compliance with the requirements ((2) and (3)). Faults can therefore be introduced between each design step.
- the transformation from the last (formal or not) model of the solution to an implementation model (4) (for example a program written in Ada language) frequently does not allow the equivalence between the two expressions to be proved.
- furthermore, the program must be generally translated (using a compiler) to obtain a program which can be run on a 'machine' (5). Faults may be introduced by an erroneous compiler. Moreover, we pointed out that errors can be obtained at run-time due to the differences in the interpretation of the semantics of the language features between the program designer and the run-time environment designer (6). Lastly, absence of faults in a program does not prove that there are no faults in the execution means (limits in microprocessor performance or memory size, faults in the hardware or in the run-time executive, etc.).

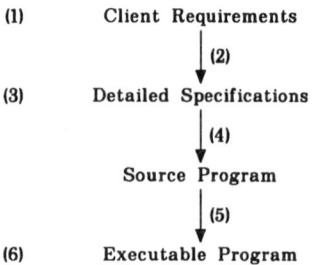

Figure 1.3: Design steps

Therefore, it is difficult to rely on the equivalence between the run-time behaviour of a program and the function required by the client as faults may be introduced during each of the software production phases.

Conclusions
The problems presented above limit the efficiency of formal methods, even if these methods are useful now and will certainly prove to be essential in the future. In particular, the verification of the non-functional aspects is not well dealt with. We pointed out that faults may still be potentially present in spite of the use of these methods. Also, a conventional approach to the problems implies high human responsibility and therefore a possible increase in the number of faults in the software produced. Moreover, the size of software tools is increasing and it seems natural that the number of faults may grow with it. This number also increases with the *complexity* of the systems. As a matter of fact, the number of behaviours for a complex system can be enormous when the combination of the numerous external events (produced by the environment) and the internal states (of the system) is taken into account. In such a situation, the undesirable states (the errors) may be numerous. As mentioned by G. Booch (Booch, 1991), *in the worst circumstances, an external event may corrupt the state of a system* (and produce an error), *because its designers failed to take into account certain interactions between the events.* This conclusion can also be applied to internal events communicated between system components.

In light of what we have just said, a serious designer who uses current design methods without completely integrating dependability requirements may produce software which does not come up to the client's expectations.

Exaggerating the distinguishing traits, two conflicting points of view concerning the fault notion can be put forward:

- that of the designer who considers that *his or her* software cannot contain faults because of the serious attitude with which he or she produced it;
- that of the client assessing the consequences of a failure of the software supplied to him.

One of the aims of this book is to bring the designers to accept the critical point of view of the clients (i.e. their non-reliance), not by judging the work produced by the designers (this is done by the measurement tools), but by providing them with **the means to master faults**. These means will be presented in the next section and developed in the other chapters.

To finally convince those software designers who would like to ignore the fault notion, we propose that they think for a moment about the Leonardo da Vinci phrase quoted by Michel Gauthier (Gauthier, 1993): 'Not predicting is already groaning'; the faults may be ignored but not their effects.

1.5 Means to master faults

In this section we will give an overall description of the means presented in this book to produce failure-free software. We will first of all introduce classes of means for dependability. Then we will present the specific utilization context, that is, the design of software written in Ada. We will also justify the reasons for using the exception mechanism as a tool for implementing error mastering means.

1.5.1 Prevent, cure and nurse

The means that we propose to the designer for taking into consideration the possible presence of faults in his or her design can be classified according to three goals:

- *Prevent*: this concerns techniques which come under the term **Fault Avoidance** and prevent the introduction of faults during design.
- *Cure*: in spite of the use of the previous techniques, faults may have been induced by design. The aim of the **Fault Removal** techniques is to detect these faults after design during the validation phase.
- *Nurse*: the aim of dependability being to obtain justified reliance in the software embedded on a target machine, the designer must admit that residual faults may still be present. For this reason, **Fault Tolerance** proposes techniques to prevent errors leading to a failure during execution.

These techniques are general. They are not associated with a special design method or a particular programming language. However we will mainly focus on the use of dependable techniques in the creation of Ada applications. In particular this language provides an implementation of an exception mechanism, allowing errors to be detected and handled.

1.5.2 Ada language

Having perceived the growing importance of software, the U.S. Department of Defense (D.o.D.) introduced the Ada language as a standard. One aim of this language is to make the design and the programming of software more efficient: easiness of the first design, production of reusable parts, etc., (Booch, 1986). Another aim is to provide features (task and time management) allowing real-time software to be programmed (Burns, 1985) (Burns, 1990). This domain concerns embedded applications for which dependability is a critical criterion. The language provides many others benefits which will not be developed in this book. Ada is now becoming a standard for industrial software design. For these reasons, we considered Ada as the language to be used to illustrate dependability principles.

Moreover, the language offers features useful for dependability. Certain concepts of the specification can be directly expressed using the language, avoiding faults due to coding. Thus, some syntactic and semantic checks can be performed if the notions of type and subtype, the direction modes (in, out) of subprogram parameters, etc. are used. For example, the assignment of an expression to a formal parameter specified in 'in' mode is detected as a fault at compile time. In addition, features corresponding to the needs stated by Software Engineering also increase the dependability. For instance, reusing a validated package prevents the introduction of faults in a new implementation. Another significant feature is the genericity. It allows *models* to be written and then customized for particular problems avoiding rewriting (and the introduction of associated faults).

Unfortunately, certain faults cannot be detected at compile time because they are caused by the semantics of the application. As an example, the compiler cannot judge whether the procedures included in a matrix management package are in compliance with the specifications since their semantics are not expressed in the language features. Thus, if the bodies of the two following specifications are inverted, this fault is not detected at compile time:

function "*"(M1, M2: **in** MATRIX) **return** MATRIX; and
function "+"(M1, M2: **in** MATRIX) **return** MATRIX;

The following extract from a program gives us another example.

subtype INDEX **is** INTEGER **range** 1..N;
T: **array**(INDEX) **of** INTEGER; ...
M:= ...; ...; get(P);
for I **in** 1..M*P **loop**
    ...
    T(I):= 2*M+I;
end loop;

If during execution, M*P becomes greater than N, then an error occurs which creates a misfunctioning because the I integer value goes beyond the INDEX range. The fault is not detected during the compilation time because the *type* feature does not allow us to express that M and P are linked by the law M*P<=N (M*P ∈ INDEX). Moreover, at run-time, the error is not detected by the evaluation of the loop index but at the evaluation of T(I) location only. This aspect can be improved by assigning the M*P expression to a variable of the INDEX type.

In conclusion, the Ada language provides means to increase the dependability of the programs produced. We will often highlight this point of view in this book. So the choice of this language is a good starting point for developing dependable software. Unfortunately, certain faults cannot be detected by the compiler and so fault avoidance, fault removal and fault tolerance techniques must be used. The Ada language offers a little-known and little-used feature: the exception mechanism. We will show in this book how this feature is useful for implementing the main fault-avoidance, fault-removal and fault-tolerance techniques.

1.5.3 Exception mechanism

The exception mechanism of the Ada language will be very frequently used to get the best out of the dependability techniques. Informal definitions of the elements involved in this mechanism are given in this section. The use of exceptions is sometimes debatable. For this reason, we will briefly present various points of view. A more formal definition of the exception and a characterization of the exception mechanism will be given in chapter 3. Other details will be provided in chapter 4 with the description of the implementation of dependability techniques with Ada.

Exceptions

An exceptional event (or **exception**) is a means for indicating that an exceptional state is reached. This notion is relatively vague as, for example, reading the end of a file can be considered as an exception if the execution of the file-processing program rarely encounters this. We would like to insist on the fact that if the time of occurrence of an exception is not planned, the exception itself is explicitly defined. The circumstances of this occurrence are generally used to name the exception (END_ERROR, STACK_OVERFLOW, CONSTRAINT_ERROR, etc.).

The notion of exception includes the notion of error. Errors have been defined as the perception of a fault through the state of the program. We can reasonably hope that such a state is rarely reached as the frequent occurrence of a design error or knowledge of the dates when this error occurs should allow us to determine the conditions which led to this undesirable state and therefore eliminate the fault at the origin of this error. In the remainder of this book, we will consider the use of exceptions only as a means for detecting and handling errors. This presentation will, however, give the reader better knowledge of this mechanism which can then be used to handle exceptional events, in the widest sense of the term.

The exception mechanism comprises first of all a means for **expressing errors**. Ada language offers predefined exceptions and allows the designers to define others.

Also, the exception mechanism is a means for **detecting errors**, undesirable states in the execution of the program. Such a detection causes an exception to be raised. The **raising** of an exception **informs the operation** which led to this state. This aspect of the exception is fundamental as it prevents the caller of the operation from ignoring the error.

The response to the raising of an exception is called exception **handling**. It generally includes statements for (Kruchten, 1990):

- reaching a well-defined state,
- reporting the problem,
- taking some recovery actions,
- continuing execution.

The Ada exception feature will be studied in more detail in this book. In this introduction, remember that it comprises a standardized mechanism for taking errors into consideration.

Points of view

Many applications with a dependability objective do not use exception mechanisms either because this possibility is ignored, or because the software implementation uses a language not offering this feature, or voluntarily.

First of all, the design of a dependable program can be envisaged using a defensive approach by 'larding' it with test statements which check if an erroneous state is encountered. This solution has major drawbacks: the result of the design becomes illegible; it mixes the usual statements with the exceptional ones, that is, those associated with the handling of errors; it does not take into account a fundamental aspect of dependability, that is, the designer may make faults and thus he or she may for instance omit test statements.

A second point of view consists in placing total confidence in the tools used and, in particular, in the validation means. Under these circumstances, taking exceptions into account may be not permitted as it is assumed that they should not be raised.

A third point of view consists in using exceptions during design either explicitly (test of an assertion and explicit raising by means of the raise statement) or implicitly (for example by defining constraint types). However, the exceptions are not conserved in the software embedded on the target computer either because we assume that all the faults have been eliminated (by using fault avoidance and fault removal techniques) or because we do not know how to handle residual faults!

Another category of designers, aware of the dependability needs, refuse to use exceptions as they consider that the mechanism is *too complicated*. This mechanism is perceived as introducing additional problems. The designers therefore try to solve the existing problems (presence of faults) by ignoring the means allowing them to be handled (the exception mechanism) which certainly does not increase the reliability of the software tools that they produce. It is of utmost importance to understand that the exception mechanism has not been added to the Ada language to create new problems but to solve problems which actually exist (Gauthier, 1993).

However, the exception mechanism is a basic feature. Its use in the dependability field requires a clear understanding of its possibilities and its limits:

- intrinsically: the capabilities of the feature itself;
- in implementing dependability techniques.

To conclude, we can say that the very limited use of the exception mechanism comes from a lack of knowledge concerning:

- the client's needs in terms of dependability: realization of the importance of the qualitative criterion of the software produced,

- the complex mechanism, that is the exception mechanism, provided to master complex problems (fault handling),
- the potentialities offered by the exception mechanism to implement numerous tools.

One of the aims of this book is to provide this knowledge and mainly to show how the exception mechanism can be used to improve the dependability of applications designed in Ada.

1.6 Presentation of the book

This book, divided into four main chapters, covers several scientific fields (dependability, exception mechanism, Ada language) and gives several points of view in the Ada software dependability field.

1.6.1 Three points of view

Fault avoidance, fault removal and fault tolerance techniques and how they can be applied or implemented with the Ada language will be explained in this book. In particular, we will show that mastering the exception mechanism during **design** improves **software dependability**.

The problems which need to be solved in the design of dependable software will be considered in this book from **a theoretical and a practical point of view**. The designer will acquire theoretical knowledge in order:

- not to have to restart studies that have already been completed leading to results that have probably already been achieved,
- to choose the most suitable means from a set of solutions with known characteristics,
- to avoid implementing one-off solutions which would require a new study for each specific case encountered,
- to make the maintenance easier by using techniques which are fully documented and known by the designer as well as by the people involved throughout the life of the software.

The study of the practical use of theoretical solutions allows:

- the theoretical aspects introduced to be illustrated,
- the constraints enforced by the features of the Ada language to be taken into account.

The practical presentation is considered from the **user's point of view** and the **implementer's point of view**. The term 'user's point of view' means the point of view of the people who use the existing practical means which implement theoretical concepts. For instance, it is the point of view of a programmer developing applications using the Ada features which implement theoretical notions. For example, the Ada exception mechanism provides a particular fault tolerance tool which can be directly used. The 'implementer's point of view' concerns the point of view of the people who implement the means (making them available for users). For instance, it is the point of view of a designer of a fault tolerance technique, not provided by an Ada language feature, used later to design a dependable application. It is also the point of view of the people creating a compiler or an Ada run-time executive. Access to the latter information is difficult, because information of this type is usually a trade secret. However, we will see that some of this information is helpful to the user. For instance, an Ada program designer must have information on exception mechanism implementation:

- to choose a compiler in accordance with the performance requirements of the application to be developed. For example, the designer of a real-time software must make a trade-off between two criteria: the execution time of the software when no errors occur and the processing time of the control transfer to the error handling;
- to efficiently use the exception mechanism knowing all the induced operations which are not expressed in the standard but which have consequences on the resulting performance of the application.

This book therefore presents three points of view: the **theory** (the concepts), the **use** of the means obtained from the concepts and their **implementation**.

1.6.2 Three domains

The subject dealt with in this book is located at the junction of three important fields: the **dependability** techniques, the **exception** mechanism concept and the **Ada** language. We will present the two first domains separately assuming basic knowledge of Ada. Then we will concentrate on the design of dependable Ada software using, in particular, the exception mechanism, mixing the three domains together.

The reader of this book should have knowledge of the Ada language. The syntax and the semantics will not be given here save information on the exception mechanism features. This knowledge can be acquired by reading the Ada standard (ARM, 1983) or more academic books such as (Barnes, 1984), (Brian, 1990) and (Gauthier, 1993). Note that the references to Ada features will be made using a special (but conventional) notation: we will put the locations in the Ada standard (ARM, 1983) between brackets. For instance [11.2(1)] refers to the 'exception_handler' syntax definition. The new features offered by the Ada95 standard (Ada95, 1995) will be considered specially concerning the exceptions. However, as the final version of this new standard was not accepted when this book was written, we could not insist on the new potentialities.

Many references to the sources of our assertions are also provided in order to help the reader who would like to study some aspects more thoroughly. The bibliography is given at the end of the book.

1.6.3 Four chapters

This book contains four main chapters plus this introduction chapter and the conclusions in chapter 6.

Chapter 2 deals with the theoretical study of the techniques which allow:

- faults to be avoided during the design stages (fault avoidance techniques),
- residual faults to be detected and corrected by analysing the code or by executing it after the design but before delivery to the client (fault removal techniques),
- programs to be produced where the occurrence of an error at run-time has the least possible effect on the behaviour (fault tolerance techniques).

Chapter 2 is very general and the techniques presented can be used with various languages.

Among the techniques above, exception mechanisms are tools frequently supplied by programming languages. A characterization of the Ada exception mechanism is given in **chapter 3**. This chapter does not provide a comparative study with others languages (given in Appendix A) but it highlights the originalities and the limits of the Ada language mechanism. This chapter should help the reader to improve his or her knowledge on the Ada exception feature.

The theoretical studies on dependability presented in chapter 2 are applied to Ada software in **chapter 4**. The Ada exception feature is specially used. We will successively present how to avoid (during the design), to suppress (during the validation stage) and to tolerate (during the execution) faults in Ada software. As this part has a practical goal, it is illustrated with Ada examples partially provided in this chapter and completely written in Appendix B.

The study of the implementation of the Ada exception mechanism is introduced in **chapter 5**. It shows the influence of the implementation choices on the performance of the applications which use such a mechanism.

This book is concluded by **chapter 6** which summarizes the possibilities and the problems to be addressed when the Ada exception mechanism is used during the design of dependable software.

1.6.4 Several readings

To sum up, this book has three dimensions. It includes **four main chapters** (chapter 2: theoretical studies on dependability techniques, chapter 3: Ada exception mechanism, chapter 4: use of dependable techniques in Ada design, chapter 5: Ada exception implementation). **Three fields** are dealt with (dependability, Ada, exception) from **three points of view** (theoretical, use, implementation).

The **dependability techniques** are presented *theoretically* in chapter 2. The Ada exception mechanism which expresses one of the techniques described, is available for the *users* (Ada program designers) and analysed in chapter 3. Other theoretical means are not directly supplied by the Ada language features. For this reason, their *implementation* will be described in chapter 4. These three points of view concerning the **dependability** domain are represented in the first column of Figure 1.4 where T symbolizes the theoretical point of view, U the user's point of view and I the implementer's point of view. The subjects (Dependability, Ada, Exception) are given on the abscissa of the graph and the numbers of the main chapters (2, 3, 4, 5) on the ordinate.

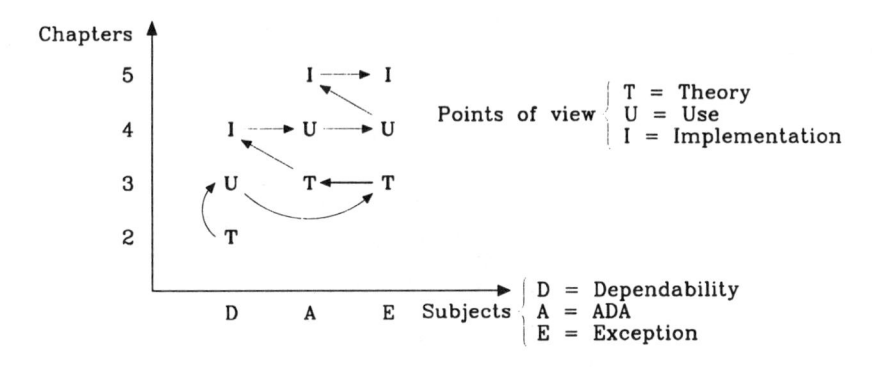

Figure 1.4: Book structure

The *use* of the **Ada language exception mechanism** for implementing dependability techniques is developed in chapter 4 (3rd line of Figure 1.4). This presentation is preceded by a *theoretical* study of the Ada exception mechanism in chapter 3 (2nd line of Figure 1.4). It is followed in chapter 5 by the description of the *implementation* of the Ada exception mechanism (4th line of Figure 1.4). This book can therefore be used to acquire knowledge in the Ada exception domain from three points of view (Theoretical, Use, Implementation).

22 Chapter 1: Introduction

The two previous paragraphs show that the book can be read from several standpoints depending on the information required. The contents follow a special logical progression shown on the graph on Figure 1.4:

- chapter 2 studies the theoretical aspects of dependability and presents the principles of the associated techniques;
- among the dependability techniques, the exception mechanism is a practical means available in the Ada language. In chapter 3, we will present this usable means and analyse it from a theoretical point of view in order to highlight the characteristics of the mechanism supplied by Ada;
- techniques other than the one offered by the exception mechanism are required for the design of dependable software. Their implementation is described in chapter 4 using the Ada language and, in particular, its exception mechanism;
- chapter 5 describes, for the Ada language, the implementation of the exception mechanism proper.

The book can be gone through in other ways depending on the reader's prior knowledge and the information sought. The structure of the book is symbolized on Figure 1.5. This figure depicts ways of accessing the contents other than the sequential access that we have chosen.

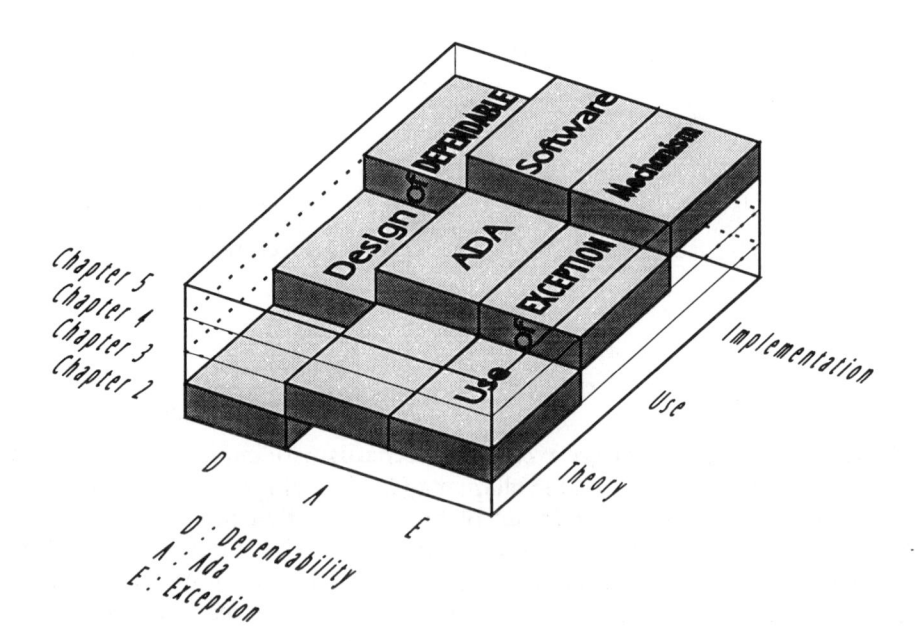

Figure 1.5: Book contents

CHAPTER 2

Fault Detection and Correction Techniques: Theoretical Points of View

We gave the definition of dependability in chapter 1: the *trustworthiness of a computer system such that reliance can justifiably be placed on the service it delivers*. This definition gives the client's point of view of a system (a software tool for us). We said that means exist for the client to measure the dependability capabilities of software. With measurements, the client evaluates a posteriori the reliance that he or she may justifiably place on a program. Our goal is quite different. We want to describe the means allowing this reliance to be obtained a priori by the designer taking the client's software dependability requirements into account during design. Of course, the use of such means by the designer will never provide absolute reliance for the client. They must be completed by measurements. The design techniques proposed in this book are not to be considered as a replacement for measurements but as complementary to them.

Firstly, to produce dependable software, the designer must be convinced that faults can exist. In section 1.4.2 of chapter 1 we detailed numerous causes of the presence of faults. Then, the designer must define the terms of reliance with the client. These terms are written into an initial contract which we will discuss in the next section. Finally the designer must use techniques to obtain the expected dependability. A general description of these techniques is given in the following sections of this chapter. Their specific use for designing Ada software will be described in chapter 4.

2.1 Definition of reliance

2.1.1 Contract

This book deals with the production of dependable software, it concerns both the software designers and the clients. In order to take the client's dependability requirements into account, we must study the relationships which should exist between the client and the designer before design begins.

Guarantees

Initially and whatever the subject of the project, the client provides requirements which are analysed by the designer to obtain functional specification defining the function to be performed by the running software. Consider a person who requires a program to compute solutions to mathematical equations and another who wants a software tool to control a railroad crossing gate. In a conventional manner (that is generally and unfortunately without taking dependability into consideration) and starting with the specification, the designer uses various techniques to produce the tool. At the end of the design, the client receives the software tool and then the following question arises in his or her mind: 'What reliance can be placed in the program produced?' To reply, the first client may use his or her tool by feeding in data and obtaining results to mathematical equations. However, he or she may have doubts about the processed output values. To increase the reliance he or she can place on the tool, the user may solve the equations himself or herself with a pencil, paper and a lot of time. After this first experiment, if the results are the same, he or she can place a *certain reliance* on the software but he or she pays for a tool to compute the results then has to do the calculations himself or herself to check their values.

To avoid such a situation, the client must express the criteria allowing the required reliance to be obtained. For instance, in the previous example, mathematical correlations may exist between the data fed in and the processed results. If these correlations are verified for specific input and output values then the user can assume that the results are correct because the behaviour of the software is in compliance with the defined reliance criteria. This approach is frequently used by physicists who like to obtain 'a rough estimate' before calculating the accurate result. This gives them an idea of the expected result. In fact they define a property which must be verified by the value obtained by precise calculations. 'The output value must be in the interval [Minimum(I), Maximum(I)]', where I is the input value, is an example of such a property.

These criteria do not define functional requirements for the software (what it has to do), or pieces of information for its implementation (how it has to do it) but other kinds of information. These criteria express **assertions** which have to be fulfilled by the software to provide **guarantees** of its correctness.

The terms of the guarantee have a different meaning than the conventional specification. For instance, consider the software used to control a railroad crossing gate. 'The gate is pulled down when the train approaches' is a functional specification. It expresses the function of the software: when approach of the train is detected the program handling must pull the gate down. 'The gate must be down when the train is passing the railroad crossing' is an assertion expected by the client. This sentence implies a state ('the train is passing the railroad crossing' and 'the gate is up') which is undesirable, that is an error in the software which controls the gate if this state is reached at run-time. Assertions are means required as guarantees by the client to help to form an opinion (i.e. to justify reliance) on software dependability.

Obligations
If the terms of the guarantee are considered after the design, they specify criteria allowing the software to be accepted or rejected. In this case, these terms are binary measurements of the reliance which the client can place on the received software. If they are used by the designer at the end of development, they are measurements of the quality of his or her work. If the conclusion is 'the software is not correct', this provides an interesting piece of information for the designer but, unfortunately, far too late.

In this book, we consider that the terms of the guarantee expected by the client must be expressed before the design so that they can be taken into account by the designer as new constraints. Fulfilling these guarantees implies **obligations** for the designer. For instance, concerning the production of the railroad crossing gate controller, the designer must manage the controller software creation with the aim of avoiding the catastrophic situation: 'the train is passing the railroad crossing' and 'the gate is up'. He or she may use means allowing the client's assertions to be proved. These obligations will influence the way the software tools are produced. They require the use of new techniques which will be presented in this book.

Assertions and assumptions
The **assertions** express properties expected from the client as guarantees and considered by the designer as obligations to be fulfilled. They concern the results (data or behaviour) provided by the software. However a software tool is not only characterized by the results produced (output values) but also by the services offered, which can be asked for, (input values) and the way of asking for them (for instance the sequencing of the service calls). To produce dependable software, the designer must have guarantees concerning the future use of the program that has to be produced. The occurrence of a malfunction may not be considered as a failure if the software is not used in the assumed way. For instance, in (Leveson, 1991) an incident is given concerning an aircraft with a flight-control system not programmed to handle a particular altitude because it was assumed that the aircraft could not attain this altitude.

Such guarantees required by the designer provide obligations for the future user. They are **assumptions** which must therefore be initially given by the client and considered by the designer at the beginning of the design phase.

For example, let us consider the railroad crossing gate control software. The train approach detection, then the processing of this signal and finally the action on the gate, take time. So the client must specify the minimum distance between the approach sensor and the railroad crossing and the maximum speed of the trains. These assumptions fix obligations for the client and allow a minimum time to handle a train approach detection to be guaranteed to the software designer.

In conclusion, dependability implies that new relationships must be established and new pieces of information communicated between the client and the designer before design starts.

Elements of the contract

In order to produce dependable software, a **contract** must be drawn up. It states both the obligations and the guarantees (Meyer, 1991) for both the designer and the client of the software. This contract adds constraints which define both assumptions and assertions to the functional specification. For instance, 'the gate must be down when the train is passing the railroad crossing' is an assertion for the client (he or she asks for this guarantee) and also for the designer (he or she is obliged to obtain this result). 'The plane's maximum altitude is A' is an assumption for the client (obligation for use) as well as for the designer (guarantee for use). The relationships between designer and client, assertion and assumption, and obligation and guarantee can be synthesized as follows:

- for the **designer**, an **assertion** places **obligations** on the realization;
- for the **client**, an **assertion** provides a **guarantee** on the software behaviour or the detection of a malfunction;
- for the **designer**, an **assumption** provides a **guarantee** concerning the software's directions for use;
- for the **client**, an **assumption** corresponds to **obligations** for use.

The initial contract, written mainly by the client and partially by the designer, specifies the assertions and the assumptions on the software, to define obligations and guarantees for each partner. The elements associated with this contract are represented on Figure 2.1.

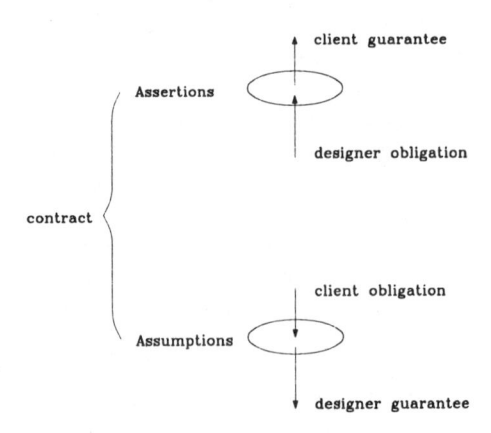

Figure 2.1: Software contract elements

Contract contents

For the client, software is judged dependable if its use, in accordance with the assumptions, verifies the assertions. The negation of an assertion constitutes a failure: the expected service is not provided. The designer, assuming correct use, must therefore produce software whose results are in accordance with the assertions (i.e. without failures).

Some clients would like to say that the contract is defined by 'everything which is not specified'. However it is generally impossible to give an exhaustive expression of the negation of the specification as it would have to define all other possible systems. It is therefore difficult to check all the possibilities. Moreover the client is only interested in the verification of the effectiveness of certain particular properties. For instance, a client may not be concerned by the fact that the railroad crossing gate is down for a long time but he or she wants to be sure that the gate is down when the train is passing. For these reasons, the contract only defines several characteristic properties linking assertions and assumptions that the software to be designed must possess.

The terms written in the contract are closer to those provided by the client's requirements than those deduced analysing these requirements and expressed in the functional specifications. The system properties expected are equivalent to the benefits anticipated by the client who requires the software realization. For example, the railway manager wants a system which assures that the gate is closed when the train is passing. It is really a requirement which justifies the necessity to have a realization of a control system. The contract terms are therefore the first pieces of information generally expressed by the client before obtaining the functional specifications. However the designer often considers the requirements expression as a step one aim of which is to allow the specifications to be produced. On the contrary, the designer of a dependable application must pay special attention to the client's requirements to detect information expressing dependability contract elements.

Note that this book deals only with elements of the contract corresponding to functional aspects. Thus ergonomic expression of a software tool will not be taken into account. Concerning temporal constraints only some remarks will be written.

2.1.2 Formalization of the contract

The contract concluded between the client and the designer defines relations between the assumptions and the assertions. Informal expressions of these relations are called **rules**. Several types of operators expressing several kinds of relations may exist.

Implication
A first simple expression is the **application** which relates a set of input values to a set of output values: $\forall\, i \in I \Rightarrow o=F(i) \in O$, where $o=F(i)$ expresses the value

obtained as the result of the function F of the software from input value i. The assumption is i ∈ I and the assertion is o ∈ O. We must highlight the fact that the previously given relation does not specify the exact value of o as the result of F(i) but it just expresses that the unknown value is a member of set O. The constraints imposed on use or on implementation are limited to guaranteeing that values belong to sets. For instance, for function ABSOLUTE_VALUE, we can state that the value to be communicated as input parameter must belong to the INTEGER set and that the calculated and returned value must belong to the NATURAL set.

Boolean relations more complex than 'belonging to a set' can be defined on the input values and on the output values. The contract is then of the following type:

$\forall$ i such that B1(i) is true $\Rightarrow$ B2(o) is true, where o=F(i).

B1 (respectively B2) is any Boolean function on the input values (respectively on the output values). For instance, if procedure F calculates the MAXIMUM and MINIMUM values (output) of a list L (input) then NOT_EMPTY(L) is an assumption on L and MINIMUM<=MAXIMUM is an assertion on the result.

Invariant

The **invariant** concept constitutes a more general relation between assumptions and assertions to define formally the rules. We will deduce progressively the definition of the *invariant* notion in 3 steps: Input-Output relations, introduction of the internal state then the generalized state.

① **Input-Output relations**

The implication relation between two Boolean functions (one on input values and one on output values) is generalized into a relation correlating values i and o by a Boolean function called INVARIANT:

INVARIANT(i,o) where o=F(i).

Thus, for the previous example of procedure F which computes the MINIMUM and the MAXIMUM values of a list L, condition MINIMUM ∈ L and MAXIMUM ∈ L specifies the terms of a contract by coupling the data (L) and the results (MINIMUM, MAXIMUM).

If F is now a program adding to a sum INITIAL_VALUE the interests capitalized in FINAL_VALUE, then the contract can state:

0 < INITIAL_VALUE <= FINAL_VALUE.

② **Introduction of the internal state**

The behaviour of many software packages cannot be only expressed in the form of relations relating only inputs and outputs (INVARIANT(i,o) where o=F(i)). This case arises for software with a *memory effect*, that is software for which the result of a service depends on earlier service requests. A stack is a typical example: two successive poppings give two different popped values. To specify this type of software and the associated contract, the **internal state** notion must be introduced. The result (o) of a function (F) depends on the input value (i) and also on the internal

state value (s). The execution of this function also acts on this state. For instance, the state of the stack is modified after a pop. If s' is the initial value of the internal state and s the final value of the internal state (after F has been executed) then the contract expresses that the following Boolean condition must be true:
INVARIANT((i,s'),(o,s)) where (o,s)=F(i,s')

Thus the first form of invariant that we presented is a particular case where s'=s.

Consider the following example: INVARIANT((i,s'),(o,s)) is defined by (s'=s) and this $\forall$ i and $\forall$ o. Such an expression is used, for instance, to define that an operation on an object must not change the state of this object. In concrete terms, if the object is programmed as an Ada package, the invariant defined on the internal state expresses that the values of the local variables of the package are not modified following the execution of an exported procedure (s'=s).

③ **Introduction of the generalized state**
The state notion can be generalized as a triplet e=(i,s,o) <input, internal state, output>. An input, respectively an output, comprises a part of a controllable state (that can be applied), respectively an observable state (that can be obtained) of a software system. A contract is expressed by the following Boolean condition:
INVARIANT(e',e)
where e' is the initial state and e the final state obtained after running the software function.

As previously quoted, the notion of invariant does not generally express the function of a system but constant properties concerning it.

To illustrate the invariant notion, let us consider a package STACK which exports subprograms POP and PUSH. The state is defined by the operation, by the internal state of the stack which can take value EMPTY, FULL or OTHER, and by the value returned. The client can limit the contract to the fact that the stack must not be empty on call of subprogram POP to supply a result. In this case, this contract is expressed by the invariant (POP, not EMPTY', data) where no constraints are stipulated on returned data value.

In general, the definition of the contract is not condensed into a single Boolean expression but is composed of a list of invariants providing assertions or assumptions on certain components of the state and correlated for instance by 'or' and 'and' operators.

Expressing an error
An invariant defines the condition allowing the client to place his or her reliance on a software tool. The negation of this invariant implies a software failure. This failure is the result of an error expressed by the state pair (e', e) such that INVARIANT(e',e) is false. This pair is a means for observing a fault. The fault at the origin of the error and the failure can be the result of:

- incorrect use. For example, where the square root of a negative number is requested. This situation comprises a specific case where only the component i (input) of the state and its initial value are considered. The INVARIANT(e',e) is reduced to INVARIANT(i');
- use which is inadequate for the current value of the internal state; for instance, a request to pop an empty stack. This situation comprises another specific case where only the initial value of the state (input and internal state) is considered. The INVARIANT(e',e) is reduced to INVARIANT(e');
- incorrect implementation giving an erroneous output value. This situation comprises a third specific case where the output value o is at the origin of the detection. INVARIANT(e',e) is reduced to INVARIANT(o);
- more complex relations between input, output, internal state and implementation. This is expressed by the general definition: INVARIANT(e',e).

The latter situation may seem extremely vague. This fuzziness comes from the fact that the link between the error notion defined precisely from the invariant and the fault notion which led to the negation of the invariant may be highly complex. For instance, if a stack is implemented using a constrained array and an index representing the top of the stack and if top of stack decrementation was forgotten when implementing the service POP (this is a fault) then an error can be detected during a call for the service PUSH (Stack Overflow). Now, the error is due neither to the use of services PUSH and POP (for instance there was a series of PUSH then POP requests), nor to an implementation fault of the called procedure (PUSH) which led to the detection of the error but due to a fault in the implementation of the POP procedure.

2.1.3 Contract and function

In this section, the difference between contract and function notions is highlighted studying a subprogram specification example. The programming level is chosen because it is well-known. We also show that the distinction of the two notions is often intuitively perceived by Ada program designers without being formalized.

Consider a client asking for the design of a subprogram which returns the last object of a given list of objects. The designer may provide one of the two following specifications:

    void function last(Object *l, Object *o)

written in C-languange, and
    procedure last(l: **in** Object_list; o: **out** Object);

written in Ada.

If a purely functional point of view is considered, the two declarations are the same because the compiler will probably manage the list passed as the first parameter of the second specification by means of an address (pointing the first object of the list out) as the compiler does for any complex data structure. In the same way, the returned object o will be possibly handled by its address. The second declaration is therefore far from the subprogram implementation requirements because this declaration contains additional information. This specification may seem to be too heavy because it needs the supplying of pieces of information which are considered as useless with a functional point of view. It requires the type Object_list and the modes in and out to be declared.

Indeed, the pieces of information added to the second declaration are not functionally required. Consequently some people may probably consider that the systematic use of the in out mode avoids useless problems to be solved. However the additional information is useful because it specifies contractual elements defining the terms of the reliance which may be placed in the subprogram.

At first, this specification expresses two *assertions*: l is an Object_list and a value of l must be given (in mode). On one hand, these assertions define *obligations* for the client: the subprogram caller must pass a value in conformance with the type Object_list at call-time. On the other hand, these assertions are *guarantees* for the designer. On the contrary for the first specification declaration, the first actual parameter communicated at call-time may be an address of an object which is not the first element of a list.

Moreover, the definition of the second parameter of the second specification expresses two *assertions*: the subprogram provides a result (mode out) whose type is Object. On one hand, these assumptions are *obligations* for the subprogram designer: the designed subprogram must return a result and the type of this result must be an Object. On the other hand these assumptions are *guarantees* for the client (the procedure caller). On the contrary for the first specification nothing specifies that o contains an address of an object which must be assigned by the function body execution. The address value may be a data to be used as done for the first parameter.

The pieces of information added to the second declaration define the following invariant:

$\forall$ l $\in$ Object_list $\Rightarrow$ o $\in$ Object

To conclude, we must insist on the fact that all the pieces of information given in the second specification are not necessary to obtain a functional definition to produce executable code. However these elements of information allow numerous checks of invariant to be done, at compile-time and at run-time. These verifications *justify* a greater reliance placed in the subprogram by the client.

The second specification declaration provides an example which would be certainly proposed by most of the Ada software designers. This example thus highlights that the contract notion is often intuitively perceived by the Ada program designers. Moreover they make out that this information induces a certain quality of the produced software tools and so increases the reliance which can be placed in these designed tools. In this book these notions as well as the associated means and the expected results will be developed.

2.1.4 Faults and design steps

Knowledge of the invariant which defines the client's reliance criterion will be considered by the designer during each step in the design to master faults which may lead to a negation of this invariant.

The aim of the fault mastering techniques is **to detect faults and to handle their effects** to avoid a failure occurring. Fault detection can be performed during the design and the effects of the fault are then inhibited by suppressing the faults. Errors can also be detected during the running of the program. The faults are then extracted in a new release of the software or their effects are masked by the operation of the program itself. The present chapter deals with these two problems (detection and correction). The contents of this chapter are however not structured around these two aspects. Indeed for the designer, these two problems are strongly coupled. Moreover the techniques used to solve them integrate the two aspects but depend on the phases of the software life cycle where fault detection and correction must be done.

Firstly, detection and correction imply the use of specific techniques during software creation. New techniques are then considered during the validation of the designed software. Finally other techniques are required to integrate defensive means into a program to be used during operation against any residual faults.

During software creation, the designer wants **to avoid faults**. On the one hand, this is obtained by preventing faults from being introduced. On the other hand, during the design steps, detectable faults must be extracted or it must be proved that potential faults have no effects on the behaviour of the program. During the validation of the complete program, the designer wants to **remove faults** which could not be avoided during the design. Finally, to increase the reliance that the clients can place on the software, the designer may add mechanisms to **tolerate faults** the potential existence of which must be assumed. These mechanisms avoid the occurrence of a failure during the operation in spite of the presence of faults in the software.

Three classes of techniques must therefore be used to produce dependable software. They are useful at three times in the life of software: fault avoidance techniques are used for the design steps, fault removal techniques are used for the complete software validation stage and fault tolerance techniques are used for useful life (embedded software). The positions of the techniques studied to master faults in the life of the software are summarized on Figure 2.2.

```
     ⟨TECHNIQUES OF⟩    ⟨ USED FOR ⟩
                       ┌──────────────────┐
                       │  Specification   │
                       │        ↕         │
   Fault Avoidance ────┼→[    Design    ] │
                       │        ↕         │
   Fault Removal  ─────┼→[   Validation ] │
                       └──────────────────┘
   Fault Tolerance ─────→[  Useful Life  ]
```

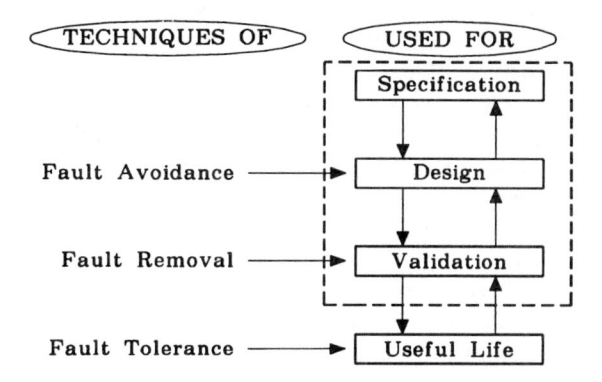

Figure 2.2: Techniques and production stages

Even though the techniques are effective at different times in the life of the software, all these techniques are used by the designer during software production. For instance fault tolerance mechanisms are introduced during the software design but are effective during (i.e. used for) the useful life of the software.

The boundary between fault avoidance domain and fault removal domain may be perceived as fuzzy because faults are *removed* during design by techniques called fault *avoidance* techniques. The partition was done considering the programming language as the means used to define the border and to split a global subject (mastering of faults during software production) into two. All actions done to master faults before programming thus concern fault-avoidance techniques. The actions applied to the designed program are in the fault removal domain. This choice is of course arbitrary but it is voluntary. On one hand the design methods and tools are numerous and change quickly; consequently it is difficult to find a common method to illustrate the theoretical principles provided in this chapter. On the other hand Ada language is now a well-known standard and so we will use it to apply in the following chapters the advice provided in this chapter to Ada programs.

2.1.5 Contents

In this chapter we will successively detail the three types of techniques.

Section 2.2 explores the various techniques used during design which allow the presence of faults to be prevented or detected and then avoided in the designed software: **Fault Avoidance**.

Section 2.3 develops the techniques applied after the design concerning the fault detection and the correction of a program: **Fault Removal**. Static analysis (analysis of the source code) and dynamic analysis (analysis by execution of the generated code) are described. The techniques presented in this section are not to be considered as a substitute for fault avoidance techniques. The detection of a fault just after the design step, where the fault was introduced, is better than a detection after the complete design of the program.

Section 2.4 deals with the production of programs for which the occurrence of an error has the least possible effect on the program behaviour: **Fault Tolerance**. This concerns fault detection and correction during operation. We will focus on the most significant techniques: 'Retry mode', 'Recovery Blocks technique', 'N-Version Programming', 'Termination mode' and mixed techniques.

In order to make the presentation of this chapter clearer, we separated into three classes (fault avoidance, fault removal, fault tolerance) the explanations of the techniques according to their use in the software life cycle. However, in practice, these techniques are used together during the software production phase and they then interact introducing new problems. For instance, the techniques used to tolerate faults at run-time are introduced at the design stage where fault avoidance techniques are considered. The interaction problems will be discussed in **section 2.5**.

The techniques presented are general and therefore not specific to Ada applications. However, knowledge of their principles is required so that they can be applied to Ada software design in chapter 4.

2.2 Fault Avoidance

2.2.1 Introduction

Hierarchy of abstraction
A system can be expressed from several points of view called **abstractions**. For example, the client's requirements, the associated Ada program and the executable program are three abstractions of one system. The translation from the second abstraction to the third one is obtained automatically using a compiler. The purpose of a design method is to help in producing the second abstraction from the first one.

Generally the expression of an abstraction needs the use of other abstractions. This process may be repeated until abstractions considered as primitive are encountered. The well-known modular approach (Parnas, 1972) consists in defining an abstraction as a structure of elements called components.

The **structure** defines the interactions between the components. Control statements (`if`, `loop`, etc.) and subprogram calls are examples of structures. An abstraction of each **component** must be provided to obtain a new abstraction of the whole system. This new abstraction is an **implementation** abstraction of the system. The change from the client abstraction to the implementation abstraction is the first design step.

Each component introduced is considered as a new system. The design process may then be repeated. It is terminated when primitive components are obtained. Primitive components are abstractions of the programming language or, more generally, of the execution tool. For instance, packages providing complex objects are primitive components if they are previously implemented; functions of the operating system are also primitive components; predefined data types and associated statements (addition, access, etc.) are other examples of primitive components.

Each iteration of the design process defines a **design step**.

The design methods then bring the designer to implement a system as a **hierarchy** of sub-systems which is generally maintained in the program produced: tree of sub-programs, of data structures, etc. Figure 2.3 illustrates such a hierarchy. The arrows symbolize the structure linking the components.

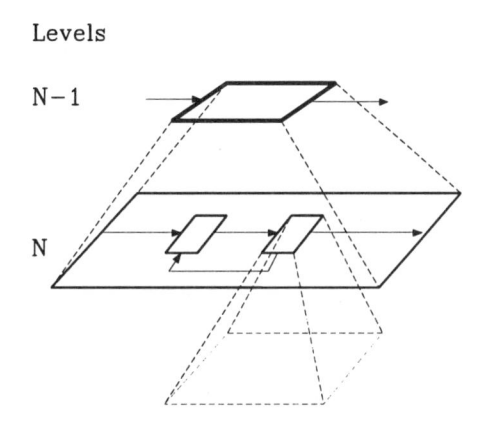

Figure 2.3: Structured hierarchy of components

This hierarchy is introduced to progressively **break down** a **complex** system, whose abstractions are far removed from those of the programming tool, into less and less complex sub-systems. This is an **abstraction hierarchy**, mainly used to compensate for the limits of the human intelligence. Indeed we are unable to master a solution without this design 'trick' because of the vast number of the components and the tangle of interactions which intervene in the final program.

The hierarchical approach to the design implies that **the designer** (or the design team) **is simultaneously a client and an implementer** as defined in section 2.1. Indeed, during a design step, the designer is a client because the current level of the design uses the components to be designed at the next step. Moreover, he or she is the designer of the components used by the higher level components. So, the components which are not the root (the global software) or the leaves (the primitive components) are used as well as implemented by designers. Consequently, to obtain dependable software, the designer must produce components such that *reliance can justifiably be placed on the service they deliver*. Then, in order to define the correctness criteria, the designer must specify for each component a contract defining assertions and assumptions required on the use (user as client) and the implementation of the component to precise guarantees and obligations. Figure 2.4 again presents a component contract using designer's vocabulary.

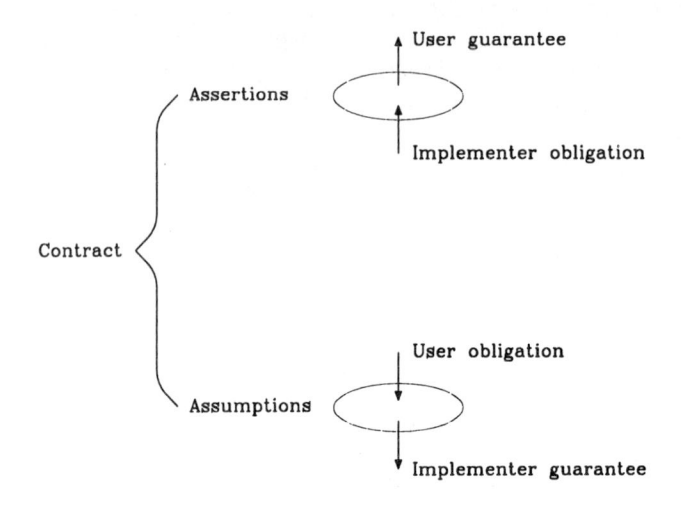

Figure 2.4: Component contract

The purpose of fault avoidance techniques is to obtain a correct solution at each step in the design. These techniques are classified into two classes which complement each other to provide this result: verification and validation.

Verification
The term **verification** is defined in the IEEE Standard Glossary of Software Engineering Terminology as follow (IEEE, 1983): the verification is the process of determining whether or not the products of a given phase of software development cycle fulfil the requirements established during the previous phase. Boehm gives an informal definition: the verification answers the question 'Am I building the product right?' (Boehm, 1984). In this domain a goal is to find a **correct method** to produce a solution, in order to avoid the faults a priori. We saw, in section 1.4.2 of chapter 1, the numerous limits of automatic methods, making a single use practically impossible. Human intervention is then needed in the design. This implies that the presence of faults is possible.

The risk of fault insertion is limited if the designer uses *well-proven methods*. The goal of these methods is similar to the one of verification, but it takes into account the fact that it is impossible to provide an automatic process. These methods constitute *guidelines* which define **the way to correctly design** a program. They do not provide an algorithm to solve any problems which may occur but provide advice to be followed by the designer to construct his or her own intellectual algorithm (his or her reasoning) in order to design a solution for his or her particular problem. We must insist on the fact that the guidelines are not associated with the problem to be solved but with the way to solve it. Simple and practical advice, which is now conventional, is to forbid global variables because they might produce undesirable 'side effects'. The use of *type* is another guideline for detailed design and programming. For instance, explicit types, contrary to data coding, prevent a variable of type T1 from being assigned by an expression of type T2 even if T1 and T2 are implemented in a similar way. The type feature allows *obligations* to be defined for the *use* of the assignment statement. Other advice concerns the grouping into a single entity (an object) of strongly correlated components: data structure as record fields, procedures in packages, etc. This gives *guarantees* for the *client* that no other correlations exist with other components of the software. Moreover if the implementation of an object is masked (private part, bodies, etc.) no intrusion is possible by the clients of the object.

In fact, these guidelines represent a **rule book** which exists for all the professions. To follow this advice does not constitute an absolute guarantee for the client but it *justifies that he or she gives more reliance* to the software produced with such methods. This field is booming because the validation of complex software is becoming more and more difficult. Many clients indirectly judge a product according to the quality of the method used to design it (the know-how).

However systematic studies in this domain are quite recent and are not stabilized. Most of the recent books on software engineering provide punctual and specific advice. In particular most of the authors who propose a means to express a system (model, language, etc.) have in mind a personal perception of the design process. However, although they develop prolifically the expression means, they only outline their ideas on the subjacent process. Some books such as (Pyle, 1991) give information about advice. This reference is particularly interesting if Ada is used as design and programming language. The advice strongly depends on the design method used and therefore on the abstraction level considered. For instance (SPC, 1991) provides advice and warnings on each Ada statement and then is useful for the programming step. So in this chapter no particular advice is provided but general techniques useful for avoiding faults during the design steps are described.

Validation

Another approach to produce dependable programs consists in checking if any faults were introduced during each design step. A validation is done after a design step, a posteriori. The term **validation** is defined by IEEE as follows: the validation is the process of evaluating software at the end of the software development process to ensure compliance with software requirements. Boehm explains that the validation answers the question: 'Am I building the right product?'. Validation and verification are complementary because, in practice, the use of a single approach does not provide an absolute guarantee. Figure 2.5 presents the two points of view.

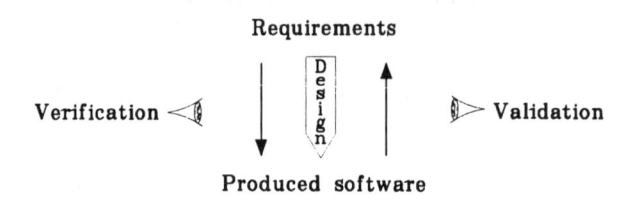

Figure 2.5: Verification and Validation

Validation means are used to detect faults after each design step in order to avoid their presence in the structure (correlation of the components) or in the specification of the components which are taken as a basis for the following step of the design. So they avoid faults being present in the final product and they must be considered as fault avoidance means.

Techniques
Our presentation of the fault avoidance means does not propose an absolute *method* to design software but several *techniques* to be used at each step in order to look at the designed software from a critical viewpoint. The aims of these techniques concern verification or validation of the software or both. They assume a functional and hierarchical design of the software so that the failure of a component (sub-program, package, etc.) will be **due to** errors in sub-components or in the structure linking the sub-components and has **effects** (consequences) on the higher components or on the components intervening in the same design stage.

The proposed techniques have the following purposes:

- to avoid the introduction of faults during a design step (verification means) or,
- to detect and then to extract faults introduced during a design step (validation means).

The common objective is to avoid the presence of faults in the design of the complete software.

We will successively explain the use of Rules, of the Failure Modes and Effects Analysis (F.M.E.A.), of the Fault-Tree Method (F.T.M.) and of the Petri Net model. We will conclude this section 2.2 by presenting the Design Review Techniques.

The methods and techniques were generally introduced from needs which do not stem from the fault avoidance domain. However, particular uses allow these techniques to be efficient fault avoidance tools. For instance, F.M.E.A. or Review Techniques were introduced to remove faults at the end of the design (fault removal) but are also of interest in fault avoidance.

The use of techniques to avoid introducing faults at each one of the design steps is indispensable. However these techniques are inefficient if the specification considered by the software designer does not fit the client's expectations. Thus the design phases must be preceded by a correct analysis of the client's requirements. A misunderstanding of the requirements would introduce in the specification a fault which must then be detected and extracted to be avoided in the complete program.

2.2.2 Requirements analysis

Importance of faults associated with requirements and specifications
A great number of faults included in software tools are due to a bad capture of the client's requirements or are due to a bad translation of requirements as specifications. Even if the system to be designed is simple, the expression of the requirements by the client and their understanding by the designer may be the origin of numerous faults. The rate of 30% of the faults is often accepted (Albin, 1982) (Eckhardt, 1991). In reality this value is higher because requirement captures and specification expressions are necessary at design time for each of the components introduced at every design step because, as previously explained, the designer is his or her own client. For instance (Chillarege, 1992) and (Bhandari, 1993) quoted that 25% of the faults occurring during design correspond to problems associated with the interfaces of components. The problems of interface between used components and implemented components are relative to requirements and specifications. Other data reinforce this opinion: (Sullivan, 1991) specifies that 30% of the faults comes from the fact that the limit values of data or the states not frequently reached are badly taken into account. This rate value is higher for systems for which interactions with hardware or software components are numerous. For instance (Nakajo, 1993) presents a control software in which 56% of the faults are coming from problems of interfacing with software components (36%) or hardware components (20%). So the designer must be aware of the importance of faults associated with requirements and specifications to avoid having these faults present before the design phase. Moreover, even if the client who expresses the requirements is at the origin of certain faults (for instance the client forgets to communicate pieces of information), it is the designer who will handle these faults.

To highlight the consequences of the faults introduced during requirement analysis, let us say that on one hand it is admitted that all the faults introduced in a software tool (whatever are their origins) multiply the costs by two, and that, on the other hand, the correction cost of a fault associated with the requirements specification is 100 times as expensive than the cost of the studies of the requirements which would allow the detection of the fault to be obtained (Boehm, 1984) (Boehm, 1989a). Therefore, even if the obtaining of correct requirements specification consumes time, this period is very useful. This moment is often considered as lost time which will provoke delays. The bad understanding of the importance of this step comes from the fact that, at first, some managers often focus on the system disposal and after on its dependability. On the other hand, for instance in Japan, obtaining a consensus between the client and the designer is very important and this phase may be long. (Tamai, 1993) gives two examples of two big software applications for which the requirements expression and the preliminary studies consume 60% (first example) and 70% (second example) of the time necessary to obtain the software tools. The authors assert that this long work then allows a very quick design and programming to be obtained. This short time is due in part to the fact that the designers were fully conversant with the client application domain.

Causes of the faults
The reasons of fault presence in the requirements specification are partitioned in three classes: bad understanding of the client's requirements, bad translation of well-understood requirements (Gaudel, 1991) and finally bad expression of a correct translation. In the first case, the bad understanding origin may be due to a bad readability of the requirements written by the client (it is a qualitative problem associated with the expression) or a difficulty to master these requirements, for instance, due to the numerous concepts which intervene in the requirements expression (it is then a quantitative problem associated with the expression and the human limits to assimilate and to correlate a great number of entities).

The writing of the Requirements Specification document is not easily done by the designer because the client firstly omits to furnish numerous pieces of information assumed by the client as well-known by the designer. It is not the reality because the designer does not generally work in the client application domain. Moreover the client frequently provides useless information because his or her objective is not the same as the designer's. For instance, the client often expresses elements about the benefits that he or she hopes to obtain when the software which must be created is used (for example, saving money thanks to the software if it intervenes in an automatic system for production) (Scharer, 1981). The designer is not interested in this kind of information but wants the description of the functions which will be done by the software system.

So, it is necessary that the designer helps the client to provide useful information: from the client's expression of the interests to possess the required software (for instance the production costs are too expensive), the client (with the designer) must deduce the objectives, that is 'what the system is to do' (for instance: reduction of the cost associated with the products buffering), to conclude by the definition of the functions which must be provided by the system to be developed (for instance relative to the buffer management). Therefore the client defines 'how the system is to work' which will be perceived by the designer as 'what the system is to do'.

Consequently, to avoid faults in the requirements specification the designer must firstly have a method to capture the client's requirements. This verification means will be studied in the next sub-section. Then, to detect and thus to extract faults introduced in spite of the use of the previous method, the obtained specifications must be examined. This validation means will be examined in the following sub-section.

Method to capture the requirements
The conventional method used to obtain the requirements is the interview. To be efficient (that is to obtain faultless specification), this work must be driven using a method. As previously signalled, the client has a point of view which is very different than the one of the designer. The client perceives the system by the new benefits that it will provide and not by the functions which must be offered by the system. At first the designer must explain the differences between these two points of view, specifying the form of the expected information. This will influence the client's presentation (Sharer, 1981). The client will then be an efficient actor in the requirements expression and then he or she will make easier the requirements specification production.

The choice of a specific method to obtain the requirements is not easy. The method must be decided taking the following criteria into account (Drake, 1993):

- a method is appropriate if it is easy to capture (that is to obtain from the client) the role of the system;
- the conceptual cleanliness: this method makes easy the understanding of the problem;
- the constructability deals with the existence of a systematic approach for formulating the requirements.

(Davis, 1990) adds some others method qualities. Its capabilities:

- to make easy the communication between the client and the designer;
- to encourage writing the documentation (which justifies the reasons of the written requirements);
- to highlight the conflicts;
- to make easy the changes;
- to provide means for partitioning, abstraction and projection (terms which will be defined later).

Among the methods used for the interviews the one proposed in (Lano, 1990) may be considered as a good example. This method aims to obtain answers for the five following questions:

- What ? What are the entities handled to define the system.
- Where ? In what part are the entities intervening (components, interface, etc.).
- When ? Define the event sequences received or produced by the system.
- Who ? Define who (operator, system, etc.) does what. This information allows the partition between the system and its environment to be specified.
- Why ? Justify the existence of the entities.

All the methods aim to highlight the boundary between the system and the environment, specifying the interface. To do it the analyst must understand the environment and not only the system to be designed (Roman, 1985).

As well as at design-time, the great number of entities handled to define a system poses a problem for the analyst. To master the numerous pieces of information and thus to avoid faults due to this quantitative aspect, he or she must organize these entities. Two complementary approaches exist:

- Definition of families of entities: the client often provides pieces of information in a disorganized way; several elements associated with one purpose are scattered in the provided information. It is necessary to group together the entities relative to a unique concept (family of entities). This phase offers a first horizontal structure of the requirements.
- Definition of abstraction levels: for one given subject, the client frequently provides various and numerous pieces of information. However, they correspond to multiple and different abstraction levels. For instance data may be perceived as an abstract entity (just defined by an identifier), or as a block (structure of elements) or as a set of bytes. Relationships exist between these various pieces of information; they are dependency relationships which must be expressed. Let us signal that this hierarchy is not the same as the one existing during design: a low level does not explain 'how ?' but specifies the answer to the question 'what ?'.

Several methods are based on this double structure (Nelsen, 1990) (Roman, 1985) (Thayer, 1990). They will not be detailed in this book but just analysed considering their principles. These methods use four operations handled by the requirements analyst (Thayer, 1990):

- allocation: precise requirements are grouped in one entity (bottom-up analysis);
- derivation: relationship from a high-level requirement to several low-level requirements (top-down analysis);
- interface analysis: defines the requirements specific to the interface of the system or of the components;
- tracing: establishment of links (references) through the requirements.

Finally a third notion which corresponds to another kind of hierarchy is defined.

It is the 'annotations of the software requirements' (ANSI, 1984). They define by means of labels the importance of the requirements: those which must be taken into account imperatively, or those which are not mandatory and which correspond to qualitative improvements.

The methods proposed to capture the requirements are often supported by tools which make easier the management of the handled pieces of information and make automatic a part of the creation of the documentation.

The elements of information to be captured are numerous, then it is important that the analyst understands the concepts of the domain before he or she starts the studies concerning the specific problem to be solved. A bad understanding of the domain is often the cause of numerous faults in the requirements specification (Drake, 1993). After this first work, the definition of the system interface must be obtained without giving details (abstract definition). This is particularly important because we signalled that a lot of the faults are due to a bad interface specification. For instance (Neumann, 1986) develops the case of the 'Three Mile Island' nuclear power station failure. A problem was due to the occurrence of four states associated with the system and the environment (including the human operator).

Even if a method was rigorously used, faults may be introduced and thus the obtained requirements specification must be examined.

Examination of the expressed requirements
After its production, the requirements expression must be examined to detect the presence of faults. The examination will concern content and form. Form criteria are independent to the specific problem handled. The negation of one of these criteria (a bad quality of the expression) is often due to a bad quality of the requirements expressed (faults in the content). For instance, an expression whose understanding is difficult may hide an erroneous understanding of the problem.

We classify the criteria associated with the form into three groups: the criteria associated with the semantics, those associated with the syntax and those associated with the management of the requirements expression.

The criteria associated with the semantics are firstly (ANSI, 1984):

- unambiguous: each requirement stated has only one interpretation;
- complete: the text includes all the requirements;
- verifiable: each requirement can be verified, that is a means exists to check if a given implementation is in accordance with the requirement;
- consistent: there are no conflicts between several requirements (no contradictions);
- traceable: the origin of each requirement must be clear;
- backward traceability: references to the sources exist;
- forward traceability: each requirement has only one reference.

Other qualities concern syntactical aspects (Lano, 1990). The requirements specification must be:

- concise: no useless verbiage;
- clear: easy to be read;
- simple: the subject is defined with a simple language;
- understandable: the subject is defined with an understandable language;
- specific: each subject concerns one aspect.

Finally, qualities are associated with specification management:

- manageable: non-excessive management expenditures;
- maintainable and modifiable: flexibility to change.

These criteria are analysed reviewing the documents as presented in section 2.2.8.

The content of the requirements specification is evaluated by means of the scenarios and prototypes.

A scenario is a sequence of interactions (a simulation of a use of the system). Created scenarios are presented to the client to know if the interactions between the system and the environment were well understood.

The prototyping is an efficient technique even if it requires development time. 'One of the main motivations for the prototyping model is the recognition that prospective users of a system are rarely able to define their requirements fully in one operation ... I Will Know It When I See It (IWKIWISI) ... A prototype provides a means for users to say more precisely what they do or do not want' (Wolff, 1989). A prototype does not provide a complete executable model of the system (because it does not aim to replace the final product) but presents a point of view (an abstraction).

2.2.3 Rules

We pointed out that during a design step, the designer must have the same critical attitude as the client to the complete software. To avoid faults, he or she must justify the reliance that can be placed on the service of each designed component. A design step must be preceded by the definition of a contract which specifies assertions and assumptions and more generally an invariant on the component to be designed. As introduced in section 2.1.2 an invariant is a Boolean function linking the initial value (before the execution) with the final value (after the execution) of the state of a component. This invariant formally expresses rules concerning the implementation (internal state) and the use (input and output) of the component. A violation of a rule is detected by a negation of the invariant. It signals the presence of an error. In this section we will first of all explain the component rule characteristics then describe their use to avoid faults.

Definition of rules
The contract associated with a component is defined by rules. A rule is an informal expression specifying a property of a component. When the component is a **data structure**, rules are defined globally or for each sub-component or between the sub-components of this data structure. For instance, 'a variable can receive values constrained by a fixed range' is a rule expression. The definition of a 'PORTRAIT' type window is another example. It requires a constraint correlating the height and the width: 'the height must be greater than the width'. An assignment statement which assigns a PORTRAIT type variable by a value which denies the rule comprises a fault. This may not immediately provoke an error if the constraint correlating the two data items is not checked, that is if the rule is not expressed as an invariant in the programming language, and if each data item does not violate its own constraints.

The *type* feature, now provided by a lot of languages, allows particular rules to be formally expressed as invariants. We gave the constrained type as an example. Some of these constraints are verified at compile-time and then they become fault avoidance means. However the type feature capabilities are limited; for instance relationships between components of Ada records cannot be expressed. In such a case informal comments expressing rules must be added and examined by the designer in order to evaluate the error presence potentialities.

Rules may be provided to correlate **data and functions**. For instance, abstract data types (Liskov, 1974) facilitate such expressions. Thus an integer set type may be defined by four functions:

```
EMPTY:   ->                             INTEGER_SET
INSERT:  INTEGER_SET, INTEGER ->        INTEGER_SET
EXCLUDE: INTEGER_SET, INTEGER ->        INTEGER_SET
MEMBER:  INTEGER_SET, INTEGER ->        BOOLEAN
```

It expresses the rules concerning the use of an INTEGER_SET. It gives assumptions on the parameter types and it asserts that no other functions allow the INTEGER_SET to be handled. This definition corresponds to a package specification in Ada:

```
package SET_OF_INTEGER is
  type INTEGER_SET is private;
  function EMPTY return BOOLEAN;
  function INSERT(S: in INTEGER_SET; I: in INTEGER)
            return INTEGER_SET;
  function EXCLUDE(S: in INTEGER_SET; I: in INTEGER)
            return INTEGER_SET;
  function MEMBER(S: in INTEGER_SET; I: in INTEGER)
            return BOOLEAN;
private ...
end SET_OF_INTEGER;
```

In the case of a **functional component**, a rule can specify static properties on its behaviour. This information does not concern the implementation of the function but its semantics. For example, consider a function which computes the `average`, the `minimum` and the `maximum` values of a list. We can assert that `minimum<=average<=maximum` without making hypotheses on the realization.

The rules may also express dynamic properties (Howden, 1990). For instance, a `TOTAL` variable which is used to sum the values included in a file, must be 'initialized' at the beginning of the program, represents a 'partial sum' in the `loop` statement used to handle each file data and then the 'complete sum' after this loop. This variable *is assumed* to be in the 'initialized' state before the execution of the loop, etc.

Dynamic rules may be used for data but also for subprograms: in a package, the call of a procedure `P2` may assume the previous call of a procedure `P1`. It is also suitable for tasks for defining sequential constraints on the entry calls.

The rules specify assertions as well as assumptions. Consider a `STACK` object defined by two functions: `PUSH` and `POP`. Rules are associated with these functions. '`STACK` is not empty' has to be true before a `POP` call. '`STACK` is not empty' is true after a `PUSH` call. However the same rule has two kinds of meaning. For the `PUSH` function it is an **assertion** whereas for the `POP` function it is an **assumption**.

Interest of rules for avoiding faults

After a design step, a component of level N-1 is described as a structure of components of level N (see Figure 2.3). The rules associated with each component of level N may be correlated in order to detect the presence of a given error or, on the contrary, the absence of this error. For instance, if a `PUSH` call is immediately followed by a `POP` call then the assertion associated with `PUSH` ('`STACK` is not empty') implies that the assumption associated with `POP` (the same one) is true. Absence of errors gives guarantees (at level N-1):

- to the designer of the level N-1 component who translates the specification of this component into structured level N components, and
- to the client of the level N-1 component, that is the designer who specifies this component.

More generally, to avoid faults, assumptions must be confirmed as true by assertions for components of the same level correlated by a structure. Howden (Howden, 1990) insists on this necessity explaining that a lot of faults come from the fact that the designer of a part of a program makes erroneous hypotheses on another part. For instance, the designer uses the value of a variable assuming that this variable was previously assigned (or initialized) by another part of the program. The sub-components (level N) of a component (level N-1) must define assumptions as well as assertions; the sub-component relationships expressed by the structure of the component design then allow the consistency between the assertions and the assumptions to be verified or not. For example, if the results produced by a sub-component are used as input for another one, the knowledge of precise rules on the parameters of the two sub-components allows some possible faults to be detected. For instance, typing of subprogram parameters partially solves this problem.

The design of a component introduces new real objects, that is, those which are formally defined completely without expecting the next design steps as for sub-components. The local variables are such real objects. Their definitions must contain the expression of the rules associated with them. For instance, the definition of a type specifies the laws governing all the values and the operations possible on all variables of this type.

The design uses also sub-components manipulating virtual information, that is, not completely formally defined. The Ada subprogram specifications are such virtual information. The formal definition of these sub-components will be provided by the following design steps. However, rules can be associated with this kind of information. In section 2.1.3 we provided an example on a subprogram specification. The coherence between the virtual and real information must be checked. This is achieved by checking that the invariant defined on the real information implies the invariant on the virtual information. For example, the use of typed subprogram parameters allows a verification to be done between the formal parameters and the real parameters. These real ones must be in accordance with the formal ones. Thus a real parameter type can be a sub-type of the formal parameter type. The compilers can check the coherence between subprogram specifications and subprogram calls. However only some syntactic checks will be done. For more semantic checks, axiomatic rules must be given, for instance, specifying the relationships between subprograms such as

```
EXCLUDE(EMPTY, i) = EMPTY
EXCLUDE(INSERT(s,i), j) = if i=j
    then EXCLUDE(s, j)
    else INSERT(EXCLUDE(s,j), i)
```

for the INTEGER_SET abstract type definition. Note that new properties such as 'an INTEGER_SET cannot possess two identical items' can be deduced from the previous one to assert new guarantees.

We said that invariants can be used to give guarantees to the designer who specifies the component (i.e. the client) by the designer who translates a level N-1 component specification into structured level N components. This is illustrated by the use of the parameter mode 'in' in Ada. Indeed the compiler checks that a mode 'in' parameter is not assigned in the subprogram body. The mode 'in' therefore specifies a request by the client and the compiler provides him with a guarantee. The analysis of the level N rules then allows the truth of the level N-1 rules to be asserted. It shows that an error (a rule negation), potentially raised at level N by the implementation, cannot occur because of constraints which were imposed by design choices (the components and their structuring). Let us again consider the sequence of PUSH then POP statements. The assertions 'the stack is not empty' and 'if the stack is empty then UNDERFLOW' are respectively associated with each subprogram. The sequencing of the two statements implies that the potential UNDERFLOW error has been avoided.

The ease with which assertions of level N can be deduced from assumptions and assertions of level N-1 and assumptions of level N depends on the characteristics of the structure which correlates the level N-1 components. The means of expression for design or programming (i.e. the language) must therefore be chosen carefully.

Ease with which rules can be handled
Some means used to design and program software make it difficult to define a clear contract or evaluate its effectiveness, taking the realization into account; other means make the expression and the manipulation of the rules easier.

For instance, *structured design* leads the designer to use frames (as loop statements, if statements, subprograms, etc.) which possess only one exit point and one branch point where execution is resumed after executing the frame. This facilitates the examination of the control flow in order to demonstrate rules expected in the contracts. It is not the case if the EXIT statement or the GOTO statement which provokes branching outside the frame are used. In these cases, it is impossible to specify where the execution of the frame is terminated and where it will be continued after the processing of the frame. If the frame is globally examined then:

- no guarantees are provided for the frame client concerning the effective exit label if several label names exist (i.e. for instance if the frame implementation possesses GOTO LABEL1 and GOTO LABEL2 statements);
- no obligations are imposed on the frame client concerning the continuation of the execution. The labels can be located almost anywhere in the program.

No precise contract can therefore be expressed in the frame specification. The use of such features to structure components implies the presence of *hidden clauses* (Meyer, 1992), that is, information which is not expressed in the contracts. Such a situation does not favour fault avoidance.

On the opposite the *abstract data type* approach, which deals with the enumeration of the only subprograms possible on a data structure, is a good (with dependability criterion) design method to structure the components. Indeed, this is a guarantee for the user of this data that involuntary *side effects* will be avoided.

These remarks show that the design and programming means must not be chosen by considering only the behaviours which can be expressed with these features but must also take into account the contract expression capabilities and the faults they prevent from being introduced.

Use of rules to avoid faults

To assert that the veracity of the properties expressed by the rules associated with the design product are established, the designer must examine the correlations between the rules associated with the components of the implementation, as client as well as implementer of components. Consider a component of level N-1 designed with components of level N (see Figure 2.3). As client of the level N-1 component, the designer must establish if the assumptions associated with the use of this component are true. As implementer of the same component, he or she must establish if the assertions associated with the services provided by this component are true.

Firstly, to specify whether the **assumptions** of the level N-1 component are true or not, the designer observes the use of this component. Its use depends on the use of the higher component at level N-2 and on the relations existing with the other components intervening at level N-1. The truthfulness of the assumptions associated with the component of level N-2 was studied after the previous design step. The assertions of the components of the same level N-1 are studied after the implementation of these components. Therefore, the designer must establish if the assumptions of level N-2 and the assertions of the other components allow the assumption concerning the correct use of the studied component to be deduced. This is obtained by correlating rules of the components taking the structure into account. Earlier, we gave a very simple example on a stack: the previous execution of a PUSH subprogram implies that the assumption 'the stack is not empty' associated with the POP subprogram is true.

Secondly, the designer of a component of level N-1 must show that the **assertions** (that he or she has to guarantee) of this component are true in accordance with his or her design choices. This is made taking the assertions of the components of level N and the structure of level N into account.

Difficulties

During a design step, the designer must not only try to find an implementation expressing a solution to the requirements associated with a component but he or she must also think about introducing the highest possible amount of information relevant to the properties that the manipulated components (control structure, data structure, subprogram, etc.) must have. When trying to find a solution as rapidly as possible, which generally is the case, expressing properties by means of rules is often considered as cumbersome for the design. This is far from the truth as these means:

- facilitate design by explicitly expressing the expected properties (verification means) and
- reduce calling the proposed solution into question at a later date thanks to immediate error detection (validation means).

The first difficulty which arises with the fault avoidance technique described concerns **the obtaining of the rules** and **their formalizations as invariants**. In particular, this work is not easy if there is only one designer who must have simultaneously to play the role of the client and the implementer.

The correlations between the rules associated with the components (of one level or of different levels of the design hierarchy) must then be done to assert that the invariants are true. Consequently, a design tool or a programming language must be chosen to express the result of the design steps looking at its possibilities to establish such correlations. Unfortunately this work has to be done manually if no tools are available and then it is difficult **to obtain exhaustive examinations**.

Consequences
The difficulty in handling invariants to deduce their effectiveness has three consequences on the way they are used in practice.

- Firstly, before starting a hard demonstration to show that an invariant is true, the designer may answer the following question: 'if the invariants of a component introduced during the design step were false, that is, if a rule relevant to this component could not be respected, **what are the consequences** on the global behaviour of the application?'. The Failure Modes and Effects Analysis (F.M.E.A.) technique presented in the next section will allow us to reply to this question. On one hand, if these consequences are serious, all means must be employed to avoid the presence of faults causing the invariant violation and to prove the absence of such faults. On the other hand, if the negation of the invariant has no effect no excessive work is necessary.
- Secondly, instead of proving that an invariant is always true it may be easier to examine if this invariant may be false, that is to answer the question: 'taking design choices into account (level N), **do circumstances exist** such as the invariant of the level N-1 component designed can be false?'. The Fault Tree Method (F.T.M.) described in section 2.2.6 aims to provide an answer.
- Thirdly, the means (model, language, etc.) used to express a solution has **specific characteristics which facilitate** the examination of certain kinds of invariants. Section 2.2.7 will consider the Petri net model as an example.

Finally, we previously highlighted the two roles of the designer (client and implementer) and we pointed out that they are a cause of the difficulty for the designer to express and to analyse the invariants. This may be solved by a review undertaken by design specialists who were not involved in the design of the program. Design review techniques will be presented in section 2.2.8.

2.2.4 F.M.E.A.

Principles

Failure Modes and Effects Analysis (F.M.E.A.) (Villemeur, 1991) is a technique used to highlight the consequences of a failed component on the behaviour of the whole program. This technique, which is normally used to examine a general system whose design is completed (scope of section 2.3), is applied here after each stage of a top-down hierarchical design of a program. If the consequences are serious, the designer of the component must pay a special attention to avoid the introduction of faults leading to this error.

Let us consider step number N of the design. Each component of level N-1 is split into interconnected sub-components at level N. This breakdown singles out the sub-components and the structure, i.e. the relations between the sub-components used to express the data flow and the control flow. Relations of cause and effect exist between the behaviour of each sub-component at level N and the behaviour of the component at level N-1 (see Figure 2.6). These relations also exist with the higher levels, up to level 0 defining the complete program. The aim of the F.M.E.A. is to use these relations to determine the consequences of the failure of a component.

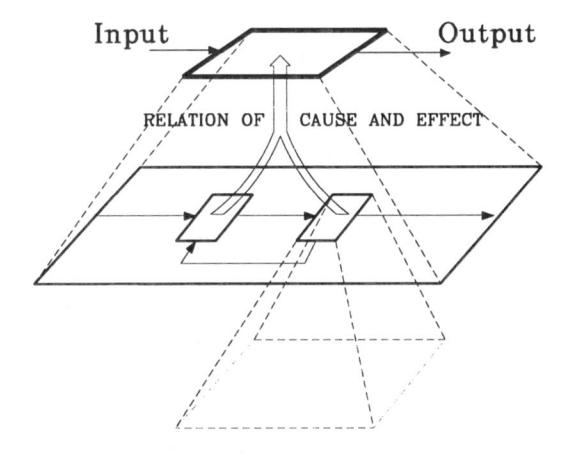

Figure 2.6: Relation of cause and effect

52   Chapter 2: Fault Detection and Correction Techniques

In this technique, the negation of a component's invariant is named component's *'failure mode'*. It defines the negation of a property expected by the user's component, that is, an error which itself can lead to a failure of the user component.

Note that as this mode does not determine the cause of the failure (the fault) but the way it is perceived. For instance, the *failure modes* of a STACK object include: 'the stack does not provide the correct value when popping', 'the stack does not memorize the value when pushing', etc. Remember that the initial contract written to specify the dependability criteria for a software component defines neither the function performed by a component nor the pieces of information about the implementation but rules (i.e. properties) which must be observed when the component is used to consider this component as dependable. The negation of a rule expected by the user of a component is then a way to consider a failure. A component failure mode is therefore a negation of one contract rule associated with the component.

Pay attention that the modes define at level N potential failures whose reality is not known because it depends on the level N+1, N+2, etc., design choices which are presently unknown.

Method

After the level N failure mode definitions, F.M.E.A. deals with the study of the effects of these failure modes on level N-1, then on level N-2, etc., then finally on level 0, that is on the global behaviour of the program. The consequences of each potential failure are then propagated in order to observe the effects that this failure would have. The F.M.E.A. approach therefore imposes that the designer establish the effects of a violation of a sub-component guarantee.

This work is done by hand using tables whose main pieces of information are:

- the identity of the analysed component (name, number, etc.),
- the functions performed by the component (specified or required),
- the failure modes,
- the possible causes of the failure (optional),
- the local effects (that is to say the consequences on the components at same design level N),
- the next higher level effects (on level N-1),
- the effects on the global behaviour (end effects),
- the failure detection method,
- the reactions to these errors.

These last two aspects are generally relative to the techniques used to tolerate faults (described in section 2.4).

A standardized (MIL-STD-1629) worksheet exists (Figure 2.7).

System	______		Date	______
Indenture level	______		Sheet	______ of ______
Reference drawing	______		compiled by	______
Mission	______		Approved by	______

Identification number	Item/functional identification (nomenclature)	Function	Failure modes and causes	Mission phase/ operational mode	Failure effects			Failure detection method	Compensating Provisions	Severity class	Remarks
					Local effects	Next higher level	End effects				

Figure 2.7: F.M.E.A. worksheet

Advantages and difficulties

The most interesting characteristic of F.M.E.A. is that this method considers a failure of a sub-component not by its causes (which depend on its future design) but by its observability and its effects. The failures defined by the modes associated with the components of level N of a design are only potential because the faults which are the causes would eventually exist only after the step N+1 of the design. However, highlighting of the effects of these failures allows the designer to be aware of the consequences of a fault provoking these failures, before he or she starts the design step N+1. So we can assume that **he or she will pay special attention to avoid faults** which provoke these failures when he or she makes his or her design. F.M.E.A. is then a verification technique.

F.M.E.A. is useful as fault avoidance means because errors are handled during the design and not after. This method is based on the *contractual approach* proposed in the first section because failure modes are expressed as rule negations. It points out the importance of the effectiveness of the guarantees associated with the sub-components to be used and then the importance of the obligations for the designer of these sub-components.

F.M.E.A. is also suitable for indicating, at each design step, the failures for which fault tolerance mechanisms have to be introduced. As we said previously, even if such mechanisms are integrated during design, they will be presented separately in section 2.4 in order to make them easier to understand.

The main difficulties with F.M.E.A. are:

- the list of failure modes is difficult to establish. If there is one designer, the difficulty is the same as the one encountered in writing the rules of the contract

for the sub-components because the two roles (user and implementer) are played by one person (the designer);
- all the information is written in natural language or expressed through given design and specification languages (for instance HOOD, SADT, etc.). This makes it difficult to process formal operations, to establish relations between the failure modes described on level N and the effects which appear on levels N-1, ..., 0. In fact, to obtain such pieces of information automatically, the failure modes and the effects must be expressed in a formal way (negation of invariants). Moreover, an operator, which deduces the effects from the causes, must be available.

F.M.E.C.A. (Failure Modes, Effects and Criticality Analysis) is a variant of F.M.E.A. that associates a probability with the failure modes and with their effects, allowing a finer analysis. It takes the criticality (severity) of the consequences of each potential failure into account.

2.2.5 Gathered Fault Combination Method

The Gathered Fault Combination Method (G.F.C.M.) is an extension of F.M.E.A. It is used to characterize potential errors of a set of interacting components regarding to their effects.

Principle
The principle of this method consists in analysing each component of level N by F.M.E.A. defining the errors of the components and their effects on the component of level N-1 and also on the components of level N. Then, the errors which have the same effects (i.e. which provoke the same failure) are grouped together.

This method is completed by using a classification in accordance with the location of the effects:

- the *'internal gathered failures'* expression (Figure 2.8) labels the groups of errors which have the same effect on the component studied. In this case we obtain error classes which are identified by their effects and not by the identifiers of each error. For instance, if the component is a stack object then an undervalued constrained size of the stack may cause a 'stack overflow' when pushing. This failure also occurs if the pop function offered by the stack object does not decrease the stack pointer.

Fault Avoidance 55

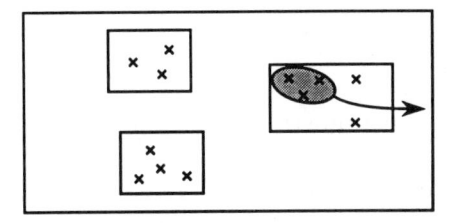

Figure 2.8: Internal gathered failures

- the *'external gathered failures'* expression (Figure 2.9) labels the groups of errors of various components which have the same effect on the studied component. In this case we obtain error classes which are identified by their effects and not by their origin (the component associated with this error). For instance, if a first component uses the stack object, it can provoke a 'stack overflow' if too many push function calls are made. The same effect can be obtained from a second component which also uses the stack.

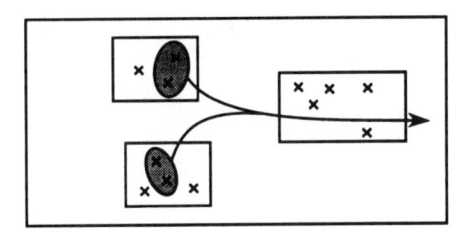

Figure 2.9: External gathered failures

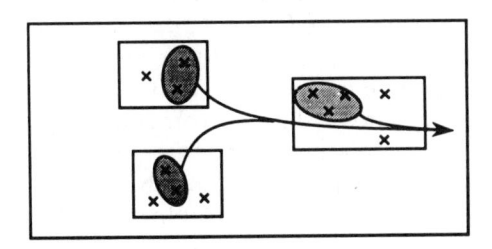

- the *'global gathered failures'* expression (Figure 2.10) labels gathered errors which have the same effect on one component. For instance the 'stack overflow' may come from implementation errors ('internal gathered failures') or from use errors ('external gathered failures').

Figure 2.10: Global gathered failures

Advantages

We said that F.M.E.A. can be used after each design step as a fault avoidance method. This method indicates the outcomes of the errors of each of the sub-components on the higher level components and then prompts the designers of the sub-components to pay attention to avoid a realization causing these errors to be introduced.

The gathering of errors which have the same effects allows the designed system to be analysed not by taking the individual error into account but by considering groups of errors classified by the fundamental criterion: the effect. The addition of labels is interesting because they specify the sub-components which are subjected to the same effects. Relationships between sub-components introduced during the design are then obtained. These relationships are not functional but come from the propagations (relations of cause and effect) associated with the errors.

The knowledge of such error relationships imposes relationships between software component designers who intervene in the creation of one application, to prevent the introduction of the faults which provoke the identified errors. For instance a 'stack overflow' may come from an under-valuation of the stack size or from too much pushing. However these two causes must be correlated because a small size is acceptable if few elements are pushed at a given moment.

The effects are considered for components of one level. The method can be extended in order to consider the effects on higher components. Then errors which cause the same effects may be correlated.

2.2.6 Fault-Tree Method

Principle

F.M.E.A. was used to indicate to the designer the consequences of a failure of a component (an error in the future designed product) on the behaviour of the program to allow him to pay attention to avoid introducing the faults producing the failure during component design. This is a verification technique. F.T.M. (Fault-Tree Method) concerns the validation process. It tries to determine if a failure of a component at level N-1 is possible taking the knowledge of the design choices at level N into account (see Figure 2.3). In particular, this method is used to check if a thought error corresponding to the negation of a rule can exist.

In reality, the basic method is more general. It deals with the study of the state of a component taking the states of the other components intervening in the design into account. An error considered as an undesirable state allows the method to be applied. We will give a general presentation of the method then we will describe its interests in preventing faults from being introduced.

Method

An *event* (vocabulary used for this technique) can be associated with each state of the software, expressing if the software is in this state or not. 'A variable is initialized', 'a rendezvous was done', 'an action is concluded' are some examples of events. Remember that an error has been defined as a particular and undesirable state which is reached by the program due to a fault. Events may therefore be associated with errors. 'Array index is out of range' is an example of such an event. Taking the design choices into account, the state of a program may be defined as the correlation of more detailed states which specify the causes. This may also be applied to errors (invariant negations) and more generally to any event. For instance, 'array index is out of range' is due to 'index value is smaller than lower bound' or to 'index value is bigger than upper bound'. The first event is the effect of the second or the third events which are the causes. **An event is thus expressed as a combination of other events** by mean of the logical operators AND (notation '·' in textual examples), OR (notation '+') and NOT (notation '-'). The **'cause' events** can also be determined in the same way. This creates an event tree called *cause tree* by some authors (Villemeur, 1991) and fault-tree when the root event is associated with an error. For each potential error of the program, a fault-tree grows as the design advances and the perception of details, specifying the causes, progresses. Note that the cause events are not necessarily errors in sub-components but a combination of events which constitute an error. For instance, for a railroad crossing controller system, the event 'the train is within the railroad crossing' and the event 'the gate is up' are not associated with an error if they are considered separately. However they provoke an error if they are simultaneously true ('AND').

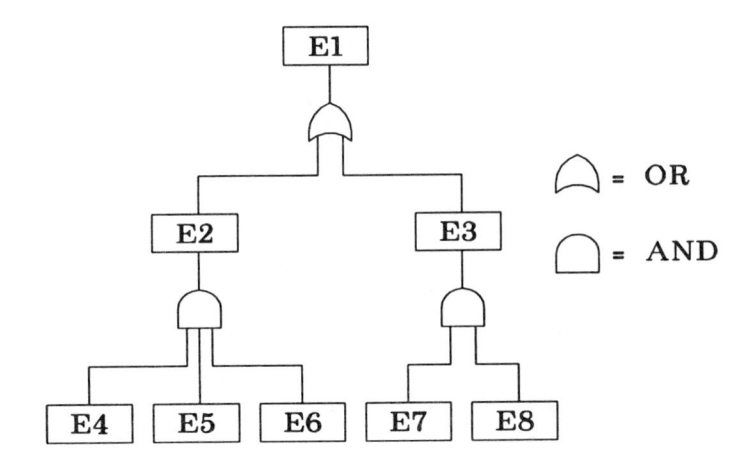

Figure 2.11: Event tree

58 Chapter 2: Fault Detection and Correction Techniques

In the example shown on Figure 2.11 event E1 is true if at least one of the events, E2 or E3, is true. This situation may, for instance, represent 'an engine does not work' if 'it is not supplied' **or** if 'it is out of order'. Another example is the 'array index is out of range' if the 'index value is smaller than the lower bound' **or** if the 'index value is greater than the upper bound'. E2 is true if E4, E5 and E6 are true. This tree allows the event set on the root (the effect) to be expressed as a logical combination of the leaf events (the causes):

    E1 = (E4·E5·E6) + (E7·E8)

If the event set on the root is associated with an error (undesirable event) producing a failure in the program, then the different combinations of events which generate this error are available. The system must be designed so that the true value is not assigned to the root event. Then, after each design stage, to progress from level N-1 to level N, the event tree grows taking the design choices introduced at level N into account. This tree is analysed using the binary logic properties to obtain more information on the potentiality of the root event, that is on the potentiality of the failure of the program.

For instance, the properties of the binary logic allow expressions to be reduced. In the previous example, if event E7 is identical to E4, the previous expression can be written as

    E1 = E4 · ((E5·E6) + E8)

We then establish that event E4 is compulsory prior to E1.

This analysis also allows contradictions to be detected, for instance, finding an event and its contrary on the same branch. This permits branches to be removed as illustrated by the two following examples (Figure 2.12 and Figure 2.13).

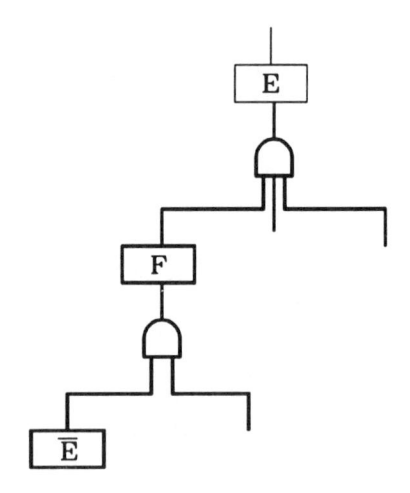

Figure 2.12: Branches removed

On Figure 2.12 event E is due to F **and** to some other events. F is due to not (E) **and** to another event. So event E exists if event not (E) exists. We deduce from this contradiction that event E cannot be true and that we can delete the subtree which stems from E (thick on Figure 2.12) and deduce the consequences on the ancestors. We thought of a component error which cannot exist taking the component design choices into account.

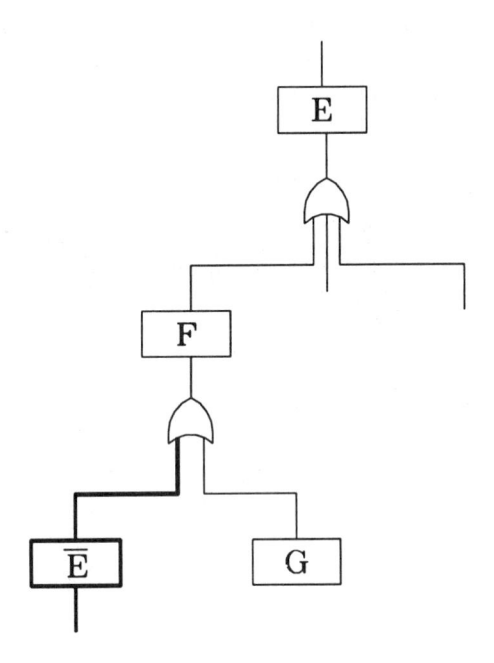

Figure 2.13: Event removed

In the second example (Figure 2.13), event E may be due to F **or** other events. F can be due to not (E) **or** G. As E cannot be due to not (E), then the branch which stems from not (E) can be deleted. If F is true and is the cause of E, it is due to the fact that G is true.

A reduction synthesizes the relations existing between a failure (root event) and its causes. This reduced form allows us to establish that:

- if the root event is *always true*, then the failure of the system is always present: the designed program is out of order;
- if the root event is *always false*, then we *proved* that the imagined failure of the program cannot occur (Leveson, 1983);
- in the other cases, it determines the smallest possible combination of causes leading to the failure (root event).

Advantages and difficulties

The tree reduction and some conclusions concerning the failures are made at each design stage. For instance F.T.M. may allow the presence of a potential fault provoking a failure of the program to be invalidated (second item of the previous conclusions). Thus its use after each design step allows this step to be judged, evaluating if it can avoid or not the failures considered as possible. If not, the current design stage may therefore be called into question before the following design step. Moreover the use of this method prompts the designer to introduce implementations preventing the events highlighted in the previous step from occurring. This is confirmed by the reduction of the tree.

However, in certain cases the tree can increase, become complex and irreducible. It then will give no final conclusions on the existence of failures or not. We must wait for later steps in the design to obtain results concerning the existence of failures.

Furthermore, the use of this method allows the fault tolerance studies to be minimized. If an event intervening at an intermediate level of the design hierarchy is always false (i.e. the potential fault does not exist) then a correction handler must not be defined. For other events, a mechanism to tolerate them may be designed and then a fault tree elaborated again to *prove* that the event can no longer provoke a failure (Hecht, 1986).

Finally, the comparison between several fault trees allows failures which stem from a single cause (one event) to be detected (Villemeur, 1991). The fault avoidance of such an event has to be specially considered.

Conclusions

The aim of the F.M.E.A. method is to observe the effects of an error associated with a component on the global behaviour of the program (i.e. of the higher component). The Fault Tree Method deals with the observation of the design choices when faced with the potential failures of the program (or of a component). These two approaches are complementary and must be used together at each design step because the designer has two roles:

- implementer of components and he or she wants to know the causes of a failure, and
- client for these components or for others and he or she wants to know the effects of a failure.

However, the application of the two methods is performed manually because no formal structure linking the sub-components and no formal behavioural model of the leaf-components are considered. If such formal information exists, more precise conclusions can be obtained. In the next section we will take the Petri Net model as an example. Note that a programming language is almost a formal means of expression (control statements, etc. to define the structure and behavioural definition of the primitive features). However, the program is obtained at the end of the design when *fault removal* techniques are used.

2.2.7 Petri nets

In this section we will show how some faults can be avoided using a formal model during design. Fault avoidance is obtained by examining the application behaviour model at each design phases. The main interest of such formal models is to detect **automatically** the presence of certain kinds of errors. However the invariant types which can be handled are specific to each model. We will take the example of Petri net as a means to model event driven systems. This model is not only interesting for multi-tasking programs because the study of a sequential software requires the modelling of both this software and its environment. The two elements progress in parallel as shown on an example which will be considered in this section. Most of the other modelling means offer numerous possibilities to detect various kinds of errors but each of them will not be examined in this book.

The Petri net model
We will only present the basic Petri net model through its graphical representation. However, concerning our application, its interest is due to the existence of a mathematical definition (Murata, 1989a) (Peterson, 1981) which allows properties to be deduced systematically.

A Petri net model is defined by *places* (circles on the figures), *transitions* (bars on the figures) and *arcs* (arrows on the figures) which connect places to transitions and transitions to places. Some places contain tokens (dots on the figures). Figure 2.14 shows an example of a Petri net. The current state of the model is defined by the location of tokens. This is called *marking*. The operation of the Petri net model must be explained briefly. A *transition may be fired* if each place which is an input of the transition contains a token. After the transition fire tokens from the input places are removed: all places which are outputs of the transition receive tokens. On Figure 2.15, two transitions were fired from the current state defined on Figure 2.14. The Petri net model has very simple features to express the structure (transitions and arcs) and the activity of primitive components (places) but it allows complex behaviours to be expressed. In reality, the model is more complicated but we will use this simplified definition to present its interests for fault avoidance.

Generic errors
At first this model is used to deduce *generic errors*. These errors are due to design faults in the studied software, but their semantics are associated with the Petri net model semantics, not only to the semantics of the software considered. From among the generic errors evidenced by the Petri net analysis, two are of specific interest in the software context: detection of deadlocks and detection of conflicts.

The first kind of errors detected by the Petri net model are the *deadlocks* which show that the **system is blocked** (lifeless). For instance, consider a two task system modelled by a Petri net (Figure 2.14). We can assume that task 1 (or 2) uses resource A and then resource B (or B and then A). The presence of a token in the place associated with the resource shows that the resource is free (i.e. can be accessed).

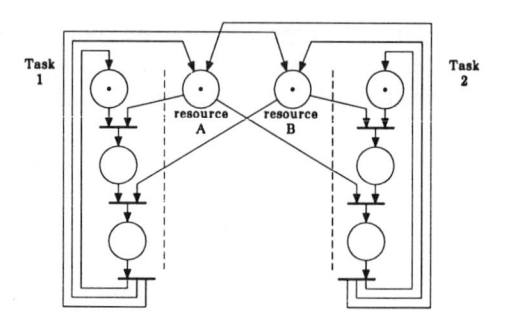

Figure 2.14: Petri net example

The running of a system designed as such may induce a deadlock. This situation is detected, for instance, by an operation of the Petri net. This deadlock situation is shown on Figure 2.15: no token can be moved. It models the fact that the system is blocked: it cannot progress. Task 1 wants resource B and then will free resource A but task 2 wants resource A and then will accept to free resource B.

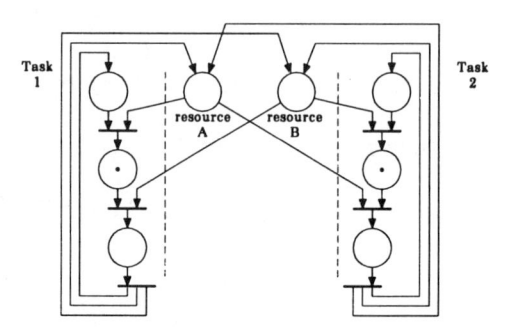

Figure 2.15: Deadlock detection

The model also evidences *conflicts*. For instance, let us come back to the initial situation (Figure 2.14). Now, if resource B is used by task 2 (the token is removed from the place associated with the resource), then the token of resource A may provoke the progress of task 1 **or** the progress of task 2. This case shows a potential **hazard** which may characterize an erroneous design.

Situations such as lifeless and hazards can be detected systematically using mathematical processes based on a matrix representation of the model. The detected errors come from the semantics (i.e. the features) of the Petri net model. Only a certain number of errors bound to the general properties are detected. However these possibilities can be used:

- to express kinds of rules such as: 'the software must react' or 'the software must have always the same behaviour';
- to verify the effectiveness of these rules.

Particular errors
A suitable use of the Petri net model for fault avoidance was proposed (Leveson, 1987) considering the basic definition of the error as an undesirable state. It consists in modelling the behaviour of the designed software and then in determining the state or *markings* (set of places where tokens are located) which represents an erroneous situation. For instance, in the model of a railroad level crossing controller, the simultaneous presence of a *token* in the place 'train is within the crossing' (P3) and of a token in the place 'gate is up' (P11) represents such an error (Figure 2.16).

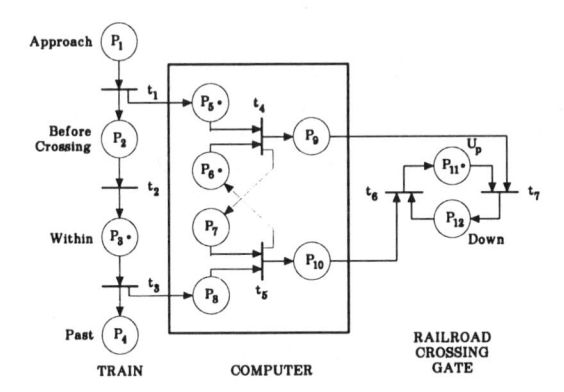

Figure 2.16: Definition of an error as a marking

Figure 2.16 presents a modelling of the system proposed by Nancy Leveson. It shows, on the left side, the model of the train's behaviour, on the right side, the model of the behaviour of the railroad crossing gate and, in the centre, the model of the behaviour of the software embedded in the computer used to control the railroad crossing gate. We want to check that the behaviour of the software is correct. This is defined by the rule: 'the railroad crossing gate must be down when the train is passing the railroad crossing'. We then make a search to find if a *firing sequence*, that is to say an evolution of the system (train, computer software and gate), can lead from the initial state to the erroneous state: presence of a token in P3 and in P11 simultaneously.

This search can be made automatically starting from the initial marking (P1, P6, P11), using tools associated with Petri net model. As this situation can be reached then the design of the system must be modified. In the example given, the introduction of a semaphore between the opening of the gate and the passage of the train can be considered. A traffic light is added to ask for the train to stop while the downward motion of the gate is not terminated. These modifications in the design must involve a new Petri net model and a new analysis of it.

In this example, time is a very important feature. The erroneous state will not be attainable if the speed of the train is low and if the controller and the gate act quickly. Timed Petri net models exist which associate time constraints or time intervals with the places or with the transitions (Bertomieu, 1991), (Ghezzi, 1991), (Kubek, 1995). Designers use these pieces of information to deduce if potential errors can exist taking the time constraints into account.

In conclusion, the Petri net model allows a formal representation of a system integrating the parallelism and the time to be achieved. For important applications, the graph handled can become huge. Then a hierarchical modelling and tools based on the mathematical theory associated with the Petri net analysis must be used. We showed that two kinds of errors can be detected: generic errors (as deadlocks and conflicts) and particular errors (specifying the errors as markings).

The use of other models will detect automatically other classes of errors and then avoid the presence of the associated faults in the complete program. Consequently **the design model must be chosen carefully** taking the characteristics of the rules written in the contract into account. If all the design models are not supported by formal definitions then they are not able to automatically detect errors.

2.2.8 Design review

We highlighted the difficulties for the designer to be simultaneously the client and the implementer of his or her components (i.e. to play two roles) and thus to have a critical attitude in front of his or her realization. The **review** consists in having the software produced examined by software design specialists (for instance other design team members) or application domain specialists (for instance the client or future users) who were not involved in the design of the software part in question.

This process is generally applied once the program has been completed as a fault removal technique. However, its use is highly efficient as a means of fault avoidance. Within this context, this approach is used at each step in the design, both on the statement of requirements of the software components to be designed and on the result of their design.

At requirement level

The aim of the review of the statement of requirements is to check that the designer has correctly understood the expression of the problem that he or she must solve. This verification is very important because a great number of the faults of the complete program comes from misunderstanding of the client's requirements. The rate of 25 to 30% is frequently accepted (Albin, 1982) (Eckhardt, 1991). This check concerns, in particular, the semantics of the problem domain. The designer must well understand the concepts which intervene in the client's domain (in particular the client's terminology). The examination also concerns the understanding of the system interface which is the cause of numerous problems (Sullivan, 1991) (Nakajo, 1993) and then the behaviour that the software to be produced must have. For this, the reviewer analyses the statement of requirements written by the designer from the client's explanation.

This analysis examines the completeness of the requirements. The reviewer makes a check to see if requirements have not been omitted, if additional requirements have not been unnecessarily introduced and if contradictions exist between the various aspects of the expressed requirements.

This analysis is performed either in an absolute manner (for example, concerning the contradictions) or, and principally, by taking into account particular specifications expressed by the client. The aim is then to establish if the requirements expressed by the designer correctly correspond to the client's expectation.

The reviewer also studies the form of the document written by the designer describing the requirements. If this text is difficult to understand, the reviewer must harbour doubts about the comprehension of the problem to be solved by the writer, that is, the designer.

At design level

The aim of the design review is to evaluate if the design proposed correctly meets the requirements declared in the previous step.

This review is conducted both by examining the results of the design (and it is then a validation technique) and by analysing the means used to obtain this result (and it is then a verification technique). Concerning these two aspects, the use by the designer of the techniques described in the previous sections (F.M.E.A., etc.) allows the reliance that the reviewer can place on the result of the design step to be increased.

Role of the reviewer

The reviewer's role is twofold:

- **to check the product** of the design work whether the product be the statement of requirements or the solution proposed;
- **to examine the way** in which the work is performed. For example, a vague expression of requirements or unevaluated design results must lead to doubts concerning the conformity of the designed software to the client's specifica-

tion. The reviewer thus attempts to detect faults in the design process which may lead to the generation of faults in the result of this design. This point of view comes down to evaluating the quality of the result of the design from the quality of the work performed.

However, the reviewer must not impose his or her way of designing from among the many possible solutions. He or she must only evaluate the reliance that can be placed on the examined design step (Pyle, 1991).

Reviewing methods
Many techniques exist for reviewing. They will not be detailed here. Their principles will be introduced presenting three classes of techniques taking their characteristics into account (Knight, 1993):

- **formal reviews**: the author presents his or her work (statement of requirements or the expression of a design). He or she is questioned by the reviewers (the client or a software specialist) who point out any problems detected;
- **walkthroughs**: the reviewers examine the result of the work and compare them with its initial expression: examination of requirements with regard to client's expectation; examination of the design with regard to the requirement specifications. These examinations are conducted in various ways. For example, the designed solution can be simulated;
- **inspections**: the reviewer checks that the solution proposed meets a certain number of criteria. First, these criteria are associated with the problem dealt with. For instance, the reviewer checks if certain specific situations considered as critical can be reached. These situations concern violation of the initial contract rules. The aim sought is then to identify faults in the writing of the requirements or in the designed software. Other criteria concern the general quality of the requirements or of the designed software (for instance, its portability or its reusability) or the general quality of the design process.

The general qualities of software are not superfluous or secondary characteristics. They are also associated with the notion of correctness. For instance, the run-time system of a software tool will no doubt vary during the life of this software. For example hardware technology changes very quickly and then the application hardware support may vary. Consequently, the dependence of the behaviour of a software component on the characteristics of a specific run-time system will lead to modifications in the behaviour of the component, modifications which may lead to errors. In certain cases, non-portability can therefore be considered as a fault in the designed software.

Likewise, the non-reusability of a component will lead to errors in the applications using this component. This non-reusability is caused, for instance, by the dependence of the behaviour of the component on the specific application where it was used when created. The reusability criterion is especially important as the use of a software component in its first application increases the reliance that the designers using this software component in other applications can place on it. If the component is not reusable, this reliance is totally unjustified. The reusability of the components is a necessary property in software engineering. It therefore implies that the non-reusability of a specific component must be considered as a fault in its design.

Reviewers are normally persons who were not involved in the design. However, the dependability objective implies that the designer must be capable of displaying the same critical attitude both towards the product that he or she designed and towards the way in which he or she produced it. At each step, the designer must have a detached view of his or her own work, similar to that of a reviewer. For instance, during the programming phases, an examination of the program before compilation or before execution comprises a good attitude.

2.2.9 Synthesis

To avoid introducing faults during design two approaches can be considered. The first approach deals with the guidelines used to produce high-quality software. We gave no general advice useful for every methods but specific advice can be found in books on design methods as, for example, (Meyer, 1988) (Booch, 1991). For instance, modularity is one of the criteria to be obtained. It implies weakly coupled components (little information is exchanged), the presence of explicit interfaces (no masked communications), etc. Some books provide guidelines for producing dependable software (Pyle, 1991).

The second approach deals with the analysis of the software at each stage in the design. Techniques allow errors to be detected at intermediate stages and therefore allow faults to be extracted and thus avoided in the software produced. Faults detected 'at the earliest' possible stage avoid important overhead costs which would be incurred when handling them if detected 'later on': fault removal at the end of the design and fault tolerance techniques to master residual faults.

We gave a presentation of the fault analysis techniques to be used. Some books or papers focus on this subject and therefore give more detailed information (Hecht, 1986), (Holloker, 1990), (Knight, 1993), (O'Connor, 1991), (Pyle, 1991), (Villemeur, 1991), (Wise, 1993).

The techniques described present various points of view on the fault avoidance problem and are therefore complementary to each other. The specification of the rules and their formalization as invariants is of general interest. The reliance placed on a software component is expressed giving, before its design, properties which must be obtained on the component produced. The rules must be correlated to demonstrate that both the assumptions and the assertions are true. Unfortunately, it is very difficult in practice to obtain such a general conclusion. Partial conclusions are therefore sought.

F.M.E.A. (Failure Modes Effect and Analysis) analyses if a potential error can lead to a failure. In particular, it indicates the effect of the violation of a rule. F.T.M. (Fault Tree Method) establishes if a potential error can exist by searching for the cause (the fault). It can be used to examine if a rule can be violated taking the design choices into account. The interest of F.M.E.A. and F.T.M. is to provide means for studying faults taking the structure and the components introduced by the design process into account. The faults are studied according to the cause and effect relations between the abstraction levels produced by the design stages.

The Petri net model was used to detect faults which concern the specification of the behaviour expressing event driven systems possibly including parallelism phenomena. We presented two uses of Petri net. The first one allows faults associated with general Petri net properties to be detected. With the second one (Leveson's approach), a marking (tokens in a set of places) is specified as an erroneous state and a mathematical process is used to check if this marking can be reached (due to design faults).

The aim of the review techniques is to detect faults in the writing of the requirements and then in the design. These techniques are used to study the results and the way in which these results are obtained. These techniques therefore analyse the designed software and the work performed by the designer.

We said in the introduction section (2.2.1) that the techniques proposed for fault avoidance have two purposes:

- to avoid the introduction of faults during a design step or,
- to detect faults introduced during a design step.

The table on Figure 2.17 summaries the main advantages of the techniques according to these two purposes.

	To Avoid Introduction	To Detect Error
Rules	X	X
F.M.E.A.	X	
G.F.C.M.		X
F.T.M.		X
Petri Net		X
Design Review		X

Figure 2.17: Synthesis of fault avoidance techniques

Some of the techniques described in this chapter are used in domains different from dependability. For instance, Petri net modelling is a conventional method for expressing the design of parallel processes. In the following sections certain techniques will also be used for fault removal and some others for fault tolerance.

2.3 Fault Removal

This section explains the fault removal methods for software already programmed. After detection, the faults are extracted to be absent in the software provided to the client.

2.3.1 Principles

In chapter 1, we listed the many reasons which can lead to the presence of faults. The techniques described in the previous section of this chapter 2 help to avoid faults from being introduced during the design but do not provide an absolute guarantee that no faults will be present. The aim of the techniques exposed in this section is to detect some of the residual faults in order to remove them. These means take two program characteristics into account:

- the program provides a complete and formal description of the software because it is defined with a programming language;
- the program is executable after its compilation.

Generally these two characteristics were not available during design: the formal models expressed at each stage provide partial descriptions of the software; a lot of informal comments written in English intervene in the expression and are not executable.

In fault removal, distinction is made between two approaches:

- the static studies which consist in analysing the program obtained without executing it (sections 2.3.2 and 2.3.3);
- and the dynamic studies which consist in analysing the operation by observing program execution (sections 2.3.4, 2.3.5, 2.3.6 and 2.3.7).

Static analysis
The aim of the static analysis is to prove that the behaviour of the program is partially or completely in compliance with the specification of the client examining the programmed software. This aim is close to one expressed for fault avoidance. However it concerns the program once its design has been completed. Some of the techniques proposed to avoid faults are therefore used to remove faults but in another way. The program defines a complete and formal definition of the software. Moreover the features of the programming language used are specific means for structuring the components introduced during the design. Finally new pieces of information are introduced at the programming step (data structure, etc.). The static analysis can be approached in two ways:

- by extracting from the program the specification or the invariants defining the dependability terms,
- by introducing these invariants into the program then checking them.

Dynamic Analysis
One of the characteristics of a program is that it can be executed. This is generally not possible for the product of the intermediate design steps. This important capability is used here. The dynamic analysis consists in comparing the realization with the specification or with the invariants defining the dependability criterion by executing the program. We present two approaches:

- the **testing methods** which consist in defining a succession of pairs (inputs, outputs) called a test sequence, deduced from the specification, and in supplying input values to execute the program and:
  (a) checking that the output values obtained by the execution correspond to the ones provided by the test sequence (*functional* or *black box* testing);
  (b) or checking that certain elements of the program are effectively used (*structural* or *white box* testing).
- the methods which consist in **adding, in the program, invariants** obtained from the contract associated with dependability terms and in verifying these properties at run-time.

Note that, even if fault removal techniques detect faults associated with the programming step or the execution means (compiler, run-time executive, used packages, etc.), they also highlight faults introduced during the design steps but which did not produce errors observed with the fault avoidance methods.

2.3.2 Static analysis: extracting specifications

The principle of the first static analysis method consists in finding a formal model of specifications from the program. Then this obtained model is compared with the one established at the beginning of the design from the client's requirements. It is a case of 'reverse engineering' process.

However, as we said in chapter 1 concerning formal specifications, only a partial specification (a point of view) is generally modelled depending on the characteristics of the model chosen. Furthermore it is frequently difficult to extract a complete specification model from the program. So this method is used to find properties written in the contract expressing the terms of the software dependability expected. Finally for industrial applications associated tools are necessary to obtain results.

Instead of these difficulties this method is interesting because it provides conclusions systematically, that is without human choices in its use. For this reason we will introduce the method proposed by T. Murata which uses Petri net models and we will develop the method presented by N. Leveson based on Fault-Tree models.

Murata's proposal
Murata proposes a technique to obtain a Petri net, which models the behaviour of the software, from an Ada program which uses tasking features. This model expresses sequencing between tasks. Then sequencing between input and output data of the software can be verified. If the sequencing obtained by extraction is not as expected, a failure is detected and the cause (the fault) must be removed.

Moreover, properties in accordance with Petri net characteristics may be checked on the extracted model as deadlocks (see fault avoidance in section 2.2.7). Unfortunately the correctness of the output values (and not only their occurrences) cannot be examined because Petri nets do not express operative treatments.

The technique used to translate an Ada program into a Petri net model will not be detailed here (Murata, 1989b).

Leveson's proposal
To obtain proofs of sequential programs, Nancy Leveson proposes an approach using Fault-Tree models (Leveson, 1983). These models are used in order to verify expected properties of the software taking the program structure into account.

A generic Fault-Tree model is associated with each language control statement. Figure 2.18 shows the tree associated with the 'if-then-else' statement. This tree is defined taking the semantics of this statement into account. The tree is generic because it defines the causes of any event such as an assertion or the violation of a rule. Generic elementary trees are proposed for each language statement. They allow an extended tree to be obtained from a program, considered as a combination of statements. Then, the generic root event is *instantiated* with a particular event as an expected assertion or an undesirable event. The reduction and the examination of the tree provides information about the occurrence potentiality of this event (see section 2.2.6) taking the program structure into account.

In the following paragraphs we will give more details on generic elementary trees then give proof of a property on an example.

An assertion (more generally an invariant) is true after the processing of an 'if-then-else' statement, if it is caused by the processing of the *then* part **or** if it is caused by the processing of the *else* part. The sentence 'the assertion is caused by the processing of a part of the program' expresses that the assertion is true due to the execution of this part and of the statements leading to this part. An assertion is caused by the processing of the *then* part if the Boolean condition associated with the *if* statement is true prior to the *if* statement **and** if the assertion is caused by the processing of the statements of the *then* part. Similar reasoning is considered for the *else* part. Then the causes of an assertion A after the processing of an *if* statement are defined by the relationships between assertions associated with the statement control (the condition) and the causes of the assertion A after the *then* and *else* part statements. Trees exist for these statements and trees can be provided for the four assertions introduced as leaves of the 'if-then-else' statement tree.

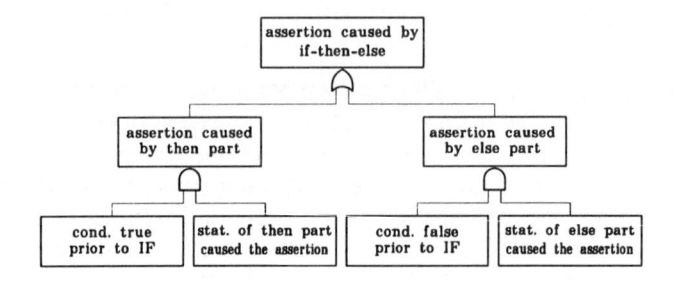

Figure 2.18: Fault-tree of the if statement

Figure 2.19 gives another example. It shows the generic tree associated with the 'while' statement. An assertion is true after the processing of a 'while' statement if:

- no loops are executed. In this case, the Boolean condition associated with the 'while' statement must be false prior to processing the 'while' statement **and** the assertion must be true due to the statements prior to the 'while' statement; **or**,
- N loops are executed. In this case the Boolean condition has to be true prior to the 'while' statement processing **and** the assertion has to be true after the Nth iteration processing.

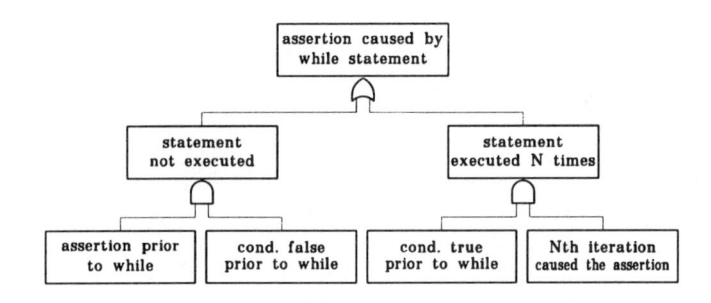

Figure 2.19: Fault-tree of the while statement

The case of sequencing of several statements is described using an example. Consider the following sequence of statements:

(1) A := SQRT(Y);
(2) B := X - 3.0;
(3) **if** A>B **then** SUB1;
    end if;

Assume that subprogram SUB1 controls an actuator and that we want to prove that the actuator is activated. To do this, we examine the assertion 'the actuator is activated' that is the assertion 'subprogram SUB1 is executed'. We search for the causes of the assertion 'SUB1 called'. This assertion is true if the execution of the previous statements (1) and (2) implies that A>B. So, due to the fact that statement (2) is always executed before (3), the assertion is true if A>X-3.0 is true, that is the statements executed prior to (1) caused the assertion SQRT(Y)>X-3.0 to be true. Figure 2.20 gives the tree obtained. If there are no previous statements, an assumption concerning the values of X and Y is obtained (SQRT(Y)>X-3.0). If previous statements were executed the effectiveness of this assumption must be studied taking these statements into account.

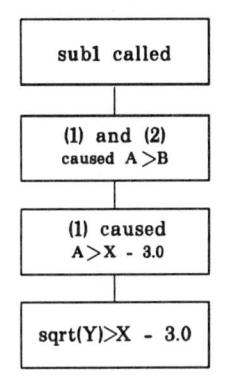

```
        ┌─────────────────┐
        │   sub1 called   │
        └────────┬────────┘
                 │
        ┌────────┴────────┐
        │   (1) and (2)   │
        │   caused A >B   │
        └────────┬────────┘
                 │
        ┌────────┴────────┐
        │   (1) caused    │
        │   A >X - 3.0    │
        └────────┬────────┘
                 │
        ┌────────┴────────┐
        │ sqrt(Y)>X - 3.0 │
        └─────────────────┘
```

Figure 2.20: Fault-tree of sequence of statements

Complex proofs can be obtained with this approach. Nancy Leveson provides a pedagogical example. Consider the following procedure:

```
procedure DIVIDE(A,B:in positive; Rem,Count:out natural) is
begin
   GET(A,B);
   if A>B then        -- T:= MAX(A,B)
      T := A;         -- S:= MIN(A,B)
      S := B;
   else
      T := B;
      S := A;
   end if;
   Rem := T;
   Count := 0;
   while Rem >= S loop
      Rem := Rem - S;
      Count := Count + 1;
   end loop;
end DIVIDE;
```

74 Chapter 2: Fault Detection and Correction Techniques

The aim of this procedure is to divide two positive integers (A and B) by the successive subtraction algorithm. It produces the quotient Count (result of the division) and the remainder Rem which are both integers. We want to establish that the program is correct: does it divide integer A by integer B? To do this, let us consider if the assertion 'quotient Count is greater than N' where N is any integer, is true after the processing of the procedure. The fault-tree obtained from the program structure analysis which has this assertion as root, is given on Figure 2.21. It is obtained using the generic elementary trees by the analysis detailed in the following paragraph.

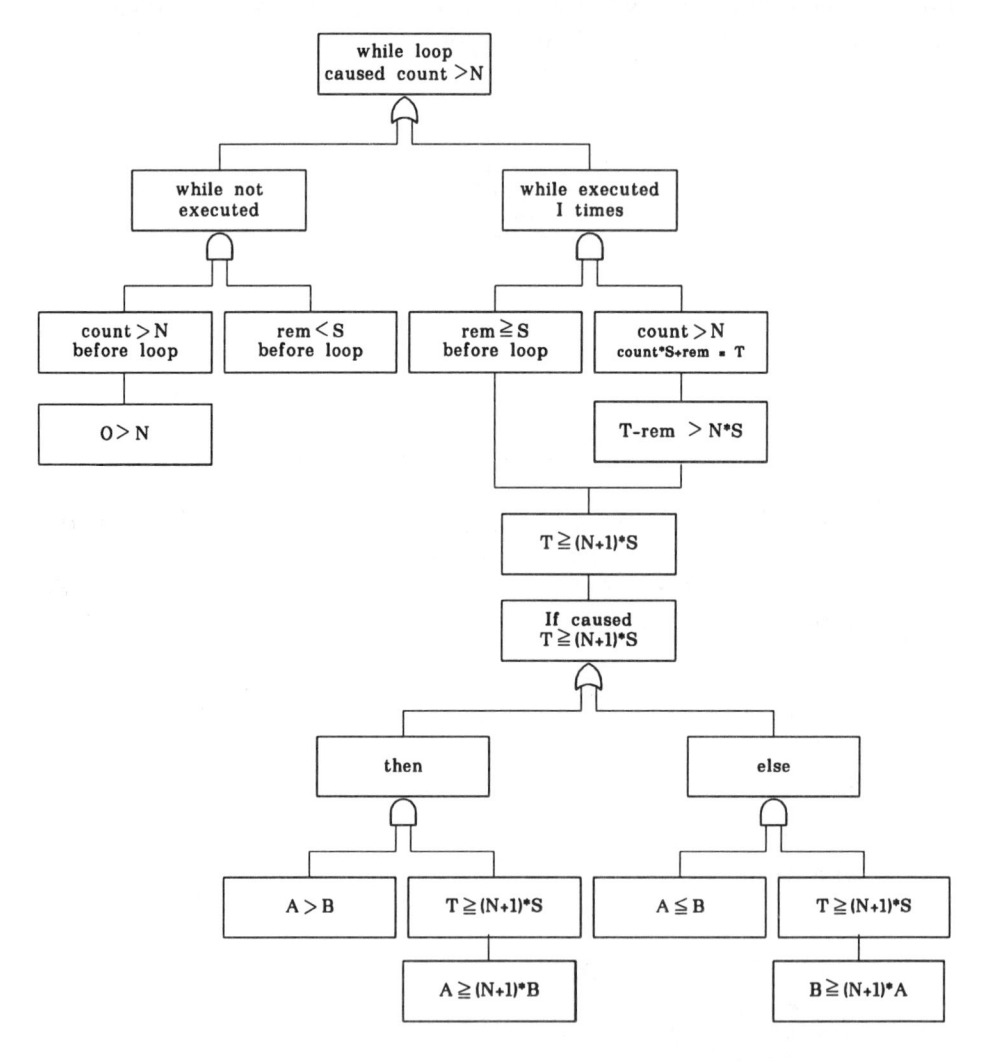

Figure 2.21: Fault-tree of an integer division procedure

The assertion is true after the processing of the procedure if it is true after the processing of the statement while. Considering the generic tree of the statement while, two cases must be examined: the loop was executed 0 times **or** I times. If the loop while was not executed to cause the assertion COUNT>N to be true, then the assertion must have been true before the loop statement was processed. As COUNT is assigned by value 0 then 0>N must be true and the Boolean expression associated with the loop statement must be false, that is T<S must be true. Such an assertion is false because the previous statements defined T as the maximum between A and B, and S as the minimum between A and B. So the loop is executed at least once.

Now let us examine the leaves of the tree corresponding to the assertion 'while executed I times'. The while statement generic tree is instantiated with assertion 'Count>N'. We must check the assertions: 'Rem>=S' before the execution of the loop **and** the Ith iteration caused 'Count>N'. Count is incremented at each loop; so there are more than N iterations and 'Rem>=S' at the Nth iteration. After N iterations 'Rem=T−N*S', so 'T−N*S>=S' must be true, that is 'T>=(N+1)*S' before the loop statement. The use of the 'if' statement generic tree provides two cases (see Figure 2.21). Consider the case of A>B. In this case, the assertion 'Count>N' implies that the data A and B are as follows: A>=(N+1)*B, ∀N<Count. This expresses that Count is the highest possible divisor. For if not, the remainder (Rem) would be greater than B!

We showed, therefore, that the program written satisfies the mathematical law, ∀ N<Count then A>=B*(N+1). Note that the same argument will be obtained with the hypothesis A<=B. This conclusion corresponds to partial proof that the program provides the division of A and B.

If the tree obtained had showed that, for certain values of N lower than Count, the mathematical law could be false then a design fault would exist in the program.

The use of fault trees therefore allows properties concerning the semantics of a program, that is invariants of the initial contract, to be proved and therefore gives total or partial proof of its correctness, that is absence of faults in its design or in its programming. If the condition had not been true, for all values of A and B, we would have underlined the situations in which the program produces erroneous results and therefore contains faults which would need to be extracted.

Generic fault-trees were provided for the tasking features (Cha, 1988) allowing real-time software to be analysed.

2.3.3 Static analysis: introducing invariant from specification

The properties obtained from the specification to define the dependability criterion have already been used as a fault avoidance means at each step in the design (section 2.2.3). We will concentrate here on their use in programming and show their interest as a fault removal tool.

Language capabilities

A compiler is generally used above all as a means for translating a source language program into a target machine language code. In addition to this basic role it is also used as a source program analyser to detect design faults in the programs. To perform analyses such as these, the semantics of the language features used must be close to those of the designed software concepts. For instance, an intuitive notion of system design is that a component receives data at its inputs and outputs the results. These output values may then be used as input data for another component. Assigning them to the output of another component is a design error. Likewise, the realization of a software component can use input parameter values and must assign values to the output parameters. Use other than this also corresponds to a design error.

These basic design notions (inputs and outputs) have equivalences in very few languages. For instance, in C language, to communicate a variable to be modified (**output** parameter), we give its address (**input** parameter). The implementation can then modify this value: the address is overwritten and the designated variable remains unchanged. Such an error cannot be detected at compile time as the address type semantics does not allow us to know if an address corresponds to input data or to an artefact to pass information associated with an output variable. Pascal language offers an improvement by means of the mode 'var' specifying that a parameter is output or input/output information. However, as distinction cannot be made between the two cases (output or input/output), the body of a subprogram can use the value of a parameter passed by mode 'var' (considered as an input/output parameter) even though the semantics of the specification consider this parameter as an output parameter, that is, whose initial value is not pertinent. Thanks to distinction between the 'in', 'out' and 'in out' modes in Ada, the compiler makes these semantic coherence checks associated with the input and output concepts.

Different **type** definitions in a program source correspond to different kinds of objects in the design product or in the client's specification. The possibility offered by languages to express these distinctions in the program texts is a means to introduce pieces of information from the specification into the problem. Typing of subprogram parameters and variables also comprises an important method for detecting design faults by the compiler. The assignment of a variable by an incompatible type expression is both a simple illustration of typing interest and shows that it is a feature indispensable for such a detection.

Parameter type and mode allow the contract binding the subprogram user and its implementer to be specified. It gives obligations for the two partners. For the user, it defines rules for correct use. For instance, an actual parameter in 'in' mode must have an initial value on subprogram call (for example, by being an 'out' mode parameter of an earlier called procedure). For the implementer, the body of his or her solution must assign parameters in 'out' mode before return to the caller. Conversely, assertions defining the contract provide guarantees for both partners. The implementer assumes, for example, use in compliance with the contract which eliminates the need to introduce cumbersome checks into his or her design (Meyer, 1992).

Through these examples, we see that languages can favour fault removal by varying degrees. To this, we can add the capability of the language to avoid faults being introduced. We mentioned, for example, the possibility of easily designing objects in the form of abstract types or the impossibility to make disorderly jumps. The features of the language thus prevent the presence of entities including *hidden clauses*, that is clauses not stipulated in the definition of the contract, which would make fault removal difficult during program analysis. For instance, use of statement exit in loops or statement return in subprograms (except as the last statement of a function) complicates the check on the effectiveness of the assignment of the values to the 'out' mode formal parameters of the subprograms before return to the caller.

Extensions

Programming languages have limited capacities for introducing specifications into the programs and tools making evaluations on the conformity of the program with regard to specification information introduced in the program are few. Let us recall here some of the work conducted by Howden (Howden, 1990). He proposes a tool to detect if one part of a program has a wrong idea (perception) about another part of the program with which it interacts. In his study, he considers that every entity must specify:

1. its *assumptions* on its environment; for instance, a task T1 using an accept statement assumes that another task of the application has an entry call statement which will be executed at some time to resume the execution of T1;

2. its *assertions* which are affirmations about its behaviour. For instance, a task asserts that it calls a specified entry call.

The proposed tool demonstrates, for an application which is considered as a set of entities, that the assumptions can be proved (or denied) by means of the assertions. An important characteristic of this method is that the responsibility for specifying and not forgetting the assertions and assumptions falls to the designer.

We will not provide more pieces of information in this chapter because they are strongly dependent on the used language. The case of the Ada language will be detailed in section 4.4 of chapter 4.

Conclusion

Introducing information concerning the specification into the program allows a compiler to be considered not only as a code generator but also as a means for detecting faults in the designed program. Definition of assertions can be imposed by the language (example: parameter modes) or proposed by it (example: intensive use of types). In the latter case, checks on non-use or under-use cannot be made. Therefore, faults can only be detected by the voluntary use of this possibility. This again shows that the quality of the design work (use of the features offered) has an effect on the quality of the program designed (fault detection).

Analysis tools are few. To overcome this drawback, the designer must make an intellectual analysis of his or her program. This is achieved using the techniques proposed (for example, the Fault Tree Method) or also by a review. For instance, before the first compilation, the designer can inspect his or her program to establish the effectiveness of general criteria such as: 'are all the real parameters associated with in mode parameters correctly assigned before the subprogram calls?'; 'are all the out mode parameters correctly assigned in the body before the return to the caller?'; 'are statements whose behaviour depends on the implementation used (for instance, the priority range for tasking or the biggest number of the float representation)?', etc. The aim of the review is also to demonstrate if the program implements properties obtained from the specification specific to the problem posed by the client. The review techniques are the ones presented in section 2.2.8.

2.3.4 Dynamic analysis: functional testing

Principles
Consider a system specified by a description of its behaviour, that is to say by the expression of the evolution of its outputs stemming from the evolution of its inputs (and of time). The aim of the design work is to obtain an expression of the realization of the system (as a program). The **functional equivalence** between the basic model (specifications) and the realization obtained (program) is made uncertain due to the human work. The aim of the functional testing is to show that the behaviour of the specified system is equivalent to the behaviour of the program produced by executing the software (target system) (Figure 2.22). Such an approach makes no assumptions on the realization of the program studied, i.e. on the design choices, because only the software behaviour is considered. For this reason this technique is also called 'black box testing'.

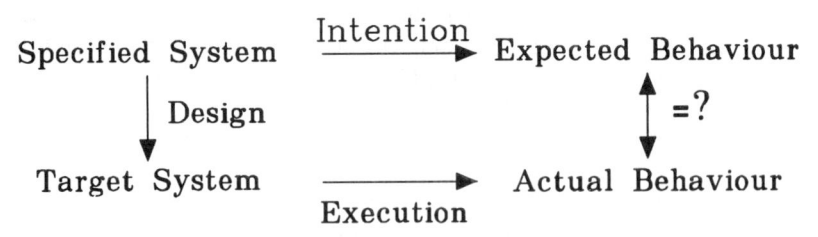

```
Specified System  --Intention-->  Expected Behaviour
       |                                  ↑
     Design                              =?
       ↓                                  ↓
Target System     --Execution-->  Actual Behaviour
```

Figure 2.22: Functional equivalence

Fault Removal

One way of expressing the expected behaviour is to provide a **test sequence**. A test sequence is a succession of pairs (inputs, outputs) values obtained from the specification of the system. More precisely, the input sequence $(i_j)_{j=...}$ applied to the specified system supplies the appropriate output sequence (o_j). Figure 2.23 illustrates the test Sequence = $(i_1,o_1), (i_2,o_2), (i_3,o_3), ...$

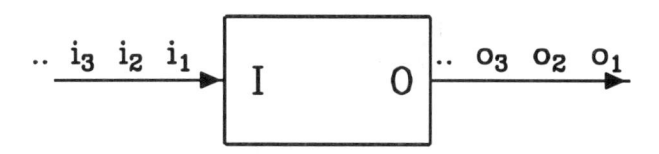

.. i_3 i_2 i_1 → [I   O] → .. o_3 o_2 o_1

Figure 2.23: (input, output) test sequence

The succession of values $i_1, i_2, i_3,...$ is supplied to input I of the designed program which gives as output the computed values $O_1, O_2, O_3,...$ They are compared to the expected values $o_1, o_2, o_3,...$ The software system is considered as correctly designed if, $\forall i, O_i = o_i$. The functional equivalence (Figure 2.22) is shown by the equivalence of the outputs (Figure 2.24).

```
                Specified System  --Intention-->  Expected Outputs
Input  <                                                  ↕ =?
                Target System    --Execution-->   Actual Outputs
```

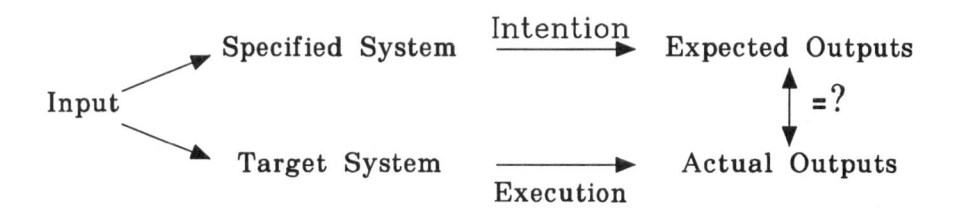

Figure 2.24: Output equivalence

Difficulties in obtaining test sequences
The definition of a test sequence poses two problems:

- how to define the input sequence,
- how to obtain the expected output sequence.

In order to check the correctness of the software system, the **test sequence inputs** must cause *all the possible modes of behaviour*. Thus, for a purely sequential application, we should find all the input sequences activating all the behavioural sequences defined in the specification. For instance, if the specification is defined by the automaton shown on Figure 2.25, the input sequence to be applied could be 'a b c a c' if the state numbered 1 on the figure is considered as the initial state.

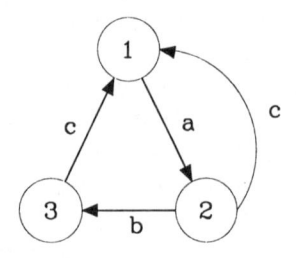

Figure 2.25: Sequential specification

However, actual problems to be solved are rarely as simple as this. The specification often defines memory effects associated with data which are not generally expressed by the automata on account of their combinational aspect. For instance, to book a seat on a train using an automatic ticket dispenser, behaviour depends on the sequence of actions performed by the user but can also depend on data such as the number of the credit card used for payment or the ticket price. For these applications, two identical input sequences lead to different outputs as the specific values associated with the events cause the system behaviour to change.

Thus, operative specifications are also combined with the sequential aspects. An input comprises an event which changes the program behaviour and also a value which intervenes in the operations (for example, arithmetic). This case arises, for instance, with a program solving a second-degree equation. The giving of coefficient value data is the only event causing the start of the calculation process the result of which, however, depends on the values effectively given.

For such programs, an exhaustive (but unrealistic) test would consist in considering all the possible values of the three coefficients of the equation. This sequence is unrealistic on account of the execution time that it implies. Also, knowledge after this test of all the possible solutions would eliminate the interest of conserving the program! A sequence which only supplies a set of coefficients for each of the typical cases (discriminant>=0 and discriminant<0) would not provide complete proof. In effect, the program designer could have introduced specific cases which do not appear in the specification. He or she distinguishes, for instance, the null discriminant case.

The **length** of the input sequence is also difficult to establish. For instance, a sequence can activate an error due to a design fault. However, this error may not immediately introduce failures of the program. It may lead to a failure in a component without affecting the global behaviour. However, extension of the sequence may propagate the error to the program outputs. The existing fault can thus be observed through program failure, that is obtaining an unexpected output value.

Another problem arises when determining a test sequence. Even if a study allows an ideal succession of input values to be obtained, the **corresponding**

output values are required. Often these values cannot be obtained directly by the specification since the client pays for a program to obtain them. This problem is called the **oracle problem** in (Courtois, 1987). It is easily solved if a reference is available. For instance, in the case of the factory test of integrated circuits, a standard circuit considered as correct is used. In the case of a new version of software associated with the same specification, we can refer to the old version already tested. Unfortunately, it cannot be done for a first design of a software product.

If new functionalities are added to a software tool, the old ones must be retested, even if the design of the first functionalities is not modified. Actually *side effects* may occur between the two parts of the implementation. For instance, in a real-time application, if new tasks are added which do not interact explicitly with the existing ones (no rendezvous, no common data), an implicit temporal influence appears. This is due to the sharing of a single microprocessor. Non-regression tests will therefore have to be conducted on the old functionalities.

Obtaining a test sequence
The first way to obtain a test sequence consists in giving random inputs i_j. However, this method does not allow *certainties* to be given for the sought equivalencies. We can only estimate that the longer the sequence, the better the *probability* of reaching this aim. Studies have been made in this area more particularly for electronic systems (David, 1980) (Thevenod-Fosse, 1981) (Thevenod-Fosse, 1983). The length of the sequences giving a test probability near to 1 (the highest value), gives rise to long testing periods. In practice, these sequences are truncated. The testing is continued through the actual use of the program by the software buyers! This is not permissible for the dependable software with which we are concerned. The '**random testing**' approach is not as good when the software tested is the one of a complex sequential system because it is difficult to provoke all the possible operations. Some improvements consist in making a '**pseudo-random testing**' taking the system's sequentiality into account. This aspect will be developed in the next section. Another improvement consists in choosing the inputs taking into account their probabilities of occurrence in practical use (DeMillo, 1987) (Thevenod-Fosse, 1991). The aim of this approach is to obtain the *most exhaustive* sequence (with regard to the user's behaviour) taking the *realistic constraints* into account (for example, the time required to execute the test).

For dependable systems, proof of the behaviour's equivalence is sought. Therefore, it is advisable to show that a test sequence is a *complete linear form* of the model of the specification. The test sequence describes a behaviour linearly (in sequence): input values imply output values. To be exhaustive a test sequence must completely express the behaviour of the software to be tested. Obtaining such a sequence is made difficult by the fact that the system's behaviour often expresses sequential phenomena.

The most **formal method of obtaining a test sequence** consists of deducing it from a formal model of the specifications. Work has been done along these lines for cases where the models are specified by automata (Saucier, 1981) (Bellon, 1985) or by algebraic formulations (Bidoit, 1987) (Bouge, 1986).

Test sequence evaluation by identification
If a test sequence cannot be obtained from the specification using a formal approach, the reverse problem can be considered. A test sequence is defined and then the following question is formulated: 'is the test sequence a *good* one?'. A test sequence is perfect if it can detect a program whose behaviour is different from the one defined by the specification. In the previous approach, the test sequence was deduced from the specification (verification). Here the test sequence is the initial knowledge (validation). The **test sequence evaluation** principle is as follows: a sequence is analysed *identifying* the models of the behaviours which are defined as correct by this test sequence. Then these models are compared with the model of the specification (see, for instance, (Abid, 1989b) (El Maadani, 1991) for systems specified with automata). If several models different from the specification model are identified then the test sequence is not good because it cannot detect programs whose behaviours are not in compliance with the specification model.

However, these formal methods (for verification or validation) are very limited, because, on one hand, they only apply to a few simple models and, on the other hand, they may generate *theoretically ideal* sequences of *practically inadmissible* length (Pham Van, 1989). In particular, for certain systems, a theoretically perfect test sequence may have a huge length.

Generally, since it is **impossible to obtain perfect test sequences**, and detect all the misbehaviours, research is limited in obtaining sequences which emphasize certain aspects of the behaviour or a predefined set of misbehaviours. Once more the contract which contains the rules specifying the dependability criterion is useful to define test sequences.

We said that software specification often involve combinational aspects, the aim of testing every combination thus generates an explosion in the length of the sequence. In order to avoid this, the set of operations is split into classes of equivalencies. The test sequence must check a representative element of each class. For instance, in the case of a program solving an equation of the 2nd degree, the test sequence must successively provide coefficients in order to obtain two real solutions, a double solution and two complex solutions. However we gave the limitations of the efficiency of such a method.

The presentation that we just have made concerns software tools to be tested from a behavioural point of view (black box testing). Only the result obtained (global behaviour of the program) is of interest. Frequently (i.e., unfortunately, always for significant software), it is not possible to obtain a complete test sequence, and the correctness of the realization cannot be proved. In this case we try to evaluate certain factors to judge the program itself instead of comparing it with the specification. This kind of test, called *structural testing* will be presented in the next section.

2.3.5 Dynamic analysis: structural testing

Principles

Structural testing is based on the structure of the program tested. The program structure comes from design choices: statements, subprograms, data, etc., that is all internal components combined to design the program. For structural testing of software, the principle consists in verifying that the internal structure of the program is 'well covered' when executed. This qualifier will be measured by what we call the **coverage rate**. This number corresponds to the ratio between the number of *elements covered* and the number of *elements to be covered*. The word 'element' depends on the form of test chosen, as will be explained later. An element may be a variable, a statement, a branch or a path. For example, the test can consist in evaluating the number of variables effectively used by executing the program.

Structural testing does not therefore evaluate the correctness of the program's behaviour but evaluates its structure considering the use of certain elements as evaluation criteria. If some elements of the structure are not used, this does not mean that the program is not correct but questions must be posed to the designer.

The structural test of a program uses knowledge of the program structure. This is why it is also called **'white box testing'**. Performing such a test requires four stages.

- First, **trial sets** are required. They are different from the test sequences because only input values are necessary. The outputs given by the execution of the program are not taken into consideration because this technique does not concern a functional study. The inputs composing a trial set can be chosen in a random way or by taking the specification or the implementation into account.
- The program to be tested is **statically** split into elements (which are portions of the code) in order to obtain a **control graph** (also known as a flow graph). This is a conventional graph where the nodes represent the *control statements* of the source code and the arcs represent the sequences of *ordinary statements*. Control statements correspond to statements which cause a transfer of control as, for instance, conditional jump instructions in an assembly language, or loop statements (such as 'for', 'while') or conditional statements (such as 'if', 'case') in a high-level language such as Ada.
- The program is executed using the trial sets. At run-time, the elements used (nodes and arcs of the graph) are **'marked'** in order to memorize the passage points taken.
- Finally, the ratio between the marked elements and the total number of elements provides the coverage rate.

Several forms of structural tests exist which depend on the chosen elements. They will be presented and illustrated using the following fragment of a program:

```
if X<=0                     -- 1
    then   X := -X;
           Y := 2;           -- 2
    else   X := 1-X;
           Y := 1;           -- 3
end if;
if X=0                       -- 4
    then   X := 1;           -- 5
    else   X := X+1;         -- 6
end if;                      -- 7
```

The associated control graph is shown on Figure 2.26.

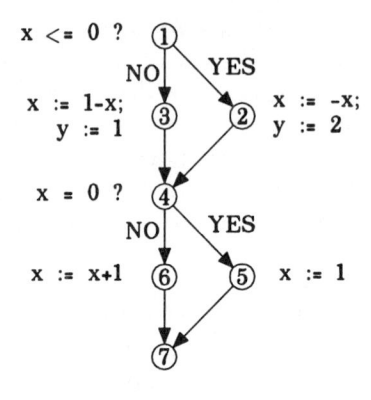

Figure 2.26: Control graph

Statement, branch, path testing

The first form of a structural test consists in supplying a coverage rate from the **statements** of the program. When the program is run, the statements used are marked. We can reasonably arrange that 'a good' trial set will give a coverage rate of 100%, which means that all the statements will be reached, i.e. executed at least once. If not, the presence of these statements must be justified and it must be explained why they have not been reached. This may be because the set of trials is insufficient. However, unreachable statements may exist if general packages are reused. These packages probably offer services more extended than the ones used. Unreachable statements are also incorporated using fault tolerant techniques. The statements introduced to recover an error are not executed because the input sequence used to raise this error is not known.

Many programming environments (like most Ada environments) integrate this form of testing.

This test considers that statements are independent without taking into account the sequential relations which exist between the program statements. These relations are expressed by the branches of the control graph. For instance, consider the fragment of program proposed to illustrate our presentation. The execution of statement x:=-x involves the execution of the statement y:=2.

A first improvement consists in verifying that all the **branches** of the control graph are taken at least once. The marked elements are the branches. Here again, if a branch is not marked, a justification is necessary. A branch which is never used can correspond to an impossible path due to an incoherence in the design or in the programming. However, it may be due to the input sequence or other reasons explained for statement testing.

This test considers that the branches are independent without taking into account the sequential relations determined by the control graph and the presence of operations on variables. Suppose, in our example, that a test indicates that all branches are covered (i.e. all the branches are used at run-time testing). The fact of having gone through path (1,2,4,5,7) (case x=0 at the beginning) cannot be proved, for we may have gone through paths (1,2,4,6,7) and (1,3,4,5,7) (tested with values x=-3 and x=1 at the beginning). What we would like to do, is to use all the possible paths.

The corresponding method consists in computing the coverage rate of the control **paths** (ratio of the number of paths effectively covered over the number of paths on the graph). A rate of 100% affirms that all the paths on the graph have effectively been processed. In general, this rate is practically unachievable, because of the excessive number of paths. For instance, Boehm provides an example containing two loop statements, two case statements and an if statement (Pham Van, 1989). He calculates that if the maximum number of iterations is equal to 12 and if a path is tested in a nanosecond, an exhaustive test would last for 4000 years!

The presence of while statements increases the complexity. The length of the paths (number of arcs) can be enormous and it may be not possible to give a bound value (even if the value is not infinite if the program execution can be terminated). So the maximum length of the checked paths is fixed to define the test trials ('basis paths' method (Pyle, 1991)).

Moreover, **all the control paths** deduced from the graph **are not execution paths**, for it is necessary to take semantic aspects into account. If we modify our example by replacing the second test statement x=0? by x=-1?, the path (1,2,4,5,7) will never be covered so there is no point in trying it.

In conclusion, no absolute judgement can be deduced from a 'coverage rate' value. A given sequence can be judged as 'good' for one criterion and 'bad' for another. Furthermore, the coverage test **evaluates a certain quality of the design and not the correctness** of the designed software. However, the structural testing is interesting for removing faults because it indicates which elements (statement, branch, path) are not used by the test. It warns the designer who must then examine the reasons for such a situation. In particular the input sequence of a test sequence used for functional testing may be applied as a trial set to examine the programming quality in addition of the behaviour correctness. The non use of certain elements may highlight that the test sequence is not complete (or there are extra parts or redundant parts in the program).

More ample information is available on structural testing in (Myers, 1979), (DeMillo, 1987), (Pham Van, 1989) and (Muenier, 1989).

2.3.6 Dynamic analysis: structured functional approach

In order to benefit from the advantages offered by the functional method (information on the behaviour) and the structural method (information on the design choices expressed by the program structure), a **structured functional** representation is used. Structured functional models are behavioural models taking the consequences of design choices into account. The aim of structured functional analysis is to establish the relations which exist between the effects of a software (its behaviour) and the causes (the structure of the program).

Debugging
The structured functional approach is first used in software design for debugging. Debugging tools are frequently used as fault removal means. The user examines program behaviour correctness taking output values and also pieces of information from the structure (such as variable values or statement pointers) into account.

A debugging tool must offer the three following features (see (Brindle, 1989) (Feldman, 1989) (Martinolle, 1990) (Tokuda, 1988)):

- isolation of an event. In particular it must be possible to express errors (variable values or statement execution unexpected, etc.) which stop the execution process,
- mastering of the progress of a program running at procedure levels, source code level or assembly instruction level to take the program structure into account and to choose the best level of abstraction to examine the program execution to facilitate its understanding,
- presentation of the various states of the variables and, in particular, the interface variables to understand the operation, that is the global behaviour.

The structured functional approach is also used for testing as described in the following paragraphs.

Definition of test sequence
We showed that functional test sequence definition is not easy. The very simple program, solving second-degree equation, illustrated this difficulty: it is not possible to try all the combination of coefficients. The choice of representative coefficients depends on the program structure. So a structured functional approach for testing seems to be an improvement.

Knowledge of the realization facilitates the test sequence generation (Chandra, 1987) and allows a reduction of its length. The method consists in grouping into equivalence classes the behaviours taking the design choices into account. We will not give more theoretical explanations but just an example to illustrate the principle. Consider a program which converts a two-character string in a positive integer. If the design distinguishes the processing operation which supplies a one-digit number from the one which supplies a two-digit number, a 'good' test must provide data belonging to each class. We can consider that a test sequence using, for example, inputs '3' and '27' is better (in terms of coverage rate) than one successively providing the values from '10' to '99'.

Studies taking the structure and the behavioural model into account may show that some parts of some components never intervene in the global operation. For example, statements of some procedures may never be executed, because these procedures are called in a particular context (with constrained parameter values). Martinolle (Martinolle, 1991) presents the case of a system designed as a hierarchy of subsystems the behaviours of which are defined as finite-state machines. She shows how to find some parts of the designed system which cannot be controlled from the outside (they cannot be activated by the inputs of the system) and also some parts which cannot be observed (the operations of which have no effect on the outputs).

This phenomenon will be found increasingly, because the software components produced are as general as possible, so that they can be reused. However, it is important to detect the unused functions in a particular program in order to avoid having to take them into account in structural testing because it is impossible to find input sequences to provoke the running of these parts, or to find output sequences to observe their impact on the global behaviour.

Test sequence validation
When a test sequence is available, its efficiency must be evaluated. For this purpose the structured functional approach is also suitable.

The aim of the functional testing is to study the correctness of software taking only its specification into account, without information on implementation. Software failures are expressed by modifications in the behaviour in front of the specification. The behaviour of each failed software may be defined by a model. As this model is different from the one associated with the specification, an input sequence for which such a model gives an output sequence different from the one provided by the model of the specification exists. A functional test sequence is then considered to be perfect if it can detect *all modifications*, that is to say, if the output values expected by the sequence are different from the ones obtained by the operation of all the models which are different from the one defined by the specification.

Unfortunately, this point of view often requires too much of the test sequence which must perceive all imaginable modifications in the behaviour. Probably, all used test sequences will no doubt be measured as being of bad performance.

However, taking the realization into account shows that certain transformations of the program behaviour are not possible and that therefore it is not indispensable to test them.

The reasoning can be extended by considering the design choices still further, by evaluating the test sequence by its capacity to detect implementation variations.

Work was initially done in this area, in electronics, under the name of *Method with Assumptions of Failures* (Thatte, 1980) (Annaratone, 1982) (Su, 1982) (Brahme, 1984). The same principle was used to study the efficiency of software test sequences. This technique, called **mutation**, consists in modifying the program to be tested by introducing a fault and executing the test sequence proposed to check if it detects this voluntary fault (Appelbe, 1988). One of the problems raised by this approach concerns the choice of modifications to be embodied.

The source program can be modified by first introducing some alterations obtained from a study of the misuse of the programming language features, that is, of the misunderstanding of the semantics of the programming language, without taking the semantics of the problem into account. For instance, the statement '`while A loop ...`' is changed in '`while not A loop ...`'. Here we assume that certain designers make mistakes between the condition to stay in the loop or to exit the loop. Another fault concerns the use of the keyboard. For instance, `X:= 1.03` may be in the program instead of `X:= 10.3`. These injected faults can be viewed as careless mistakes or programming faults caused by incorrect use of the statements.

A second class of injected faults is deduced from the semantics of the problem. The assertions associated with the components of the program are analysed and the statements of these components are modified in order to make these assertions erroneous (violation of invariants). For example, if a procedure computes the values of parameters A and B where A must be lower than B, we modify the statements so that the value assigned to A is higher than the value assigned to B. Then the program is executed using the test sequence in order to check its efficiency to detect this fault.

Fault detection

We said that the input values of a test sequence must activate internal operations to detect faults but must also propagate the errors outside (to produce failures) allowing the faults to be observed on the output parameters. The observability problem is frequently solved by adding observation variables as program output parameters. These variables are not maintained during normal operation but only added so that internal behaviour of the program can be understood. This technique requires the addition of new output values (those of the observation variables) to the test sequence.

To avoid introducing observation outputs in the realization to be observed outside by comparing the values produced with the ones expected by a test sequence, observation and examination means can be incorporated into the program during design. This is obtained using invariants. **Invariants** are added to components involved in a program. They express rules of the contract associated with each component.

This solution has several advantages. First, an invariant offers the possibility of detecting an error immediately and not afterwards by means of the results obtained. Additional input values are not required to propagate errors towards the outputs. So, the introduction of invariants associated with components at design time allows the size of the test sequence to be limited because the internal errors are signalled by the inside of the program. It therefore gives a location for the fault. In addition, it allows an error to be signalled which could not be seen from outside the system.

For example, consider a STACK package providing the procedures PUSH and POP. Assume that the realization of the POP procedure does not decrement the STACK_SIZE (local variable not accessible from outside). By using the test sequence:
```
PUSH(X);
POP(Y), Y is equal to X;
```

this error cannot be detected. By associating the assertion '*STACK_SIZE is decremented*' with the procedure POP, this error will be signalled.

The errors are detected by the local invariants put in the components of the program and not by verifying the *external assertion*: 'the computed value is equal to the expected one'. This avoids the estimation of several output values for the test sequence because the errors will be detected by the local assertions. Of course, invariants can be added to the main procedure to increase the checks. However, we must point out that invariants define general properties between input and output variables whereas a test sequence pattern gives an absolute relationship between precise values of a (input, output) pair.

Fault location
A test sequence is used to detect the presence of faults. If such a situation occurs, the designer must remove the fault. For this, he or she must locate it. Multiple faults may produce a single effect. The use of the Gathered Fault Combination Method (G.F.C.M.) during design evidenced some of these independent causes and is therefore useful as a Fault Removal technique.

However, if an error is the result of a combination of independent events (which are not necessarily errors), the Fault Tree Method will provide pertinent information to facilitate the location of these causes.

It is obvious that location is easier for design faults intervening at one level than for faults causing errors propagated through several components obtained from many design levels. For this reason, the test must follow the inverse process to design. The lowest level components are first tested before being assembled into higher level components, etc., up to complete program level.

2.3.7 Dynamic analysis: introducing invariants

We mentioned the difficulty of obtaining the output values (the oracle problem) to create a test sequence. At first this difficulty can be due to the fact that the computations made by the program are bulky. The program was designed because human calculations would take too long. In this case, we may not try to calculate the expected outputs as we only want to verify the consistency of the computed outputs with **properties** deduced from the specifications or expressed in the contract established to define dependability criterion. For example, if the minimum, average and maximum values of a set are computed by software, we assert that these values must rise (minimum <= average <= maximum). The test will then consist in providing inputs and checking this assertion without checking the correctness of each separate output value.

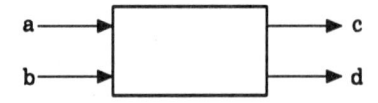

Figure 2.27: Time constraints between input and output values

Estimating output values is frequently impossible for specifications involving temporal aspects. Consider, for instance, the system shown on Figure 2.27 which must have the following property: *if the 'a' signal is applied before the 'b' signal then the 'c' signal will occur before the 'd' signal*. The input sequence 'a,b,a,b' can furnish the output sequences 'c,d,c,d' or 'c,c,d,d' depending on the delay between the assignments of the input values and on the duration of the system reaction, that is the time required to provide the output values after input reception. A test sequence therefore cannot a priori provide an expected output sequence if temporal pieces of information are not specified. In this situation, the introduction of invariants, obtained from specifications, could be contemplated.

Moreover, a test pattern constitutes a *punctual and explicit* evaluation of the correctness of a system: an output value is examined at a time determined by the test sequence. On the contrary, an invariant may *continuously and implicitly* check this correctness. Consider, for instance, a new property of the previous system, linked to the values of the input and output data: 'V(a)<V(b)=>V(c)<V(d)', where V(s) is the value associated with the 's' signal. For a test sequence of such a system, the check concerning the outputs (V(c)<V(d)) must be explicitly added to each pair (V(a), V(b)) so that V(a)<V(b). On the contrary, the property expressed by the introduction of the invariant is evaluated *automatically*.

We also showed the interest of associating invariants with the components introduced in the design of a software tool in particular to reduce the complexity of the test sequence. The choice of the programming language is here again important as it can favour the expression of the invariants checked during run-time or not. Thus, the definition of a constraint type in Ada if it can allow memory space to be limited, favours especially detection of assignment errors during run-time checking the invariant 'the assigned value must belong to the range specified by the constraint type'.

Usually, the validity of invariants is verified on line, i.e. immediately at runtime. In (Dillon, 1990) another technique is proposed. A graph of the paths used is generated at run-time. This graph is close to the one described for the structural testing (see section 2.3.5). Whereas the control graph represents all the possible behaviours of the program, the generated graph corresponds to the particular execution performed. The graph is then executed with symbolic information obtained from assumptions (such as two values V1 and V2 where V1<V2) and the assertions are checked.

Note that the introduction of executable invariants can modify the behaviour of the software. For instance, it can involve time overheads and so change the sequential order of the task sequencing (order of the rendezvous) in case of an application which uses multi-tasking. It must be checked that invariants do not introduce such a modification (Cheng, 1989).

2.3.8 Dynamic analysis: execution means dependency

The dynamic analysis methods conclude that a software is correct showing the reality of criteria by means of software execution. For functional testing, the criterion is the equivalence between the expected behaviour (described by the client's specification) and the obtained behaviour (actual behaviour). For structural testing, the criterion concerns the real processing of program elements (statement, branch, path) towards those provided by the program. The reality of these criteria is evaluated by means of the designer's execution tools associated with the language: compiler, run-time executive, hardware. These means constitute the execution environment (or run-time environment).

For a given language, numerous environments are provided by various manufacturers. Thus the environment used by the client may be different from the one considered by the designer for testing. If the actual behaviour of the language statements varies according to the environments, the actual behaviour of a software application may be multiple. Consequently, the conclusions on the software correctness obtained by the designer may not be valid for the client.

The programming languages have numerous features whose fuzzy definition allows various behaviours to be provided by language environment implementers. This fuzziness is necessary to give freedom degrees to the execution environment designers to take implementations constraints (such as hardware constraints) into account. Thus, the precision of the float numbers is not specified for numerous languages. We signalled in section 1.4.2 that implementation variations are due to abstract definitions of the features of the languages whereas the implementers must provide a specific execution environment.

In section 4.4.2 of chapter 4 we will show that such a situation exists for the Ada language. So the client must have a tempered reliance in the correctness of a software tool (or a software component) if this correctness is established by test methods (Motet, 1995). This conclusion does not mean that these methods are not efficient. They are useful to detect numerous errors. However they must not be considered as infallible tools.

2.3.9 Synthesis

During the design stages, techniques must be used to avoid faults in the designed program. In section 2.2, we presented means to avoid or detect and then extract the faults during the top-down design steps. Unfortunately the practical use of the proposed techniques does not guarantee absence of all faults in the software produced. After the design phase we must therefore eliminate residual faults in the program using Fault Removal techniques.

In this section, we made a distinction between static analysis, which consists of an off-line check of the behaviour of a program, and dynamic analysis, which consists of an examination of the software by its execution.

Synthesis of the techniques

Two classes of techniques are proposed for **static analysis**. The aim of the first one is to extract pieces of information associated with the specification from the source program. In practice only some properties can be proved. These means are very interesting for ensuring the effectiveness of partial but critical properties which are given in the contract defining the client's reliance criteria. The second technique consist of program text analysis to detect mismatching between pieces of information resulting from the specification and introduced in the source program and elements used for programming and resulting from choices made by the designer. We highlighted the importance of the analysis done by the compiler. Fault detection then depends on the capabilities of the language features to allow the elements of the contract between the user and the implementer of a component to be written into the program. We pointed out that certain Ada features facilitate the expression of such a contract. However, the use of these features is not obligatory and furthermore, only certain aspects can be expressed as we will detail in chapter 4.

Faults can also be detected by running the program (**dynamic analysis**). Functional testing consists in defining a test sequence which is a sequence of pairs (input value, expected output value). The output values supplied by running the program by applying input values are compared with the expected output values. We mentioned the difficulty in establishing an exhaustive test sequence. First of all, the input sequence must activate all possible behaviours defined in the specification. Also, the output values are sometimes difficult to estimate if the program was written to calculate them (oracle problem).

Another test approach takes into account the structure of the program by examining if a set of elements (statements, branches, paths) are used during execution. Lastly, we mentioned that adding invariants into the program components facilitates the detection of certain faults by avoiding, in particular, the need to propagate the errors of these components to the program outputs (to create a failure).

We concluded by signalling that sometimes the execution means may have various effects on the program behaviour. Therefore the equivalence between the expected behaviour defined by the client specification and the behaviour obtained with the designer execution environment may not be maintained with the client execution environment if it is not the same. These circumstances must relativize the efficiency of testing methods.

Techniques for validation or for verification
Due to the existence of the numerous techniques to remove faults, the designer may ask for the best one. An answer needs a previous remark. Before presenting the Fault Avoidance techniques, we required two types of means (see section 2.2.1):

- validation means which evaluate if the program is in compliance with its specification;
- verification means which examine if the program was designed in the correct way.

The first point of view judges the quality of the program produced whereas the second one allows judgement to be made on the quality of the designer's work assuming that bad work (i.e. presence of faults in the work process) generally implies incorrect software (i.e. faults in the program produced).

For instance, the aim of the functional testing is to evaluate if the software is in agreement with the specification supplied by the client whereas the structural testing measures the way in which it was produced. For example, the designer must justify the existence of unused control paths. A test sequence can therefore be used to evaluate the software or the way followed for its realization.

To judge the efficiency of a technique, we must first specify its aim, that is, to what will this technique be applied: the software produced or the means of producing it? For example, the efficiency of a test sequence may be measured (test sequence evaluation) according to its capacity:

- to identify variations in the behaviour of the software (identification technique); the sequence capability is thus measured as a validation means or,
- to identify variations in its realization (mutation technique); the sequence efficiency is here evaluated as a verification means.

Each of the Fault Removal techniques described replies to one of the requirements as defined in the Figure 2.28.

94 Chapter 2: Fault Detection and Correction Techniques

Analysis	Techniques	Validation	Verification
Static	Extracting Specification	X	
	Introducing Invariants	X (1)	X (2)
Dynamic	Functional Testing	X	
	Structural Testing		X
	Structured Functional Testing	X	X
	Introducing Invariants	X (1)	X (2)

Figure 2.28: Synthesis of Fault Removal techniques

Invariants can define:

- either properties of the complete software, taken from the contract drawn up by the client (1);
- or properties of the software realization components. For example, preconditions define hypotheses on component utilization rights. The negation of an assumption detects incorrect use of the component and therefore comprises verification means (2).

We pointed out the respective pros and cons of the proposed techniques. As no ideal technique exists, various methods are used together. However, even the use of all the techniques provided does not guarantee that no faults will be present. For these reasons we will describe in section 2.4 a set of means for detecting and handling on-line errors which can occur during the useful life of a system (fault tolerance).

2.4 Fault Tolerance

Requirements
In the preceding section we showed that it is difficult to know whether software is free from faults or not. Consequently, residual faults may be present after the design and the programming of the software.

Also, a software tool can be correct in its development context but generate errors due to its real run-time context. For instance, the software can be embedded into a machine with a lower memory size or a processor which runs at a different speed. In the specific case of a multitask application, variation in processor performance may lead to a different sequencing of the tasks which could cause an error. These types of error are due to the absence of a sufficiently explicit *contract* concerning the program execution means.

Lastly, in spite of the accurate definition of the specifications of the software run-time environment, errors may be generated due to the violation of these specifications by this environment (which is not under designer's control). This violation may be the result of various elements with which the software interacts: run-time support (for instance, erroneous behaviour of the hardware due to ageing); process controlled by the software; the operator; etc. For instance, we can cite the introduction of incoherent data or noncompliance with the sequencing of actions which can be performed on the software. In these situations, the software although correct must be robust against these errors, even if it is not the cause of these errors.

Aims
For all these reasons, fault tolerance devices must be included in the software applications. The aims of such devices are:

- **to detect the errors** occurring **in operation** associated with the program faults not previously extracted or associated with the bad use of the software tool and then
- **to handle these errors** to have the least possible effect on the program behaviour when it is **embedded** (i.e. in operation on the client's target machine).

The fault tolerance devices are introduced during design, during which Fault Avoidance methods are also used. We have however placed the fault tolerance presentation apart as the aims and the techniques used are different. We will see in section 2.5 that the three points of view (avoidance, removal and tolerance), intervening in the development of dependable software tools, interfere.

In the first section we will deal with the principles of the means required for the design of a fault tolerant system (detection, perception, location, diagnosis, correction, recovery). In the following sections we will describe the techniques for implementing fault tolerance mechanisms. For each of them we will present the implementation of the above principles.

In this chapter, the techniques studied are general. They are not specific to a given language. In the following chapters Ada will be considered. In particular the Ada exception mechanism (used as an error handling feature) which facilitates the implementation of the presented techniques will be studied in chapter 3. The implementation using Ada will be detailed in chapter 4.

2.4.1 Principles

The fault tolerance techniques presented later will use several general principles introduced in this section: detection, perception, location, diagnosis, correction, compensation and recovery.

Detection - Perception
An error is defined as an undesirable state reached by executing a program. An error allows a fault in the program to be perceived. The erroneous state has an identity (the error identifier) and a condition defining the circumstances which cause the program to 'fall' into this state. This condition is the negation of an invariant explaining a property concerning the expected operation. For example a variable value must be within a given range. If, during execution of an Ada program declaring such a variable, the value of this variable is out of its range (negation of the invariant), the program detects this error immediately (CONSTRAINT_ERROR) when the value is assigned. We must insist on the fact that the invariant is a means for detecting an error and not the fault which is at the source of the error. In the previous example, the cause of value overflow is not identified.

The notion of an invariant detecting a fault seems not to be evident for everybody. For instance when programming in C language, the fault may be detected not at assign time but only if an explicit test is programmed or if the variable is used as an array index generating a 'STORAGE_OVERFLOW'. In other situations, the program continues to run without signalling the existence of a fault as the state of the program is not considered as erroneous.

Bringing error detection as close as possible to fault location facilitates fault tolerance technique implementations (diagnosis, correction, recovery). The presence of invariants to detect errors avoids error contamination. For instance, without using *preconditions*, a subprogram called with erroneous parameters can start its execution and modify caller variables before an error is detected.

The detection of an error can generate several **perceptions** of it. Detection consists in identifying an error when an invariant is violated, whereas the perception of an error is defined by the way (including the identity) in which the error is identified without knowledge of the specific invariant which is at the origin. In Ada, for instance, if an exception is propagated by a procedure, the body of the procedure may be at the origin of the detection whereas the calling procedure only perceives the occurrence. Likewise, when an error occurs during a rendezvous, it is detected by the server task and perceived both by this server task and its calling task (exception propagation). The calling task does not detect the error, but it perceives it.

Location - Diagnosis
The purpose of location is to find the erroneous element(s). It helps in establishing a diagnosis, that is to say, in getting to know the causes of the error. Location and diagnosis will allow the fault to be corrected or allow its effects to be limited.

A program is composed of a set of components and a control structure used to relate these components (loop, if-then-else, while, declare, etc.). This construction results from the design choices. Location of an error can be made in a component or in a structure. We will group these two notions together under the term **frame**.

As a result of nesting frames, an error can be perceived at a high level of abstraction even though it comes from a low level frame. In this situation, the diagnosis is complex on account of the loss of significance and of the masking of the lower levels by the realization. For example, if an ARRAY_OVERFLOW error is generated by calling a procedure in a package STACK, this error makes no sense to the caller who cannot know that the package implementation uses an array.

The detection of an error in a frame does not imply that the frame is the source of the error (i.e. it may not contain a fault). An error may be caused not by the implementation of the frame but by its use. Unfortunately, the last use of the frame (which has detected the error) is not necessarily the only cause of the error. Generally, we must take into account the previous actions performed by the user frames. For example, it is not the last pushing action which causes the STACK_OVERFLOW error but the summed effects of the previous pushing and popping actions.

Correction - Compensation
In order to obtain dependable software, errors must be handled. However, faults cannot be corrected as was done during and after design (fault avoidance and fault removal). In effect, the program cannot modify itself at run-time extracting the fault but it can modify the control of its processing if means to handle errors are provided during design. The aim of this handling is **to inhibit** or **to limit the effects of an error**. A perfect correction prevents an error from being visible from outside, i.e., the error has no effect on the external behaviour of the program.

The correction modes for an error occurring in a frame can be classified according to two criteria: the place of detection with regard to the frame and the reliance placed on frame design.

Detection can be made inside (internal) or outside (external) the frame. For instance, detection is internal if achieved by a test on a data item (such as a variable or a parameter) used by the frame. This can be obtained by checking membership to a domain. For example, Ada typing allows such implicit checks to be done when variables are assigned.

98 Chapter 2: Fault Detection and Correction Techniques

Consider now a subprogram which has a formal 'out' mode parameter of type T. If it is called with an effective parameter which is of sub-type ST then the added constraint is evaluated after the call. This is the external detection of an error.

The **reaction** to the detection of an error depends on the reliance placed on the frame which detects the erroneous execution of the program. Two situations can occur:

- it is considered that the frame does not contain the fault which is at the origin of the error. Incorrect use (for instance the providing of erroneous data) is assumed. In this case, the same frame is re-executed with other data. This corresponds to a **transient fault** corrected by a time replication of the execution of the same function;
- it is assumed that a fault is present in the frame. Another frame (a **'spare frame'** or backup) which is implemented differently and which has the same functionality is then executed. This corresponds to a **permanent fault** corrected by a functional replication.

A third point of view must be given. The frame and the 'spare' treatment(s) are executed in parallel and the result is deduced from the results provided by each of the parallel processing operations. For this technique the word 'spare' cannot be used to qualify the added treatments because all of them are executed. This solution does not use means to detect errors (inside or outside) and to correct their effects. Its aim is to produce a result which is estimated as correct after an 'average' calculation on the results produced. This calculation must **compensate** for the presence of erroneous results if they occur. For instance, it can be implemented by a majority vote (the value provided by the majority of treatments is chosen) or a weighted average (suppressing the spurious values) of the values provided by each treatment. In such an approach, the error is not detected but compensated for.

The Figure 2.29 sums up the different situations.

DETECTION / TREATMENT	Internal	External	Error Compensation
Same Treatment			
Other Treatment			

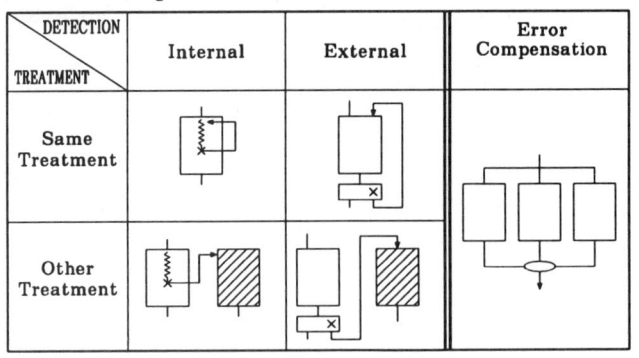

× : Error Detection
▨ : Spare Treatment

Figure 2.29: Classification of correction techniques

The techniques associated with the boxes in the table of Figure 2.29 will be developed in the next sections.

Recovery
By definition, the current state of the application is erroneous when an error is detected. A treatment (the same or another one) must be recovered once the erroneous state has been corrected. The treatment must restart its execution from a **safe state**, that is to say a state which is foreseen in 'normal' operation. In practice, this state is defined by an execution context (instruction pointer, local variables, etc.).

Correction and recovery means are not independent as we will show in the following sections. This is why some authors (Anderson, 1981) place these two notions under the single term 'recovery'.

Several techniques are used to implement recovery. They can be classed into two categories in accordance with the direction chosen to resume normal operation.

- **Backward recovery** consists in returning to a state which the program has already been in. This solution corresponds to a 'back timing' simulation (Anderson, 1979) because the software execution seems to come back in the past. A trivial example of this kind of recovery is the *reset*. The backward recovery principle is simple because it allows resumption independent of error identity. We will show that the techniques implementing this principle are, however, cumbersome because the use of *recovery points* obliges the context (state of the program) to be saved and sometimes restored even without errors.
- **Forward recovery** consists in going to a *new* faultless state. For this, the application must possess enough knowledge on the error and on its own operation to perform the correction and the recovery. As a previous context is not saved (as with 'backward recovery'), the application must compute a new context. The implementation of such a technique is more complex, but it does not burden operation if there are no errors.

Hierarchy
Generally the software design requires the introduction of several levels of abstraction. Often these levels are maintained in the implementation of the solution (i.e. in the program). For instance, in Ada, they are encountered in the breakdown into frames (procedures, tasks, packages, blocks, etc.). A program is then expressed as a hierarchy of frames correlated by control structures. In section 1.4.1 of chapter 1, we pointed out the fact that the notions of fault, error and failure are **relative to one frame of the hierarchy**. We said that a propagation phenomenon exists. A fault in a frame may induce an error and then a failure of the behaviour of the frame. If this frame is included in another one, the failure may

provoke an error and then a failure of the higher frame, etc. This characteristic of the architecture of the programs designed must be compared with the principles that we have just presented.

First of all, detection can be made at a given level but it must be possible to perform correction at a higher level. In this case, the bottom-up propagation of the error to the calling functions must lead to a change in the identity of this error. In effect, this error has a different meaning depending on the level where it is perceived and information related to the level is required to make an accurate diagnosis. For instance, exception CONSTRAINT_ERROR raised by an incrementation statement used in the body implementing procedure PUSH can be translated for the caller as a STACK_OVERFLOW whereas the same exception will be converted into STACK_UNDERFLOW in the case of procedure POP. These exceptions can be renamed again according to the stack utilization semantics and propagated up to the level performing handling.

The example above also shows the importance of error identity with regard to choice of a correction technique. For instance, error STACK_OVERFLOW implies incorrect use (too many pushings). Procedure PUSH could be used but in a different manner. The correction must therefore be applied to the frames using the stack. However, an error named ERROR_ON_STACK should qualify incorrect implementation. Another treatment, or even another stack, must be used.

Object approach

The two classes of techniques proposed (execution of another function or execution of the same function with different data) are used at a hierarchical level and are suitable to a functional approach. An 'object-oriented' design poses new problems.

First, when a backup function is called after failure of the original function has been detected, the previous calls to the failed function or to other functions are not called into question. If, for an object-oriented design, the detection of a failed action of an object leads to the creation of a new object, it must be placed in the same state as the abandoned object. In effect, unlike a function where the local variables are allocated on call and freed during return, the object attributes are remanent and represent the current state of this object. Initializing the state value does not consist in copying the internal data structures as a different implementation has no doubt led to different attributes.

Secondly, if a function is considered as correctly implemented and if the error is due to incorrect use, as the variables at call level or at higher levels are visible, they can then be modified before the next call. However, in the case of an object-oriented design, the state of the object can only be modified if functions were explicitly provided (for instance, a reinitialization procedure for an object STACK).

The problems raised above do not occur if the technique named 'error compensation' is used. Thanks to this technique, the values of the attributes of the various examples of the object are updated simultaneously each time the object's actions are called.

Fault Tolerance 101

Conclusion

In this section we presented the general fault tolerance principles separating the various notions (detection, perception, location, diagnosis, correction, compensation and recovery) in order to make them more understandable. For the techniques which implement these principles, this separation is not so simple because constraints exist between the notions. For instance, some fault tolerance techniques do not require detection means: N-version programming which matches error by a compensation principle is an example. In addition, the choice of the recovery mode is conditioned by the correction technique used.

We have chosen to describe the various techniques in accordance with their recovery modes. For each of them we will show how the principles are implemented.

After the presentation of the backward recovery techniques (section 2.4.2) we will discuss two correction techniques associated with this recovery mode: the Recovery Blocks in section 2.4.3 and the Retry mode in section 2.4.4.

We will then describe two techniques using forward recovery: Termination mode in section 2.4.5 and N-versions programming in section 2.4.6. Characteristics of the techniques described can be used together in applications; some examples will be given in section 2.4.7.

2.4.2 Backward Recovery technique

Backward recovery requires the implementation of execution context saving and restoring mechanisms. The most popular technique is known under the name of **'recovery cache'**. After an error has been detected, this mechanism (Randell, 1975) allows the previously safeguarded variables defining the context to be retrieved in their initial state.

A **recovery point** is defined as a location where the context required by the recovery technique is safeguarded. In order to save memory space, this mechanism must only take into account the variables actually modified between the last recovery point and the next one. Several recovery cache strategies exist. In all cases, the subsequently modified variables are copied from the main memory (i.e. the variables used without fault tolerance mechanism) in a cache (1) which is a special part of the memory.

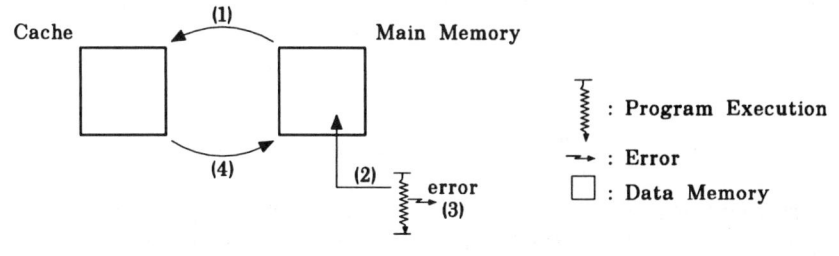

Figure 2.30: First backward recovery implementation

102   Chapter 2: Fault Detection and Correction Techniques

In the first solution (Figure 2.30), the updates of the variables are done in the 'main memory' (2) during normal processing. If an error occurs (3), the values stored in the cache are transferred to the main memory (4).

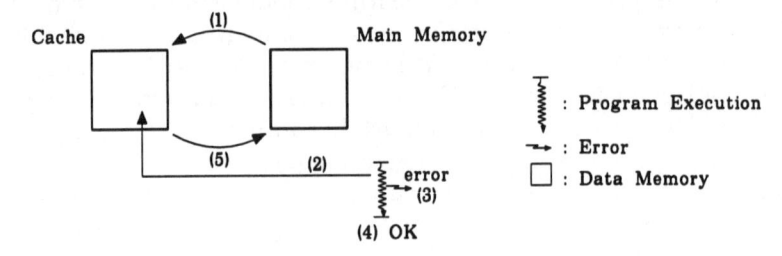

Figure 2.31: Second backward recovery implementation

Another possibility (Figure 2.31) consists in adopting a strategy 'symmetrical' to the previous solution. During execution, the new values of the modified variables are temporarily stored in the cache (2). If an error occurs (3), the main memory already contains the initial values so no action is necessary. On the contrary, if execution is successful (4), the memory must be updated (5). The advantage of this technique is that it only modifies the values in the memory if there are no errors. There is no degradation (even temporary) of the integrity of the data during execution. However, the first technique is quicker if there are no errors, because it does not require updating at end of execution.

We said that the software design and the programming lead to the use of nested frames (sub-programs, etc.). The hierarchical structure of the programs influences the recovery technique implementation. If recovery point 1 exists in a first frame (see Figure 2.32) and if this frame calls a second frame which defines its own recovery point 2 then, when exiting the second frame, the recovery context of the calling frame must be restored. This requires a stack mechanism to manage the recovery caches.

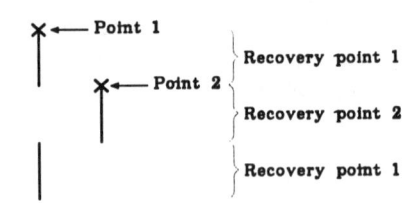

Figure 2.32: Frame nesting and recovery points

The recovery technique is used in the case of 'backward recovery' correction. Two examples of such correction mode will be given: Recovery Blocks (section 2.4.3) and Retry Mode (section 2.4.4).

2.4.3 Recovery blocks

Definition

The 'Recovery Blocks' technique (Randell, 1975) consists in attempting the execution of a frame called **alternate**, then in evaluating the result of this attempt by an assertion called **acceptance test** and finally in executing a rescue block which is *an other alternate* if the preceding alternate fails.

The initial state of the data is re-established before the execution of the rescue alternate using a recovery cache mechanism. The syntax definition proposed by Randell to express recovery blocks is as follows:

```
<recovery block>     ::= ensure <acceptance test>
                         by  <primary alternate>
                              <other alternates>
                         else error
<primary alternate>  ::= <alternate>
<other alternates>   ::= <empty> | <other alternates>
                         else by <alternate>
<alternate>          ::= <statement list>
<acceptance test>    ::= <logical expression>
```

A simple recovery block structure is:
```
ensure T
  by P
  else by Q
else error
```

where T is the acceptance test condition, P the primary alternate and Q the alternate routine *attempted* if P does not 'fulfil its contract' defined by the T condition. We emphasize the fact that in this technique the **same data** are used but with a **different treatment**.

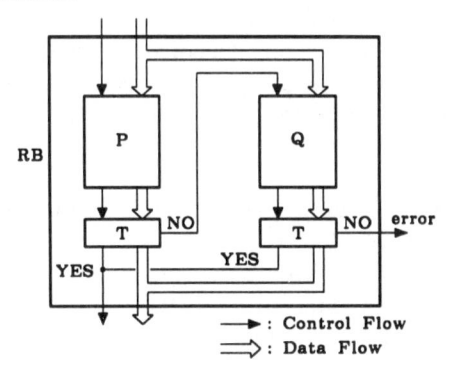

Figure 2.33: Recovery Blocks

Figure 2.33 gives a graphical representation of the previous example and illustrates this technique. The structure authorizes nested recovery blocks: an alternate (P or Q) can be implemented as a recovery block (RB on the figure) itself.

Characteristics
Nothing is forecast in the Recovery Blocks technique to give (to the system using the block) the identity of the alternate which has effectively produced the result. It could be judicious to keep a trace of the Recovery Block execution to discover which alternates have failed, in order to facilitate their maintenance (Kanoun, 1987) (Anderson, 1981).

If we consider the treatment and its rescue treatments globally, the whole constitutes a software component where the error occurrence is masked.

To increase the performance it could be interesting to dynamically change the execution order of alternates after a certain number of failures in the execution of the first alternate and of issues of the second. This allows execution-time to be saved in the following executions. Such a solution is only suitable if the alternates are equivalent, that is if they have the same behaviour and do not implement a mode of operation by graceful degradation.

This technique does not provide error diagnosis. Consequently the spare alternate must re-execute the complete operation. It cannot use intermediate results which were correctly processed by the erroneous alternate. If there are any useful intermediate results, they must be taken into account by making another breakdown of the frames to be recovered. For instance a frame P can be split into P1, P2 and P3. The recovery blocks technique is then used on each of them.

The following paragraphs deal with how to obtain alternates and acceptance tests. We will conclude by presenting problems induced by a multi-task context.

Obtaining alternates
First it is desirable that different design teams form and produce the different alternates. Moreover, different algorithms may be used to solve a problem or even different releases of the same algorithm. In this case the last release constitutes the primary block, i.e. the one executed first.

On one hand, the alternate common specification must be sufficiently precise in order to obtain alternates with the unique specified behaviour. On the other hand, it must not be too constrained to avoid similar designs. Two points of view can be considered:

- the first one consists in giving specifications without information concerning the implementation. We then assume that, statistically, different teams will produce varied solutions. This assumption can however be refuted if an 'obvious' design exists. In this case, similar errors can appear (Avizienis, 1984). Backup alternates will then be ineffective as they will have the same fault;

- the second consists in fixing implementation constraints to force the diversity of the solutions. This can be achieved by imposing various design methods (functional, object-oriented, etc.) or by defining different versions of first design level or by choosing various programming languages which offer different features. This solution can itself lead to different designs or avoid the presence of similar errors due to the features of the language.

Another problem concerns the size of the function which must be protected: is it better to have one large function P or to break it down into several ones P1, P2, ..., Pn? A specification which is too large will introduce alternates with overlong codes which may lead to the overstepping of the time constraints in the case of successive failures of extensive alternates.

If time constraints exist, successive alternates can use algorithms which are less and less sophisticated, that is increasingly rapid, to produce results which are less and less accurate. This is especially valid if numerical calculations are required. This design implements a degraded mode of the service.

The alternate implementation problem will also arise for implementing the N-version programming technique which we will discuss later.

Acceptance Tests

The aim of the Acceptance Test is to decide if the result provided by an alternate is correct. It defines the terms of the contract allowing a justified reliance to be placed on the result delivered. The Acceptance Test is thus an invariant. It must have *enough* pieces of information to estimate the expected result in order to judge the validity of the provided result. A rough solution would consist in evaluating once more (with another implementation) the expected values. However, such an Acceptance Test is likely to be slow and it would then appear to be an alternate itself! Moreover, this solution is closer to the error compensation done by the N-version programming technique. A compromise must be found so that an Acceptance Test only verifies the pieces of information *necessary* for the detection of an erroneous or valid result. We again come up against the difficulties encountered in expressing the contract.

Another problem arises. An Acceptance Test conclusion requires the execution of the contract expression. As *we must rely* on an Acceptance Test to decide on the acceptability of an alternate, the **dependability of the acceptance test** must be greater than the dependability of the alternates. For example, it should not indicate that a correct result is incorrect or, more important still, that an incorrect result is correct. Increasing the sophistication of an Acceptance Test has two consequences:

- it increases the reliability of the result checked and therefore the conclusion provided (correct/incorrect alternate);
- it increases the risk of introducing faults during its design and therefore the risk of errors occurring in the operation and thus reduces the reliability of the result.

A contradiction therefore exists. The Acceptance Test design choices result from a compromise between the low complexity and the high efficiency of the error detection for which it is responsible. In practice, the Acceptance Tests are relatively simple. They express: constraints on values, comparisons between several parts of the result, likelihood-comparisons with previous results, etc. They are deduced from properties associated with the specifications. They lead to a problem similar to the one encountered when introducing specifications into the realization to perform structural-functional testing.

Different acceptance tests can be associated with different alternates (Banâtre, 1981). This is suitable if alternates provide degraded services. In such a situation, the decrease in the accuracy of the results and the tightening of the time constraints, imply more flexible (less constrained assertion) and quicker acceptance tests. The succession of pairs (alternate, acceptance test) constitutes a series of self-testable components.

Concerning **real-time software**, the Acceptance Test is augmented by a watch-dog timer that monitors if an acceptable result is furnished within a specified period (Hecht, 1986). All alternates have a given time for execution. This time may be the same for all the alternates. If the primary alternate oversteps the time limit (infinite loop for instance), the alternate execution is stopped and the execution of a following alternate is begun after the reset of the timer. If the last alternate exceeds the time limit, the frame is considered as being erroneous. Therefore, a maximum time is imposed for the execution of the frame. It is defined by the specification of the behaviour of the frame (which is implemented by each of the alternates). The effective maximum frame running time is equal to the product of the maximum time given to each alternate and the number of alternates. This run-time value must be lower than the specified maximum value. So if, for a part of the program judged to be critical, a certain redundancy is necessary and implemented using Recovery Blocks, the maximum time required to execute a frame increases with the number of alternates. A certain compromise must therefore be found between safety performance and time performance (speed). We wish to point out that different times for the alternates (for instance decreasing times) can be envisaged.

When an Acceptance Test is associated with a function, this one is called **self-checked** function.

Recovery Blocks for a multi-task software
The use of Recovery Blocks techniques for communicating sequential processes (multi-task program) poses a new problem concerning resumption. Let us consider the example shown on Figure 2.34. It represents from left to right the evolution of the execution of three processes (or tasks): P1, P2, P3. A character 'X' signals the moment when the recovery cache technique is processed at a recovery point to save a process context. The vertical dotted lines express the communication or synchronization moments (for instance using a rendezvous).

If a sequential block of a process P3 fails (at present time), then it must recover the context in (1). As it has made a communication or a synchronization S1 with another process (P2) between the recovery point (1) and the present time, the resumption of this block (by an alternate) induces the need to go backwards through process P2 to the recovery point (2). Process P2 had established a communication or a synchronization with P1 (S2), so the backward movement in P2 must generate a backward movement in P1 to the recovery point (3). It implies backward movement of P2 to (4) (due to S3) and then backward movement of P3 to (5) (due to S4)! This phenomenon, called '**domino effect**', is mentioned in (Randell, 1975).

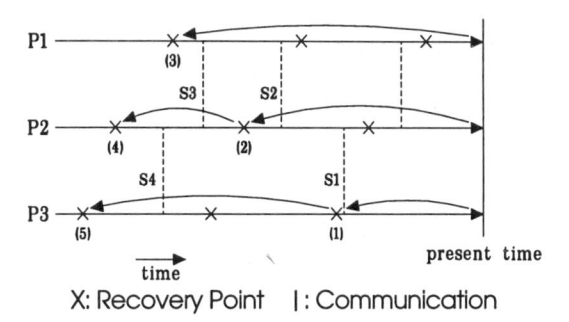

Figure 2.34: Domino effect

A solution to this problem consists in:

- adding recovery points just before the communications,
- introducing a task which knows the sequential order of the recovery points and the task communications or synchronizations. When an error occurs, this task can identify the processes to be recovered and their recovery points. These points are not necessarily the last ones as shown on Figure 2.34.

Rather than asking the designer to introduce a supplementary task, it would be interesting to integrate the recovery function into the real-time kernel which already controls the communications in order to provide a dependability-oriented real-time kernel.

2.4.4 Retry mode

The 'Recovery Blocks' technique is based on the idea that the data provided for the component are correct, but that an error may come from an incorrect realization of the component. The 'Retry Mode' technique is useful if an error is not due to the implementation but to the values of the associated parameters, that is to say, to incorrect use of the component (in terms of *contract*). Its principle consists in re-executing the **same implementation** with different values for the parameters (retry).

108 Chapter 2: Fault Detection and Correction Techniques

However the implementation may use environmental pieces of information not specified as parameters (for instance global variables). These pieces of information might be modified by the previous erroneous execution. Consequently, the environment context must be saved before first execution and restored before the following execution done with new parameters. This is made using the **recovery** techniques given in 2.4.2.

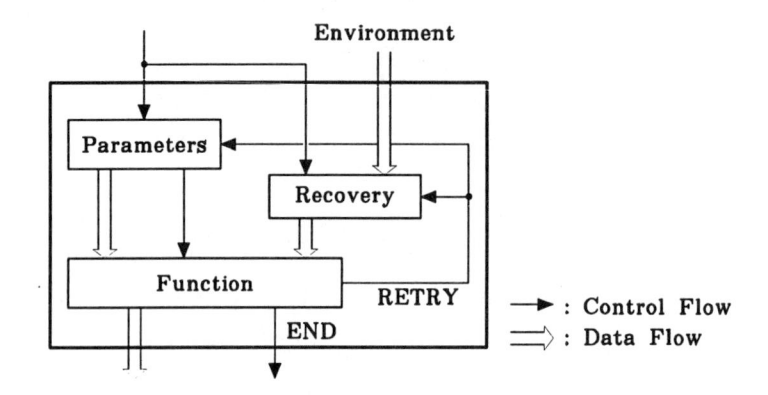

Figure 2.35: Retry mode

Figure 2.35 provides a graphical representation of the Retry Mode technique. To illustrate the behaviour of this technique, consider a reading function. It supplies an integer value (for example: 1995) from a string of characters representing the digits (for example: '1995') given as parameter using the keyboard. Before function execution the keyboard buffer is empty, then it contains the parameter value (characters pressed on keyboard). If an error is detected by the reading function operation (for example if data '19Z5' is provided), retrying this function with newly entered data as parameter must be preceded by flushing the keyboard buffer which constitutes the environment (**recovery** action).

Note that it appears that certain variables must not be restored by the recovery action in order to take the previous erroneous executions into account during the handling. For instance, in the previous example, we can introduce a variable which counts the number of tries: this variable may not be reset. When its value reaches a specified (maximum) number of tries, another treatment is executed. This last implementation is in line with the Recovery Blocks principle and so is not a 'pure retry mode'.

In the Retry Mode technique, the **detection** of an erroneous parameter value is made at the beginning, at the end or during the execution of the function. The detection means come from the rules of the contract associated with the function concerning the expected values of the data. For instance, this detection can be made by preconditions which express constraints on input parameters. In the example the keypressed characters must be in the range '0'..'9'.

The program may also possess means to **correct the parameters**. For example, if a function monitors an electrical braking system, taking periodically the value of pressure given by the driver into account, a precondition can express that the new value is bound by a range deduced from the previous value handled. If bad use (the driver brakes too hard risking that the wheels become blocked) or a bad realization (of other parts involved in the car control system) generates a value very far from the previous one, the correction function can give, as a correct value, the bound of the range which is the closest to the value assumed as erroneous.

The two techniques presented in the previous sections use the 'backward recovery' principle. The techniques of 'termination mode' and 'N-version programming', presented in the two following sections, use the 'forward recovery' principle: in case of an error the software state does not go back to a previous state but the execution is resumed from a new safe state.

2.4.5 Termination mode

The 'termination mode' principle consists in executing another treatment Q after the detection of an error in a frame P.

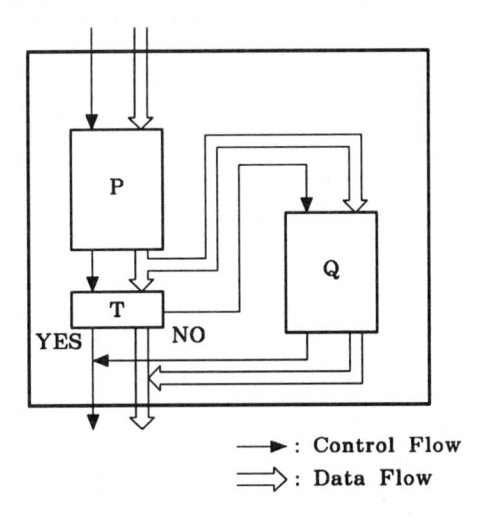

⟶ : Control Flow
⟹ : Data Flow

Figure 2.36: Termination mode

Figure 2.36 gives a graphical representation of this technique. T represents the means used for error detection. This figure is close to Figure 2.33 which illustrates the Recovery Blocks technique. An essential difference lies in the fact that the initial data used by frame P are not restored before the start of function Q (which continues with the current data). So function Q must be a function which **corrects the effects** (and not the fault) of P. For instance it completes the operations not performed by P.

Q uses the results produced by P and so there is no 'backward recovery'. Therefore, the objective of function Q is not to provide another version of P (with the same specification as P) but to **handle an error** occurring in P **compensating for the work** not done by P.

While the 'recovery blocks' technique does not require **diagnosis** because the following alternate starts in a safe state (in the initial one), it is necessary for use of the 'termination mode' because the handling function starts in an erroneous state. The work to be done by Q depends on the progress of function P before error detection. The aim of the function Q is to **complete** (to compensate) the part of the function effectively and correctly fulfilled by P. The termination mode is therefore theoretically faster but more demanding on the designer than the Recovery Blocks technique.

2.4.6 N-version Programming

Principles
The philosophy of the N-version technique consists in **compensating for an error** instead of detecting and correcting it. Several realizations (or versions) of a function are executed in order to **mask** an eventual error occurring in any one of the realizations.

This technique is defined in (Chen, 1978) as *the independent generation of N>=2 functionally equivalent programs, called versions, from the same initial specification*. These N versions supply N results which must be compared in order to give a single (correct) result. It can be deduced either by a majority vote mechanism (if N>2), or by a more complex law. Figure 2.37 shows the principle of this technique.

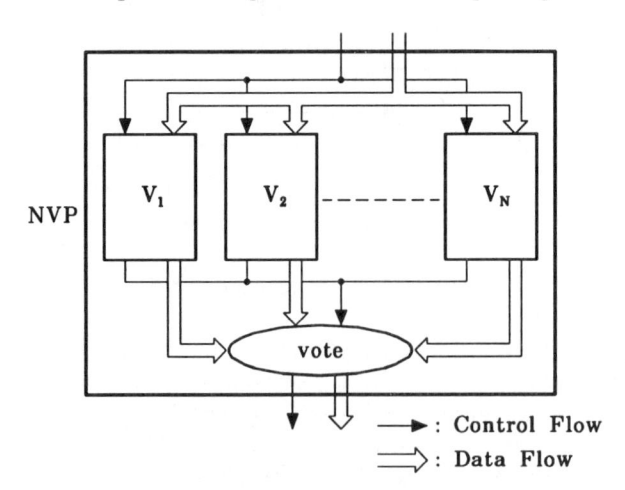

Figure 2.37: N-version programming

The term 'compensation' was also used for the 'Termination mode' technique but with different semantics. Whereas for N-version programming the technique compensates implicitly the occurrence of an error, for the Termination mode the compensation must be realized explicitly by the designer providing a function Q to complete the work not yet realized by the erroneous function P.

The N-version technique seems also to be close to the Recovery Blocks technique. In particular, the problems encountered to obtain different versions are similar to the ones encountered to obtain alternates. However two main differences exist:

- the N versions are executed unconditionally, whereas an alternate of a recovery block is executed if the previous one failed;
- the result of a recovery block is accepted using invariant checks on the computed value, whereas a result of a version is not judged individually: the correct result is obtained by comparing all the results provided by all the versions.

Vote algorithm
The aim of the vote algorithm is to give a correct value from the values provided by the versions. This algorithm depends on the type of the information on which the vote is made, i.e. the type of the result of the versions:

- for Boolean results (for instance, orders delivered to binary actuators) a conventional majority vote can be performed. The result given will be the one which appears the most often;
- for numeric results, a simple vote which furnishes the most frequent value is in general impossible. The versions provide values which are probably distinct. For instance, this problem occurs when floating results are processed with various numerical methods because of the variety of precisions. Two classes of votes, adaptive and explicit, must be contemplated:
  (a) in the *adaptive* vote, the result of the vote is a weighted sum of results supplied by the different versions. The evaluation of the weights depends on the acceptability of different results. A small weight will be assigned to a result judged incoherent when compared with the others;
  (b) the *explicit* (or non-adaptive) vote consists first in determining an average or median value from the results obtained, then in choosing the value supplied by one of the versions which is the closest to the average one.

Relations between the voter and the versions
The relations between the voter and different versions require specific mechanisms for practical implementations:

- the implementations of the versions are different, so are their execution times. Thus the voter must possess a synchronization mechanism for these different versions. This mechanism can take time constraints into account, in particular, in order not to wait indefinitely for the results of a version which is too slow or which is blocked. Consequently, the voter must be able to provide the correct result after receiving only some of the results computed by the versions;
- the voter may take into account only a significant part of the result instead of all the pieces of information which composed the data provided by the versions. This case occurs if, for instance, the out parameters of the versions are correlated parameters, or if some parameters are not considered as important, or if we want to simplify the vote;
- the voter's role may not be limited to determining the correct result but it may provoke an action on erroneous versions. 'Intelligent' voters (Hourtolle, 1987) must be able to detect faulty versions in case of disagreement between them, to stop these versions or to put them back in phase in accordance with comparison indicators.

However, the N-version technique inherently assumes that the voter's dependability is excellent. We have mentioned various problems already formulated for the Acceptance Test of Recovery Blocks. In particular, the theoretical principles lead to design sophisticated voters whereas the dependable criteria encourage the implementation of simple solutions. So a compromise has to be found.

The N-version programming technique masks faults so that they are not perceived by the other modules which will use a 'good' result obtained by estimation. In the case of two versions only, a voter is not able to determine which one of the two versions is wrong and so cannot give an estimated result if the result expected is Boolean. Two versions giving a Boolean result only allow error *detection* and do not give an 'average' of the different results.

An extended presentation of N-version programming is available for instance in (Kanoun, 1987). Applications of the N-version technique can be read in (Tso, 1986) and (Kelly, 1986).

2.4.7 Mixed techniques

In practice, fault tolerant software sometimes uses a mixed technique strategy. The aim is to draw on the advantages of each of the techniques and to correct their disavantages. For example, the electrical flight control system of the Airbus A320 (Rouquet, 1986) (Briere, 1990) tolerates design faults by using the technique called *N-Self-Checking Programming* (Laprie, 1987). In the same way as with the Recovery Blocks technique and N-version programming, a common specification leads to several implementations created by different design teams. All the versions are embedded and are executed but the spares are only used if problems arise, that is

Fault Tolerance 113

an error is detected. Every version or every group of versions is self-checked (Arlat, 1990), that is, possesses an acceptance test. By analogy with the vocabulary used in hardware design, this technique corresponds to an *active dynamical redundancy*.

A first application of this approach can be as follows (see Figure 2.38). The N versions are executed in parallel (but the N results are not compared). If any errors are detected in the first version (V1) by means of its acceptance test (AT1) then the result of the version is not acceptable and therefore the conclusion of the acceptance test (AT2) of the following version (V2) is considered, etc. So every version is self-checked and the first correct version result (with regard to its acceptance test) is supplied. This solution combines the advantages of the N-version (parallelism of the computation saves time) and of the recovery blocks (detection of the failed versions facilitates maintenance).

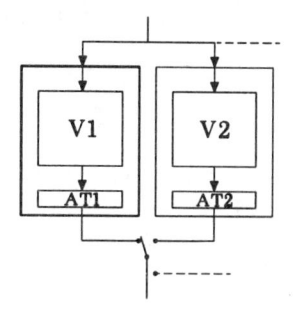

Figure 2.38: N-self checking

All combinations of self-checks and votes between versions are possible. To avoid complex self-checking, the results of the different versions may be compared two at a time. If the results are different, they are not considered (even if one is probably correct) the conclusion of the following group of two versions is examined, etc. Figure 2.39 represents such a structure. N-version time savings are made, the assertion to accept a result is very simple (comparison) and the groups of two versions containing an erroneous version are detected.

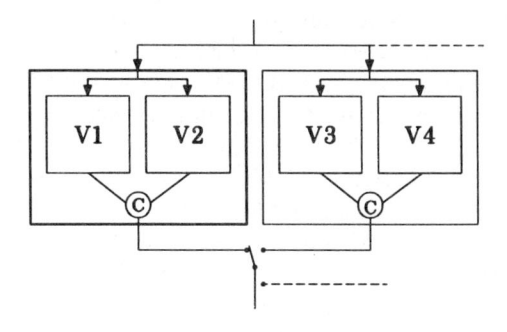

Figure 2.39: Mixing fault tolerance techniques

Numerous other mixed techniques exist. We pointed out in section 2.4.4 dealing with the retry mode that a variable, containing the number of tries of the function, can be introduced to avoid an infinite loop. Of course this variable must not be recovered at each retry. The counter value check is an assertion to accept or not the retry. Another implementation of the function may be executed if the counter value reaches the limit. A recovery blocks technique is then associated with the retry mode technique.

2.4.8 Synthesis

In this section we have described the principles and the techniques allowing fault tolerance to be introduced into the programs during their design to avoid failures during their execution.

First we described the principles of the actions involved in fault tolerance. We successively studied: detection and perception, location and diagnosis, and correction and recovery.

Next, we presented the main techniques to design fault tolerant applications by implementing the principles described. Some techniques do not include all these principles. For example, N-version programming does not try to detect and handle an error but tries to compensate for it, just as there is no diagnosis in case of Recovery Blocks.

Let us resume the characteristics of the techniques in order to compare them.

With the Recovery Blocks technique or the N-version programming method, several versions of the function exist. The first technique executes the versions one at a time until one is found which produces a result considered as correct by an acceptance test. However, for the second technique, all versions are executed a priori, in parallel. The correct result is then estimated by means of a vote function. The difference between these two techniques lies in the fact that one highlights erroneous versions (Recovery Blocks) whilst the other one masks the errors (N-Versions). If an error appears in one or more versions and if the run-time system physically allows parallel execution of the versions, then N-version programming will be quicker. However, on a single processor machine, execution of the N versions can be long and unnecessary if the correct execution of a single version produces an acceptable result. Nevertheless, establishing the correctness of the result by an acceptance test seems more complex than using a vote function. The choice of a solution in terms of performance depends therefore on the complexity of the function performed compared with the complexity of the acceptance test.

The Termination Mode may appear to be close to Recovery Blocks as a second function is undertaken if the execution of the first function is detected as erroneous. However, in Termination Mode, the second function does not have the same specification as the first one. It does not start its execution after having recovered the execution context which existed when the call to the erroneous function was made (backward recovery). The second function executes a new treatment with the current context (forward recovery). This function will therefore complete (and not necessarily restart) the work performed by the erroneous function. This technique imposes that the backup function performs a diagnosis before compensating for the unperformed part of the operation. Making a diagnosis and defining the compensation with regard to the result of the diagnosis are the main difficulties encountered in using this technique. However, its interest is that it takes into consideration the work correctly performed by the erroneous function instead of globally discarding its contribution. This technique also avoids the implementation of recovery mechanisms.

The previous techniques are based on a strong hypothesis: the error comes from the realization of the function. On the contrary, the Retry Mode technique applies to the case where the error is due to incorrect use of the function. The realization of a single version is then required. However, in addition to the implementation of a backward recovery mechanism retrieving the initial run-time context, a software device must allow erroneous parameters to be corrected.

We concluded the presentation by showing that various techniques are frequently used together to get the best out of the characteristics proper to each technique.

The techniques were presented without making assumptions on the means used to implement them such as the programming language and the features it includes. The use of the Ada language for this implementation will be studied in chapter 4.

2.5 Integration

2.5.1 Introduction

In this chapter, fault detection and correction were studied considering the software application designer's viewpoint. However, to be run, software applications require hardware and other software comprising the executive environment: computer, real-time kernel or drivers, etc. In section 2.5.2, we will discuss the problems raised by the integration of these various components to obtain a dependable executable system.

Furthermore, we separated the various problems and solutions posed by dependability as follows: 'fault avoidance' (section 2.2), 'fault removal' (section 2.3) and 'fault tolerance' (section 2.4). These three tasks are integrated into the design process. They are carried out at different times, during design for 'fault avoidance' and at end of design for 'fault removal'. 'Fault tolerance' was presented as being a later step. It however influences the design architecture. Also, to design tolerant software 'fault avoidance' and 'fault removal' techniques must be used. We will show that the specificities of tolerant software influence the use of these techniques. In section 2.5.3 we will look at fault analysis used as fault avoidance techniques applied to fault tolerant programs. Section 2.5.4 addresses the problems posed in testing fault tolerant software.

Another important and critical aspect particularly concerning real-time systems is the measurement of their performance. We will show in section 2.5.5 the additional difficulties in making these measurements when fault tolerant techniques are introduced (integration of fault tolerance and time constraints).

2.5.2 Dependability of a system

Generally a system is made up of a hierarchy of components involving hardware and software features. These components interact to a great extent. For instance, an application written in Ada, is executed on a microprocessor and calls software kernel primitives and uses hardware resources (such as memory).

To obtain a dependable system, each component of the program must of course be studied independently using fault avoidance, removal and tolerance techniques and then put together. However, this is not sufficient because other components are concerned. For example, the use of a microprocessor which contains a fault or of a real-time kernel whose behaviour is different from that expected, may cause a failure in the application. The relationships between the components of the application (program and execution means) must therefore be examined.

The hierarchical aspect of a system allows an error to be detected at different levels. For example, if the application wants to create a task dynamically, the kernel must store in a table the task code start address and other pieces of information associated with the task management. If this table is full, the request may cause an 'array overflow'. This can be detected by the microprocessor (segmentation violation), by the kernel (test instruction) or by the application (test statement). A fault-tolerance mechanism can be provided at microprocessor or kernel level (by dynamically increasing the size of the array) or at application level (by killing other tasks). The definitions of fault, error and failure, given in section 1.4.1 of chapter 1, are relative to an abstraction level. An error detected by the microprocessor or by the kernel (for instance a division by zero or a demand for synchronization with a non-existent task) may not be corrected at this level and will lead to a failure at this level that (if signalled) is considered as an error by the application (the higher level) which may or may not tolerate it.

This example illustrates that the different levels of the design must coordinate their activities in the dependability domain in order to ensure the cohesion of the different means used. For instance, writing statements in the application to kill tasks is not necessary if the kernel has a mechanism to dynamically allocate its task management table. The design of a fault tolerant system can lead to detection and correction redundancy at the different levels which could turn out to be useless or even dangerous if the techniques are not deliberately coordinated. For example, the hardware can detect a floating point division by zero and correct it by providing the highest positive or negative value. In this case, the software does not perceive the error although it was at the origin of the error and so some corrections could have been foreseen. However, the fact that low levels tolerate higher level errors could be useful (robustness). The introduction of fault tolerance at kernel level can be illustrated by the RMX286 real-time kernel (RMX286, 1988). It dynamically increases the size of the 'mailboxes' used for communications between tasks if the designer of the application underestimates their size.

2.5.3 Fault analysis and fault tolerant systems

In this section we will discuss the use of fault analysis techniques for fault tolerant software.

The **Failure Modes and Effects Analysis** (F.M.E.A.) method defines the effects of the potential failure of a software component, used during a design step, on the global behaviour of a program. This technique highlights the effects of a failure resulting from a component design error. This information therefore draws the attention of the designer (fault avoidance) and the persons in charge of the validation (fault removal) of this component. The global behaviour of the software application is obtained by analysing the consequences of the failure of a component through various functional elements (components and interaction structures) comprising the software during design. It assumes that the behaviour of these elements is correct.

The use of fault tolerance techniques has led elements for dependability to be added to the functional elements (intervening in the operational definition). The aim of the added elements is to master errors by limiting the propagation phenomenon of the effects. By using F.M.E.A., we can therefore present the effects of the failure of an element assuming the efficiency of the tolerance devices. Note that a tolerance mechanism often partially handles the error (a correction or a compensation) which is completed by other treatments in the higher levels obtained from design. Thus, effects are propagated into several hierarchical levels of the design product.

The dependability point of view must incite the designer to have a critical attitude towards the tolerance device itself. The **Event Tree Method** consists in establishing the effects of a failure. It is useful for examining the two possible conclusions of each tolerance device: its success (behaviour without failure) and its failure. From the failure of a functional element (initial event), we will study its effect through the functional elements or the ones introduced for dependability. For the latter, we will successively consider their success and failure hypotheses. In the two situations, we will specify the resulting global behaviour. Figure 2.40 shows such a situation from the nuclear domain proposed by Villemeur (Villemeur, 1991). The top line gives from left to right the succession of functional or added elements affected by the failure. The right column defines the possible global behaviours of the system according to the success or the failure of the elements. Let us look at the example shown on the figure.

118   Chapter 2: Fault Detection and Correction Techniques

The initial event is the rupture of a primary pipe of a nuclear power station. If this event occurs, it modifies the mission of a tank shared by the two connected systems. If this element fails then the meltdown occurs (global behaviour). If the mission is a success then the mission of the power system must be examined, etc.

Rupture of a primary piping	Mission of the tank shared by the 2 systems	Mission of the power system	Mission of the security injection system	Mission of the enclosure aspersion system	Sequences

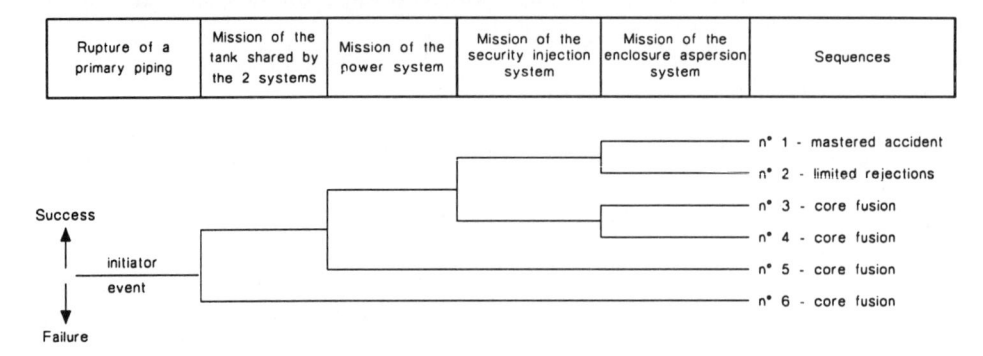

```
                                                            n° 1 - mastered accident
                                                            n° 2 - limited rejections
                                                            n° 3 - core fusion
Success                                                     n° 4 - core fusion
  ↑     initiator                                           n° 5 - core fusion
  ↓     event                                               n° 6 - core fusion
Failure
```

Figure 2.40: Event Tree Method

The Event Tree Method is therefore a method for analysing the effects of a failure taking the possible failure of introduced tolerance devices into account. It especially highlights the sequences of functions leading to unacceptable behaviours of the application which can lead to an increase in the avoidance and removal work and the modification of the fault tolerance devices.

2.5.4 Testability of fault tolerant systems

We separately and successively presented the three domains relevant to the life of a fault ('fault avoidance', 'fault removal' and 'fault tolerance'). However fault tolerant mechanisms are introduced during a design stage. Faults must therefore be avoided and removed during and after this stage. We previously established a first relationship between 'fault avoidance' and 'fault tolerance': failure analysis techniques are used to locate the critical points which require the introduction of a fault tolerant mechanism. Furthermore fault tolerant applications must be tested (fault removal). Consequently 'fault tolerance' and 'fault removal' are correlated. Here we will show that the introduction of fault tolerant mechanisms makes the software more difficult to test.

Remember that a test sequence must provoke two actions:

- operation of the program by applying input values to it (controllability),
- observation of the program's behaviour by comparing its output values with the expected values (observability).

Problems

To test tolerance mechanisms, input sequences would be found to activate the redundant parts of the code introduced to tolerate an error. However, they cannot be found and these parts will never be executed because the way to place the software in an erroneous state is unknown. If it would be possible, the associated fault could be searched and corrected immediately. Take for instance the case of additional alternates of a 'Recovery Blocks' implementation and the correction function of a 'Termination Mode' implementation. It would be impossible to assert that these added parts operate correctly.

Consequently, it is not possible to execute these parts of the code and it is pointless to try to find the sequence of input values causing the error. In particular for 'white box testing' (or structural testing) the statements or the paths used for tolerance mechanisms will never be executed and the 'coverage rate' values will be low.

This situation is equivalent to the one encountered during integrated component testing (software or hardware). Some of the functions provided will never be used. So a test sequence activating the operation of such functions needs not be searched for because it does not exist.

In the case of 'black box testing' (or functional testing), if a design fault exists and if it generates an effectively tolerated error, this error is not observable outside and it cannot be detected by the test sequence. Two drawbacks can be highlighted:

- the test sequence does not detect the error. So the fault will remain after the program has been delivered;
- the supplied software may not tolerate a new error since it already uses the tolerance function.

In order to illustrate the second drawback, consider the examples of Figure 2.41 showing two fault tolerant implementations of software S assuming that box A is erroneous.

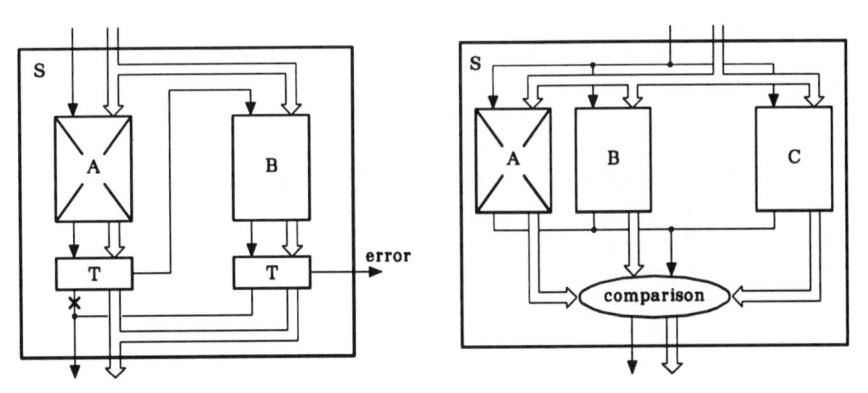

Figure 2.41: A new error

A test sequence considers S software as correct because the tolerance mechanisms are efficient. The software is then delivered to the client. However in both situations, if an error occurs during execution of B, when in operation, then it will generate a failure of software S. So S is not fault tolerant even if its design foresaw that it would be. In this case, the designer and the client place unjustified reliance on the software.

Solution
A 'white box' test can be performed (to show the internal states) or errors injected during the 'fault removal' stage in order to test the tolerance mechanisms.

Testing fault tolerance mechanisms is difficult because a good design (without errors) may not allow an error to be provoked (that is to occur). One technique consists in injecting faults (Arlat, 1990). For instance this is done providing inputs to the program that are not expected in the specification. For example, we provide an input sequence over a short period of time with a higher frequency than the one specified in order to know if the software can tolerate 'bursts of traffic'. This corresponds to a 'robustness test' on the use of the system and on its implementation (efficiency).

Another way of injecting faults consists in modifying the program in order to obtain *mutants* as described in section 2.3.6. The efficiency of the fault tolerance mechanisms is judged by applying the test sequence associated with the initial program. If the mutants fulfil the test sequence (they run successfully), we consider that the tolerance mechanisms are efficient.

2.5.5 Measurement of performance

Two kinds of measurements made on dependable software must be studied:

- the first one concerns the measurement of the dependability of a program. It was introduced in section 1.3 of chapter 1;
- the second one concerns the measurement of the real-time performance of a software tool into which fault tolerance mechanisms were introduced. This aspect will be discussed in this section.

Evaluation of the performance of real-time software or rather the compliance with the performance specified in the client's requirements is a widely studied subject. Generally it is based on the study of the system's behaviour which is, for instance, modelized with temporal modelling. The introduction of elements proper to fault tolerance makes this measurement more difficult. Firstly, the place (and the time) of error occurrence is not predictable so the global operation (normal + correction) is difficult to forecast and measure. Therefore a theoretical study is difficult. The same applies to a practical study. The fault injection problems as those described in the previous section are found again when studying measurements.

The difficulty in obtaining a measurement depends on the fault tolerance technique chosen. For instance, the maximum time can be predicted in the case of an N-version implementation that has a voter with a watchdog monitoring the version execution time. For the recovery blocks technique, this measurement is generally impossible unless a watchdog is added to the acceptance test (Hecht, 1986). However, real-time languages allow time constraints on the execution of statements to be expressed but in a limited way. So the detection of an error in case of non-conformance makes the implementation of techniques using watchdogs quite difficult.

The problems that we have just mentioned are relevant to sequential programs. The aim is to measure the impact of a fault on the temporal performance of the software. The presence of a fault will modify (lengthen) the execution times. For multi-task programs running on a monoprocessor, this study must be completed by a global study of the software. What is the impact of modifying the execution time of the part of a task on the whole program? The presence of a fault in a task may increase its processor utilization time because of the correction handling. For instance, it can generate starvation phenomena for lower priority tasks. The increase in task processing time due to an error can change the sequencing (order) of actions performed by the tasks. Sometimes it can lead to the non-conformance with system requirements. Therefore it is important to be able to check that the fault tolerance mechanisms do not modify this order. This aspect will not be developed. To study this you can refer to the work of Cheng (Cheng, 1989).

Under the term 'mechanism' we not only mean corrective actions but also actions executed even if there are no faults, like the actions needed to save the context (see section 2.4.2 dealing with recovery cache) or to detect an error (see chapter 5).

2.6 Conclusion

In this chapter, we presented dependability techniques classing them into three sets: Fault Avoidance, Fault Removal and Fault Tolerance. These techniques must be used in a complementary manner to tend towards 'zero fault software' justifying the reliance that can be placed on it.

In the presentation, we developed general problems and proposed logical solutions without attempting to discuss practical implementation of these solutions. Implementations for software programmed in Ada will be developed in chapter 4. We will see that the exception mechanism offered by Ada is often used.

This use however requires good knowledge of the syntactical characteristics (which are supposed to be known) and the semantical characteristics of this feature and, in particular, the potential that it offers and its inherent limits. This will be covered in chapter 3.

CHAPTER 3

Characterization of the Ada exception mechanism

In chapter 2, we presented the fundamental principles of dependability and the methods and tools used to take these principles into account during the program development steps. Among the methods we mentioned the necessity to possess means for error expression, detection (notion of invariant associated with designed components) and handling. These three elements are available in the Ada language by using the *exception mechanism*. In this chapter we will especially deal with this mechanism.

In chapter 4, we will present how dependability techniques must be considered to design dependable Ada programs. The Ada exception mechanism will be frequently used. Consequently, good knowledge of the exception mechanism features provided by the Ada language is required. Thus this chapter provides a characterization of the Ada exception mechanism. In particular, the possibilities and limits of this feature are discussed.

3.1 Introduction

In this first section we will give an informal introduction of the exception and exception mechanism notions then a description of the software designers' points of view concerning these notions. Lastly, a plan of this chapter will be presented.

3.1.1 Exception, exception mechanism

The notion of exception concerning the associated concepts (Goodenough, 1975) and their availability via the programming languages is fairly old (as PL/1 (Veillon, 1971) and CLU (Liskov, 1979)). Concerning Ada, the handling of exceptional situations (the interest of which was mainly demonstrated by the work of (Bron, 1976)) was considered during the definition of the language (Ichbiah, 1979)

Introduction   123

to provide a mechanism from the first versions (Ledgard, 1981). It was improved for the recent version (ARM, 1983) and is modified in the new standard (Ada95, 1995). This shows both the importance of this feature and the discussions that it still provokes.

An exception is generally defined as a means for expressing an exceptional situation which occurs during the running of a program. An exception handler can be associated with it. This handler is executed following the detection of the exceptional state (called exception raising) and the abandoning of the processing in progress. On completion of the exception handling, normal processing is resumed.

These conventional definitions consider the exception concept or the exceptional state concept as primitive and intuitive. This is also the point of view which is expressed in the standard (see section 11(1) and 11(2) of the standard (ARM, 1983)). Although these definitions are acceptable for a literary introduction, they are however rarely expressed more precisely and give rise to much discussion which does not deal with the root of the problem as the original notion is not formalized. In the following sections, we will come back to the definition of the term *exception*, the other elements comprising the *exception mechanism* and the nature of these notions.

3.1.2 Designers' points of view

The exception mechanism is rarely used by software designers and this mainly for two reasons:

- the notions of exception and exception mechanism are poorly understood and,
- the possibilities of using this mechanism are poorly known.

These imply that the exception mechanism is often considered by the program designers as an artefact introducing further complexities into the problem to be solved. Designers believe that they can (or even must) avoid its use.

Software designers can be divided into fours classes on the basis of their points of view towards the exception mechanism. Designers consider that:

- the exception mechanism was introduced by Ada language designers to solve problems specific to the language;
- the exception notion is not useful because the designed program will never raise exceptions;
- the exception mechanism may be used to detect errors during program debugging but must not be maintained in the embedded software;
- the exception mechanism seems to be useful but how to use it and in what circumstances.

The study of each viewpoint is interesting.

Solving a language problem
The Ada program designers of the first class think that the Ada language designers have added exceptions *to solve certain problems inherent in the language itself*. This impression is often due to the fact that the exception notion is introduced into literature or training courses by presenting predefined exceptions. The software designers do not perceive exceptions as being a reply to a design requirement but as introducing additional complexities imposed by the language itself. At best, they generally reject the mechanism and, at worst, the language itself.

In the absence of exception mechanism use, exceptional situations are dealt with by larding the programs with nested test statements making them illegible and by not underscoring the exceptional aspect of certain states of the application. In addition to these drawbacks, this point of view is fundamentally unacceptable from a dependability viewpoint. In effect, the implicit and mandatory detection of exceptional situations is not possible. Only states whose occurrence has been explicitly provided for by the test statements will be detected. Thus, the use of a language without this mechanism may lead, for example, to the following situation: a program causing an array to overflow may prolong or even complete its execution without indicating this fact.

For this class of designers, we can argue that the exception mechanism has not been introduced to create new problems but to solve problems which actually exist (Gauthier, 1993).

My software is dependable
Designers of the second class place *total reliance in the software* that *they* design and in the components and the means for execution that they use. In this situation:

- the 'predefined exceptions' of the language and the exceptions raised by the modules used are judged as unnecessary. In effect, these designers consider that the run-time environment and the packages used cannot reach exceptional states as they were well designed and are correctly used;
- the use of 'user exceptions' during the design of a program is considered as unnecessary and dangerous and is therefore prohibited. In effect, for these designers, expressing exceptions in a program is the same as admitting their fallibility or their incapacity to design correct programs.

In the case of the Ada language this choice was made for example for the SPARK project. It is fully justified here due to the existence of a validation tool. The semantics analysis tool which was itself written in SPARK was validated. However, only a subset of the language can be used. The designers then have a limited number of features at their disposal which notably impoverishes the means of expression provided by Ada.

The bans of the SAFE-ADA project are not so hard. This project allows user exceptions (but not predefined ones) to be used. The predefined exception ban assumes that a tool exists to prove the impossibility of the raising of such exceptions. This project was brought out in order to use the Ada language for the design of avionics software (Holzapfel, 1988). More recent studies concerning the EFA (European Fighter Aircraft) temper these proposals by allowing the use of exception mechanisms but by logically imposing the following rule: 'all possible exceptions shall be handled' (Welz, 1992).

Many other designers hold a fairly similar point of view. They suppose that an exception cannot occur in *their* software. However, they generally do not have the necessary validation means. Their point of view is unacceptable by the client who can only place very limited reliance in the software that they produce. The association of numerous exceptions with Ada objects (packages, subprograms) does not measure a low quality of the design of these objects. For instance 427 packages (on 505) provided by G. Booch (Booch, 1987) to define basic abstract data types, declare 2 or 3 exceptions (Schwille, 1993).

Detection means

The third class of designers only use the exception mechanism as *means for detecting an erroneous situation*. As we will see, the Ada language offers facilities to achieve this. For example, the declaration:

type FINGER **is new** INTEGER **range** 1..5;

not only facilitates the expression of the concepts of the problem but also increases the dependability of the programs including it. This is due both to the checks made at compile time and to the CONSTRAINT_ERROR exception raised if a value assigned in a variable of this type exceeds the range.

For these designers, exception handling consists then in displaying a message on the screen to indicate this error. The associated fault is corrected during a next step in design or maintenance.

The possibility for the program to handle exceptional situations itself and to resume current processing is not used. If the point of view of these designers is acceptable to facilitate debugging (fault removal), it is not so in the case of an embedded software which must be dependable. Indeed, in this situation, the operator can of course interact with the program at run-time but he or she can no longer act on the program contents itself. We can imagine the distress of an aircraft pilot and speculate on what we should advise him to do if a message such as 'ERROR IN ENGINE CONTROL procedure' is displayed. If an exception occurs in an embedded software, action on the behaviour of the program can only be performed by the program itself. This action may be implemented in an exception handler.

Also, limiting the use of the exception mechanism to software fault removal implies that the error detection means must be suppressed in the embedded software. But, extracting or inhibiting the exceptional situation detection statements in the final version of the software may modify the behaviour of the application. Costly *non-regression tests* are then indispensable (Pyle, 1991).

To prevent the exception mechanism from being activated, means offered by the Ada language (the pragma SUPPRESS) are used to inhibit the raising of the exceptions. The use of this option and the absence of exception handling are extremely dangerous as the pragma SUPPRESS does not eliminate the faults but only the checks allowing the errors to be detected. For example, a design fault may cause a value not included in the range defined by a type to be assigned to a variable of this type. This fault will generate an error (abnormal state of the content of the variable and therefore abnormal state of the software execution) which will not be immediately detected by the execution if the check is suppressed. The execution may therefore be erroneous (section [11.7(18)] of the standard). We wish to point out here that the meanings of the qualifier *erroneous* are slightly different in the Ada standard and in dependability. In the dependability field, erroneous operation is operation leading to the occurrence of an error. This can possibly lead to a failure (behaviour not in compliance with specifications). In Ada standard it defines that the effect is unpredictable (section [1.6(7)]).

Exceptions provide opportunities but not miracles
Lastly, the fourth class of designers includes those who are aware of the *potentialities of the Ada exception mechanism*. However a good many of these designers do not get the best out of these potentialities. This comes generally from the fact that they have not assimilated the nature of the exceptions or the characteristics of the exception mechanism. The aim of this chapter is to provide this knowledge.

A small number of designers, aware of the potentialities of the exception mechanism, hope to be provided with a miracle tool which will help them to find correct responses to unforeseen circumstances. This unfortunately is not the case: the mechanism adds no further intelligence to the program other than that provided (that is programmed) by the designers (Gauthier, 1989).

These four viewpoints highlight the fact that the definition of a new concept (in our case the exceptions) made available by means of a tool (the Ada language exception mechanism) is only a first step. The designers must also have knowledge to understand and master the concept and the tool implementing it. An invention is one thing, understanding and using it is another matter.

3.1.3 Plan

The aim of this chapter is to provide help in understanding and mastering the exception mechanism offered by the Ada language.

This objective will be reached by presenting the *characteristics* of this mechanism. To achieve this, we will look at the nature of the exceptions (section 3.2), their expressions (section 3.3), the modes for associating an exception handler with an exception (section 3.4), the raising (section 3.5) and the handling of an exception (section 3.6). The effect of the mechanism on the concurrent features of the language will be tackled in section 3.7.

This knowledge is indispensable to get the best out of the exception mechanism for implementing dependability techniques. This will be presented in chapter 4.

The basic presentation, syntax and semantics, of the Ada exception mechanism is not recalled in this chapter. If this knowledge is not acquired, the reader can refer to books on the language including (Watt, 1987), (Mendal, 1992), (Gauthier, 1993).

As signalled in chapter 1, the basic mechanism features (ARM, 1983) will be mainly used. However the additional possibilities offered by the new standard (Ada95, 1995) are studied and the differences are highlighted.

Lastly, the introduction of this chapter is the occasion to point out the existence of an exception mechanism in other languages and real-time kernels. We will from time to time underline these other solutions in order to improve the understanding of the one offered by Ada. However, our aim here is not to present a comparative study. This is proposed in appendix A.

3.2 Nature of an exception

The aim of this section is to give accurate and general definitions of the exception and of the exception mechanism and also the associated terminology. These definitions are illustrated by some examples relevant to the Ada language. The Ada language exception mechanism is analysed in detail in the following sections.

The presentation made is derived from the formal work by Flaviu Cristian (Cristian, 1982). We admit that the point of view selected is specific to the dependability field. We will point out other approaches in order to clearly express the effect of the context considered.

3.2.1 Specification invariant

In this section we will go back to the notion of invariant introduced in section 2.1 of chapter 2, focusing on its definition in Ada programming context.

Definitions
The definition of a module (or a component) depends on the selected abstraction (see section 2.2.1). Distinction is made for example between the *specification abstraction*, giving the behaviour expected of the module and the *implementation abstraction*, defining its realization. A hierarchical breakdown obtained from design generally offers various implementation abstractions (Parnas, 1972).

An abstraction is defined by:

- an *abstract formal state* the possible values of which define a set of *abstract states* and by

- *transitions* between the abstract states caused by a request for an operation supplied (*exported*) by the module.

An abstraction definition can be represented explicitly by graphical modelling (finite state machine, Petri net, etc.) or more implicitly by a textual program. Consider, for example, the following module (the Ada specification of the package SIMPLE) containing a single operation (ABSOLUTE_VALUE):

```
package SIMPLE is
  procedure ABSOLUTE_VALUE( V:         in  INTEGER;
                            ABSOLUTE:  out POSITIVE);
end SIMPLE;
```

A procedure call is a means to control the module and to change its abstract formal state value by a transition. The abstract formal state defines the means allowing the module evolution to be observed. In the case of a procedure specification, the observation means are the parameters which define the inputs and outputs of the module. For the considered example, an abstract formal state of this module is therefore defined by the (V, ABSOLUTE) pair.

By abuse of language we will frequently call abstract state (respectively abstract formal state) simply *state* (respectively *formal state*) in the remainder of this chapter.

The call for the ABSOLUTE_VALUE operation (that is the procedure) causes a change from a state of a given value (v,.), where v ∈ INTEGER and '.' expresses 'whatever the value of the second parameter is', to a new state of value (v, absolute).

An exhaustive specification could be defined by the abstract automaton of the module by giving the transitions for each of the integer values v of V. For the considered example we would then obtain a correspondence table: (v,.) -> (v,absolute) for all values v in INTEGER. This would be a true sequential automaton in the case of a package specification containing several procedures or variables which would then be used in the definition of the state.

The giving of the table (or generally the automaton) makes an implementation, that is the definition of the body of the package, unnecessary. In effect, for all values v of V we would obtain the corresponding value of the ABSOLUTE parameter. Also, the expression of these transitions is often not known as the client hopes to obtain them once the module has been made thanks to execution by a computer.

As detailed in the introduction of chapter 2 (section 2.1), the reliance placed in an operation of a module is evaluated by a contract. This contract is not defined by the set of the expected transitions but in the form of an **invariant** defining a Boolean condition on the set of the transitions, that is between all initial states (e') of the module and the **expected** states (e) after execution of an operation P offered by the module. This invariant is called **INVARIANT/P(e',e)**. It is not a definition of the behaviour of the operation P of the module but it expresses a property that this behaviour must have. INVARIANT/P is then defined by:

INVARIANT/P = {(e', e) such that INVARIANT/P (e', e) is true }.

INVARIANT/P expresses the set of the transitions (e', e) which are in conformance with the contract, without defining how e is obtained from e'.

Invariant expression in a programming language
The expression of a specification in a given programming language first of all defines the expected behaviour. This is generally done *informally*, for instance, through identifier names (ABSOLUTE_VALUE for example). The non-formalism of the information elements on the behaviour implies the impossibility of exploiting them by means of an analysis tool. In particular, these specifications are not executable making the expression of a body necessary.

A specification defined in a programming language also gives an invariant expressed formally by means of the features of the language. For example in Ada, the parameters of a subprogram introduce information concerning the properties that the behaviour of the subprogram must have. First, the parameters define the abstract formal state. Thus, the abstract formal state of the ABSOLUTE_VALUE procedure of the SIMPLE package is a pair (V, ABSOLUTE). Second, the types associated with the parameters specify all the values that the states can take (v $\in$ INTEGER and absolute $\in$ POSITIVE). Third, the parameter modes (in, out and in out) constrain the possible transitions:

- the definition of the semantics of the Ada language specifies that the value of an in mode parameter is unchanged after the execution of the subprogram. Thus, for the ABSOLUTE_VALUE procedure, for each transition, the value of the v component of a final state is the same as that of the initial state;
- the language standard imposes that the value of an out mode parameter of a subprogram be assigned by the execution of this subprogram. Also, the provided result does not depend on the initial value of the real parameter. This applies to the ABSOLUTE parameter of the ABSOLUTE_VALUE procedure. Consequently, for each transition, the ABSOLUTE component of the formal state can have any initial value.

Figure 3.1 shows the constraints added by specifying the in and out modes in the specification of the ABSOLUTE_VALUE procedure.

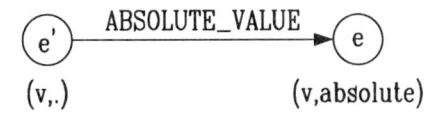

Figure 3.1: Abstraction and in and out modes

130 Chapter 3: Characterization of the Ada Exception Mechanism

To conclude, the specification of a subprogram introduces three classes of information (number of parameters, types of the parameters, modes of the parameters) expressing constraints on the behaviour that this subprogram must follow. These elements form the subprogram **specification invariant**.

Thus, the specification invariant of the ABSOLUTE_VALUE procedure is obtained from the Ada specification definition of this procedure and the semantics of the language:

**INVARIANT/ABSOLUTE_VALUE = {((v,.), (v, absolute)) where
v ∈ INTEGER and absolute ∈ POSITIVE}.**

This example shows that the accuracy of the specification invariant depends on the information given by the designer (for example by choice of types). It is also highly dependent on the features of the language used for programming: for example taking into account the number, the types and the modes of the parameters for the Ada procedures.

3.2.2 Standard Domain

The specification of a subprogram does not give a formal expression of its expected behaviour. Consequently, after implementation, it is not possible to confirm the absolute correctness of the execution. However, as shown in the previous section, expected properties can be deduced from the subprogram specification and expressed in the form of a specification invariant. This defines a contract as correlations which should exist between the state obtained after execution (e) and the state prior to execution (e') of the subprogram.

Let us consider an **implementation** I of the operation P of a module and therefore another abstraction of this module. We call **Standard Domain** of P (abbreviated SD/P) the set of initial states e' such that, **after execution of implementation I of P**, we obtain a state e in compliance with specification invariant INVARIANT/P:

SD/P = {e', e'-I(P)->e and INVARIANT/P (e',e) is true}

For example, let us consider the following implementation of the ABSOLUTE_VALUE procedure.

```
procedure ABSOLUTE_VALUE( V:            in    INTEGER;
                          ABSOLUTE:     out   POSITIVE) is
begin
   ABSOLUTE := V;
end ABSOLUTE_VALUE;
```

The INVARIANT/ABSOLUTE_VALUE definition obtained in the previous section allows us to affirm that SD/ABSOLUTE_VALUE is the set of (v,.) such that v ∈ INTEGER before execution and ABSOLUTE ∈ POSITIVE after execution, that is, **on account of the implementation** (ABSOLUTE := V;) such that v is POSITIVE. Hence:

SD/ABSOLUTE_VALUE = {(v,.) / v ∈ POSITIVE}.

For any v ∈ POSITIVE value, the result obtained by the implementation of the ABSOLUTE_VALUE procedure will be considered as correct with regard to the expected properties expressed by the specification invariant deduced from the subprogram specification.

3.2.3 Exception Domain

Definitions

For any state e' not belonging to SD/P, execution of P leads to a state e such that INVARIANT (e', e) is false. In this case, the properties wanted (i.e. expected by the contract) are not obtained.

The **Exception Domain** ED is defined as the complement of the Standard Domain:

ED = ¬ SD

For our example:
ED/ABSOLUTE_VALUE = {(v,.), v ∉ INTEGER or (v ∈ INTEGER and v <= 0)}.

Let us insist on the fact that the states of ED are those for which we can affirm that the result provided by the considered implementation is incorrect. This does not mean that the results obtained from a SD state are correct with regard to the informal client's requirements but simply that they are in compliance with the specification invariant and are considered as reliable by the client. This shows the importance of the contract drafting to be done by the client and to be expressed by the designer in the program specification.

Let us consider the following new implementation:

```
procedure ABSOLUTE_VALUE ( V:         in   INTEGER;
                           ABSOLUTE:  out  POSITIVE) is
begin
   if V <= 0 then ABSOLUTE:= - V;
            else ABSOLUTE:= V - 1;
   end if;
end ABSOLUTE_VALUE;
```

SD/ABSOLUTE_VALUE is the set of (v,.) such that v ∈ INTEGER before execution and ABSOLUTE ∈ POSITIVE after execution. If V>=2 or V<0 then

ABSOLUTE ∈ POSITIVE. If V=0 or V=1 then ABSOLUTE=0 and so ABSOLUTE ∉ POSITIVE. We then obtain:

SD/ABSOLUTE_VALUE = {(v,.) / v ∈ INTEGER and v different from 0 and 1}.

Thus values (v,.) such that v ∉ INTEGER or v = 0 or 1 define ED. The processing of the ABSOLUTE_VALUE of the integer values V strictly greater than 1 gives admittedly a positive result (ABSOLUTE) (therefore in compliance with the specification invariant of the procedure) but not correct: for example, the ABSOLUTE parameter has value 2 when parameter V has value 3.

Note that this implementation, different from the first one (ABSOLUTE:=V;) gives a different ED set. The Exception Domain is therefore strongly related to the implementation and does not only qualify the use of the operation as was proposed in the first publications (Bron, 1976), (Goodenough, 1975).

The Exception Domain depends on the implementation of the operation of the module and also on the specification invariant. If we now consider the following new specification:

```
procedure ABSOLUTE_VALUE ( V:         in  INTEGER;
                           ABSOLUTE:  out INTEGER) ;
```

and the first implementation (ABSOLUTE:=V;), then ED is defined by the condition: v ∉ INTEGER.

The states of the Exception Domain are called **exceptional states**. The definition of Exception Domain shows that the exceptional states do not represent unimaginable situations as they can be accurately expressed with regard to the specification and the implementation defined by the client and by the designer through his or her programming.

Exception Domain and dependability

The execution of an operation P from a state e' of the Exception Domain places the module in a state e such that the properties linking e' and e are false. e' is therefore an undesirable state to execute P. The specification invariant defines the means for observing these kinds of states. The implementation specifies transition from e' to e and therefore the cause giving value e of the formal state from value e'.

The Exception Domain states of an operation P define errors of P due to implementation faults or utilization faults (invariant concerning only initial state e') and observed on account of the formal information elements supplied by the specification of P. The Exception Domain is therefore a means for expressing a set of errors.

The under-utilization of the features offered by the programming language for the subprogram specification or the unavailability of such useful features gives invariants with low constraints. This case arises, for example, if constrained types are not used to define the subprogram parameters when this piece of information is available or if all parameters are defined as in out mode when their specificity

Nature of an exception   133

(input or output) is known. Therefore, for a given implementation, the Standard Domain is a set which is larger than it should be. The Exceptional Domain is thus smaller. The number of **errors detected** is therefore reduced. Many faults can thus exist (implementation or utilization faults) which are not observable as not transformed into errors. Dependability requirements make the behaviour of an optimistic designer priding himself in a smaller Exception Domain inadmissible. The faults exist even though they are not detectable. Their effects will be increasingly difficult to master as detection moves away from their origin.

If the implementation constraints are insufficiently taken into consideration this also implies that the Standard Domain will be too large and the Exception Domain smaller than it should be. For instance consider once more the following procedure:

```
procedure ABSOLUTE_VALUE( V:           in    INTEGER;
                          ABSOLUTE:    out   POSITIVE) is
begin
  if V <= 0  then ABSOLUTE:= - V;
             else ABSOLUTE:= V - 1;
  end if;
end ABSOLUTE_VALUE;
```

The ED1={(v,.) such that $v \notin$ INTEGER or $v = 0$ or $v=1$}. If the implementation is not considered then SD2={(v,.) / $v \in$ INTEGER} and so ED2={(v,.) such that $v \notin$ INTEGER}. Thus the procedure is called in its Exceptional Domain with V=1 as first parameter in the first case, and in its Standard Domain in the second. However in this last case the result ABSOLUTE=0 $\in$ POSITIVE will be signalled at run-time.

This situation is therefore totally different from the previous one. In this case, exceptional states whose existence was not anticipated are added to the exceptional states previously identified by the designer. We would like to insist on the fact that this does not mean that they appear by magic, but that, although existing in the program and detected by it, they were not identified by the designer. This omission may be due to the difficulty in mastering the complexity of the program implementation behaviour and in particular in exhaustively defining the Standard Domain and then the Exception Domain. These situations correspond to *unanticipated errors*.

As the invariant considers the state of the subprogram at call-time and the state obtained after execution, detection of utilization faults or pure implementation faults comprise specific cases:

- the first situation (detection of utilization faults) is detected by an invariant concerning only the initial state, a *precondition*;
- the second situation (pure implementation faults) is detected by an invariant concerning only the final state, a *postcondition*.

3.2.4 Generalization of the Exception Domain to implementation

As we pointed out, an implementation of an operation constitutes another abstraction of this operation. This **implementation abstraction** has an abstract formal state often qualified *internal state* (E) which generally extends the formal state (e) of the specification abstraction. This state incorporates local variables in the case of package bodies and Ada subprograms.

Take procedure P specified by:

procedure P(I: **in** TI; O: **out** TO);

The **specification formal state** of P is defined by (I, O). If the implementation requires two local variables A and B, the **implementation formal state** is defined by a 4-tuple (I, O, A, B). If A is initialized by value a' and B is not, an initial value e' = (i',.) of the specification state produces an initial value E0 = (i', ., a',.) of the implementation state.

Each transition between model states associated with the behaviour of the specification abstraction ((i',.)->(i', o) for the previous example) is made more precise in the implementation behavioural model by intermediary transitions between internal states. These transitions are fired by executing the operations used in the implementation.

Let us consider the following implementation example of P:

```
procedure P (I: in TI; O: out TO) is
        -- defines the formal state of initial value e'
   A, B... -- completes this state into formal state E
begin --initial state E0 (dependent on e' and possible
        --initialization of local variables)
   P1(I, A);   --expected state E1 after P1 execution
   P2(A, B);   --expected state E2 after P2 execution
   P3(B, O);   --expected state E3 after P3 execution
end P;        --expected state e (dependent on E3)
```

The behaviour of the implementation abstraction is shown on figure 3.2.

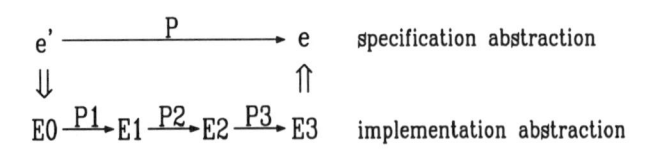

$$e' \xrightarrow{P} e \quad \text{specification abstraction}$$
$$\Downarrow \quad\quad \Uparrow$$
$$E0 \xrightarrow{P1} E1 \xrightarrow{P2} E2 \xrightarrow{P3} E3 \quad \text{implementation abstraction}$$

Figure 3.2: Implementation abstraction

As with the specification abstraction, an implementation abstraction behavioural model rarely exists exhaustively. Such a model should, for each value i' of I, give the sequence of the four values E0 = (i',., a',.) E1 = (i',., a'',.), E2 = (i',., a'', b'), E3 = (i', o, a'', b'). Its existence would also make the implementation of the used procedures Pi unnecessary as for all values e' = (i',.), value e = (i', o) would be known.

In practice, only a property on the behaviour can be supplied by means of a Boolean function on the internal state values. An **implementation invariant** of procedure P is a Boolean function on (E0, E1, E2, E3). For example: I(E0) + A(E1) > B(E2) + O(E3) where X(Ei) represents the value of component X of state Ei.

Beware, this is not an invariant on the specification of operations Pi used in the implementation but on the specific use made by P of these operations. For example, if X, Y and Z are three variables or formal parameters of the INTEGER type and if statement

```
X : = Y + Z;
```

is expressed in the implementation, then invariant:
MINIMUM (Y, Z) < X < MAXIMUM (Y, Z)
is not true for all additions but is specific to the implementation context of the subprogram containing this assignment statement. We wish to check, for example, the constraint: 'Y and Z have opposite signs'.

Supposing that the implementation of operations (P1, P2, P3) involved in the design of the original operation P has been performed, we can define the **Standard Domain of the implementation** of P, that is, relevant to the formal state E and to the implementation invariant, then the associated **Exception Domain of the implementation** as described in the previous section.

By the same way, the Exception Domains can be defined for the specifications and the implementations of operations Pi.

The definition of the Exception Domain conserves its general nature, only the abstraction level and therefore the definition of the formal state change.

3.2.5 Exception Domain and Ada

The examples chosen to illustrate the formal state notion required to define the Exception Domain used information relevant to the data appearing explicitly in the specifications or the bodies of the Ada subprograms (parameters, local variables). The Ada language features involved in the definition of the formal states and the Exception Domains will be studied in section 3.3. However, we would like to point out at this stage that the Ada language semantics also associates, as a component of the formal state, information relevant to control. This is the **termination state**. Its value, delivered at the end of the execution of the implementation of an operation is: either *normal termination* or *abnormal termination*.

This new component of the formal abstract state is necessary as the evaluation of the invariant on the data supposes that the execution of the operation concerned has been completed (or 'normally terminated') and therefore that a state e has been reached from the initial state e'. However, the language semantics declares that the execution of certain implementations may not be terminated after the sequencing of the statements described in the body has been completed. This case arises if one of the operations of the body is executed in an exceptional state. The execution of the following statements turns out to be unnecessary. If it is impossible to bring value of the implementation formal state into one of the states of its Standard Domain (for example, if there are no exception handlers), the execution of the enveloping operation will not be considered as completed. This is an abnormal termination.

In Ada, the specification invariant involved in the definition of the Standard Domain of a subprogram includes therefore the fact that the termination state of this subprogram must have the *normal* value. Thus, in case of *abnormal* termination of the execution, the state preceding the subprogram call belongs to the Exception Domain.

This component of the formal state and therefore this part of the invariant are not explained by the syntax but are expressed in the semantics defined by the standard [11(1)] [11.4(1)] [11.4.1(4)]. Thus, the call for procedure ABSOLUTE_VALUE with value '5a3' as first parameter places the call for this procedure in a state belonging to its Exception Domain on account of the negation of the invariant (concerning the types) defined explicitly by the subprogram specification. If the execution of the procedure with an integer value for the first parameter places one of the actions called by the body in its Exception Domain and if normal termination cannot occur (for example because the body has no *exception handlers*), then the procedure will also be in an Exception Domain state, due this time to an abnormal termination.

3.2.6 Exception mechanism

Exception
An **exception** of an operation of a module is a concept identifying a state or a set of states of the Exception Domain associated with the operation.

We are conscious of the fact that the definition chosen is very precise: exceptions are introduced here as means for expressing states leading to the negation of the properties associated with the specifications, taking implementation into account. This point of view can be considered as limited when compared with the one defining the exceptions as means for describing *rare situations defined by the specification* of the problem. The exception mechanism is then used to extend or generalize the operations (Goodenough, 1975). This last definition is chosen in many books on Ada. It has the advantage of not overloading an implementation, which under most circumstances turns out to be simple, with specific cases complex to deal with. The following example is typical.

```
function "/" (DIVIDEND, DIVISOR: in FLOAT) return FLOAT is
begin
   return DIVIDEND/DIVISOR;
exception -- DIVISOR = 0
   when CONSTRAINT_ERROR =>
      if DIVIDEND > 0.0   then return FLOAT'last;
                          else return FLOAT'first;
      end if;
end "/";
```

Our presentation can be seen as a specific case as we hope that the negations of the invariant, in fact the program errors, will not be numerous. The definition is however very different and greatly influences the developments which will be described. In effect, defining exceptions as rare states is the same as considering these states as an integral and explicit part of the requirements. The exception mechanism is thus a technique used, for example, to highlight *specific cases* and to simplify the description of the most frequently executed behaviour. There is therefore a fundamental difference between this point of view and ours. We will not discuss this here but we will underscore in this chapter some of the consequences induced.

Lastly we would like to point out that proposals exist to quantify the rarity using probabilities integrating the occurrence frequencies of exceptional situations and their handling times (Cheriton, 1986). This is a temporal approach: a state which occurs infrequently (an error for example), but whose handling is very bulky is considered as an 'ordinary' state whereas a state which can be reached relatively frequently, but whose handling is short (an end of file for example which requires the file to be closed), is considered as 'exceptional'. We will not use this point of view either.

We can therefore see that at present agreement has not been reached on the definition of the term 'exception'. The definition chosen is however suitable for handling the error concept associated with dependability which is the subject of this book.

More than one exception can have the same name in several locations of a program as it is for the variables, parameters, subprograms, etc. They concern various entities. To allow exception identifier and exception identity notions to be distinguished, the package Ada. Exceptions introduces a private type Exception_Id and subprograms which have parameters of this type. In particular

```
function Exception_Name(Id: Exception_Id) return String;
```

returns the textual identifier associated with the exception identity. Conversely, if E is an exception then E'Identity defines the identity of E.

Exception occurrence
An exception defining a state (or a set of states) is a static notion. The execution of an operation from one of the states of its Exception Domain is called the **occurrence of the exception** associated with this state.

The notion of exception and exception occurrence are now distinguished syntactically in the new standard. The package Ada.Exceptions explicitly provides a limited private type Exception_Occurrence and subprograms having parameters of this type. This distinction is necessary because the two concepts are different:

- an exception defines a static notion (state) whereas
- an exception occurrence is a dynamic notion. For instance one state is reachable several times during a program execution. Then there are one exception and several occurrences.

One exception occurrence is associated with a single exception. Its identity is obtained by means of

function Exception_Identity(X: Exception_Occurrence) **return** Exception_Id;

provided by the new standard.

Exception raising
The **raising** of an exception during the running of a program is a mechanism signalling the occurrence of an exception to program execution, that is the fact that an operation has been executed in its Exception Domain. This indication could be reported by modifying data such as the value of a parameter (error code) as is done in many microprocessors (example: overflow or underflow bit of arithmetic operations) or real-time kernels. In the Ada language, the mechanism acts not on the data but on the control and on the state. The execution is diverted from the block of statements, containing the operation which raised the exception, to the **exception handler** associated with it (if it exists). As we will develop later, absence of **association** places the operation comprised by the block of statements in its Exception Domain (by abnormal execution termination state), thus reiterating the raising process at user block level of the block in question. This is the **propagation** phenomenon.

Here also the use of the exception mechanism is specific and we admit this. Other authors propose uses which may seem to be less restrictive. However, this generally concerns the use of a technical tool, not based on principles, to implement designs sometimes improper. This type of use is one of the causes of the suspicion that many designers have toward the exception mechanism, considering it, for example, as a means for reintroducing the use of the 'goto statement'.

3.2.7 Overview

The scenario developed to present the nature of the Ada exception mechanism shows that this mechanism is defined by four characteristics:

- the means for expressing an exception and, in particular, for defining exceptional states (belonging to the Exception Domain),
- the means for associating a handler with an exception,
- the means for raising an exception and connecting to the exception handler,
- the means for handling the exceptional situation: the exception handling itself and the normal execution resumption mode.

These four characteristics appear twice in the life of an Ada program: during its design (syntactic aspect) and during its execution (semantic aspect). For example, the language offers features to express an exception during design, the semantics of these features defining the means for detection made during execution. On account of the strong correlation between them, these two aspects will not be separated in the plan followed by our text but distinction will be made between them in the writing of the sections. Sections 3.3 to 3.6. will successively deal with the four characteristics mentioned. In these sections, only the sequential programming will be considered. Concurrent programming will be dealt with separately in section 3.7.

3.3 Expressing an exception

This section describes the features that the Ada language offers for expressing an exception. We will successively examine the *predefined* exceptions and the *user* exceptions.

3.3.1 Predefined exceptions

Development
A study of the languages and real-time kernels (see appendix A), which incorporate an exception mechanism, shows a change in the definition of the predefined exception identifiers, change which the Ada language has followed.

The first tendency consisted in **characterizing the cause** of the exception by partitioning the Exception Domain and, more exactly, **in detailing the abnormal termination situations** with regard to the implementation, that is the faults. We can cite for example the SIGILL (illegal statement) and SIGBUS (bus error) exceptions of the Unix kernel. These details are not related to the specification of the operations raising them but to the implementation. In practice, they are difficult to handle as the language does not have means for acting on the causes.

However, it is generally possible to act on their effects by performing for example substitution handling. From the predefined exceptions in the Ada language, only STORAGE_ERROR belongs to this class. It is related to an abnormal termination detected by the Ada run-time environment. The STORAGE_ERROR identifier is not associated with a specific operation as most of the operations offered by the language can cause memory allocation requests.

After this, the identities of the predefined exceptions were brought **closer to the specifications** of the operations and therefore the **specification invariant** notion and the contract notion. As these invariants are generally defined as various conditions linked by logical OR operations, the Exception Domain can be partitioned and several exceptions can be associated with a given operation. Thus a real-time kernel such as the Intel RMX offers 120 exceptions.

With the Ada language, many conditions composing the invariant can be verified at compile-time significantly reducing the number of predefined exceptions and their raising potentiality. For example, the coherence of the operand types of the arithmetic operations or the coherence of the elements of a task entry call (existence of the task and the entry, parameter mode and type) are checked at compile-time. Conversely, as the primitives of the real-time kernels are called by languages not incorporating these primitives as features (C language for example), not many verifications are made at compile-time. This requires a high number of checks at run-time and therefore, frequently, a large list of exceptions. In Ada, dynamic checks are still to be done in spite of the compile-time verifications. For example, the fact that the result of an expression is a value in the range defined by a type or not cannot be detected at compile-time as it requires the evaluation of the expression performed at run-time. Exception CONSTRAINT_ERROR raised by an addition whose result exceeds the defined number representation limits is an example of an exception due to the negation of an invariant defining the numerical type.

The preliminary version of the Ada language distinguished between exceptions ACCESS_ERROR, DISCRIMINANT_ERROR, INDEX_ERROR and RANGE_ERROR which were associated with separate operations whilst expressing the same invariant: non-compliance with a constraint. For this reason, these exceptions were combined under the single CONSTRAINT_ERROR label (Winkler, 1981). This example illustrates an additional change consisting in the use of **a single identifier for the parts of the exception domains belonging to separate operations**. In the same way, the NUMERIC_ERROR identifier which incorporated DIVIDE_ERROR, OVERFLOW and UNDERFLOW will disappear from the new standard (Changes, 1995) under the CONSTRAINT_ERROR label.

This therefore shows that more interest is given to the logical definition of the exception, in terms of errors associated with the specification, than in an accurate designation of the cause of its raising, that is in terms of faults associated with implementation.

Characterization

An executable Ada application is composed of the application code generated by the compiler and the executive which mainly implements the language semantics. For example, an arithmetical expression on float numbers is translated into a sequence of calls to the services of the executive performing the '+', '-', '*' and '/' operations. The executive is implemented using the hardware (processor, arithmetic coprocessor, memory, etc.) and the software (task and memory managers, etc.). The executive specification is called the **Ada Abstract Machine** (ARTEWG, 1991) (Motet, 1994) (Motet, 1995) (see Figure 3.3). The Ada Abstract Machine is a machine capable of interpreting the Ada language semantics and, in particular, the basic operations provided by the language (arithmetical operations, access to an element of an array or a record, assignment, etc.).

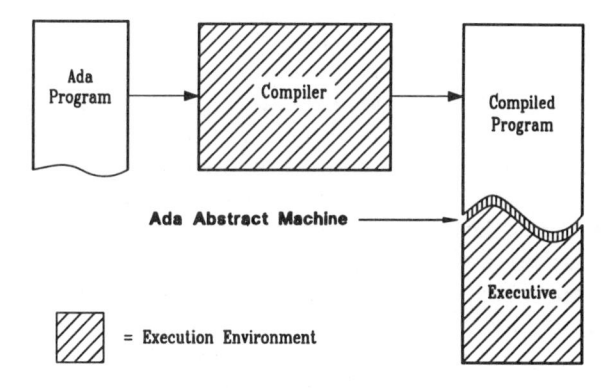

Figure 3.3: Ada implementation

One of the important assets of the Ada language is the definition in the standard of invariants for the operations of the Ada Abstract Machine. For example, 'a divisor must be different from zero' defines a constraint for the execution of the '/' operation. The invariants concern the specification or the implementation. Exception Domains are therefore associated with the operations and with the implementation of the Ada Abstract Machine. Thus, exceptional states can be detected and exceptions specific to the language raised: these are the **predefined exceptions**.

Classification

The abstract machine offers two types of operations: basic operations and constructors.

Basic operations are for example operations on numerical expressions, assignments, etc. The invariants associated with the basic operations are mainly the specification invariants of these operations. We can mention for example the exception CONSTRAINT_ERROR (or NUMERIC_ERROR in the old standard) when it is associated with numerical operations. As the implementation of the basic operations may require dynamic memory allocation, exception STORAGE_ERROR expresses the occurrence of a state of the Exception Domain of the implementation of these operations.

In addition to the basic operations, the language offers **constructors** to create and handle new objects. Predefined exceptions are associated with these constructors thanks to the invariants attached to their definitions. The invariants cover both the specification and the implementation fields.

First, the language allows the **construction of new objects to be specified** whether these are subprograms or data structures. In the first case, the typing of the subprogram parameters induces assertions concerning utilization (call of subprograms). Thus, incompatibility in the assigned values (parameters of 'in' mode) or the returned values (parameters of 'out' mode) causes the exception CONSTRAINT_ERROR to be raised. Typing is a means of integrating additional constraints into the Standard Domain and therefore increases the Exception Domain, that is the capacity of the sub-program to detect errors. For data structures, evaluation of the conformity of the value of the index of an array with regard to its definition is a good example.

The specification of the parameter 'in' and/or 'out' modes may lead to the implicit detection of an exceptional state. For example, if a formal 'out' mode parameter is not assigned on completion of subprogram execution, exception CONSTRAINT_ERROR is raised. This example clearly illustrates the fact that the exception notion (via that of the Exception Domain obtained from the Standard Domain) can involve both specification and implementation. The subprogram is called in an exceptional state if the execution of its implementation ends without assignment of a parameter specified as being in 'out' mode.

The semantics of the subprograms supposes the existence of a stack in the implementation model (stack machine): pushing of context during calls and popping on return to caller. Thus, the specification of a subprogram implies the possible raising of exception STORAGE_ERROR which occurrence depends on the implementation characteristics (memory size, memory optimization of generated code, etc.).

Constructors also exist for the **implementation of objects**. They authorize (or even require) supply of constraints involved in the definition of the invariant attached to this object. For example, to implement a procedure, the use of subtypes for the parameters of the subprograms called allows a more specific use of the subprograms to be specified as shown in the example below:

```
procedure A (...) is
  subtype ST is T range ...;
  V: ST;
begin
  ...
  B(V);
  C(V);
  ...
end A;
```

where B and C have parameters of type T in 'out' and 'in' modes respectively. If, after the execution of B, parameter V has a value belonging to T and not to ST then the negation of the implementation invariant introduced by means of ST leads to the raising of exception CONSTRAINT_ERROR.

The use of the constructor function is another example. The definition of this constructor includes the verification that the execution of the body is concluded by the execution of the return statement. Otherwise, exception PROGRAM_ERROR is raised.

3.3.2 User exception

In the previous section we introduced the fact that good use of the Ada language constructions allows implicit detection of many erroneous states. This is obtained by expressing information coming from the specifications using the features of the language. This aspect is one of the main arguments for choosing Ada as programming language. In effect, if dependability is the dominant criterion, a language must be selected for its facility to express certain concepts and also for its capacity to show any faults introduced.

However, certain semantic data of the application are not intrinsically related to the features offered. For example, the Ada language does not provide primitive constructions defining a graphic window of the portrait type (height greater than width). The primitive operations of the language will not detect a state which makes the width larger than the height. These situations must be expressed by user exceptions and explicitly detected.

Specification
For the subprograms exported by a package (expressing for example an abstract data type), the exceptions raised are defined in the specifications as follows:

```
package EXAMPLE is
  E1, E2, E3: exception;
  procedure P1 (...);
end EXAMPLE;
```

Procedure P1 can raise predefined exceptions such as CONSTRAINT_ERROR because of the invariant expressed by its declaration (see previous section) in addition to the user exceptions introduced (E1, E2, E3).

Note that the name of a **user exception is not syntactically associated with a subprogram**. Thus, if a second procedure P2 is exported by the package EXAMPLE, only a pertinent choice of the exception names allows this association to be implicitly specified. The syntactical association of the names of the exceptions raised by a subprogram was examined during the definition of the Ada language as this exists in other languages (LTR3 (de Bondelli, 1984), CLU and PL/I). It was rejected on account of the heaviness of the compiler implementation (Rationale, 1986) which should have analysed the propagation paths. However, as we will see later, the propagation paths are established dynamically. The executive should then conduct a coherence check between the declared exceptions and those which are effectively propagated. This syntactical association also poses problems in the case of predefined exceptions. For some of these predefined exceptions, the raising of an exception by an operation depends on the run-time environment implementation. For instance to implement arithmetic operations the stack may be used (and then STORAGE_ERROR should be associated with these operations) or not (using the microprocessor registers). The lack of syntactical attachment between exceptions and subprograms of packages implies that for all calls to any subprogram of a package, for which only the specification is known, we should consider the handling of all the exceptions defined in the specification of this package.

What is even more impeding, is the fact that **no invariant** explaining the causes of the raising of the user exceptions **is expressed in the declaration** (package specification). Moreover, the user exceptions must be raised by the body and propagated. The raising of a user exception defined in the specification of a package should therefore express an *abnormal termination* (value of the *termination state*). The user exception identifiers would informally specify the cause of the *abnormal termination* of a subprogram of this package. These would be exceptions related to the implementation abstraction and propagated at specification level. But, from the designer's point of view, the exceptions declared in the specification of a package are generally associated with the specification abstraction of its operations. The impossibility of associating an invariant with the specification of a user exception is one of the major limits of the language which admittedly is not specific to Ada. Let us point out however that tools based on Ada exist to get round the language limits in this field. For example, further constraints expressed in the specifications as formal comments (--¦ ...) can be added to the type definition as shown in the following example written in ANNA (ANNotated Ada) (Luckham, 1990):

```
subtype LINE_POSITION is INTEGER range 1..24;
subtype COLUMN_POSITION is INTEGER range 1..80;
type PORTRAIT is record    HEIGHT: LINE_POSITION;
                           WIDTH: COLUMN_POSITION;
end;
--¦ where P: PORTRAIT => P. HEIGHT > P.WIDTH;
```

After all operations modifying a variable of the PORTRAIT type, the associated invariant is evaluated. If it is false, exception ANNA_ERROR, predefined by the ANNA tool, is raised. Annotations can be associated with the subprogram declarations to specify the constraints on the values supplied ('in' mode parameters) -defining the initial state e'- and the values obtained ('out' mode parameters) -defining the final state e-. An example of a specification invariant written in ANNA is associated with the following procedure P.

```
procedure P(X: in T; Y: in out T; Z: out T);
--| where in (X<Y), out (Z<Y);
```

Rare situations

The exception notion has been defined as a means for expressing contradictions with regard to the specifications considering the implementation (Exceptional Domain). We stated in the introduction (section 3.2.6) that a different definition exists for exceptions: it expresses *rare* occurrence states defined in the specification. In this case, exceptions must be raised when these states are reached. If not, that is if an exception is not raised when the program execution is in such a rare occurrence state, the program state belongs to its Exception Domain which must therefore be expressed using another exception. This corresponds to the *strong propagation annotation* of the ANNA language illustrated by the following example:

```
OVERFLOW: exception;
procedure PUSH(X: in ITEM; P: in out STACK);
--| where SIZE(P)=MAX => raise OVERFLOW;
```

If the precondition SIZE(P)=MAX is true (where SIZE and MAX were defined previously in the Ada program or in formal comments) and if exception OVERFLOW is raised by PUSH procedure execution then this procedure has been called in its Standard Domain: the effective behaviour is in compliance with the expected behaviour. If in the same situation (SIZE(P)=MAX), execution of PUSH is not terminated by a propagation of exception OVERFLOW, then the procedure PUSH will be in its Exception Domain which is indicated by the raising of exception ANNA_ERROR predefined by ANNA tool.

To conclude, even if the exception mechanism is used as a technique making rare situations easier to handle, the non-raising of an exception in such a situation comprises an error. This must be detected by means of an exception, in our sense of the word.

Implementation: exception associated with specification

User exceptions declared in the specification of a package and raised by the body of a subprogram correspond to Exception Domain states communicated at subprogram call level by means of the propagation phenomenon offered by the Ada exception mechanism. First, these states can be detected by the primitive constructions used in the implementation (predefined exception) by propagating the exception under another name. The following example illustrates this situation.

```
procedure PUSH(X: in ITEM) is
begin
   TOP := TOP+1;
   STACK(TOP) := X;
exception
   when CONSTRAINT_ERROR =>
           raise STACK_OVERFLOW;
end PUSH;
```

where TOP and STACK are local variables of the package body exporting the procedure PUSH.

Detection can also be provided explicitly by means of the test of a Boolean expression whose parameter is the data representing an abstract formal state of the package. Example:

```
procedure PUSH(X: in ITEM) is
begin
   if TOP=MAXIMUM then  raise STACK_OVERFLOW;
                 else   TOP := TOP+1;
                        STACK(TOP) := X;
   end if;
end PUSH;
```

Note that for the two implementations of procedure PUSH, exception STACK_OVERFLOW detected by the body expresses membership to the Exception Domain associated with the specification of the problem (limited size stack), the invariant of which ('push an element in a full stack') could not be expressed in the subprogram specification. This justifies the propagation of the exception under its name.

Exception CONSTRAINT_ERROR could have been propagated by the two implementations: implicitly in the first implementation omitting the exception handler and explicitly in the second implementation by 'raise CONSTRAINT_ERROR;'. It would have signalled the occurrence of an exceptional state. However, propagating exception STACK_OVERFLOW reflects a change from the Ada Abstract Machine semantics which is at the origin of the detection (array overflow), to the user semantics which handles the stack (stack overflow). With no invariants attached to the user object specification, the name of the user exception supports the major part of the information specifying the circumstances of its raising.

The second implementation is close to the notion of invariant: the test placed as the first statement may be considered as a precondition evaluation. A test placed at the end of a procedure body would be perceived as a postcondition (check of the output parameter values) or an invariant (linking the output parameter values and the initial values of the input parameters).

Exception associated with implementation
Exceptions specific to an invariant associated with the implementation are detectable by styles of programming which seem to be quite similar to the ones provided in the previous sub-section as shown in the following examples:

```
procedure A(...) is
  subtype ST is T range ...;
  V: ST;
begin
  B(V); -- if V is in T but not in ST then CONSTRAINT_ERROR
  C(V);
exception
  when CONSTRAINT_ERROR => raise E;
end A;


procedure A(...) is
  V: T;
begin
  ...
  B(V);
  if not INVARIANT_ON(V) then raise E; end if;
  C(V);
  ...
end A;
```

Regarding the examples given in this sub-section and in the previous one, dealing with exceptions associated with implementation or with specification, the syntactical constructions are therefore the same for the two cases. This uniformity can lead to confusion between the two sorts of exceptions. This comes from the impossibility of describing a user invariant in a subprogram specification.

To limit the ambiguities the exceptions related to the implementation should be defined in the body and possibly propagated by a single new name specifying that they represent an *abnormal execution termination*. For instance FAILED_PUSH raised by a procedure PUSH of an unlimited size STACK, corresponds to implementation errors such as use of a constrained array to implement the stack or STORAGE_ERROR raising due to a memory size overflow. However, the propagation phenomenon offered by the Ada language does not prohibit exceptions declared in the body from being propagated outside of the body in the form of anonymous exceptions.

148   *Chapter 3: Characterization of the Ada Exception Mechanism*

Scope - Visibility
For identifiers, the scope and the visibility of the user exceptions follow the rules defined for variables. However, on account of the propagation phenomenon, an exception can exist outside of its scope: it becomes anonymous. It then expresses the *abnormal termination* of the Exception Domain of the operation which propagates it. On account of this, it is not associated with an assertion of the operation specification and the choice of considering that it no longer has a (user exception) name is logical.

However, as we will see, the exception can recover its identity, which is not acceptable with regard to the same definition. Other languages have adopted a different solution, more satisfactory for this latter point, which consists in explicitly giving a common predefined name to exceptions which go beyond their scope (example FAILURE) (Liskov, 1979). This solution identifies a subprogram which terminated abnormally without specifying the cause. The cause therefore cannot be found during the bottom-up propagation through the design hierarchy.

This can be implemented in Ada by systematically adding the 'when others => raise FAILURE;' clause and by declaring the user exception FAILURE so that it is visible in the complete program. Also, to make this solution efficient, the exception handlers must not raise locally declared exceptions as they would lead to the propagation of anonymous exceptions.

Static definition
Due to the static definition (established at compile-time), there is only one example of an exception declared in the specification of a non-generic package. If this package expresses an abstract data type, all objects of this type will raise the same exception. This situation is illustrated in the following example.

```
package P is
  E: exception;
  type T is ...
  ... -- exported subprograms
end P;
...
with P;
O1, O2, O3: P.T;
```

There is only one exception E raised by the operations executed on the three objects O1, O2 and O3. To obtain different exceptions, a generic package must be defined as follows:

```
generic
package GP is
  E: exception;
  ... -- exported subprograms
end GP;
```

Expressing an Exception 149

The type is defined in the GP package body. The declarations:
```
with GP;
package O1 is new GP;
package O2 is new GP;
package O3 is new GP;
```
then define three objects with three separate exceptions: O1.E, O2.E, O3.E.

Dynamic life
The coexistence of a static definition (that is, established at compile-time) and a dynamic life (due to propagation) of the exceptions has far-reaching consequences. A new propagation may return an anonymous exception to within its scope where it will recover its identity. An example is given in (Rationale, 1986).

```
package D is
   procedure A;
   procedure B;
end D;

with D;
procedure OUTSIDE is
begin
   ...
   D.A;
   ...
end OUTSIDE;

with OUTSIDE;
package body D is
   ERROR: exception;
   procedure A is
   begin
      ...
      raise ERROR;
      ...
   end A;
   procedure B is
   begin
      ...
      OUTSIDE;
      ...
   exception
      when ERROR => ...
   end B;
end D;
```

This example shows that exception ERROR can be propagated by procedure A to procedure OUTSIDE (caller). In this situation, the exception (previously called ERROR) becomes *anonymous* since it has gone out of its scope (out of the package body scope). It can only be handled by the exception choice others of the *exception structure* of procedure OUTSIDE.

Moreover, this example shows a curious situation: the exception that became anonymous comes back to within its scope after having gone out of it. It occurs if the procedure B is called. In this case, the anonymous exception propagated by OUTSIDE to B will recover its name.

This phenomenon is not satisfactory. It cannot be avoided but it can be mastered either by defensive programming (see definition of exception FAILURE above) or by an analytical approach using a tool detecting frames propagating anonymous exceptions (Bundy, 1993).

Other consequences relevant to the static and dynamic aspects of the identity of the exceptions must be given. The static definition means that, in the following example, there is only one single exception E which is propagated with its name along the call sequence even though the declaration is internal to the recursive procedure P (Bert, 1982):

```
procedure P (...) is
   E: exception;
begin
   ...
   if not C then raise E; end if;
   P(...);
exception  -- handling of the exception raised by
           -- raise E or propagated by P(...)
   when E =>  ...
              raise; -- propagation
end P;
```

In particular, in the case of generic packages, as an exception is defined on instantiation (at compile-time) and not during elaboration (at run-time), only a single exception exists in the following recursive procedure (Mendal, 1992):

```
generic
package GP is
   E: exception;
   ...
end GP;
```

```
with GP;
procedure RECURSIVE is
  package NP is new GP;
begin
  ...
  RECURSIVE;
  ...
end RECURSIVE;
```

However, if a frame C1 is nested in a frame C2, the declaration by these two frames of an exception of same identifier E clearly specifies two separate exceptions with the same name (static declaration of Ada identifiers). Thus, exception E propagated by frame C1 to the second frame C2 cannot be handled by the statements which follow the guard 'when E =>' of C2 but only by 'when others =>' because it has become anonymous in a frame defining another exception with same name. The following procedures give this example:

```
procedure C2 is
  E: exception;
  procedure C1 is
    E: exception;
  begin
    ...
    raise E;
    ...
  end C1;
begin
  ...
  raise E;
  ...
exception
  when E        =>... -- handles E of C2
  when others   =>... -- handles E of C1, and the others
end C2;
```

This chosen solution is logical with regard to the definition of the Exception Domain: even if the identity of the exceptions is unique, the associated invariants and operations are different and the exceptions are therefore different. These problems in any case require meticulous attention on behalf of the designer.

In the light of this last example, a remark already made concerning predefined exceptions can be repeated and justified. If exception E is replaced by a predefined exception, the behaviour of the software will be different because of the unicity of the exception in this case. This difference is questionable. An exception is admittedly defined by an invariant but it is also defined by an operation and an implementation (by circumstances). Consequently, even for predefined exceptions, the two propagations correspond to two exceptions in our definition. For this, it is desirable to impose the re-raising of predefined exceptions which cannot be handled locally, with an identifier defined by the user: 'when CONSTRAINT_ERROR => raise STACK_OVERFLOW;' or 'when CONSTRAINT_ERROR => raise FAILURE;'. The same reason can be used to justify the advice not to explicitly raise predefined exceptions (SPC, 1991).

The raising of an exception with a new name causes a new exception to occur. Example: 'when E => raise MY_ERROR;'. This is not the case if renaming is used. In effect, the definition of the exceptions is static, that is performed at compile-time. Thus, there is only one exception in the following program but with different names (P.E and MY_ERROR) in the two parts of the program.

```ada
package P is
  E: exception;
  ...
end P;
with P;
...
MY_ERROR: exception renames P.E;
```

Generic implementation
The realization of module implementation models is an important requirement of modern design. Such a model expresses the implementation of the operations of the module assuming the existence of certain means such as basic operations or types (for example defining an abstract object). The implementation model concept can be expressed in Ada using genericity. As this feature contributes towards the way in which the modules are implemented, its relation with the exception notion must be examined.

The following example defines a generic package giving the procedure EXPORTED which can raise exception E.

```ada
generic
  type GENERIC_TYPE is digits <>;
  with procedure GENERIC_PROCEDURE(X: in out
                                      GENERIC_TYPE);
package GENERIC_PACKAGE is
  E: exception;
  procedure EXPORTED(Y: in out GENERIC_TYPE);
end;
```

The implementation of the procedure EXPORTED uses the procedure GENERIC_PROCEDURE and the type GENERIC_TYPE as follows:

```
package body GENERIC_PACKAGE is
   ...
   procedure EXPORTED(Y: in out GENERIC_TYPE) is
      Z: GENERIC_TYPE;
   begin
      ...; raise E; ...
      GENERIC_PROCEDURE(Z);
   end EXPORTED;
end GENERIC_PACKAGE;
```

The presence of a generic type as a parameter of the procedure EXPORTED makes it difficult to obtain its Standard Domain and therefore its Exception Domain. The formal state is defined by the singleton (Y). The values of Y must belong to GENERIC_TYPE. The invariant is deduced from the in out mode of the parameter: if the initial value of Y is Yin ∈ GENERIC_TYPE then its value after execution must be Yout ∈ GENERIC_TYPE.

The following simple but erroneous reasoning must be rejected: let us consider the most general case, that is, instantiation with float; suppose that we know how to show that the invariant is always true, i.e. whatever the value Yin ∈ float of Y, the value of this parameter is Yout ∈ float after execution of the procedure EXPORTED. This allows no conclusions to be made on the other instantiations. For example, if the instantiated type is:

```
type WATER_TEMPERATURE is float range 0.0 .. 100.0;
```

a real parameter may have a value in the range [0.0,100.0] on call of procedure EXPORTED and the result of executing this procedure may be a value which belongs to type float but located outside this range.

The designer of a generic package can only add specific constraints to the set of acceptable values in the generic type specification by comments. The executable constraints must be expressed in the body part of the package body as shown in the extract of the program which follows.

```
package body GENERIC_PACKAGE is
   ... -- EXPORTED procedure body
begin
   if GENERIC_TYPE'last - GENERIC_TYPE'first > 3.0 then
        raise BAD_INSTANTIATED_TYPE;
   end if;
end GENERIC_PACKAGE;
```

Chapter 3: Characterization of the Ada Exception Mechanism

The check that the real type given is in compliance with constraints is conducted on instantiation of the generic package. Thus, the following instantiation causes the raising of the exception BAD_INSTANTIATED_TYPE.

```ada
...
subtype MY_TEMPERATURE is float range 36.0..41.0;
procedure TAKE(T: in out MY_TEMPERATURE);
package MY_PACKAGE is new
                    GENERIC_PACKAGE(MY_TEMPERATURE,TAKE);
```

Exception BAD_INSTANTIATED_TYPE signalling nonconformity must be added to the package specification.

Raising exception E of the GENERIC_PACKAGE expresses that a state of the Exception Domain of the specification or the implementation of procedure EXPORTED has been reached. Procedure EXPORTED also propagates exceptions raised by the execution of GENERIC_PROCEDURE. At GENERIC_PACKAGE compile-time, these exceptions are not visible. They will be anonymous in the body of EXPORTED on execution of this procedure. They express abnormal termination of the execution of the GENERIC_PROCEDURE. However, propagation in the frame calling procedure EXPORTED can allow them to recover their identities as shown in the following example.

```ada
package FOR_INSTANCE is
  type T is float range 10.0 .. 20.0;
  ERROR_IN_P: exception;
  procedure P (X: in out T);
end FOR_INSTANCE;


with FOR_INSTANCE, GENERIC_PACKAGE;
use FOR_INSTANCE;
procedure EXAMPLE is
  package NEW_PACKAGE is new GENERIC_PACKAGE(T, P);
  X: T;
  ...
begin
  ...
  NEW_PACKAGE.EXPORTED(X);
  -- can raise FOR_INSTANCE.ERROR_IN_P
end EXAMPLE;
```

This phenomenon represents a singular situation. Abnormal termination of the execution of a subprogram (raising exception ERROR_IN_P of procedure P which instantiates GENERIC_PROCEDURE) of the implementation of the procedure EXPORTED creates the occurrence of an anonymous exception in this procedure (EXPORTED). The propagation mechanism causes the raising of the exception in the procedure EXAMPLE calling the procedure EXPORTED associating a name with it (FOR_INSTANCE.ERROR_IN_P). If it is used explicitly, this effect allows a mechanism resembling generic exceptions to be implemented.

```
generic
   type GENERIC_TYPE is digits <>;
   with procedure GENERIC_PROCEDURE
                                 (X: in out GENERIC_TYPE);
   --! with GENERIC_EXCEPTION: exception;
   --! raised by GENERIC_PROCEDURE when INVARIANT is denied
package ...
```

A use such as this is acceptable if the exception expresses an exceptional state of the specification of procedure GENERIC_PROCEDURE and if this state cannot be defined simply by using the Ada features relevant to the parameters (number, type, mode). In this case, the comment must explicitly express the INVARIANT whose evaluation must appear in all implementations of procedures used on instantiation as real parameters.

This same phenomenon may however have dangerous side effects. Indeed, the procedure passed as generic parameter may raise exceptions proper to its specific implementation and not associated with its specification. The implementation must then propagate an exception with a common name (as FAILURE) qualifying the general abnormal termination state notion of this procedure.

3.4 Association

The raising of an exception causes the termination of the execution of the current frame and connection to the associated exception handler if it exists. These aspects will be studied in section 3.5. In the present section, we will characterize the associations which may exist between exceptions and their handlers by means of three criteria.

- With what is the exception handler associated?
- By what is the exception handler associated?
- What is the effect of non-association?

3.4.1 With what is the exception handler associated?

Two features of the Ada language provide two ways of characterizing the association of an exception handler with an exception:

- exception handler of frames expresses an internal association and,
- the propagation mechanism expresses an external association.

Internal association

First, the association can be fixed statically inside the frame where the exception is raised. The exception is handled locally, independently of the use of the frame. For example:

```
procedure P is
   ...
begin
   ...
   raise E;
   ...
exception
   when E => ...
end P;
```

This association is suitable if the handling of the exception is independent of the operation utilization context. For example, if the result of a numerical calculation provokes an exception CONSTRAINT_ERROR to be raised on account of an attempt to exceed the number representation, the handling of this exception may return the highest allowable number. The example given in section 3.2.6 illustrates this situation. Moreover this example shows that although the choice of the executed handler is independent of the call, the result of the handling can depend on it. This is obtained on the example by using parameter values.

If the handling depends on the operation utilization context, an exception is generally propagated so that it can be handled by the caller of this operation (see next sub-section). This is a good solution if the exception really corresponds to a specification invariant violation and not to an implementation invariant violation. We saw previously that Ada programming can lead to confusion between these two situations as certain conditions of the specification invariant must be evaluated by means of statements placed in the body. This may lead to erroneous choices for the association. Thus, an external association is often systematically chosen by the designers if different reactions are required when exceptions are raised during different uses of the operation. To design this, the caller is structured for example by means of the 'declare' feature. To illustrate this situation, let us consider exception E raised by operation A called at two locations in the following extract.

```
begin
   ...
   declare
      ...
      A;
      ...
   exception
      when E => ...  -- handler 1
   end;
   ...
   declare
      ...
      A;
      ...Y
   exception
      when E => ...  -- handler 2
   end;
end;
```

A different handler (1 or 2) will be executed if exception E is raised, depending on the call location of A. However, this solution may make the programs illegible and in addition often corresponds to a design error.

The association was chosen outside of the operation body as the designer did not know how to make this association inside A (to highlight the dependency of operation A), as well as taking the changing behaviour of the exception handling into account. A first solution of this problem is obtained by introducing an intermediary object (PA) exporting operation A. The handler of exception E raised by A is inside A. Due to the presence of the local variables in package PA, the handling of exception E can be not uniform if the handler takes the value of these variables into account (that is dependent on the state of object PA).

```
begin                package body PA is
   ...                  ... -- variables representing the state
   A;                   procedure A is
   ...                  begin
   ...                     ... -- raises E
   A;                      exception
end;                        when E => -- handling dependent on state
                         end A;
                      end PA;
```

Thus, even if one handler exists, the two handlings of exception E raised during the two executions of procedure A can be different as the state of object PA is different. This approach can be used if A is a procedure which adds an element in an object 'queue'. If overflow is detected, the exception handling can consist in increasing the size of the queue or extracting certain elements. The choice can depend on the state of the queue (current size, value of elements, etc.) and the number of occurrences of the exception.

The previous solution shows that the internal static association offered by the syntax of the language nevertheless allows variable behaviours to be obtained on execution.

External association

The language also gives explicit means for defining external associations: the propagation mechanism. Thanks to this mechanism, the caller's handler is considered. This possibility allows exception handlings to be defined depending on the call context. Propagation is programmed either explicitly using the raise statement in an exception handler or by the absence of an exception handler. In the following section we will justify why the first solution is desirable: the exception handler can then simply be written:

```
when ... => raise;
```

The use of the propagation mechanism has drawbacks or at least requires specific precautions. First, the association of an exception handler must not be omitted in the frame using the operation raising the propagated exception. Also, if the reaction is always the same and if the subprogram propagating the exception is called at numerous locations, many calls for the exception handling subprogram will be observed.

The association of a single exception handler with an exception raised by an operation, globally in a program, is therefore interesting. This association can be expressed in Ada by not placing the exception handler in the frame where the operation raising the exception is used but by attaching it to the definition of the operation itself.

```
procedure OPERATION is
  E: exception;
  procedure UNSAFE_OPERATION is  -- can raise E
    ...
  end UNSAFE_OPERATION;
begin
  UNSAFE_OPERATION;
exception
  when E => HANDLER;
end OPERATION;
```

Thus, whereas frames calling UNSAFE_OPERATION must repeat 'when E =>HANDLER;', calls to OPERATION no longer require the handler call.

This solution enables the programming of various exception handlers without access to the body of the subprogram propagating the exception (UNSAFE_OPERATION). If this subprogram is in a package defining an object (OBJECT) whose data structure of type OBJECT_TYPE, is a parameter of the subprogram, then the procedure OPERATION can be defined by:

```
with OBJECT; use OBJECT;
package body SAFE_OBJECT is
   ...
   procedure OPERATION(O: in out OBJECT_TYPE) is
   begin
      UNSAFE_OPERATION(O);
   exception
      when E => HANDLER(O);
   end OPERATION;
end SAFE_OBJECT;
```

where HANDLER is a subprogram of the SAFE_OBJECT package.

For this solution, the exception is always handled outside the structure which caused it to be raised (the UNSAFE_OPERATION of OBJECT). It can nevertheless act on the object on which the erroneous subprogram (UNSAFE_OPERATION) operated.

Declarative part

We would like to remind the reader of a specific case encountered in Ada: the exceptions raised in a declarative part are propagated and therefore not processed by a local handler. This requires some comments and special attention on behalf of the designer. For instance, take the following example:

```
procedure ACTION_ON_PORTRAIT(WIDTH, HEIGHT: in POSITIVE);
   DELTA: POSITIVE := HEIGHT-WIDTH;
begin
   ...
end ACTION_ON_PORTRAIT;
```

If the value of parameter WIDTH is greater than or equal to that of parameter HEIGHT, exception CONSTRAINT_ERROR will be raised at the location of the call for this procedure in the calling subprogram. However, the implementation below causes the raising of the same exception in the body of procedure ACTION_ON_PORTRAIT. This exception can then be processed by the exception handler inside this procedure.

```
procedure ACTION_ON_PORTRAIT(WIDTH, HEIGHT: in POSITIVE);
  DELTA: POSITIVE;
begin
  DELTA := HEIGHT-WIDTH;
  ...
exception
  when CONSTRAINT_ERROR => ...
end ACTION_ON_PORTRAIT;
```

These two subprograms seem to be functionally equivalent. They are however different if the exception notion is considered. For the two subprograms, the two parameters of the procedure define its specification formal state (e). The variable DELTA completes this state to give the implementation internal state (E). The exception raised by the first subprogram expresses the impossibility to change from specification state value e' to implementation state value E0 (see vertical arrow on Figure 3.2 of section 3.2.4). This means that the procedure was incorrectly used and the exception must therefore be handled by the caller. Whereas, the exception raised by the second version corresponds to the impossibility to change from state E0 to state E1 by executing operation P1 (DELTA:=HEIGHT-WIDTH;). This represents membership to the implementation Exception Domain. The exception of the erroneous implementation must be handled inside the body of the procedure. To conclude, this example again shows that taking the exception notion into account influences the design choices.

3.4.2 By what is the exception handler associated?

The exception propagation mechanism is often badly used and overused due to confusion between the two following questions:

- 'with what is the exception handler associated?'. This question was dealt with detail in the previous section and,
- 'what performs this association?'. That is, 'which entity realizes this association?'.

Here is discussed the answer of the second question. Four solutions exist which are successively examined.

Inside the frame, by the frame
When the handler of an exception E is placed in a frame as defined in the following extract,

```
begin
  ... -- raise E
exception
  when E => ... -- handler for E
end;
```

the exception handler of E is associated with the frame (reply to question: 'associated with what?') and by the frame itself on account of its syntax (reply to the question: 'associated by what?').

Outside the frame, by the frame
A propagation due to raising in the exception handler of a frame as illustrated in the following extract,

```
begin
   ... -- raise E
exception
   when E => raise;
end;
```

indicates that the frame ('by what?') expresses an association with an exception handler located outside ('with what?').

Inside the frame, from outside the frame
We have already pointed out the drawbacks of propagation: risk of forgetting the association of an exception handler or duplication of calls of the subprogram handling the exception if the calls to the subprogram propagating this exception are many. The use of the propagation mechanism must therefore be reserved for situations where it is indispensable, that is when the execution context of the operation which propagated the exception is necessary. In this case, the handlers must be dynamically assigned by the callers. Unfortunately, the propagation mechanism is often used incorrectly by the designers because they do not know how to associate a specific handler with the inside of the operation concerned (reply to question: 'with what?'), and how to make this association from outside the module exporting this operation (reply to the question: 'by what?'). Kruchten (Kruchten, 1990) has proposed a solution called 'Zero-Exception'. Among other things, it has the merit of providing the designer a method to adapt the program that he or she has designed using propagations. Let us describe its principle.

The list of exceptions of the specification of the package defining an object which exports operations need not exist as the exceptions are not to be propagated; they must be handled locally. This list is transformed into the generic procedure definitions as follows:

```
generic
   with procedure E1_HANDLER;
   with procedure E2_HANDLER;
package GENERIC_OBJECT is
   type OBJECT_TYPE is limited private;
   procedure OPERATION(O: in out OBJECT_TYPE);
      ...
end GENERIC_OBJECT;
```

Chapter 3: Characterization of the Ada Exception Mechanism

In Kruchten's proposal, in the body of the subprograms exported by the package (such as OPERATION), the statements raising exceptions Ei are replaced by calls for subprograms Ei_HANDLER. However the exception mechanism can be conserved by maintaining the exception raisings and by calling the generic procedures as handlers (when Ei => Ei_HANDLER;).

In all cases, the creation of a particular object imposes communication of specific exception handling procedures on instantiation as follows.

```
procedure MY_OBJECT is new GENERIC_OBJECT
           (E1_HANDLER => HANDLE1, E2_HANDLER => HANDLE2);
```

where HANDLE1 and HANDLE2 are procedures which were defined by the program creating MY_OBJECT.

This solution replies to the two questions highlighted in the introduction of this section as follows:

- 'with what is the exception handler associated?': with the body of the operation. In effect, the procedures Ei_HANDLER are called inside the body of the object's operations.
- 'by what is the exception handler associated?': by the entity performing instantiation, that is via the outside of the object created.

The solution is extended to allow the handlers (generic and therefore instantiated) to act on the object data structure. The following example illustrates this solution:

```
package OBJECT is
  type OBJECT_TYPE is limited private;
  generic
    with procedure E1_HANDLER (ON: in out OBJECT_TYPE);
    with procedure E2_HANDLER (ON: in out OBJECT_TYPE);
  package OPERATIONS_ON_OBJECT is
    procedure OPERATION (ON: in out OBJECT_TYPE);
       ...
  end OPERATIONS_ON_OBJECT;
private
    ...
end OBJECT;
```

The associations of exception handlers are performed from the outside of the object and are achieved on instantiation. However, the associated handler cannot be modified during execution. Consequently, and if behaviours dependent on the object utilization context are required, a procedure grouping the complete set of possible behaviours must be defined and communicated on instantiation. We have already pointed out that this situation can be encountered in practice. For example, in the case of overflow of a stack or queue object constrained by a maximum size, this size may be first of all increased, then the oldest elements may be deleted if the exception raisings are reiterated (see a solution in section 3.4.1).

This difficulty will be overcome by using the *access_to_subprogram* feature offered by the new standard. The following type can then be declared:

```
type HANDLER is procedure (PIECES_OF: INFORMATION);
```

where INFORMATION is a previously defined type. It declares a type (named HANDLER) of the set of procedures having an 'in' mode parameter of type INFORMATION.

The subprograms can thus have a formal parameter of type HANDLER which may be referenced in the exception handler as follows.

```
procedure OPERATION (...; A_HANDLER: HANDLER) is
   SOME_INFORMATION: INFORMATION;
begin
   ...
exception
   when E => A_HANDLER(SOME_INFORMATION);
end OPERATION;
```

A real handler of varied nature can be assigned during various OPERATION calls.

Outside of the frame, from outside the frame

The last case to be studied to conclude the four possible situations in reply to the two questions ('with what is the exception handler associated?' and 'by what is this association performed?') consists of an association with an external handler by an external frame. This association characterizes the handling of non-anticipated exceptions.

Now we will only briefly discuss the question: **'when did the association occur?'**. Even if syntactic associations with a frame exist, no check for the presence of an exception handler for each exception raised in the frame is made at compile-time. Thus, and on account of the propagation phenomena, the effective association of an exception handler with a given exception is generally dynamic, that is performed on execution and not at compile-time. The justification of this solution adopted for the Ada language will be developed in chapter 5. This is a major cause of difficulties concerning both the analysis of the effects of raising exceptions and the proving of programs using the exception mechanism.

3.4.3 What is the effect of non-association?

The voluntary non-association of a handler with an exception in a given frame (or subprogram) generally leads to the propagation of the exception. The exception is implicitly raised at frame call location. Specific cases concern the task and package bodies [11.4.1(7-8)]. The propagation phenomenon also exists in the case where non-association is caused because the existence of the exception is not forecast (qualified non-anticipated). Whatever the cause, propagation of exceptions requires means to master it.

Non-anticipated exceptions
First of all, the taking into account of an exception must be as close as possible to the location where it is raised (and so its cause). The taking into an account of an exception does not necessarily imply its handling. It expresses only the perception, by the running of the program, of the occurrence of an exception, that is its existence. It can be expressed explicitly by propagating this exception. For this, anticipated exceptions which appear in the specification must be propagated explicitly by:

```
when E1 | E2 | E3 => raise;
```

Note that the language allows programs such as:

```
procedure P is
  E: exception;
begin
  ...
exception
  when E => raise E;
end P;
```

to be written.

This explicit exception propagation is naturally not recommended as it leads the reader of the procedure to think that the exception E appears in the specification of the object exporting operation P whereas, in reality, it becomes anonymous.

For non-anticipated exceptions, it is preferable that their taking into account be immediate and their propagation voluntary. This kind of propagation must avoid the presence of anonymous exceptions and indicate the abnormal operation termination character. Indeed, non-anticipated exceptions were not identified by an invariant of the operation (by definition) and are therefore not attached to an exception identifier. This propagation can be programmed in Ada by:

```
when others => raise FAILURE;
```

FAILURE must be declared so that it will be visible in the complete application, for example in the specification of a package shared by the team of designers.

Handling by default

Most of the solutions proposed in this section (3.4) do not locally associate handling by default. If no association exists, the exceptional state is propagated to the hierarchically higher levels until an associated handler is found. Another point of view consists in explicitly propagating the association to the lower design levels (Zero-Exception technique discussed in section 3.4.2).

We would simply like to say that here the solution proposed for the Zero-Exception technique can be extended by using by-default formal parameter for generic operations in order to obtain handling by default. For example, this handler could be a procedure causing the raising and the propagation of an exception FAILED_OBJECT which should then appear in the object specification as expressed below:

```
package OBJECT is
  type OBJECT_TYPE is limited private;
  FAILED_OBJECT: exception;
  procedure DEFAULT (ON: in out OBJECT_TYPE);
    -- raises FAILED_OBJECT
  generic
    with procedure   E1_HANDLER(ON: in out OBJECT_TYPE)
                     is DEFAULT;
  package OPERATIONS_ON_OBJECT is
    procedure OPERATION(ON: in out OBJECT_TYPE);
      ...
  end OPERATIONS_ON_OBJECT;
private
  ...
end OBJECT;
```

3.4.4 Case of data

The association of a handler with an exception depends on the statement frames. The Ada language provides no specific features for expressing the definition of an exception from the negation of an invariant on a data structure, that is an invariant applicable to all operations using this data structure as parameter (specification invariant) or as local variable (implementation invariant).

This can however be implemented. The data structure must be considered as an abstract data type and programmed by a package specifying the operations which are possible on the data. This package can either specify the exceptions which will be propagated by the operations using the data or declare exception handler generic procedures, procedures which must be specified on instantiation (see 'Zero-defect' technique).

To conclude this brief section concerning data and exception handling let us signal the existence of Ada meta-languages allowing formal comments to be associated with data types either to provoke the raising of an exception predefined (ANNA (Luckham, 1990)) or to execute a given handler ((Cui, 1990)), if an invariant provided in the formal comments is violated at run-time.

3.5 Raising

In a programming language an exception is a means for defining an exceptional state or a set of exceptional states (Exception Domain). The raising of an exception is an artefact of a language to signal the occurrence of an exception when the program is running, that is the fact that an operation has reached a state of its Exception Domain.

3.5.1 Predefined exceptions

Detection means
An executable application is composed of statements generated by the compiler, after program analysis, and executive statements implementing the Ada Abstract Machine run-time environment (see section 3.3.1). These two parts can detect the occurrence of certain exceptional states of the program and activate the mechanism signalling this. On one hand, checks related to constraint type variables are generally made in the generated code (raising of CONSTRAINT_ERROR). On the other hand, the terminated state of a task whose entry is called is detected by the executive (raising of TASKING_ERROR). In effect, the check on the data associated with the calling task code, which must raise the exception, does not allow a conclusion to be made on the state of the called task.

The location where a given exception is detected can vary according to the run-time environments. For example, a by-zero division can be detected by evaluating the divisor in the code generated by the compiler, or by the microprocessor (therefore by the executive).

The effective raising of a predefined exception frequently depends on the application but may also depend on the run-time environment (compiler and executive). For example, the raising of exception STORAGE_ERROR is related to the size of the application, to the physical memory of a machine (executive), to the efficiency of the memory manager (executive) and the efficiency of the code generator (compiler). Problems and solutions related to the implementation of the exception raising and detection mechanism will be detailed in chapter 5.

Masking

We pointed out in the introduction to this chapter (section 3.1.2) that certain designers think that they do not need exceptions, including predefined exceptions. Considering their programs as correct with regard to the Ada Abstract Machine, that is they consider that their programs cannot reach states in their Exception Domains, they use the **pragma SUPPRESS** with the causes of the predefined exceptions as parameters.

On the one hand, this practice frequently shows ignorance concerning the relations which exist between the causes and the identities of exceptions. This is justified by the fact that these pieces of information are not grouped together but scattered throughout the standard. To provide this knowledge, a synthetic and exhaustive presentation is given below (Enumeration of the circumstances of predefined exception raising).

On the other hand, these designers often use the pragma SUPPRESS in order to avoid designing exception handlers and to increase the performance of their applications. These two points of view are dangerous and incorrect for three reasons. First, using the pragma SUPPRESS does not suppress the existence of the exceptional states expressing the errors but only their detection. If such a state is reached, the program will be erroneous and can continue its execution without indicating the fact or can go later into another exceptional state which is a consequence of the original state. Also, the efficiency of this pragma is not imperative for implementing the Ada run-time environment

(Rationale, 1986), that is an exception can be raised in spite of this. This freedom in implementation was given for performance reasons. In effect, to avoid detection of exceptions raised by the microprocessor, the executable program must contain many calls to detection mechanism masking and unmasking instructions, mechanism generally implanted in the circuit, and therefore slowing down the execution (Rationale, 1986). The use of the pragma SUPPRESS can thus, at limit, give a result contrary to the initial objective which was to improve performance. In all cases, its use is dangerous as it does not eliminate the problem (presence of faults leading to errors) but only the need to consider it.

The static definition of exceptions and the static action of a pragma (which is a compilation directive) imply that the masking of a predefined exception is attached to a syntactic frame. Consequently, the implementation of dynamic maskings and unmaskings, that is dependent on the execution state, cannot be considered.

Enumeration of the circumstances of predefined exception raising

In this part we will give the circumstances under which a predefined exception can be raised. In the standard, the general information is grouped together, in [11.1], but the details are scattered throughout the manual. In addition, the classification given in [11.1(4)] is indexed by exception identifiers and not by Ada features. This means that it is difficult for the designer to know the predefined exceptions which can be raised using a given feature.

This section proposes a synthesis of the causes raising exceptions. No definitions or examples are given in this part of the text. However, references to the standard are associated with each feature.

Even if the number of Ada predefined exception identifiers is small, the circumstances under which a predefined exception can be raised are numerous because the Ada language voluntarily imposes numerous checks at run-time. We will successively study the following aspects:

(1) declaration, (2) evaluation, (3) assignment, (4) parameter passing, (5) dynamic object allocation, (6) tasks, (7) genericity. We will conclude (8) with the exception PROGRAM_ERROR concerning erroneous execution cases. The words given in italics and between brackets correspond to the pragma SUPPRESS parameters allowing the detection of the studied exceptions to be inhibited. We will give them repeating our warning concerning their use.

1) Declaration

For the declaration of an initialized object, the initial value must be in compliance with the object type [3.2.1(16)], the declaration of a subtype must be compatible with the referenced type [3.3.2(9)]. CONSTRAINT_ERROR is raised if the results of the checks are wrong (*RANGE_CHECK*).

It is also checked that the declarative elements declaring the entities used were elaborated. Elaboration of:

- a subprogram body before the subprogram call, a task body before task activation, a unit body before the generic unit [3.9(8)];
- a package body before the call of exported subprogram [7.3(4)].

If not, PROGRAM_ERROR is raised (*ELABORATION_CHECK*).

2) Expression, operation, identifier evaluations

The use of attributes on discrete types [3.5.5] (VAL, SUCC, PRED, VALUE) can generate exception CONSTRAINT_ERROR if the effective parameter is not a value of the basic type or if the result of the attribute function does not belong to the specified domain (*ACCESS_CHECK*).

Exception CONSTRAINT_ERROR can also be raised by the evaluation:

- of a name that has a prefix if type of prefix is an access type and if value of the prefix is a null access value [4.1(10)] (*ACCESS_CHECK*),
- of an indexed component if an index value does not belong to the corresponding type range [4.1.1(4)] (*INDEX_CHECK*),
- of an array slice if any of the bounds of the discrete range does not belong to the index range of the prefixing array [4.1.2(4)] (*INDEX_CHECK*),
- of the discriminant values of a variant component in a record if this record does not have this component [4.1.3(8)] (*DISCRIMINANT_CHECK*),
- of a null string literal if the lower bound does not have a predecessor [4.2(3)],

- of a record (or array) aggregate if a sub-component of the aggregate does not belong to the subtype of this sub-component [4.3.1(3)] [4.3.2(11)] (RANGE_CHECK),
- of a logical operator on the arrays if a component of an operand that does not have any homologues exists [4.5.1(3)] (LENGTH_CHECK),
- of a concatenation, if the upper bound of the result exceeds the range of the index subtype [4.5.3(6)] (RANGE_CHECK),
- of the exponentiation of an integer if the exponent is negative [4.5.6(6)] (RANGE_CHECK),
- of a type conversion if the result of the conversion is not in compliance (fails to satisfy...) [4.6(12)&(13)] (LENGTH_CHECK),
- of a qualified expression if the operand value does not belong to the subtype denoted by the type mark [4.7(3)] (RANGE_CHECK),
- of a return statement if the value of the returned expression does not belong to the result subtype [5.8(6)] (RANGE_CHECK).

Remark: the use of a deferred constant before its complete elaboration is a case of erroneous execution [7.4.3(5)].

Note that in the new standard 'ACCESS_CHECK dereference now covers the case of selected_component, indexed_component, slice and attribute' (Changes, 1995).

The execution of a predefined operation on numeric types previously raises NUMERIC_ERROR and now CONSTRAINT_ERROR if the mathematical result is not a type value or if it is not in the range of the type safe numbers (case of float numbers) [11.1(6)] : [3.5.4(10)] and [4.5(7)] for integer type; [3.5.6(6)] and [4.5(7)] and [4.5.7(7)] for real type. An implementation is not required to apply this rule if the result of this operation is intermediate and if the final result of the expression evaluation is correct [11.6(6)] and [4.5.7(7)] (OVERFLOW_CHECK).

This same exception is raised by the division, rem or mod operators if the right operand is zero [4.5.5(12)] (DIVISION_CHECK).

CONSTRAINT_ERROR is now raised instead of NUMERIC_ERROR. This choice is better because distinction between the two exceptions led to questions such as: 'why must the evaluation of INTEGER'PRED(INTEGER'FIRST) raise CONSTRAINT_ERROR [3.5.5]?'

As the difference between RANGE_CHECK and OVERFLOW is fuzzy, the suppression of OVERFLOW in the new standard was discussed. It was maintained for upward compatibility and to take into account specificities of machines.

3) Assignment

The assignment of an expression to a variable raises CONSTRAINT_ERROR if the result of the expression does not belong to the variable type [5.2(4)] [3.5.4(12)]. For array assignment, the size of the two arrays must be identical. If not, the CONSTRAINT_ERROR exception is raised [5.2.1(2)]. (RANGE_CHECK or LENGTH_CHECK)

4) Parameters

Exception CONSTRAINT_ERROR is raised at the location of a subprogram call if the value of an effective parameter (different from the scalar or the access types) does not belong to the formal parameter subtype [6.4.1(10)]. (*RANGE_CHECK*). For scalar and access types see sub-section 8).

5) Dynamic objects

An allocator evaluation can raise STORAGE_ERROR if memory storage is insufficient.

CONSTRAINT_ERROR can also be raised by the execution of statement new caused by the evaluation of the qualified expression, by the elaboration of the subtype or by the initialization of the allocated object [4.8(13)]. (*STORAGE_CHECK*)

6) Tasks

Exception TASKING_ERROR can be raised:

- by the completion of a task during its activation (exception raised during its activation or abort statement) [9.3(3)] [9.3(7)];
- by calling an entry of a completed task, or of a task completed before accepting the call [9.5(16)] [9.7.2(6)] [9.7.3(5)], or of an abnormal task, or of a task which becomes abnormal during the rendezvous [9.10(7)] [11.5(5)] (no suppression of checks).

Furthermore, an exception raised during a rendezvous (within an accept statement) is propagated to the calling task at the location of the call [11.5(4)].

CONSTRAINT_ERROR is raised if the index of the entry of a family is not within the specified discrete range [9.5(16)]. (*INDEX_CHECK*)

7) Genericity

During generic package instantiation, exception CONSTRAINT_ERROR is raised if the homology rules for the formal objects [12.3.1(1)], the formal private types [12.3.2(5)], the formal array types [12.3.4(6)] or the formal access types [12.3.5(2)] do not check out the respective constraints. (*RANGE_CHECK*)

8) Exception PROGRAM_ERROR

When all the alternatives of a select statement are closed and there is no else part, exception PROGRAM_ERROR is raised [9.7.1(11)].

This same exception can be raised if:

- an attempt is made to reach an object (subprogram call, task activation, generic instantiation elaboration) whose body has not yet been elaborated [11.1(7)] [3.9(8)] [7.3(4)]; (*ELABORATION_CHECK*)
- the end of a function is reached without return statement or exception [6.5(2)] (no suppression of checks).

PROGRAM_ERROR can also be raised by the code generated by the compiler if this compiler was capable of detecting erroneous situations or incorrect order dependence cases.

The execution of a program is erroneous [1.6(7)] if:

- its effect depends on which particular parameter passing mechanism is used by the implementation for parameters whose types are arrays, records or tasks [6.2(7)];
- the values of scalar or access type parameters are not in compliance with the parameter specifications [6.4.1(8)]: before the call, the membership of the value of an effective parameter to the formal parameter type is checked for the in and in out mode parameters; after the body achievement, the membership of the value of a formal parameter to the type of the corresponding effective parameter is checked for the out and in out mode parameters;
- the assumptions made on access to shared variables are not respected [9.11(6)];
- the value of a discriminant of an unconstrained record variable is modified during an assignment [5.2(4)];
- representation clauses or implementation dependent features have led to multiple address clauses for unity overlays [13.5(8)];
- two access variables exist on one object which is freed by the first one and then accessed by the second one [13.10.1(6)];
- the type's properties are violated by means of unchecked conversion [13.10.2(3)];
- an error arises when the execution checks are not made (pragma SUPPRESS) [11.7(18)].

The list of all the incorrect order dependence cases (12 cases) is: assignment statement [5.2], bounds of a range constraint [3.5], component association of an array aggregate [4.3.2], component of a record aggregate [4.3.1], component subtype indication [3.6], default expression for a component [3.2.1], default expression for a discriminant [3.2.1], expression [4.5], index constraint [3.6], library unit [10.5], parameter association [6.4], prefix and discrete range of a slice [4.1.2].

However the standard [1.6(10)] specifies that a compiler is authorized to generate the code that raises exception PROGRAM_ERROR if it can recognize that a construct is erroneous or that it contains an incorrect order dependence. It is also authorized to generate the code that checks these errors at run-time. The cases quoted above are therefore likely to raise exception PROGRAM_ERROR. Authorization is not an obligation. So an erroneous program can continue its execution even if an error exists. Such a situation is not acceptable for dependable software. The designer should know what the compilers do or do not do in such cases. The designer must take this information into account when choosing an Ada environment for development.

As highlighted in the new standard, 'the execution of any construct raises STORAGE_ERROR if there is insufficient storage for the execution'. The raising of this exception is unpredictable because 'the amount of storage needed for the execution is unspecified'.

The new standard authorizes the Ada language implementers to define their own rules for the pragma SUPPRESS.

Other exceptions can arise because of the utilization of predefined packages (specified in the standard). For instance, if the predefined package CALENDAR is used, exception TIME_ERROR can be raised if:

- the TIME_OF function parameters do not form a proper date,
- the '+' or '-' functions involve out of range values [9.6(6)].

These packages are only given because they are frequently used. We will not study them in this chapter that only deals with exceptions proper to the basic language features.

3.5.2 User exceptions

Detection

Even if a lot of exceptional states are detected implicitly by the features of the language, causing the raising of predefined exceptions, other exceptional states must be defined explicitly by the designer by means of user exceptions. As the Ada language has no specific features for defining invariants, additional tools (such as ANNA), or specific design methods (such as abstract data types) must be used to facilitate detection.

In all cases, the exception is raised after the evaluation of a Boolean expression implementing an invariant by calling the raise statement.

```
if not C then raise E; end if;
```

The use of this construction has given rise to much debate and is dealt with in paragraph 3.5.3 under the title of connection to the exception handler. Let us reconsider the definition of an exception to explain its correct utilization. Take the following program extract:

```
procedure P is
   ...
begin
   A1(...);
   A2(...);
   if not C then raise E; end if;
   B(...);
exception
   ...
end P ;
```

The body of procedure P is an implementation abstraction with an implementation abstract state whose definition contains, for example, local variables the values of which change during the execution of the called components (here subprograms A1, then A2 and then B). An expected sequence of these state values represents a specification of the implementation abstraction behaviour. A condition combining the parameters of this state (symbolized by C) gives a local evaluation of an invariant on this abstraction. Thus, the 'if not C then raise E; end if;' statement is only present to detect a negation of the implementation invariant and to signal this by raising an exception.

However, if the test statement was placed in procedure P to evaluate the correctness of the behaviour of A2 (post-condition), the least we can say is that this design is clumsy according to the definition of the Exception Domain. The test must be attached to procedure A2 (and not to that of P) by the definition of a procedure SAFE_A2:

```
procedure SAFE_A2(...) is -- can raise E
  procedure A2(...) is
    ...
  end A2;
begin
  A2(...);
  if not C then raise E ; end if ;
end SAFE_A2;
```

The implementation of procedure P then becomes:

```
procedure P is
  ...
begin
  A1(...);
  SAFE_A2(...);
  B(...);
exception
  ...
end P;
```

Although detected by SAFE_A2, exception E can be handled by P according to the expressed handler association.

Masking

There are no language features to express the masking of user exceptions. This can be implemented by adding a Boolean variable, representing a request for exception masking or not, to the invariant evaluation test.

```
if not MASKING and then not C then raise E; end if;
```

As with predefined exceptions, its use may be dangerous as it leads to loss of all traces of detection. This is a cause leading the use of the pragma SUPPRESS for predefined exceptions to be considered as contrary to the language philosophy (Rationale, 1986).

However, deferring the raising of the exception instead of the detection often gives practical benefits. This requirement exists first of all for the critical sections. In this case, it may be necessary to conclude the execution of a program section in order, for example, to free a resource that the program is using before analysing and correcting the error. Memorizing the existence of an error and deferring its handling may be also required if an exception is raised by the call of a subprogram exported by an object and if the following statements use other objects: the erroneous object can be corrected or substituted later. Raising delayed also exists if the duration of the exception handling is unacceptably long whereas the briefness of reactions is imposed by the specification of the problem.

A solution called 'Omega Strategy' (Kruchten, 1990) allows detection and memorization of the occurrence of an Exception Domain state. It also allows the locations where this previous occurrence can lead to the raising of an exception to be specified. Its principle is as follows: the private type associated with the data structure on which operations are exported by a package defining an object (or component) is augmented by a list of Booleans expressing if the object was (at least once) in an exceptional state.

```
package OBJECT is
   type OBJECT_TYPE is limited private;
   E1, E2: exception;
   ... -- exported subprograms
private
   type OBJECT_TYPE is record
      OBJECT_STRUCTURE: STRUCTURE_TYPE;
      E1, E2 : boolean := FALSE; -- Added Booleans
   end;
end OBJECT;
```

In the bodies of the exported subprograms, after evaluation of the invariant detecting an exceptional state occurrence, the private structure Boolean value is modified instead of raising the corresponding exception:

```
if not C1 then THE_OBJECT.E1 := TRUE;
```

where THE_OBJECT is a formal parameter of the type OBJECT_TYPE of the subprogram.

An additional procedure is exported, causing the raising, if necessary. Its body is defined in the body of the package OBJECT by:

```
procedure TEST_AND_RAISE(THE_OBJET: in OBJECT_TYPE) is
begin
  if THE_OBJECT.E1 then raise E1;
  elsif THE_OBJECT.E2 then raise E2;
  -- ...
  end if;
end TEST_AND_RAISE;
```

THE_OBJECT.Ei may be assigned by FALSE before the raising of Ei to specify the reset of the memorization.

Note that this solution hierarchically structures the exceptions. In effect, if the THE_OBJECT.E1 and the THE_OBJECT.E2 conditions are simultaneously true, only exception E1 is raised at the first call of the procedure TEST_AND_RAISE.

The 'Omega Strategy' technique can be extended to implement a temporary masking mechanism with memorization of detection and raising if necessary during or after unmasking. For this, the MASKING identifier is introduced into the definition of the private type OBJECT_TYPE:

```
type OBJECT_TYPE is record
  OBJECT_STRUCTURE: STRUCTURE_TYPE;
  E1, E2: boolean := FALSE;
  MASKING: boolean := FALSE;
end;
```

A masking procedure is exported. Its body is defined in the body of the package as:

```
procedure MASKING(THE_OBJECT: in out OBJECT_TYPE) is
begin
  THE_OBJECT.MASKING := TRUE;
end MASKING;
```

In the exported operations, the evaluation of an invariant C1 becomes:

```
if not C1 then
  if THE_OBJECT.MASKING then  THE_OBJECT.E1 := TRUE;
                        else  raise E1;
  end if;
end if;
```

If the subprogram is in a state of the Exception Domain, and if a masking request was made previously (THE_OBJECT.MASKING=TRUE), the occurrence of the exceptional state is memorized (THE_OBJECT.E1:=TRUE;). If no masking requests were made, the exception is raised (raise E1;). An unmasking procedure applied to the object THE_OBJECT is exported. Its body is:

```
procedure UNMASK(THE_OBJECT: in out OBJECT_TYPE) is
begin
  THE_OBJECT.MASKING := FALSE;
  if THE_OBJECT.E1 then raise E1;
  elsif THE_OBJECT.E2 then raise E2;
  -- ...
  end if;
end UNMASK;
```

This causes the raising of the exception with the highest memorized priority (hierarchization). The occurrences of the other exceptional states are not however lost. In addition, future detections of exceptional states will lead to the raising of the associated exception (`THE_OBJECT.MASKING:=FALSE;`) until the masking procedure is called again.

Due to the declaration of a single MASKING identifier, the examples given concern the global masking of the exceptions of an object. Finer mastery is obtained by introducing as many MASKINGi identifiers as there are exceptions Ei.

3.5.3 Connection to the exception handler

The raising of an exception in a frame terminates the execution of this frame and passes control to the part of the exception handler associated with the frame (`exception...end;`), if it exists. The execution is then resumed at this point to search for a specific exception handler (`when E=>...`) or to cause a propagation if one is not found.

The break in the execution sequence follows the 'termination mode' described in section 2.4.5 of chapter 2. This break has been and still is the subject of much discussion. The main criticism made is that it leads to a break in the structure of statements by adding implicit exit points in the form of disguised branching (goto).

We can first of all put forward the unicity of the branch point as an argument. However, the basic justification is more essential as it comes from the concept of the exception itself. Let us take the example of procedure P given in section 3.5.2. It may seem easy to avoid the use of the `raise` statement by *correct* use of structured programming as follows.

```
procedure P(...) is
  ...
begin
  A1(...);
  A2(...);
  if not C   then   ...  -- exception handler
             else   B(...);
  end if;
end P;
```

This solution leads however to the non-explicit mixing of two aspects: the implementation of procedure P (actions in the Standard Domain as defined in the procedure specification) and the handling of the exceptional situations associated with the Exception Domain states of the implementation of P. The first advantage of the exception mechanism is that it syntactically marks the difference between these two notions by the program structure (exception part).

Also, if several state evaluations are required within the body of a subprogram, the structured design implies the nesting of tests which rapidly make the developed program illegible. Presence of multiple invariant evaluations is current in dependable applications: check of the change of the implementation state with regard to the automaton defining the properties of the expected behaviour of this implementation.

Moreover, nesting of blocks using the statement 'if not C then EXCEPTIONAL; else NORMAL; end if;' leads to loss of control over the program whose normal treatment structure is split up. The following example illustrates such a situation. '...' represents the normal treatment and '///' the exceptional handlers.

```
procedure A is
begin
   ...
   if not C1 then
      ///
   else...
      if not C2 then
         ///   -- (0)
      else...
      end if;
      ...      -- (1)
   end if;
   ...         -- (2)
   if not C3 then
      ///
   else...
   end if;
   ...
end A;
```

Lastly, programming such as this does not allow the abnormal termination state notion of implementations requiring propagation of the exception raised by the failed operation to be easily handled. For example, try to modify the body of procedure A to take into account the impossibility of correcting an error in the statement block (0). In effect, this implies not performing (1) then (2) and then the following statements. This may be solved using a `return` statement but this manner is not recommended because it introduces output locations not explicitly defined in the structure.

178   Chapter 3: Characterization of the Ada Exception Mechanism

3.6 Handling

The handling of an exception must make a diagnosis of the circumstances of the exception raising in order to specify the state of the Exception Domain. Then, it must

- either perform corrective action to resume current (that is not exceptional) treatment placing the program in a state of the Standard Domain,
- or leave the program in the Exception Domain due to an abnormal termination of the implementation. This is achieved thanks to the propagation mechanism.

To perform these three actions (diagnosis, correction and propagation) the exception mechanism provides means to allow the state of the system to be known, means to act on this state and a resumption mechanism. We will successively examine these three points symbolized on Figure 3.4.

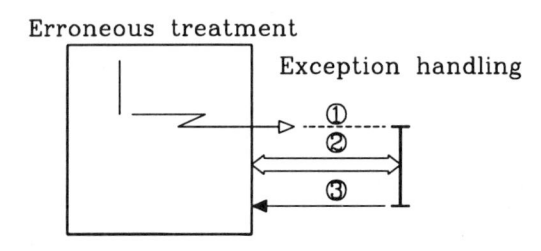

Figure 3.4: Relations between erroneous treatment and exception handling

3.6.1 Initial state

The state in which a program is found on initialization of the exception handler execution is defined by the control and the data.

Control
Concerning control, as the Ada language explicitly separates the bodies of the frames from their exception handlers, the location of the current statement is clearly defined.

```
begin
   ...
exception -- <- Here
   ...
end;
```

This location is then specified by the exception's identity:

```
when E1 => ...
when E2 => ... -- <- Here, for instance
when E3 => ...
```

However, no information concerning the identity of the faulty statement is given. This information may possibly be returned by the Exception_Information function offered by the new standard (Ada95, 1995). Presence of this information or not depends on the choice made by the Ada run-time environment implementers. We can however hope that it will be frequently available. In effect, the standard specifies that information useful for debug must be produced without however specifying its nature.

Data

The state of a program is also defined by the data. With the Ada language, these are the set of variables visible by the exception handler without other details. In effect, the raise statement does not allow typed parameters to be communicated to the handler. This possibility is not provided in the new standard (Ada95, 1995), although under discussion. This omission means that information pertinent to the diagnosis must be found from among all the accessible data. The exception handler must therefore examine the local variables of the subprogram whose body raised the exception and the local variables of the package containing this subprogram. This (bulky) set of data creates strong coupling between the current treatment and the exception handler (Yemini, 1985). Also, due to the absence of parameters this coupling is not explicit.

A partial solution consists in attaching great importance to the study of the Exception Domain. This allows the Exception Domain to be partitioned into classes of states related to the same circumstances (to the same diagnosis). In this case, we no longer associate an exception with an operation but a list of separate exceptions specifying the class of the current state.

Let us point out that the new standard partially solves this problem. It proposes a package (Ada.Exceptions) which provides a procedure (Raise_Exception) causing the raising of the exception labelled by a message to be supplied.

```
procedure Raise_Exception( E: in Exception_Id;
                           Message: in String := "");
```

This exception raises a new occurrence of the exception identified. The value of this message can be obtained in the exception handler thanks to the Exception_Message function.

```
function Exception_Message(X: Exception_Occurrence)
          return String;
```

180 Chapter 3: Characterization of the Ada Exception Mechanism

The messages are of string type only. Generalization to any sort of type cannot be considered on account of the propagation mechanism. In effect, an exception can be propagated outside of its scope and becomes anonymous. In such a situation, non-predefined parameter types could leave their scope and therefore become meaningless.

A simple example of use:

```
-- Ada95 program extract
File_Not_Found: exception;
...
Raise_Exception(File_Not_Found'Identity,
                "Bank accounts not found");
...
Exception
When Not_Found_Error: File_Not_Found =>
    Put_Line(Exception_Message(Not_Found_Error));
...
```

Abnormal termination cases
If an exception is raised following an abnormal termination of the implementation of a called operation (propagation to the caller), the value of the data used by the caller (actual parameters and global variables) may be not defined on completion of the execution of the called operation. This is the case, for example, of the value of the actual parameters associated with the formal out mode parameters of the subprogram propagating an exception. The specifier (or the implementer) of the operation is recommended to give precision on the state of these values, that is explain the effect that execution of an abnormally terminated implementation should have (or has). This effect is generally expressed in the form of a property. For example: 'the value of the parameter is unchanged'. This property appears in the form of comments accompanying the operation. A tool such as ANNA is here again useful as it allows the formal expression of this state (property on the values) to be added to the program and the check that the effective value obtained during execution is in compliance with these properties to be done at run-time. The specification below is an example of what is qualified as *weak exception annotation*:

```
procedure INVERSE(A: in out MATRIX);
--| where raise CONSTRAINT_ERROR => A = in A ;
```

If exception CONSTRAINT_ERROR is raised and propagated by the execution of procedure INVERSE, the value of parameter A must remain unchanged. If it changes this is signalled by the raising of the predefined exception ANNA_ERROR.

Knowledge of the state of the execution of a program is indispensable for implementing error correction techniques. The Ada language gives precise information concerning control. For data, special attention must be paid as:

- the subprogram designer generally does not know the values of the actual parameters returned by a called subprogram because these values depend on the exception raising location in the called subprogram and on the recovery actions made by the exception handler of the called subprogram before propagation;
- moreover the language does not impose many constraints on the run-time environment implementers. For example, no assumptions can be made concerning the real values of the out mode parameters obtained after the propagation of an exception instead of the knowledge of the body of the subprogram which propagates the exception [6.2(12)];
- the language does not provide the Ada program designers with many means for using data with the exception mechanism.

3.6.2 Handling

Common handling

The Ada language exception mechanism initially directs the control to the handler specific to each exception by means of the 'when ... => ... ' clause. In applications, the requirement for partial handlings common to each exception is however very frequent. For example, for a system controlling an automated workshop, the control software must place the controlled system in a defined state (stop of machines, etc.) before starting a self-correction. This can be programmed in Ada by placing the call for a same subprogram in each handler of each exception. Although this solution is functionally correct, it does not facilitate mastery over the problem. In effect, the unicity of a part of the handler is not shown by the program structure. To deduce the presence of a common treatment, the handler of each exception must be examined.

A solution syntactically highlighting the initial sharing of the statements has been proposed for cases where the common part corresponds to the start of the exception handling (Rosen, 1986). It can be adapted to also describe final common handlings:

```
begin
 ... -- raises an exception
exception
  when others =>
    ... -- initial common handling
    begin
      raise;
    exception
      when EXC1 => ... -- specific handling
      when EXC2 => ...
      when others => ... -- (1)
    end;
    ... -- final common handling
end;
```

The first clause 'when others' allows all the exceptions to be handled in a single way. Then the statement 'begin raise; exception ... end;' provokes the re-raising of the same exception for which a specific handler (EXC1 or EXC2) or a common one (others) is provided. Then the control comes back to the nesting frame which gives a common final handling.

The statements placed in the second clause 'when others' (1) can have the same structure (...begin raise; exception when ... end; ...). This frame constitutes a second part of the common handling for exceptions different from EXC1 et EXC2. The process can thus be reiterated.

The features offered by the new standard (Ada95, 1995) greatly simplify this solution. First, a handler 'when' clause can specify a formal parameter (choice_parameter_specification). ERROR_ON_STACK and ERROR are two illustrations in the following example:

```
-- Ada95 program extract
when ERROR_ON_STACK: OVERFLOW | UNDERFLOW => ... -- (1)
when ERROR: others => ... -- (2)
```

Thus the exception handler (1) (or respectively (2)) can use the formal ERROR_ON_STACK (or respectively ERROR) parameter. This parameter is of the Exception_Occurrence type offered by the standard Ada.Exceptions package. It can be used in the handler and in particular communicated as procedure parameters. Its real value is a constant depending on the exception effectively handled (OVERFLOW or UNDERFLOW (respectively or others)).

The value of the string representing the exception is obtained by

```
function Exception_Name(X: Exception_Occurrence)
           return String;
```

Common handlings are therefore easy to design as shown in the example below:

```
...  -- Ada95 program extract
exception
when ERROR_ON_STACK: OVERFLOW | UNDERFLOW =>
    COMMON_HANDLING;
    if Exception_Name(ERROR_ON_STACK) = "OVERFLOW"
        then   INCREASE_SIZE;
        else   MESSAGE_TO_OPERATOR(ERROR_ON_STACK);
               Reraise_Occurrence(ERROR_ON_STACK);
    end if;
end;
```

We would like to point out that Exception_Name function often returns not a shortened name but an expanded name starting with a root library unit. The procedure

procedure Reraise_Occurrence(X: Exception_Occurrence)

raises again the exception whose occurrence is passed as parameter.

Interactions with current treatment
As the execution of the current frame is abandoned in Ada after the raising of an exception, the exception handling acts only on the current state via the data. In Appendix A we will present other tools (see for example RMS68K by Motorola and the primitive ptrace by Unix System V) which consider the exception handling as a task which also acts on the control of the erroneous treatment by, for example, resuming the execution of several statements of the treatment before taking back control (exception monitor task). This allows correction protocols to be defined. However, the primitives proposed by these tools are of a very low level as they act on the language control structures (instruction level). In practice, their use is very difficult. The principle is nevertheless very interesting and will be used (in chapter 4) in the applications to implement correction techniques but handling more abstract entities.

3.6.3 Return

Termination Mode
On completion of the exception handling, execution of current treatment is continued according to the termination mode which principles were presented in section 2.4.5 of chapter 2. The frame which raised the exception is abandoned and the execution is resumed in the calling frame after the call statement.

Remember that in the Ada language, a termination is qualified as normal or abnormal. Normal means that the exception handling was capable of bringing the program back into a Standard Domain state whereas abnormal identifies an Exception Domain state. An Exception Domain state is expressed in Ada by absence of a handler for the raised exception in the body implementing the operation or by the raising of a new exception (or of the same exception thanks to 'raise;') inside the exception handler.

The return mode chosen for Ada is the subject of much discussion. The two modes

- **retry** by which the handler which raised the exception is completely retried and,
- **resume** by which the execution of the erroneous frame is resumed at the statement which follows the one which raised the exception,

again use all or part of the operation which provoked the exception raising. They are qualified as '**resumption**' modes (Meyer, 1990). The supporters of the 'resumption' mode put forward the argument that this choice allows the termination situation to be clarified: the implementation of an operation is concluded either by a success (possibly after several tries) or by a failure (impossible to find means to correctly execute the implementation). However, in Ada, the erroneous body is not re-executed but replaced by the exception handler.

These discussions frequently show the confusion which reigns between the exception concept and the specific mechanisms which can be associated with it. These two aspects are clearly separate as certain authors offer, for example, solutions integrating the three termination modes (retry, resume, termination). To further illustrate this distinction, we must point out that the termination mode offered by Ada does not prevent other modes from being implemented with this language as we will see in the following chapter.

Caller state
On return from a subprogram, whose body raised an exception, the caller state can:

- belong to the Standard Domain, if the called subprogram has an exception handler the execution of which does not caused the propagation of an exception;
- belong to the Exception Domain if the called subprogram has no exception handler or if it contains one whose execution caused the propagation of an exception (the same or another one).

The subprogram call mechanism is frequently used in design as a means for descending (in the sense of increasingly detailed abstraction) into the Standard Domains (top-down phenomenon). The propagation mechanism causes a bottom-up phenomenon in the Exception Domains. This phenomenon can be interrupted by using an exception handler which transfers the subprogram state from its Exception Domain to its Standard Domain.

Let us consider for example the function FIND which returns value TRUE if it finds a certain item and FALSE if not. Failure to find the item is a situation belonging to the Standard Domain of FIND. Failure may be caused by the fact that the sought item is missing (implementation Standard Domain state) or the incapacity of the implementation to carry out the search. In the latter case, a state of the implementation Exception Domain is transformed into a state of the Standard Domain of the function thanks to the exception handler as follows:

```
function FIND(...) return BOOLEAN is
   ...
begin
   ...
   return FALSE;
   ...
exception
   when others => return FALSE;
end FIND;
```

The following program extract describes a situation where the implementation exceptional state is not handled locally by a return to a state of the implementation Standard Domain but is propagated to the caller.

```
exception
   when others => raise FAILURE;
end;
```

The propagation changes the termination parameter of the caller's formal state (e) to the 'abnormal termination' value. This state has other components whose values stem from the latest values of the implementation state (as symbolized by the vertical arrow 'E3=>e' on Figure 3.2). Statements can precede the propagation in order to place adequate values in the other components to facilitate the handling of the exception by the caller. Consider for example a procedure inversing a matrix passed by parameters:

```
procedure INVERSE(M: in out MATRIX);
```

If an exception is propagated by the body of this procedure, the value of the communicated parameter may have been modified. It will therefore not be possible to prolong the execution by calling another inversion procedure. To find the initial value, the exception handler can return the original matrix value before propagating the exception.

```
procedure INVERSE(M: in out MATRIX) is
  SAVE: MATRIX := M;
begin
  ...
exception
  when others => M := SAVE;
                 raise FAILURE;
end INVERSE;
```

The aim of these treatments is to place the values of the parameters of the formal state, other than that of termination, in a safe state (with regard to the specification invariants).

3.7 Concurrent programming

As tasking features are not currently used, they will be studied separately in this section. The characteristics of the Ada exception mechanism in a multi-task context are complex and must be underlined.

3.7.1 Predefined exceptions

In this paragraph we will give information on predefined exceptions and tasks.

An exception raised in the body of a task induces normal achievement of the erroneous task, possibly after the exception has been handled [11.4.1(8)]. This is applicable to both predefined exceptions and user exceptions.

A task (called 'mother task') can activate one or more tasks of the application. When activation is impossible for a certain number of these tasks, whatever the reason or the number, a single exception is raised in the mother task (TASKING_ERROR) [9.3(3)&(7)]. This choice is justified in (Rationale, 1986) by considering that it is not important to know the reason: whatever the circumstances, the mother task execution cannot be continued and another operation must be considered.

During a rendezvous between a server task (the one that contains the accept statement) and the calling task (of the service offered by the first one) several events can occur apart from normal execution:

- an exception is raised and not handled by the execution of an accept body. In this case it is re-raised after the end of the accept statement. Moreover, the same exception is propagated to the calling task which would then know that its request was not completely satisfied [11.5(4)];
- one of the two communicating tasks is aborted by a third task (abort statement) during their rendezvous. If the calling task is aborted, the server

task normally completes its rendezvous; if the called server task is aborted, the predefined exception TASKING_ERROR is raised in the caller task [11.5(5) & (6)];
- the request for communication by a calling task is made with a server task which has already been ended or is abnormal (aborted for example). In this case, exception TASKING_ERROR is raised in the calling task [11.5(2), 9.10(7)].

An exception can be non-anticipated. Consider the following example which defines a server task (Leverrand, 1982):

```
select
   when G>=0 => accept E1;
or
   when G<0  => accept E2;
end select;
```

Under certain circumstances, this application is *erroneous* [1.6(6)] because it makes assumptions on the implementation (incorrect order dependence and no pre-emption). Indeed if G is a shared variable, its value can be modified by another task between the evaluations of the two guards: G is negative before the evaluation of 'G>=0' and then becomes positive before the evaluation of the guard 'G<0'. Under these circumstances, exception PROGRAM_ERROR is raised as all the alternatives of the select statement are closed [9.7.1(11)]. The same effect is obtained if G is a function using and assigning a remanent variable (for example a global variable or a local variable of the body of the package exporting G).

3.7.2 User exceptions

Each task, independently of the others, has its own formal state. An invariant can be defined on this state and an Exception Domain obtained. Each task is then considered as a sequential process and is studied independently of the other surrounding tasks. It can raise exceptions. Exceptions of this type were dealt with in the previous sections.

If we now consider the complete application, that is all the tasks, it introduces other states which express **contextual relations**, i.e. between the tasks of the application. Synchronization between tasks is an example of this. An invariant on the states of this type expresses a property concerning the relations that the tasks must have between each other. For example, 'a rendezvous between tasks A and B can only occur if a rendezvous between tasks C and D has been previously concluded' expresses such a property. Note that this example illustrates an invariant which concerns the control and not the data. A Standard Domain then an Exception Domain and user exceptions are deduced from the invariant. For instance, an exception defines a sequencing error in the synchronizations between the tasks of an application.

To illustrate this and to study the capacities of Ada, let us consider a petrol pump system including three tasks: PUMP, CUSTOMER and OPERATOR. The task PUMP can accept a TURN_ON request from the OPERATOR, a START_PUMPING request and a FINISH_PUMPING request from the CUSTOMER. The OPERATOR task can accept a CHARGE request from the PUMP. The rendezvous features allow properties between portions of tasks to be expressed. For example, petrol will only be delivered by the PUMP task after a PUMP.START_PUMPING call made by another task. However, neither the Ada task specifications nor their bodies allow **properties** to be specified **on the relations between the tasks** themselves.

- First, the petrol pump centre management software designer cannot specify (without implementing the body) that the PUMP task can only initially accept a TURN_ON request. The Ada task specification only contains the list of the entry identifiers. No property is expressed on the order of the accepted services. These relations can be deduced by analysing the implementation.
- Second, it is not possible to specify that the TURN_ON service offered by the PUMP task must only be supplied to the OPERATOR task. This information does not appear in the PUMP task design either. In effect, in the rendezvous mechanism, the service task cannot constrain the identity of the callers. Thus, a design error could allow the CUSTOMER task, managing the interactions with the clients, to turn on the PUMP, which would be a serious design fault.
- Third, the sequential relations authorized between the various service requests cannot be expressed in Ada. Consequently, any corresponding design faults cannot be detected at compile-time.

However, these types of relations exist in the **contract** written by the client and given to the designer to define the properties which must be respected by the software: initially, the PUMP must accept TURN_ON from the OPERATOR then it must accept that the consumer starts to fill his or her tank (START_PUMPING) then accept that he or she stops filling to then call the OPERATOR to manage payment (CHARGE). Lastly, the process is reiterated (PUMP turn on, etc.). These properties define an automaton which first describes a sequence of states correlating the software tasks and, second, the operations P which can be enabled in each state before going on to the next state.

To take design faults into account, means must be available which, as execution progresses, checks that the designed software is compliant with the changes described by the automaton and which raises an exception if a nonconformity is detected. This detection mechanism can be implemented by a **monitor task** which:

- is informed of the changes in the states of the application tasks (call for a given entry, wait on an accept statement for a request on a given entry, etc.)
- and collates these changes with the automaton defining the expected properties.

Concurrent Programming 189

The monitor task and the automaton can be created manually or obtained automatically from using a specification language. TSL (Task Sequencing Language) (Helmbold, 1985) (Luckham, 1987) is a good example of such a tool. It was produced to make the description of the expected sequence easier, then to introduce this description by formal comments placed in the Ada programs and finally to translate these comments in an automaton manipulated by a monitor task. The following comments illustrate the fuel pump system example (derived from (Helmbold, 1984)).

```
task CUSTOMER;
task PUMP is
   entry TURN_ON;
   entry START_PUMPING;
   entry FINISH_PUMPING;
end PUMP;
task OPERATOR is
   entry CHARGE(AMOUNT: in MONEY);
end OPERATOR;
--+ when PUMP accepts OPERATOR at TURN_ON
--+    thenPUMP accepts CUSTOMER at START_PUMPING
--+       => PUMP accepts CUSTOMER at FINISH_PUMPING
--+       => PUMP calls OPERATOR at CHARGE
--+ before PUMP accepts OPERATOR at TURN_ON;
```

The sequencing relations which must be expressed in the form of properties do not only concern the rendezvous. These are general temporal relations between the occurrences of the actions of the tasks composing the program.

The reader may ask: 'why add sequential relations between tasks when the rendezvous play this role?'. To reply to this question, let us re-examine the implementation of procedure P (a component) proposed in section 3.2.4. Even if the designer is sure that each procedure (sub-component) P1, P2, P3, taken separately, correctly calculates expected results, he or she cannot affirm that the sequence of procedure calls defined in the body of P will produce the P output values desired. This doubt is obvious as soon as the body of the procedure becomes bulky; it is recommended in all cases if dependability is considered as an important criterion. The designer wishes to justify the reliance in his or her implementation by supplying an invariant on the values of the implementation states (here E0, E1, E2, E3; see Figure 3.2). For a subprogram implementation (here P), these values are the results of subprogram calls (here P1, P2, P3) intervening in its body. The invariant is a Boolean function expressed by means of operations. For example, in the case of integer results: arithmetic operations, comparisons, etc. An invariant associated with an implementation of a component is a Boolean function expressed by means of operations on the results of the sub-components used to design the component.

A multi-task application introduces a new complexity besides numerical results: the sequencing of the dates of the occurrence of the results. A multi-task application is therefore analysed by contemplating the sequencing of the actions that it produces and thus, in a first step, by omitting the numeric results that it calculates. For example, only the activation of an actuator is considered and not the value communicated to this actuator.

A task is firstly made up of blocks of statements which do not express interactions with other tasks (such as assignment, loop, if-then-else). These blocks will be called sub-components. Secondly a task contains statements defining correlations between tasks (rendezvous statements). The application which is the studied component is therefore constituted of correlated sub-components.

Let us be precise about the two types of relations linking the sub-components. The designer of a multi-task application expresses sequential relations between sub-components of each task taken separately (sequencing of sub-components of a task) and also between sub-components of several tasks of the application (using rendezvous).

Let us now examine the sub-component results which are of interest. Statements contained in these sub-components are other than those specific to tasking and are considered only in terms of time required to execute them. The results produced by execution of sub-components are then of the *time* type. The time is the data used to define the state of the application. The relations of sequencing are the operations considered. On examining each task separately, the designer is certain of his or her results in terms of time: if two statements (or sub-components) are placed in sequence, the date of execution end of the first one is equal to the date of execution start of the second one; the start date for the execution of a sub-component is lower than the sub-component execution end date. Also, if a designer examines a rendezvous, he or she will know the value of the result in terms of time: the sub-component which follows an entry call is executed *after* the sub-component placed in the called rendezvous.

However, designers cannot affirm that the sequencing of the set of tasks which compose their application is exactly as desired. They must justify the reliance that can be placed in the application by supplying an invariant on the values handled, that is, on the dates when certain actions of sub-components (such as a sub-component execution end) are performed. This invariant combines the dates by means of new operations, the simplest of which is the precedence relation ($t1$ before $t2$). Thus, the example of the invariant associated with the petrol station task specification does not operate on the sub-components (as the rendezvous does) but on the occurrence dates of actions judged as characteristic, that is, here, the dates on which the rendezvous are effective.

3.7.3 Handling

Introducing an invariant into a task or a set of tasks is a means for detecting that the application has reached an exceptional state. An exception can be raised. If the exceptional state defines a contextual error, the task which raised the exception is not at the origin of the error as the cause is shared between various tasks. The aim of this section is not to present the implementation of error recovery techniques in Ada multi-task applications (this will be discussed in the following chapter) but to give the capacities and the limits of the Ada language features to perform this type of handling.

When an exception is raised in a task body (and not in a frame nested in the body of the task), the exception handler is executed and then the task achieved. Unfortunately nothing is directly informed of such a situation. It would be useful for instance to start another version of the task. The exception handler must therefore elaborate a replacement or warn a management task of its termination. In both cases, time is required to activate a spare task and exception TASKING_ERROR could be raised in the calling tasks.

To avoid this exception raising, task attributes ('CALLABLE, 'COUNT) can be used. But this must be done carefully for they do not give durable knowledge on the real state of a task (Leverrand, 1982) (Burns, 1985). The values of these attributes are only 'valid' at the time of their evaluation. Thus, the task using an attribute, calling for a rendezvous (as in the following example), might be unpleasantly surprised by the raising of exception TASKING_ERROR because it thought that the T.E was still callable after the evaluation of T'CALLABLE (if TRUE). Despite this precaution, an abortion of the called task or an exception in the called task can intervene during the time which elapses between the attribute evaluation and the task entry call.

```
if T'CALLABLE then   T.E;
end if;
```

If the violation of an invariant associated with the inter-task relations is detected by a task, this task would want to communicate this exceptional state by causing the raising of an exception in a target task. The first version of the Ada language provided a statement allowing a task to cause the raising of exception FAILURE (which was then predefined) in a designated task T (raise T'FAILURE;) (Ledgard, 1981). This statement could be used as asynchronous communication means. This use considered as undesirable and problems relevant to implementation (Rationale, 1986), led to the suppression of this feature.

As for the subprograms, the membership of a called server task to its implementation Exception Domain can be communicated to the calling task using the propagation mechanism provided by the rendezvous. To defer the raising in the caller task, without losing the occurrence of the exception, the 'Omega strategy' can be adapted by storing detection in the field EXCEPTION_OCCURRENCE of the object on which the service was performed.

```
SERVER_TASK:...
  ...
  accept E(THE_OBJECT: in out OBJECT_TYPE) do
    begin
    ...
    exception
      when others=> THE_OBJECT.EXCEPTION_OCCURRENCE:=TRUE;
      end;
  end E;
  ...
```

3.8 Conclusion

In this chapter we first of all gave an accurate definition of the exception notion then showed how it is interpreted for the exceptions offered by the languages (predefined) or for expressible exceptions (user).

The characteristics of the Ada language exception mechanism were then studied in detail. The Ada exception mechanism is often described in books by defining only the syntactic and semantic aspects of this feature, that is by repeating the descriptions given in the standard without proposing an analysis. In this chapter, we highlighted the potentialities and the limits of this mechanism.

This knowledge is indispensable to use the exception mechanism intelligently, and, in particular, to implement dependability techniques. The exception mechanism is in fact a primitive tool which is often used in an isolated manner even though, combined with other features of the language, it provides solutions for complex dependability requirements. The implementation of dependability techniques in software designed in Ada is described in chapter 4.

CHAPTER 4

Dependable Ada Software

4.1 Introduction

In this chapter we will deal with the use of the techniques presented in chapter 2 for Ada programs. This language has several specific features which make it easier to obtain dependable software but which are not associated with general dependable techniques. We can quote for instance the use of packages which allow design faults to be avoided by reusing improved components. Other examples concern the features allowing specification or design concepts to be directly expressed in Ada: an abstract object (such as an abstract data type) is implemented by a package (Golsack, 1985); Ada offers task management capabilities, useful for programming a design which express communicating processes (Burns, 1990). The program (or a part of the program) can therefore be obtained by an automatic translator tool or in a systematic way by the programmer.

We will not approach these aspects or the methods used in 'Software Engineering' whereas they can also have a positive effect on the design quality. For example, top-down design methods allow software containing a lower error rate to be obtained, (although this is not their primary purpose) because they help the designer to master the problem to be solved.

Even if Ada provides many interesting features, some of the other features must not be used or special attention is required to obtain dependable software if they are used. These will be discussed in section 4.2.

The main goal of this chapter is to describe how the techniques detailed in the second chapter can be used for Ada programs. We will follow a plan close to the one used in that chapter. This will make it easier for the reader to refer to the theoretical presentations. We will show the possibilities of the Ada language as far as error detection and fault extraction are concerned: during the programming (Fault Avoidance, section 4.3) and during the validation of applications written in this language (Fault Removal, section 4.4).

In section 4.5, we will present the implementation of the Fault Tolerance methods in Ada which consist in limiting the consequences of a residual fault (undetected by Fault Avoidance and Fault Removal methods) on the behaviour of an application.

This chapter has an applied character. We will illustrate it with examples developed in Ada. Significant parts of the examples are inserted into the text whereas the complete programs can be found in appendix B.

We studied the Ada exception mechanism in detail in chapter 3. We showed the benefits of this mechanism for expressing and detecting errors. It also offers means for reacting to the occurrence of errors (the exception handler). For these reasons, the Ada exception mechanism will be frequently used for implementing dependability techniques.

4.2 Problems associated with some Ada features

The aim of this section is to warn the Ada application programmer about the use of some features of the language. Even if the language offers very interesting possibilities (which will be presented throughout this chapter) for developing dependable applications, it also provides means the use of which is contrary to dependability objectives.

We will not propose here an exhaustive study which would require a complete book but we would like to warn the designers so that they do not have a too idealistic view of the Ada language. Comprehensive company reports have been dedicated to this subject. For instance (SPC, 1992) and (Wichman, 1989), which are in the public domain, can be read. Information of a more synoptic character is given in (Holzapfel, 1988), (Pyle, 1991) and (Wichman, 1990). After reading these documents, the designer is quite disappointed as it seems that only several statements can be used without taking risks. This is true not only for Ada but also for other languages for which studies as systematic as the ones conducted on Ada have been rarely carried out. Two positions can be considered:

- use none of the features in question. This may be necessary for programming applications whose dependability is highly critical;
- use these features being aware of the risks. In our opinion, this point of view is not contrary to dependability requirements if absence of errors which can be due to these features is clearly demonstrated for the application using them.

These features will be discussed in section 4.2.1.

Some other features are not dependable as their behaviours differ with the runtime environment used. Here again, an exhaustive study would be extremely large (Motet, 1994). The hazardous behaviours of these statements will be introduced in section 4.2.2.

The potential variations of the hazardous features may imply variations of the application behaviours. This poses new problems in front of dependability requirements. For instance the behaviour of a software can be considered as correct by tests done with a run-time environment and can fail with another (Motet, 1995).

Lastly, in section 3.5.1 of chapter 3, we described in detail the features of the Ada language which can lead to the raising of predefined exceptions. In section 4.2.3, we will discuss the effect of the exception mechanism on other features of the language. The aim of this section is also to warn the reader that, as the Ada exception mechanism is a complex tool, its use cannot be taken in an isolated manner but must be considered together with the other features used in the program.

4.2.1 Unsafe features

The use of certain statements is not recommended. The **goto** statement being the most well known. Its use prevents us from easily ascertaining the statements causing exit from a frame (location of the goto statement) and therefore the causes of these exits, and the execution resumption location. To get to know the control flow, the program text must be analysed, statement by statement, as the goto statement does not respect the nested frame notion which forces the designer to write a structured program.

Likewise (and contrary to the opinion given in (SPC, 1992)), we are against the use of the **exit** statement. It does not compel the designer to explicitly express the exit conditions in the frame specification. We therefore prefer use of the **while** statement. The same reasoning justifies the placing of only one **return** statement at the end of each **function body** instead of peppering these statements throughout the body.

Concerning the data, the possibility for a subprogram to use and modify the values of the **global variables** must not be used. It creates side effects. Reading the specification of a subprogram (list and modes of its parameters) does not give information on access to the global variables.

Use of the features listed above is inadvisable as it makes the program difficult to master by its designer and therefore increases the risk of introducing faults into its design.

The **comments** themselves must be used discerningly. The body of a procedure can be changed to provide another behaviour without the comments placed in the header being modified. Comments are also often incorrectly used or, rather, overused in order to make up for a program which is difficult to understand. For instance, a part of the comments associated with the procedures sometimes comes from the fact that the procedure identifiers are not sufficiently explicit (for example, because they have been abbreviated); comments are given on variables to indicate additional constraints which should have been expressed by introducing a subtype; comments are added to facilitate comprehension of the control flow because the use of the statements (such as `goto`) lead to an unstructured program. In all these situations, comments are introduced to compensate for lack in programming quality and are therefore means which could be used incorrectly.

4.2.2 Hazardous features

Some features of the language lead to unpredictable behaviour for the applications using them. We will distinguish between *erroneous execution, incorrect order dependencies* and *unportable features*.

Erroneous execution
'The language rules specify certain rules to be obeyed by the Ada programs, although there is no requirements on Ada compilers to provide [...] detection of violation of such rules' [1.6(7)]. If the program does not obey these rules, the execution will be unpredictable. These are erroneous execution cases.

The designer must pay careful attention to ensure that these rules are not violated or to avoid the use of certain possibilities of the language leading to these violations:

- do not use the UNCHECKED_CONVERSION generic function [13.10.2(3)];
- do not use two variables which have access to a given object if procedure UNCHECKED_DEALLOCATION is called [13.10.1(6)];
- do not handle shared variables in multi-task applications [9.11(6)] or check that the assumptions [9.11(4)] and [9.11(5)] are true;
- do not use the pragma SUPPRESS [11.7(18)] to inhibit the raising of exceptions;
- check that no variables are used without being initialized [3.2.1];
- 'address clauses should not be used to achieve overlays of objects or overlays of programs units; a given interrupt should not be linked to more than one entry' [13.5(8)] ;
- the program behaviour must not depend on a particular 'parameter passing mode' (by copy or by reference) [6.2(7)]. Therefore, the designer must not make the assumption that a specific mode has been chosen by its run-time environment;
- a variable which is a component that depends on discriminants of an unconstrained record variable must not be assigned [5.2(4)], except if conformity of assigned expression type has been proved.

Incorrect order dependencies
Certain precise rules are defined in the standard. Observance of these rules by the program is not mandatorily checked by the compilers and can lead to erroneous

executions. However, the standard does not impose that different parts of some given constructs be executed in a given order [1.6(9)]. The run-time environment implementer can therefore make choices and impose order constraints. The Ada program designer must not assume a specific choice. More precisely, the behaviour of his or her program must not vary with different effective implementations.

In section 3.5.1 of chapter 3, we listed the incorrect order dependency cases. The designer must therefore not use the constructions concerned or check that the variety of possible orders has no effect on the behaviour of his or her program.

Unportable features
Certain features of the language can create portability problems for the applications using them. The effect of these features varies according to the run-time environment (compiler, run-time executive) used. The non-portability of a software tool must be considered as unacceptable for a dependable application as some of the behaviours generated may not be in compliance with those required by the specification. The portability requirement is mandatory if the software developed is widely distributed on a commercial scale as the designer cannot know the characteristics of all the existing or future execution means: hardware and run-time executive (Motet, 1995).

The Ada application designer must first be aware of the problem, then, to take the dependability criterion into account, he or she must choose from the following:

- not use the features in question. This solution, if it is applied systematically, greatly limits the means of expression offered by the language. Also, if, in the absolute, certain features can have varied behaviours, the constraints on their use, defined by the program, may oblige them to have a constant effect for this specific program. In this case, it is a pity not to use them on principle;
- use the features with hazardous behaviours adding reinforcements around the features constraining them so that they will have a unique effect;
- use these features examining if, for the application concerned, their variations in behaviour have an effect on the global behaviour of the application.

Without proposing a systematic study, we will give here some examples to demonstrate the existence of the problem and the means for handling it.

As a first example, let us look at numbers. These are absolute mathematical objects whose implementation on a computer is limited by the technological facilities (such as the number of bits or words used). For instance, in mathematics, there is an infinite number of integers whereas the type **INTEGER** represents a finite number of integers (INTEGER'FIRST..INTEGER'LAST) which is variable according to the implementations. Use of type INTEGER is therefore not acceptable as an application using high value integers may raise exception CONSTRAINT_ERROR for some implementations and not for others. Type INTEGER is also frequently used not to express the mathematical object 'set of integers' but to code other objects. In particular, in this case, the constraints on the values of these objects must be mandatorily defined. Example:

```
type SHOE_SIZE is new INTEGER range 21..45;
```

Other portability problems exist concerning **float** numbers. To prevent float number calculation programs from having variable behaviours, and therefore giving variable results according to the implementations, accuracy must be explicitly defined (see *Model Numbers* [3.5.6(3)]) and operations '=' and '/=' must be used with care: 'is 0.999..9 equal to 1.0 or not?'.

Most hazardous behaviours concern features associated with **task** management. For example, consider the following statement:

```
select
   accept A do ... end A;
or
   accept B do ... end B;
end;
```

If several calls have been made to the two entries A and B, rendezvous A or rendezvous B will occur. The effective choice depends on the implementation [9.7.1(6)]. A specific implementation policy may have significant effects on the behaviour of the application. For instance, if the rendezvous is made systematically with the called entry appearing first in the list of select statement entries (for example A), the second service (B) will never be handled even if old requests exist.

The rejection of this statement for a multi-task application is practically impossible. The designer must therefore use it and ask himself the following questions:

- 'for my application, can the utilization circumstances of this statement lead to a hazard?'. If the reply is no, the statement can be used. In the example considered (select statement), this case occurs if we demonstrate that entries A and B can be called indeterminately (which justifies the use of the select statement) but that there is no more than one request at a time. If the reply to the first question is yes, the following question must be asked;
- 'for my program, do the varied behaviours of the feature have an effect on the global behaviour of the application?'. If the reply is no, its use is acceptable. However, if the reply is yes, other statements must be used to replace the statement in question, or reinforcements must be implemented to constrain the application to produce only a single effect.

For considered example, an arbitration policy must be explicitly programmed which expresses the choice to be done. Example:

```
select
   when B'count = 0 =>accept A do ... end A;
or
                    accept B do ... end B;
end;
```

In this program the service B is privileged because A entry calls are served if and only if there are no B entry calls. However we signalled in section 3.7.3 that the attribute COUNT can induce hazardous behaviours because the number of calls on an entry is a data shared between the server task and the caller tasks.

4.2.3 Impact of an exception on the other features

We described in section 3.5.1 of chapter 3 the Ada features which provoke exceptions to be raised ((1) on Figure 4.1). In the present section we will approach the impact of the exception use on the other features of the language ((2) on Figure 4.1). This knowledge is necessary because a bad use of a tool (here the Ada exception mechanism) which aims to facilitate fault mastering, may introduce new faults.

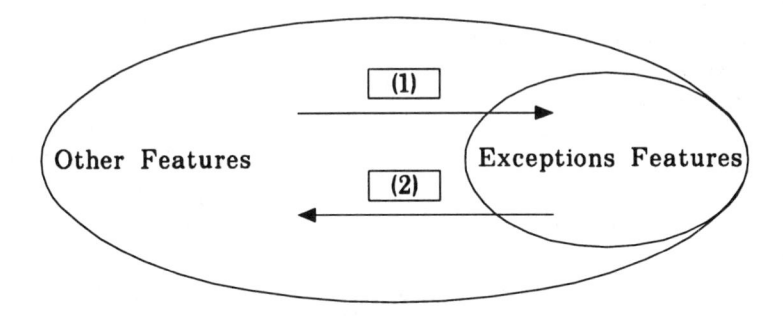

Figure 4.1: Exception and other features relationships

We have chosen to present the consequences of the use of the exception mechanism on the other features from two points of view: the local consequences expressing the consequences of an exception on a feature and the global consequences on a set of features. For instance, if an exception is raised by a statement it can have an effect on the behaviour of the statement itself and also on the frame which contains this statement (example: frame termination). The two following subsections address this problem and give a few examples. They do not comprise an exhaustive study but draw the reader's attention to the existence of these problems.

Local consequences

Let us study, for instance, the consequences of an exception raised during the evaluation of an expression written at the right-hand side of an assignment statement. The normal execution of this statement involves the modification of the value of the variable written at the left-hand side of the assignment statement. What happens if an exception is raised during the execution of this statement?

If, during the assignment of an expression to a variable, an exception is raised by the evaluation of the expression or by the assignment itself (incompatible subtypes), the value of the variable is unchanged [5.2(4)]. This case arises with the assignment of an array [5.2.1(2)] when it is made by one statement (A:=B;). However, the designer must be wary of the behaviour modification of his or her program if successive assignments to the components of an array are considered instead of a single global assignment. As a matter of fact, if we consider the following declarations:

```
B: array(1..30) of INTEGER;
A: array(1..30) of POSITIVE;
```

the effect produced if B(10)=-1 is different in the two following examples:
```
A:=B;
```

and
```
for I in B'RANGE loop
   A(I):=B(I);
end loop;
```

In the first case, array A will be unchanged but, in the second case, the values A(1)..A(9) will be modified before the raising of the exception CONSTRAINT_ERROR. This must be taken into account in order to adapt the correction handling.

Moreover, certain evaluation orders are not defined by the language standard. So no assumptions must be made on the values of certain variables even if they were logically assigned by a syntactically preceding statement! For instance, let us consider the following extract of program ((Carid, 1988) p.100):

```
B: array(1..30) of INTEGER;
A,D: INTEGER;
...
begin
   D:=30;
   if A = D/(A-3) or A = B(50) then ...
   ...
exception
   ...
```

The evaluation order of the operands associated with the **or** function is not defined. If A=3, exception CONSTAINT_ERROR previously NUMERIC_ERROR due to a division by zero and exception CONSTRAINT_ERROR caused by an index of B out of range can be raised. In addition, if the latter exception is raised, there is no guarantee on the value of D because B(50) can be evaluated before assignment to D is performed, for an optimization made by the compiler.

A similar problem is encountered in case of component assignments of a record aggregate:

```
... (A => X, B => Y, C => Z) ...
```

The evaluation order of the expressions (X, Y and Z) assigned to the different components (A, B and C) is not defined ((Carid, 1988) p.80 and (Ada_comm, 1989) AI-00189). Some components could have been modified and some others not if an exception is raised.

As a first conclusion we can remark that the Ada language has avoided the snag introduced by the C language: the coupling of assignment and evaluation.

```
B=(A=I++);
```

The example above, written in C language, induces the modification of the 3 variables I, A and B by the same statement. So, if an exception is raised, we do not know if one of the intermediate assignments (I and C) was performed or not. In Ada, this statement is translated by the three following statements:

```
I:=I+1;
A:=I;
B:=A;
```

Unlike the previous case (optimization), the Ada compiler cannot change the order of the statements because the assignments are order dependent.

A similar problem is encountered for the use of subprograms. Their execution can cause modifications to variables. If this execution is interrupted by the raising of an exception, we do not know which variables are modified. This situation is encountered:

- if the subprogram modifies global variables,
- if the subprogram has parameters of mode **out** or **in out**. The values of the actual parameters depend not only on the place where the exception is raised (were the statements that assign the formal parameters performed?) but also on the passing mechanism of the parameters: the use of the references during execution or the copies at the end of normal execution. Unfortunately, we said that no specific modes can be assumed.

Global consequences
The global consequences of an exception on the other elements of a program **depend on the place where the exception is raised** (execution of the statements or elaboration of the declarations) and on **the nature of the frame** in which the exception is raised. The standard (chapter 11) is presented in the same way. It can be summarized by:

1. an exception raised when executing the statements of a frame which does not have a handler for this exception [11.4.1] [11.5(4)], initially leads to the termination of the current frame and also has the following consequences:
   (a) the propagation of the same exception for a subprogram body, a block or package body which is not a library unit,
   (b) the propagation of the same exception for an **accept** statement, immediately after this statement for the called task and at the entry call location for the calling task,
   (c) the abandoning of the main program for a library unit package or for the main program itself,
   (d) the completion of the current task for a task body. This can have indirect consequences on the other tasks: raising of TASKING_ERROR in the tasks waiting at a call of an entry of the completed task, etc.;

2. an exception raised during the elaboration of the declarations will end this elaboration. Moreover its effect is [11.4.2]:
   (a) the propagation of the same exception for a declarative part of a subprogram body, a block statement or a package body which is not a library unit,
   (b) the abandoning of the main program for a library unit package or for the main program itself,
   (c) the completion of the current task for a task body and the raising of the exception TASKING_ERROR at the task activation location.

4.3 Fault Avoidance

In chapter two we presented software analysis methods allowing the notion of errors to be considered during the design. We will see in sections 4.3.2 to 4.3.4 how these techniques can be applied to Ada program design, in particular using the exception mechanism. Moreover, we will show how correct use of the Ada features avoids many design faults (section 4.3.1) or facilitates fault detection by the reviewer (section 4.3.5).

4.3.1 Use of Ada features

A language is often judged by the software tool designers on its capacities to express concepts used during program design. In this case, the judgement criterion considered is programming rapidity. For dependable programs, the language features must be examined with, as criterion, the capacity to avoid or detect faults.

We showed in section 4.2 that certain features must not be used or must be used only when many precautions are taken as they may lead to unexpected behaviours of the program using them. In this section, we will show that the Ada language offers many features favouring fault avoidance during programming. Due to these features, the choice of the Ada language over other programming languages justifies the higher reliance that the client can place on the programmed software.

We would like to insist on the fact that in this section the language is judged independently of the applications using it. However, in the following sections, fault avoidance techniques will be applied to Ada programs. Nevertheless, it is important to previously evaluate the dependability of the tool (that is of the language) used to program the applications that we want to be dependable.

Advice given in this section is mainly deduced from the lists proposed in the report (SPC, 1992) and the authors' experience. This advice is classed according to two criteria as a function of the dependability requirements:

- **understanding of the program**. The designer of a program often handles a considerable amount of information (syntactic or semantic) which is expressed in the program. Incorrect interpretation of this information is, during programming, the source of many faults. For this reason, the language or specific use of this language must favour the comprehension of this information;
- **avoiding the introduction of faults when writing** programs. The use of certain features avoids faults not associated with the problem to be solved but proper to the programming activity.

We will see that the use of certain features helps in obtaining the two objectives given above.

Understanding the program
The comprehension of a program is made easier by improving its readability (textual entities used) and by highlighting the semantic information on the conceptual entities used by the program.

Readability is first of all improved by adopting a standard format for presenting program texts. This is obtained for instance by indentation and alignment. Example:

```
type OPERATION is ( PUSH,     POP,       ADD,
                    SUBSTRACT, MULTIPLY,  DIVIDE);
```

The names of the variables must be easy to understand. For this, several words can be used separated by underscores. In all cases, abbreviations must be prohibited. However, names used to build other names (such as indexed components or selected components [4.1]) introduce very long strings for identifying objects. This excessive length is also detrimental to readability. An explicit but shorter name is obtained by using the 'renames' feature [8.5]. An example is given in the standard for exception SEQUENTIAL_IO [14.2.3]. This feature can also be used to give a new name with more precise semantics than the old one in its utilization context.

For constructions allowing this, optional names placed at the end of the text expressing the construction must be repeated. The constructions concerned are: specifications and bodies of subprograms, packages and tasks. This visually shows the textual limits of the construction without it being necessary to examine the alignment or the nesting of other constructions. For the same reason, names must be associated with blocks, loops and exits. Example [5.5(12)]:

```
SUMMATION: while NEXT /= HEAD loop
             SUM  :=  SUM + NEXT.VALUE;
             NEXT :=  NEXT.SUCC;
          end loop SUMMATION;
```

Code formatting is also useful for **understanding the semantics**. This possibility is at present used by indenting the control structures. This could be used more frequently and more generally. In the following example, alignment of 'in' and 'out' strings, defining the parameter modes, highlights the input parameters and the output parameters.

```
procedure INVERT( GIVEN:          in     MATRIX;
                  INVERSED:       out    MATRIX;
                  CORRECTLY_DONE: out    BOOLEAN);
```

As for the other identifiers, the names selected must belong to the semantics of the problem addressed. In particular, identifiers such as DATA or RESULT which can be applied to any context must be avoided. In order to clearly mark the active aspect of the subprograms and entries, their identifiers must be verbs.

Declaration of constants is to be preferred to the direct use of the values of these constants. For example:

```
SQUARE_METRES_PER_FLOOR : constant INTEGER := 780;
...
TOTAL_SQUARE_METRES := SQUARE_METRES_PER_FLOOR *
                                    NUMBER_OF_FLOORS;
```

instead of

```
TOTAL_SQUARE_METRES := 780 * NUMBER_OF_FLOORS;
```

In effect, in the second text, value 780 defines no semantics. We do not know what it represents. Also, a single constant value may be found at two locations in the program with different semantics (that is representing two non-equivalent notions).

The Ada language also offers many useful features for expressing abstract entities. These entities can then be handled as such, without the need to detail the structures (possibly very complex) that they represent. This abstract information greatly facilitates the understanding of the program semantics. Three fundamental examples can be cited:

- a **type** includes under a single name the definition of a data structure (record, array, etc.) and a set of values. We can thus handle the data-objects without specifying the associated data-structures. This possibility is, for instance, used to define subprogram parameter types;
- the definition of the **specification of a subprogram** gives a minimal abstract view of an action. The subprogram can then be called without having to know the details of its implementation (that is its body);
- **specifications of packages** are useful for defining abstract data types. Data-objects can thus be handled thanks to the operations that they offer (that is the subprograms exported by the packages) without the need to know the details of the data structure.

It is indispensable to define as many Ada entities as there are conceptual entities. For example, two types must be declared to define two data-objects even if their representations (that is their data-structures) are the same. Example:

    subtype SHOE_SIZE **is** INTEGER **range** 28..49;
    subtype TEMPERATURE **is** INTEGER **range** 28..49;

or

    type SHOE_SIZE **is new** INTEGER **range** 28..49;
    type TEMPERATURE **is new** INTEGER **range** 28..49;

If two separate identifiers are not declared, confusion will be possible between different conceptual type variables in the programming.

The **specialization** notion can be explicitly expressed using subtypes for the data and thanks to the instantiation of generic packages or by declaring a package providing more specific services and using a more general package. These constructions provide additional information useful for understanding the program.

We have already pointed out that the use of **comments** to provide information on the semantics of the program must be limited to information which cannot be expressed using the features of the language. 'Bad code should be improved not explained' (SPC, 1992).

Avoiding programming faults

First of all, the use of the means offered by the language to facilitate the understanding of the program being written favours fault avoidance. For example, writing optional names for loop, block and exit statements and at the end of the specifications and the bodies of the subprograms, packages and tasks avoids 'end' being forgotten or incorrect nesting of control structures.

As programming requires partial or total manual acquisition, **typing errors** are always possible. The use of constant values can lead to many faults of this type. These faults are avoided if constant identifiers are declared and used instead of constant values. We must point out that most of these faults cannot be detected at compile-time, in particular for values associated with predefined types. The declaration of private types or limited private types in package specifications means that the constant identifiers must be declared in the specifications and the value given in the private part ('deferred constants' [7.4.3]). Package users cannot define constants of this type as the type structure is private.

The use of explicit values instead of attributes leads to the same sorts of faults which can be avoided in the same way. Thus, the extract:

    for I **in** Set_Of_Persons**'range loop**
       ...
    end loop;

is preferable to
    for I **in** 1..10 **loop**
       ...
    end loop;

as values 1 to 10 may not correspond to the bounds of the range which indexes the Set_Of_Persons array.

The faults thus avoided are not limited only to typing faults. They could be more general programming faults such as incorrect comprehension of semantic information (value of a constant or an attribute). Lastly, we would like to point out that the last example does not highlight the iteration on Set_Of_Persons and therefore does not facilitate the understanding of the program.

The Ada language offers features encouraging the writing of reusable actions (subprograms), groups of actions (packages) and data (abstract data types). New design and new programming obviously imply an increase in the risk of introducing new faults, reuse on the contrary reduces this risk. These features therefore avoid fault introduction.

Other features require or encourage the description of entity specifications. The program using these entities will thus contain less utilization faults. The most conventional example is the subprogram specification. As the package specification used to define abstract data types does not allow the private data structures to be directly handled, it avoids faults associated with this handling. Type definitions also favour global handling of complex data structures (for instance, for subprogram parameters) whereas handling each component may lead to incoherent data structure values. For instance, the very simple statement:

```
A := B;
```

can express the assignment of highly complex data structures. If the assignment is made component by component, some of them could be forgotten.

A specification also facilitates the understanding of an object by giving only the pertinent information. The mass of other information is hidden in order to prevent the user from being 'submerged' with information.

The use of blocks limits the scope of the variables and therefore prevents these variables from being used outside of the part of the body where they have a meaning. Thus, a body can be structured into blocks not to add statements required for execution but to favour fault avoidance.

An alternative for the case statements must not use a discrete range. In effect, the type of the expression used to select an alternative can be modified by adding values between the bounds of the range. In this case, the designer may forget to modify the programming of the case statement when he or she wanted different actions for the added values. This fault is avoided if all possible values are listed in the alternatives.

4.3.2 Failure Modes and Effects Analysis (F.M.E.A.)

Remember that the F.M.E.A. technique consists in studying the effects of an error defined by its observation (the violation of rules) and not by its cause (the internal elements which provoked it). In a conventional top-down approach, each stage of the design expresses the **implementation** of an 'N-1' level component as the structure of 'N' level sub-components. The sub-components only are specified (their design will be dealt with in the following stage). The F.M.E.A. technique therefore analyses the consequences of an error occurring in an 'N' level component on an 'N-1' level component. To do this, the errors must be **associated with the specification** of the sub-components as we do not know their design (which will be defined at level 'N+1'). The Ada language clearly makes the distinction between specification and design (the body). However we saw in section 3.3.2 of chapter 3 that it has limited capabilities for associating the specification of errors with the specification of the features provided by the language.

First, it is impossible to express, using Ada features (except informal comments), that an error can be raised by subprograms and task services. The Ada syntax does not allow exceptions to be declared in their specifications. We highlighted the consequences. A **predefined exception** propagated by a procedure might not be handled by the user frame which could ignore this eventuality. Even if the name of the exception exists during the propagation (predefined exceptions do not become anonymous), the associated semantics of the error is lost. For instance, if CONSTRAINT_ERROR is raised by the procedure POP or the procedure PUSH, it may correspond to a stack underflow in the first case and to a stack overflow in the second case. The CONSTRAINT_ERROR identifier cannot be considered for applying the F.M.E.A. method because this exception defines a cause (an array index is out of range for instance) and does not specify the 'failure modes' (stack overflow or stack underflow). Moreover, we pointed out in section 3.3.1 that the list of predefined exceptions raised by each of the Ada features may depend on the considered implementation of the run-time environment. We therefore propose to associate with each procedure 'X' an exception such as 'PROCEDURE_X_FAILS' which propagation is obtained by writing the following clause in its exception handler:

```
when others => raise PROCEDURE_X_FAILS;
```

The described phenomenon is much more alarming when **user exceptions** are declared locally and not handled in a procedure. They produce **anonymous exceptions**. The fact that an anonymous exception can be raised by a procedure call makes the F.M.E.A. method difficult to use because the consequences of the very fuzzy failure 'the procedure does not work' must be examined. Moreover, we stated that an exception can come back into its scope (section 3.3.2) where it regains its original name and where it can provoke the propagation of another exception. Unfortunately the F.M.E.A. method does not deal with a case such as this, the body of the procedure studied being unknown as only its specification is considered.

With tasks, an exception which occurs in an accept statement is propagated to the calling task [11.5] which can ignore the potentiality of this occurrence because this information is not in the rendezvous specification. For an exception declared locally in a server task, an anonymous exception is propagated. The remarks concerning the difficulties in using the F.M.E.A. method for subprograms are also true for services provided by tasks.

For packages, the designer of the application can declare the user exceptions that can be raised by the package subprograms in the specification part. However it is impossible to know which subprogram raises which exception. Examples can be seen in the TEXT_IO package specification [14.3.10]. The following specification of the conventional stack package is another example [12.4(5)]. The association between OVERFLOW and PUSH, and between UNDERFLOW and POP, is not explicit and so must be added with informal comments.

```
generic
   type ITEM is private;
package ON_STACKS is
   type STACK(SIZE : POSITIVE) is limited private;
   procedure PUSH(S : in out STACK; E : in ITEM);
      -- raises OVERFLOW
   procedure POP(S : in out STACK; E : out ITEM);
      -- raises UNDERFLOW
   OVERFLOW, UNDERFLOW : exception;
```

```
    private
      type TABLE is array (POSITIVE range <>) of ITEM;
      type STACK(SIZE : POSITIVE) is
        record
           SPACE    : TABLE(1..SIZE);
           THE_TOP  : NATURAL := 0;
        end record;
    end ON_STACKS;
```

To conclude, the use of the F.M.E.A. method requires the use of packages including exception specifications. The application is then defined as a tree of packages. Such a program structure is obtained, for instance, by using the abstract machine method (Booch, 1986) or the HOOD method (Lai, 1990). The nodes of the tree provide exception lists. The F.M.E.A. method consists in studying the propagation of each exception from a node to the root. To do this, predefined or anonymous exceptions must be avoided.

Some tools exist whose principles are close to the F.M.E.A. method. They establish the exception paths due to the propagation phenomenon. They therefore study the effect of raising an exception on the higher components of the hierarchy developed during the design (Bundy, 1993).

4.3.3 Fault-Tree Method

The Fault-Tree method can also to be used during top-down design, to analyse the causes of a possible error taking the implementation into account. We saw that this method (see section 2.2.6 of chapter 2), coupled with the binary logic, allows an error to be expressed as a combination of events of the lowest level (causes). If it can be reduced to a FALSE event, the imagined error cannot occur.

The elaboration of a fault-tree from an Ada program was proposed by Nancy Leveson (Leveson, 1983). We gave examples in section 2.3.2. We propose to use this method:

- to detect the cause of an error to adapt the exception handling with the aim of correcting the effect of the error (fault tolerance),
- to show that the occurrence of certain exceptions is impossible and therefore that it is useless to declare them in the specification. Indeed these unnecessary exceptions will require substantial studies and costs both which serve no purpose.

To illustrate this point, consider procedure SIMPLE_EXAMPLE using package ON_STACKS which provides procedures PUSH and POP and can raise exception UNDERFLOW:

```ada
with ON_STACKS; -- defined in previous section
with TEXT_IO;
procedure SIMPLE_EXAMPLE_MAIN is
   package IIO is new TEXT_IO.INTEGER_IO(INTEGER);use IIO;

   package INTEGER_STACK is new ON_STACKS(INTEGER);
   use INTEGER_STACK;

   S : STACK(50);
   I : INTEGER;

   procedure SIMPLE_EXAMPLE(ELEMENT:in out INTEGER) is
      use TEXT_IO;
   begin
      PUSH(S,ELEMENT);
      POP (S,ELEMENT);
   exception
      when OVERFLOW =>
         PUT_LINE("Stack Overflow...");
   end SIMPLE_EXAMPLE;
begin
   -- ...
   GET(I);
   SIMPLE_EXAMPLE(I);
   -- ...
end SIMPLE_EXAMPLE_MAIN;
```

A handler is not provided for exception UNDERFLOW in procedure SIMPLE_EXAMPLE. If this exception is raised by this procedure, it will be propagated to the user frame. The user frame (SIMPLE_EXAMPLE_MAIN) wonders what caused the exception to be raised. Let us study the possible causes of the occurrence of this exception.

A fault-tree associated with this example is shown on Figure 4.2.

Fault Avoidance 211

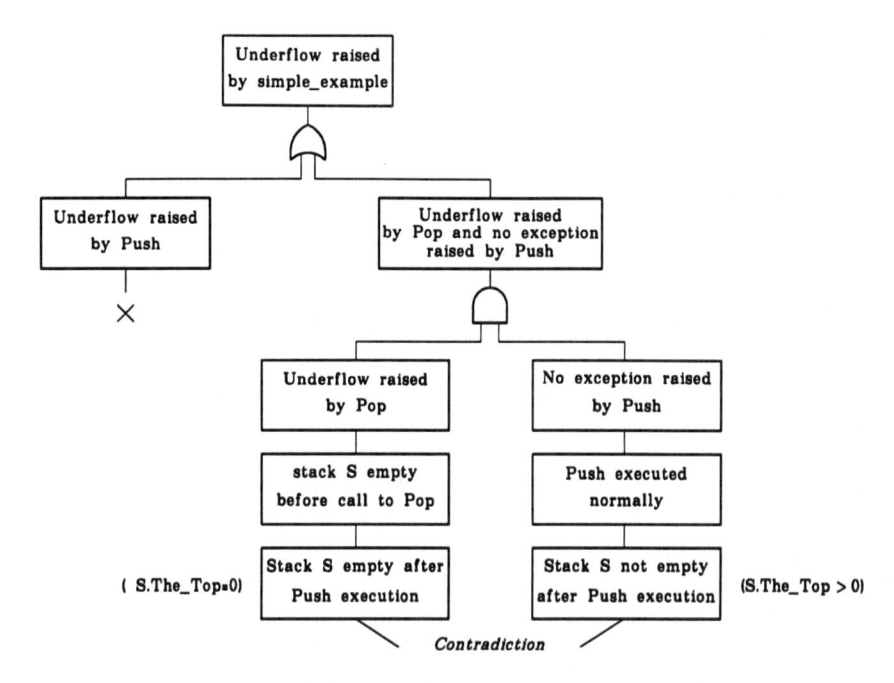

Figure 4.2: Exception Underflow cannot be raised

Fault tree diagram:
- Top: "Underflow raised by simple_example" (OR gate)
  - Left branch: "Underflow raised by Push" (marked with X)
  - Right branch: "Underflow raised by Pop and no exception raised by Push" (AND gate)
    - Left: "Underflow raised by Pop" → "stack S empty before call to Pop" → "Stack S empty after Push execution" (S.The_Top=0)
    - Right: "No exception raised by Push" → "Push executed normally" → "Stack S not empty after Push execution" (S.The_Top > 0)
    - Contradiction between the two bottom conditions.

This tree is obtained from the following reasoning on the source code. One of procedure SIMPLE_EXAMPLE statements (PUSH or POP calls) can raise exception UNDERFLOW. Procedure PUSH cannot raise such an user-defined exception (cross in the Figure 4.2). This is not specified by procedure PUSH but deduced from its implementation. Let us study the case of the exception UNDERFLOW raised by the POP call. This is only possible if the previous statements (PUSH call) has not raised any exceptions **and** if exception UNDERFLOW is raised by procedure POP. The first condition (no exception raised by PUSH) implies that PUSH was executed normally and therefore that **stack S is not empty** (after this PUSH execution). The second condition (UNDERFLOW raised by POP) implies that **stack S was empty** before the POP call (deduced from the source code). The passage from *If S is empty* to *then exception UNDERFLOW is raised* is not in the specification (we deduce it from the code analysis).

We therefore obtain a **contradiction** which proves the **impossibility to raise exception UNDERFLOW**.

In this simple example we showed how to use the Fault-Tree Method on a sequence of (two) statements to detect the impossibility to raise an exception. Nancy Leveson also proposed (Leveson, 1983) the process for the **if** and **loop** statements. A fault-tree model must be provided for the exception part of a frame although it would be necessary for an exception handler to raise an exception itself as illustrated in the following example:

```
procedure A is
begin
   ...
   ...
exception
   when X =>  ...
              raise Y;
end A;
```

Exception Y due to the calling of A can be raised by the handling of exception X which occurred in the body of A. It also could have been raised directly in this body and propagated since no exception handler was provided ('when Y => ...' does not exist).

Unlike the conventional control statements (if, while, etc.) it is difficult to establish the cause of transfer of control to an exception handler. This transfer of control can be caused either directly (by a raise statement) or by propagation by numerous statements in the body of A (this is where the problem lies). This analysis proves to be particularly difficult in the case of predefined exceptions. For instance, exception STORAGE_ERROR can be raised by numerous statements of A.

In practice, it seems to us that the use of a Fault-Tree method to take exception handlers into account should be reserved for simple Ada programs (this is why, as far as we know, no tools are available). This is due to the fact that the language does not impose the specification of the exceptions and does not possess means to explicitly express invariants. For instance, the '*Stack is not empty*' post-condition after the execution of PUSH and the '*execution of POP on an empty Stack raises the exception UNDERFLOW*' precondition would be sufficient to easily deduce that the exception UNDERFLOW cannot be raised by Simple_Example.

4.3.4 Petri net

Remember that the Petri net (Peterson, 1981) is a formal model allowing communicating sequential processes to be represented. Work has already been done to express Ada programs with Petri nets (de Bondelli, 1983). Obtaining this model allows design errors, such as deadlocks and conflicts, to be detected by exploiting the properties associated with the model (Murata, 1989). This was developed and illustrated in section 2.2.7.

The exception handling feature seems to make the modelling more difficult. This is due to the fact that the Petri net model requires the specification of all the possible transitions whereas the exceptions technique does not presuppose knowledge of the starting state (the place where the exception is raised) but only of the reached state (the beginning of the exception handler). The aim of this model is however to express and study the parallel aspects of the systems. The sequential parts of the program and also the exception handler parts must be merged into a single transition if more precise information is not required.

This problem occurs for **predefined exceptions** when the Ada program does not specify the places where these exceptions are raised. For instance, exception STORAGE_ERROR is not raised because of the Ada program but because of its execution on a given machine (with a limited-size memory for the stack area). It also depends on the used run-time executive which more or less optimizes the use of the stack area. This is due to the fact that these errors correspond to a level of abstraction different from the one of the application.

For **exceptions defined by the user**, the use of the `raise` statement corresponds to transfer of control to the exception handler which is easy to model by a transition. If there are no local exception handlers, the exception is propagated. Control is transferred therefore to the first exception handler encountered in the enclosing frames. This propagation can be represented by a Petri net model which enables the nesting phenomenon to be described.

For an exception raised during a rendezvous (and not handled locally), a transition must allow a token to be put at the place which defines the beginning of the exception handler of the calling task and a second token at the place which describes the beginning of the exception handler of the called task. Figure 4.3 shows a model of this type.

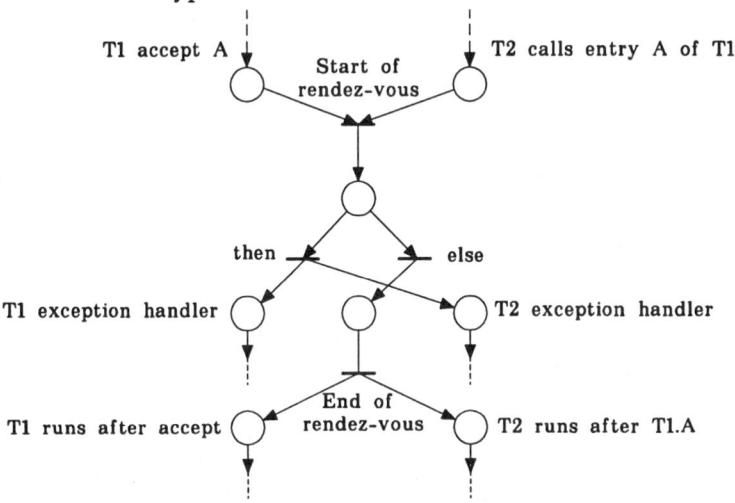

Figure 4.3: Petri net and exception

The *Backward Graph* technique, which establishes if a certain *marking* (set of states) can be reached or not, is useful for studying if certain exceptions can be raised. This is done checking if the state specifying the statement which raises a given exception can be reached by a *firing sequence* from an *initial marking*. We gave in section 2.2.7 an example of such a process for a railroad crossing gate controller.

4.3.5 Design review

The **requirement review** is independent of the programming language used as carried out prior to design.

The aim of the **design review** is to evaluate if the result of the design correctly meets the requirements. We said that this evaluation concerns the result itself and also the way in which it was obtained. These examinations depend to a great extent on the design method chosen.

On completion of the design, the system produced must be programmed. The **program** can be generated by an automatic tool. Generally, the program obtained only comprises a skeleton of the final program. Elements expressed informally in the design model must be programmed manually. Also, in most cases, transition from design to programming is mainly done manually. There is therefore a step between the design model and the program.

The reviewer will examine the result of this step (that is the program) and also the way in which the step was made (that is the programming work).

The judgement given by the reviewer will be favourable both for the program and the programming step if **the program entities correspond to those which appeared during design**. These entities concern both the structuring of the treatments and the data. A counter-example would consist in doing a top-down design supplying a structured sub-problem tree (for instance, by means of algorithmic statements) then in writing a single gigantic procedure instead of nested procedures calling each other. This solution conserves the intermediary abstraction levels which appeared during the design even if these are not useful for execution. Let us also point out that if including procedure bodies is preferred to procedure calls to increase temporal performance (program running speed), this is obtained automatically in the generated code, by the compiler, by using pragma INLINE [6.3.2] added to the Ada program.

We said in section 4.3.1 that the Ada language offers features facilitating the expression of abstract design objects both for the data (types, packages as abstract data types) and actions (subprograms, tasks, packages). These features must therefore be used so that the conceptual objects will explicitly appear in the program.

The quality of the programming work is also judged on **the facility to understand the program**. The reviewer justly considers that a program which is difficult to understand no doubt reflects the fact that the programmer's ideas were unclear. In section 4.3.1, we described the means for improving the readability and the comprehension of program semantics. We also described the means to avoid faults by getting the best out of the features offered by the language.

The use of other fault avoidance techniques (F.M.E.A., etc.) by the programmer will be appreciated by the reviewer who will note that the programmer is aware of the need to avoid faults in the program that he or she produces. The reviewer will therefore place justified reliance on the programmer's work and therefore on the software tool produced as a result of this work.

4.4 Fault Removal

Fault detection can be performed after programming by using the following means:

- certain **analysis techniques used for fault avoidance** on the program during creation. These techniques are used here on the complete program. This is the case, for instance, with the Fault-Tree Method. The verification of the property of an Ada program is given as an example in section 2.3.2 of chapter 2. These techniques were detailed in the previous section (4.3) and thus will not be exposed again;
- **compilation**. The role of the compiler is not limited to a syntactic check and generation of the code corresponding to the source program. A compiler also performs semantic checks on the use of the features and on the objects introduced by the designer. The capacity of the compiler to detect program faults therefore depends to a great extent on the use of the Ada features during programming. The capabilities of the Ada language in this domain will be described in section 4.4.1;
- **program testing**. Whereas the first two means make static analyses on the program, testing requires the execution of the program. A test can only be performed therefore after successful compilation and thus comprises an additional method. The functional test considers the executable program as a 'black box' and is therefore independent of the programming language used. Several remarks are however required and will be developed in section 4.4.2;
- structural (or 'white box') testing analyses the syntactic structure of the program and especially forms a judgement or raises questions concerning the way in which the program was designed without evaluating the correctness of its execution. No information specific to Ada programming will be added. However, the aim of structured-functional testing is to activate the program structures to detect the violation of invariants specified in the program itself. In section 4.4.3, we will study the means offered by the Ada language for expressing such **invariants**.

4.4.1 Compilation

Fault avoidance and fault removal tool
The program written in Ada is the entity that we have chosen to mark the boundary between fault avoidance and fault removal techniques. The fault removal techniques apply to the Ada program and to its derivative, the executable program; the fault avoidance technique applies to the entities handled during design before the complete program is obtained.

216 *Chapter 4: Dependable Ada Software*

Now, the Ada language can be used as a means of expression during design. Also, numerous sorts of objects written in Ada during design are compilable without being executable. The compiler is therefore a fault avoidance tool as it detects the faults which occur during a design step. This approach is favoured by the means that Ada offers for expressing specifications such as: separate subprogram specifications (in top-down design) and package specifications (in bottom-up or parallel design) [10.2].

The faults detected by the compiler, which will be listed in this section, are therefore faults which also can be easily avoided if Ada is chosen as means for expressing the design and if the compiler is used for analysis.

The faults detected at compile-time have been divided into two groups: those associated with the basic features, whose detection is systematic, and those associated with the features allowing new objects to be created and whose detection depends on the way in which the feature is used.

Basic features

Intensive use of feature type favours detection of many faults relevant to the incorrect use of operations. For instance, a variable of type T1 cannot be used as a parameter of a procedure when expected formal parameter type is T2. This is especially true for assigning a type T2 expression in a type T1 variable. A type is therefore not only a means for identifying a data or program structure (task type) as 'two type definitions always define two distinct types, even if they are textually identical' [3.3.1(8)]. A type defines a nature of entity which allows the coming checks to be obtained.

For this reason, the use of enumeration type is preferred to the definition of constants of an existing type. For example:

```
type COLOUR is (WHITE, BLUE, RED, GREEN, YELLOW, BLACK);
```

instead of

```
WHITE : constant INTEGER := 1 ;
BLUE  : constant INTEGER := 2 ;
...
```

With the second declaration, the expression BLUE+YELLOW would be a static expression of value 7 whereas with the first declaration, a fault is detected. It is corrected for instance by writing the function '+' which gives value GREEN as the result of the expression BLUE+YELLOW.

In section 4.3.1, we stated the benefits of defining constant identifiers to prevent erroneous values from being written. Also, if a constant identifier appears in a statement which would lead to its modification (left member of an assignment, real parameter associated with an 'out' mode formal parameter, etc.), this fault would be detected by the compiler. Lastly, type coherence checks are made for typed constants. Thus, if two constant identifiers have the same constant value but of different types, they cannot be interchanged in the program by inadvertence. For instance, if TEMPERATURE and SHOE_SIZE are previously defined types, the constants defined below cannot be used one instead of the other:

```
WATER_MINIMUM_TEMPERATURE: constant TEMPERATURE  := 28;
                                                 -- Celsius degrees
BABY_SHOE_MAXIMUM_SIZE:    constant SHOE_SIZE    := 28;
```

Faults associated with statements and systematically detected by the compiler are few. Let us cite the case of the loop statement: the compiler signals a fault if a statement of the loop body tries to modify the loop parameter identifier [5.5(6)].

Features for creation
Ada provides features to create new entities. These features offer means which, when they are used, generate checks by the compiler. The aim of this subsection is to demonstrate the way in which these features must be used to increase fault detection.

The Ada programmer expresses fragments of the functions by using subprograms. The accurate definition of **parameter modes** ('in', 'out', 'in out') instead of the systematic use of the 'in out' mode provides the compiler with information for conducting checks. For instance, a formal parameter of the 'in' mode must not be assigned in the body of the subprogram.

If the alternative 'when others =>' is not used in a **case** statement, the compiler checks if an alternative has been effectively written for each expression type value defined by the case statement.

If an **aggregate** is used to assign a **record** type identifier instead of a sequence of assignments (component by component), the compiler will detect the situation where aggregate value components have been omitted.

If, in a given context (for instance, in a part of a subprogram), we want to associate additional subprograms with a type, the compiler will not have the information to check if the subprograms are not also used outside the planned context. For instance, variables associated with the initial context can be communicated as parameters of new subprograms. The use of **derived types** [3.4] (possibly with constraints) detects these faults. **Derived subprograms** can be used with derived type parameters [3.4(11)] but specific subprograms can be added. Their use with initial type parameters is detected as a fault by the compiler.

Packages are currently used to define abstract data types. Type private or limited private (to be chosen with knowledge of the facts) make the structure inaccessible and therefore prohibits the basic operations associated with the structure [7.4.1(2)]. Type private also prevents all new operations on variables of this type other than subprograms exported by the package. The violation of this inhibition is detected by the compiler.

Conclusion

Ada offers many features for expressing wanted properties (for example, a 'in' mode formal parameter must not be modified) or affirmed properties (for example, an assignment modifies the value of the variable which is the left member). If these features are used advisedly, the compiler makes numerous checks and is therefore an efficient fault detection tool. However, this result is only obtained if a programming style is used intentionally by the designer.

In particular, a great amount of information on the properties is often placed in the program comments and comprises visual fault detection means which are not very efficient. However, if they appear explicitly in the program structure, they could give rise to many checks conducted at compile-time (and at run-time, as we will show in section 4.4.3). Thus, the caricatured specification below is permissible from a syntactic viewpoint but is not permissible for designing a dependable program.

```
procedure HOW_MANY_SHOES(SIZE: in out INTEGER;
NUMBER: in out INTEGER);
```

If the body of such a subprogram modifies parameter SIZE or if a call of this subprogram is written with value -321 as first parameter, or if the two actual parameters are switched, no faults will be detected at compile time.

4.4.2 Test

A software tool is tested to check that, at run-time, its behaviour corresponds to its specification. The test process detects software failures. The designer must then find where the fault is located in the program in order to extract it. We will show that the use of exceptions in an Ada program can facilitate or complicate the debugging of the program. Beforehand we must tackle the consequences of the existence of hazardous features in the Ada language on the test process.

Test and hazardous features

We signalled in section 4.2.2 that certain features of the Ada language have behaviours depending on the run-time environment used. An Ada application programmed with these features may be unportable: this application possesses various behaviours according to the used run-time environment. This make complex the test process of such a software because, even if a test shows that the application behaviour is the expected one, this conclusion may be not valid with another run-time environment. Now,

- the designer frequently does not have the final execution means. For instance, when a plane control software is developed the hardware system is designed at the same time;

- the run-time environments of the application users may be numerous. This is the case for large-scale distribution software tools;
- the run-time environments frequently change during the application life because new releases are provided (run-time executive, hardware, etc.) to take the technology improvements into account.

The test process would be preceded by a study on the sensitivity of the application to the variations of the execution means. Even if the problem is now clearly posed and means to solve it were proposed (Motet, 1995), an industrial tool characterizing the application sensitivity to the hazards of the Ada language has to be produced.

Exceptions for testing

Initially, the use of exception handling can **facilitate the detection and the location** of an error and therefore the correction of faults in the program. An exception which is never handled may be propagated to the operating system (if it exists) which does not have the information to locate such an error. A simple use of the exception mechanism consists in associating the following exception handler with each frame (where X is the name of the frame):

```
    ...
    exception
       when others => TEXT_IO.PUT("Exception in X");
                      raise;
    end X;
```

The **raise** statement allows the error to be propagated and then permits the tree of frames that led to this error to be obtained (statement PUT). Other pieces of information defining the state of each subprogram (for instance, values of parameters, values of characteristic internal variables) can be displayed on the screen by the handler. Some Ada run-time environments implicitly use this technique. They supply this tree by completing it with internal information that the programmer cannot access (e.g. source line number where the exception was raised). This provides information on the state of the software at the time when the error is detected. Such pieces of information is available by

```
    function Exception_Message(X: Exception_Occurrence)
              return String;
```

offered by the new standard. The function returns the text associated with the exception raised by

```
    procedure Raise_Exception( E:       Exception_Id;
                               Message: String:="");
```

or information specific to the run-time environment (such as the source line number of the raising) if a conventional raise statement is used. So the previous exception handler can be replaced by

```
Exception
  when Error: others =>
     Text_IO.Put_line(Exceptions.Exception_Message(Error));
end;
```

Test of exception handlers
In the previous subsection, we showed that exceptions are useful for the debugging. Then they are not used in the embedded software because no corrections or compensations are made by the provided handlers. In practice, the use of exceptions is interesting for handling detected errors (Fault Tolerance). However, faults may be introduced during handler programming. In order to check if the exception handler is functionally correct, **the test must activate these exceptions**.

Exceptions can be used to handle infrequent events (exceptional). For instance, when reading a sequential file, exception handling can be activated by an end of file reading operation. In this case the exception represents a state rarely reached by the execution of the program. This state can be achieved easily during a test (for instance using a file with a small number of records) and the exception handler can be executed.

However, if an exception handler is used to handle an error, it should be practically impossible to provoke this error by furnishing input data for the software. Indeed if a sequence of input values allowing this state to be reached is known, this exception defines a rare event and not an error. We would have to modify the program in order to avoid the fault. For instance, if we explicitly know how the embedded program can raise exception STORAGE_ERROR (predefined) or exception BUFFER_FULL (user-defined), this proves that there were implementation or design faults (insufficient stack memory or buffer size too small) that had to be corrected (by increasing the size of the memory or of the buffer). A test that consists in watching the software behaviour after having reduced the size of the memory or of the buffer would have no real significance since the real execution context is not present. The exception would be raised within an environment which is not that of the complete system. For instance, exception STORAGE_ERROR raised by a program embedded in a hardware system in which the memory has been reduced will perhaps be raised during calls for procedures, whereas in reality it would be raised by pushing in the stack due to several interrupts with higher priorities.

One of the **problems of the controllability** of a software tool to bring it to an erroneous state often comes from the fact that the program itself prevents it from reaching this state. For instance, the inputs of a component (subprogram, etc.) are limited by the possible values of the outputs of other components supplying information to it. A solution consists in taking the component out of its environment in order to test it separately (unit test). This poses certain problems:

- the state that we are trying to reach may never occur when the component is considered in its environment. We are therefore trying to solve problems which do not exist. For instance, if a program only uses several functions of a complex package, certain exceptions of this package will never be raised simply because of its specific limited use;
- the circumstances in which the exception is raised may not be the ones encountered when the component is integrated into the application (as we stated for exception STORAGE_ERROR);
- the correction or compensation obtained from the exception handling operation may be efficient when taken out of its environment, but it may generate another error when the tested module is placed in its context. Let us suppose, for instance, that the reaction of a buffer task to exception BUFFER_FULL would be to dynamically grant extra memory space. Even if this handler was well designed and tested as such but separately, its integration into the complete system may cause exception STORAGE_ERROR to be raised if the extra memory is granted in the stack.

Another problem concerns the **observability of program execution**. Remember that a test sequence is composed of pairs (inputs, outputs). The expected output values (the ones of the sequence) are compared to the ones supplied by the executed program. During the test, an exception may be raised by the execution of the program. However, if the exception handling can prevent a failure from occurring (self-correction) then the error is not perceptible from the outside. Therefore we cannot affirm that the exception was raised and the exception handler tested because the behaviour is the same if the exception raising occurs or not. In order to verify it, we must add statements giving this information to the program. The designer must especially make sure that these statements do not modify the software behaviour (Cheng, 1989).

4.4.3 Introducing information stemming from the contract

The execution of a program by means of a test sequence may lead a component of this program into an erroneous state (that is into an exceptional state, in the sense given in chapter 3). This state comes from a component utilization or design fault which was not detected during program design. Unfortunately, this situation occurs frequently either because there are no unit tests (that is on each component) or because they are not exhaustive. The erroneous state of a component implies that the program is in an erroneous implementation state (see section 3.2.4 of chapter 3). However, the erroneous character of this implementation state (belonging to the Exception Domain) may not lead to an erroneous state of the program. Let us illustrate the situation by Figure

3.2 of chapter 3. The value of implementation state E can be different from expected value E3 whereas the deduced specification state of E is the one expected (e). This shows an erroneous state of a component (P3) or of its use which is not perceptible from the outside: the output values supplied by the program are those expected by the test sequence; executing the program has not produced a failure.

However, input values supplied later may cause the erroneous state of a program component to be propagated to an erroneous state of the program indicated by the output values.

The test sequence was deduced from the specification and the contract (defining the dependability terms) given by the client. It cannot assess the information produced by the components as these are the result of design choices which are not known by the client beforehand. However, to obtain dependable software, the designer defines contracts for each of the components involved in the program. The properties expressed in these contracts can be placed in the program during design. In this case, at run-time, the reality of the properties (true or false) can be verified. The negation of a property of a component is signalled, for instance, by the propagation of an exception (see section 4.4.2) or a display followed by stop of program execution. Thus, if the state of a component becomes erroneous and if this fact is detected by evaluating the properties associated with this component, the erroneous state of the program implementation is immediately signalled.

The aim of this section is to show the capacities (possibilities and limits) of the Ada language to express invariants in the programs. We will first show that the basic features of the language are not only useful for performing operations but that they implicitly associate properties with these operations which are checked at run-time. We will see later that the language also allows properties to be associated with new created objects, that is with those whose semantics is specific to the problem to be solved.

The properties expressed are at first associated with a specific state, independent of the other states and transitions leading to or from this state. They are often called *assertions*. This assertion is named a *pre-condition* for the properties of a state preceding the execution of an operation and *post-condition* for the properties of a state following the execution of an operation. We will also examine means useful for expressing the general properties linking all states of a component. In this case, the transition notion is not taken into account. These properties are frequently called 'invariants' even though this is a specific case of the general definition proposed in section 2.1.2 of chapter 2.

Properties associated with basic operations
The Ada language provides basic operations associated with **predefined types** [3.3.3(3)]. The standard describes both the function of these operations and the properties concerning them. The violation of a property causes the raising of a predefined exception. Although the number of predefined exceptions is low, the circumstances under which they are raised are many. They are described throughout the standard and are grouped together in this book in section 3.5.1 of chapter

3. This high number of checks allows us to state that the **Ada language is a dependable tool** independent of the way in which it is used in the applications. This aspect is important, as it would be illusory to design sophisticated mechanisms to make a designed application dependable if the dependability notion is not considered when choosing the tool used on completion of the design (the programming language). This assertion does not mean that the execution means, that is the run-time environment (compiler and run-time executive), are dependable; this is however the case for the Ada language on account of the imposed certification constraints. The language dependability assertion only specifies that the dependability requirements have been considered during the definition of the language, that is to say its semantics integrate the property notion and the execution means must evaluate the properties associated with the features of the language.

Without wishing to repeat the list of errors associated with **predefined exceptions**, we would like to point out that: while some errors are well-known (example: division by zero, index to access an array component is out of range), others are not so notorious (example: the variables used in an expression must have previously assigned values except in the case of implicit initialization [3.2.1(9-14)]); most of the predefined exceptions are associated with specifications of operations whereas the raising of STORAGE_ERROR is highly dependent on the run-time environment implementation (see section 3.3.1 of chapter 3).

Properties implicitly associated with created entities
We have already said several times that the Ada language provides, in addition to the data predefined types and associated basic operations, features for building new entities (data structures and operations). These constructors implicitly associate properties with the created entities which are checked at run-time. Knowledge of these associations is interesting as the best use is got out of the basic mechanisms of the language before searching for new means to express the properties.

New **data structures** are defined by means of types, subtypes and derived types. The associated constraints specify only those values which are acceptable. For a variable of a given type, the modification of its value is preceded by a check that verifies that the new value effectively belongs to the constraint domain. For discrete types, constraints can however only be defined as ranges, which is insufficient. To extend this possibility the techniques proposed in the next subsection must be used. However, the 'range' constraint and the subtype notion favour the hierarchical structuring of discrete data sets whilst allowing the subtypes to inherit the operations associated with the types from which they are derived.

```
type       BENEFITS is range 0..100;
subtype    FIRST_TAX_BRACKET   is BENEFITS range 0..10;
subtype    SECOND_TAX_BRACKET  is BENEFITS range 11..50;
subtype    THIRD_TAX_BRACKET   is BENEFITS range 51..100;
```

Specific **subprograms** can be associated with each subtype (in addition to the subprograms associated with the type BENEFITS). When the subprograms are called, the values of the parameters must belong to the corresponding ranges.

The parameter mode ('in', 'out', 'in out') must be defined in the subprogram specification ('in' by default). The following property checks are thus performed:

- an actual parameter associated with an 'in' or 'in out' mode formal parameter must have a value when the subprogram is called;
- an actual parameter associated with an 'out' or 'in out' mode formal parameter must have a value on completion of the execution of the body of the subprogram.

Also, the definition of the formal parameter types in the specification of the subprogram means that the following property is checked: the values communicated on call or handled in the body of the subprogram must comply with the constraints defined by the type.

If the designer knows that to implement a subprogram, specific use of the called subprograms implies new constraints, then the subtype notion is useful for declaring the local variables of the subprogram body as shown in the example below:

```
procedure P(X: in T; Y: out T) is
   subtype ST is T range ... ;
   LOCAL: ST;
begin
   P1(X, LOCAL);
   P2(LOCAL, Y);
end P;
```

Concerning the **task** entry calls, the designer can assert that a call must be accepted immediately or at latest after a delay D. These properties can be expressed directly in Ada as follows:

```
select                              select
        T.E;                                T.E;
else    raise ERROR;                or      delay D;
end select;                                 raise ERROR;
                                    end select;
```

The alternative `delay` of the `select accept` statement gives a means for expressing that an entry must be called before a fixed delay.

In the same light, even if a designer estimates that he or she has expressed all the possible values of an expression in the alternatives of a **case** statement, he or she can add

```
when others => raise ERROR;
```

so that the negation of the expected property ('all possible values have an associated statement sequence') will be signalled (also see the example given in the standard [5.4(7)]).

Explicit association of properties with created entities
Certain properties expressed by the designer are not supported by the features of the language. In effect, the properties of the features are associated with the semantics of the language whereas entities introduced during the design of the application correspond to different semantics. In this case, we must examine how means to check such properties can be implemented with the help of the Ada language features.

First, properties are generally expressed by means of data. Very few concern the **control**. In this case, auxiliary variables are often used to note the evolution of the control path and read its state. For example, a variable local to the body of a package is updated when a subprogram exported by this package is called. We will come back to this aspect at the end of this subsection to examine the case of multi-task applications where task sequencing master is a crucial requirement.

We have insisted on the many benefits of **types** in particular concerning the check that the values of the variables of a type belong to a set of values defined by the type. This set of values is dynamic as elaboration is performed at run-time. For example: the values of the bounds of a scalar type range are evaluated on execution. Thus, the following declaration is allowed:

```
procedure P(X: in T) is
  subtype ST is T range F(X)..G(X);
  ...
```

where F and G are two functions returning values of scalar type T.

Types with discriminant offer another means for expressing a dynamic construction of types (see example given in the standard [3.7.1(11)]).

Even if many properties can be expressed by the correct use of types, all properties cannot be defined by using types alone. For example the set 'all even integer values between 1 and 100, or 200 and 300' cannot be specified by a type. To obtain an Ada expression of such a property, complex Boolean expressions must be defined.

We propose to use an ASSERT procedure raising exception ASSERT_ERROR if the property is false at time of evaluation.

226 Chapter 4: Dependable Ada Software

```ada
package ASSERTION is
  procedure ASSERT(PROPERTY: in BOOLEAN);
  ASSERT_ERROR: exception;  -- raised by ASSERT
end ASSERTION;


package body ASSERTION is
  procedure ASSERT(PROPERTY: in BOOLEAN) is
  begin
    if not PROPERTY then raise ASSERT_ERROR;
    end if;
  end ASSERT;
end ASSERTION;
```

Thus by using operators on the Boolean expressions, complex properties can be evaluated. For instance the fact that a value belongs to the set of integers previously defined is checked as follows:

```ada
subtype LARGE is POSITIVE range 1..300;
subtype FIRST_PART is LARGE range 1..100;
subtype SECOND_PART is LARGE range 200..300;
...
VALUE: LARGE;
...
ASSERT(  (VALUE/2 = 0) and
         (VALUE in FIRST_PART or VALUE in SECOND_PART));
```

Moreover, the checks associated with the type concept concern only one entity (one variable of the considered type) whereas many properties concern the correlation of multiple variables. For example, if A and B are two parameters of a procedure P, the specification of P can require the assertion A<B as a condition at the end of processing procedure P. This property can be expressed using the procedure ASSERT as follows:

```ada
...
ASSERT(A<B);
end P;
```

The solution proposed has a major drawback which did not exist when types are used. The fact that the value of a variable belongs to a set of values defined by the type is a property which is implicitly (no procedure calls) and permanently checked. Procedure ASSERT is suitable if local evaluations of the properties are required. This technique is however unacceptable in other circumstances. In effect, the program would become unreadable (by the multitude of ASSERT calls) because the functional aspects would be mixed up with the evaluations of the properties and, last and not least, the designer may forget to write a call for procedure ASSERT at the location where an error occurs (negation of the property).

If a property is associated with a single variable, then the variable is defined as an abstract data object by means of a package exporting the operations which can be performed on the object. Example for a stack:

```
generic
   type ITEM is private;
package STACK is
   STACK_UNDERFLOW, STACK_OVERFLOW: exception;
   procedure PUSH(X : in ITEM);
   procedure POP(X : out ITEM);
end STACK;
```

The data structure defining the stack is inside the body of the package. The bodies of the exported procedures contain the statements evaluating the properties. For example, the body of procedure POP first checks that the stack is not empty (and raises exception STACK_UNDERFLOW if it is empty). An object is defined by instantiation of the package.

```
package WORK_TO_BE_DONE is new STACK(WORK);
```

where type WORK is assumed to have been previously defined in the program. The use of an object such as

```
WORK_TO_BE_DONE.PUSH(PHONE_WILLIAM);
```

implicitly introduces the evaluation of the associated property (here stack not full).

As the local variables of packages are remanent, the earlier state is conserved on each call of an exported subprogram. We can thus easily implement the general **invariant** notion introduced in section 3.2 of chapter 3.

Procedure ASSERT can evaluate a condition concerning several objects. For example:

We must always have the relation A<B in the whole frame.

In this case, the condition must be checked each time A or B is updated. For instance, this check would be induced by the statement:

```
A:= B - 2*A;
```

To solve this problem, we propose that A and B are no longer data (memory elements) but 'objects' which are correlated with an assertion (A<B). In order to implement this approach in Ada, variables (A and B) are considered as tasks of a

single type (BUFFER) which has two entries (READ and WRITE). We could replace this type of task by a generic package exporting two procedures (READ and WRITE). This package will be instantiated on the creation of each variable. We have chosen a task type assuming that variables (A and B) are shared in a multi-task application.

Let us give general information on the principles before examine details of the programming. A request for assigning (that is writing) a value X in the variable A is made calling A.WRITE(X) where A is the associated task. It involves a call for checking the assertion (X<B), if and only if the other entity (B) was previously assigned at least one time. Of course, such an implementation is not acceptable if hard constraints exist on temporal performance and if the variables to which a property must be associated are numerous. We give this solution especially as an exercise in style.

Now let us comment the programming. This program uses the procedure ASSERT from the package ASSERTION previously defined in this section. In the given example, variables A and B will be of type RESOURCE. The package RESOURCE (given in section B.2.1. of appendix B) manages the access (READ and WRITE) to the values of the variables used in the invariant. First this package imposes a write operation (to initialize the variables) then gives guarantees that the read and/or write operations are not made simultaneously.

Variable assignment is made by calling the procedure which has the same name as the variable and the variable is read by calling the function which has the same name. For example:

A:= '$'; is replaced by   A('$');
...:= ...A; is not modified ...:= ...A; However A is a variable in the first statement and a function in the second one.

A and B are defined in the package A_LESS_THAN_B as a RESOURCE of the CHARACTER type. The use of these variables can raise two exceptions: INIT_ERROR if read is attempted on an uninitialized variable and A_GREATER_THAN_OR_EQUAL_TO_B if the assertion A<B is not true. A_INIT (respectively B_INIT) is true if A (respectively B) was initialized.

As the problem is symmetrical for A and B the examination of function A and procedure A is sufficient to understand the solution proposed.

Remark that the package CONTROL_ASSERT is introduced in order to differentiate between function A and resource A in A.READ call inside function A.

```
with ASSERTION; use ASSERTION;
  -- previously defined
with RESOURCE;
```

```ada
package A_LESS_THAN_B is
  package CHARTASK is new RESOURCE(ITEM=>CHARACTER);
  INIT_ERROR: exception;
  A_GREATER_THAN_OR_EQUAL_TO_B: exception
              renames ASSERTION.ASSERT_ERROR;
  A_INIT, B_INIT :BOOLEAN :=FALSE;
  procedure ASSERT(B: in BOOLEAN) renames ASSERTION.ASSERT;
  package CONTROL_ASSERT is
    A,B:CHARTASK.BUFFER;
  end CONTROL_ASSERT;
      -- the following functions A and B return the
      -- value of the variables using the same name
  function A return CHARACTER;
  function B return CHARACTER;
      -- the following procedures A and B assign the
      -- parameter value to the variable using
      -- the same name
  procedure A(X:in CHARACTER);
  procedure B(X:in CHARACTER);
end A_LESS_THAN_B;

package body A_LESS_THAN_B is
  package body CONTROL_ASSERT is
  begin
     null; -- to start the two tasks
  end CONTROL_ASSERT;
  function A return CHARACTER is
    X: CHARACTER;
  begin
    if A_INIT then
       CONTROL_ASSERT.A.READ(X);
       return X;
    else
       raise INIT_ERROR;
    end if;
  end A;
  function B return CHARACTER is
    ... -- idem with B instead of A
  end B;
  procedure A(X: in CHARACTER) is
  begin
    ASSERT(not(B_INIT) or else X<B);
    CONTROL_ASSERT.A.WRITE(X);
    A_INIT:=TRUE;
  end A;
```

```
    procedure B(X: in CHARACTER) is
      ... -- idem with B (resp. A) instead of A (resp. B)
    end B;
  end A_LESS_THAN_B;
```

A complete example of the use of this package is given in section B.2.3 of appendix B (procedure TEST_INV). This example shows that this approach makes the use of the variables (A and B) not easy (or at least special).

Anna and TSL tools

We are agreed that the proposed solution is quite cumbersome. It requires the introduction of many additional elements into the Ada program. A more elegant solution consists in introducing the properties as comments in the Ada program by means of a formal language (and not in English). Then, a preprocessor automatically generates the statements required for the checks. Even if these statements are bulky, the source text written by the programmer is still easy to read.

We will now briefly present two examples of languages allowing assertions to be expressed with formal comments. ANNA (ANNotated Ada) (Luckham, 1990) and TSL (Task Sequencing Language) (Helmbold, 1985) were developed at Stanford University. Tools allow a static analysis of the properties and the generation of supplementary Ada code in order to check the properties at run-time.

First, assertions can be used to increase the constraints associated with **types**. Thus we can easily express a correlation between two components of a record structure. Example:

```
  type PORTRAIT is
    record
      HEIGHT: INTEGER range 1..24;
      WIDTH:  INTEGER range 1..80;
    end record;
  --| where P: PORTRAIT => P.HEIGHT > P.WIDTH;
```

It defines that, whatever the value of the variable P of type PORTRAIT is, the invariant P.HEIGHT>P.WIDTH must be true.

It is also possible to specify an enumeration type which is not continuous. For instance, here variable X is even:

```
  X: INTEGER range 1..10;
  --| X mod 2 = 0;
```

These constructions allow variables to be linked together:

```
  U, V : INTEGER := 1;
  --| U <= V;
```

This possibility is especially used for **subprogram parameters**. It allows us to distinguish between the input and the output values of parameters. Example, before execution of P we must have the relation X<Y and after execution of P the relation: the output value of Y is less than the one given as input.

```
procedure P (X: in T; Y: in out T);
  --| where
  --|   in  (X<Y),
  --|   out (Y< in Y);
```

If **packages** are used, the state of the package or of one of its components can be handled globally. Thus, if a subprogram of a package P specifies **out** (P'STATE = **in** P'STATE) then the calls of the exported subprograms must not modify the state of the package (i.e. the values of the local variables).

The correlations between subprograms are made by axiomatic definitions. Example:

```
--| axiom
--|   for all S: STACK'TYPE; X, Y : ITEM =>
--|     S [PUSH(X); POP(Y)] = S;
```

specifies that the stack S is unchanged after a PUSH call followed by a POP call.

The conditions and the consequences of raising an **exception** can be specified (see sections 3.3.2 and 3.6.1 of chapter 3).

As far as **tasks** are concerned, the properties handle events. At first, a task expresses an expected sequencing of the events performed. The following example specifies that a philosopher, after its activation (first event), must think and eat (events occurring in an undefined order) before terminating (last event).

```
?P : PHILOSOPHER;
whenever any activates ?P then
   ?P performs THINKING and
   ?P performs EATING
before ?P terminates;
```

On execution of any task of the PHILOSOPHER type, the TSL run-time system checks that the expected sequence is effectively the one run.

Properties can also describe relations expected between events which concern several tasks. We examined the following example, which formally expresses the relations which exist between the OPERATOR, PUMP and CUSTOMER tasks of a petrol pump system, in section 3.7.2.

```
    when PUMP accepts OPERATOR at TURN_ON
      then PUMP accepts CUSTOMER at START_PUMPING =>
      PUMP accepts CUSTOMER at FINISH_PUMPING =>
      PUMP calls OPERATOR at CHARGE
    before PUMP accepts OPERATOR at TURN_ON;
```

At run-time, rendezvous will occur between the three tasks. The sequencing of these rendezvous is compared with the expected sequencing (that is the one defined using formal comments). The violation of the property raises a predefined exception (ANNA_ERROR).

The properties introduced for the debugging of programs as a Fault Removal technique can be kept in the embedded programs if the time constraints allow this, i.e. if the delay due to the comparison between the expected and real behaviour is acceptable. These properties allow errors to be detected as close as possible to their origin and then to be corrected by means of the Fault Tolerance techniques presented in the following section.

4.5 Fault Tolerance

In this section we will study ways of using the Ada language (and particularly the exception mechanism) in order to implement the Fault Tolerance techniques. These techniques consist in limiting the consequences of a residual fault which was not avoided during the design and not detected and removed during debugging or operational checking. These techniques can also be used for *defensive programming* purposes: protection against external faults (coming from a new release of a used package, or erroneous data provided by a sensor, etc.). In this section we will successively describe:

- the way of detecting and locating an error (section 4.5.1),
- the implementation of the techniques in Ada: Retry, Recovery Blocks, N-version programming, Exception Monitor Task (sections 4.5.2 to 4.5.5),
- the use of common error handling (section 4.5.6),
- the normal behaviour recovery points (section 4.5.7).

4.5.1 Detection, location, diagnosis, perception

The query functions on the state of the entities handled by the program execution are **error detection** means. The language offers some of these functions for certain features. For instance, evaluation of attribute CALLABLE for a task can detect an erroneous state (a task is not callable) and then prevent a call leading to an error which would be detected by the raising of exception TASKING_ERROR. The

designer can, in addition, add such query functions on the state of the entities that he or she creates. Consider for instance, a package STACK which exports the STACK_EMPTY Boolean function. A specific state is detected explicitly (check statement), for example by:
```
if not STACK_EMPTY then POP(X);
end if;
```

The query functions and the exceptions are two additional tools. The first must be used for prevention purposes, that is if the erroneous situation is considered as probable. In this case, its handling is a specific functional case and not an exceptional case.

Invariants are implicitly associated with Ada features. Their violation provokes the raising of predefined exceptions They are useful for **detecting** design errors as stated in section 4.4.3. This avoids the insertion of explicit and numerous check statements into the program and makes the program much more readable and dependable because checks cannot be omitted. The use the subprograms exported by a package which specify user-exceptions, corresponds to the same situation.

Implicit detection and exception raising are also useful because in certain situations check statements cannot be programmed to examine the validity of a property. For instance, the remaining memory size is not available because this information cannot be exploited (the memory size used by Ada features at run-time depends on the run-time environment and is not known). Exception STORAGE_ERROR is therefore necessary. The same applies to the user-exceptions of a package because the private variables of the package (e.g. index of a stack top) cannot be accessed.

The use of exceptions also avoids useless checks. Consider, for instance, a program that makes a lot of integer divisions. Suppose that the divisors are never equal to zero, but that this is not proved. For safety reasons we can make a test on the divisor before each division. This will increase the volume of the code and the execution time although the divisors will never be equal to zero. The use of exceptions avoids all these drawbacks but nevertheless provides a reaction, just in case.

Readability may be reduced because of **location** needs. The smaller the frame with which the exception handler is associated, the higher the accuracy of the cause. The use of small frames can make the program unreadable as it may not be easy to distinguish between the statements proper to the normal behaviour and the statements added to implement of fault tolerance techniques.

The **diagnosis** associated with exceptions poses a real problem because a given exception name can cover several causes. This especially concerns predefined exceptions. For instance, exception CONSTRAINT_ERROR can be due to the index overflow of an array, a subtype variable value out of its range, etc. It seems that the use of very narrow frames would allow a single diagnosis to be given but this is not obvious. For instance, the following statement can raise a CONSTRAINT_ERROR in three cases:
```
A(i) := expression;
```

1. i does not belong to the range of array A, or

2. the evaluation of the expression raises CONSTRAINT_ERROR, or

3. the result of the expression is not consistent with array A component type constraints.

Moreover, the difficulty in establishing a diagnosis is increased because of the exception propagations. If, in the preceding example, the expression calls a function which raises exception CONSTRAINT_ERROR without handling it, this exception is propagated. Thus it will be handled at the frame which contains the assignment statement including the expression which called the function, even though the cause is associated with the function implementation. There is a risk that the designer may consider that the exception is caused only by the overflow of index i and therefore provide an unsuitable handler.

For this reason, we have recommended several times that the names of propagated exceptions be specified, in particular by systematically changing the names of predefined exceptions. This is obtained by:

when ... => **raise** X;

where X accurately defines the semantics of the error. If the identifier of this exception is not visible (anonymous exception), it is preferable to have a name specific to subprogram P, such as FAILURE_IN_P, or a general name, such as FAILURE, and visible throughout the program, thus specifying the failure of a called subprogram and not a basic operation. For this, exception handlers are completed by:

when ... => **raise** FAILURE_IN_P;

or

when ... => **raise** FAILURE;

In this case, statement
```
A(I) := J + K * F(L) ;
```

can raise:

- exception CONSTRAINT_ERROR on account of the structure defined by the statement (array index out of range, overflow of intermediary results of arithmetic operations, value assigned not in compliance with type of array elements) which can be corrected by acting on this structure (modification of value I, etc.) or
- exception FAILURE_IN_F on account of the services used (call for function F).

The raising of an exception signals the detection of an error. The program can perceive it or not, that is take its occurrence into account. For instance, the body of a subprogram can raise an exception that it does not perceive if it does not have a handler associated with this exception.

As far as the **perception** of an error is concerned, we can distinguish between three cases:

1. An error can be *masked*, that is to say, its occurrence within the frame is not perceptible outside the frame. This is achieved by an exception handler associated with the frame (**when** ... => ...) which does not propagate an exception voluntarily or not (by the **raise** statement or a new exception raised during the handling).

2. An error can be *perceived from outside* the frame by propagation if:

   - no exception handlers are provided (special case for tasks),
   - an exception handler cannot make a complete correction and again raises an exception to indicate this,
   - the execution of an exception handler involves an error which generates the raising of another exception,
   - the declarative part of the frame cannot be elaborated.

3. An error may occur but *not be seen*. Ada authorizes the suppression of the checking of (implicit) assertions associated with predefined exceptions by means of **pragma** SUPPRESS. However, if such an assertion is false, the execution will continue and may provoke progressive damage that will be difficult to repair. For instance, the suppression of the INDEX_CHECK verification [11.7(8)] on the index of an array, can generate modifications in the memory which are not immediately perceptible, but which may later give aberrant results. With this example, we can illustrate another phenomenon: some checks cannot be suppressed. For instance, if the microprocessor monitors a segmented memory (e.g. INTEL processors) and if a data segment is associated with each task, then the suppression of the INDEX_CHECK limits the uncontrolled access to the segment; an exception is raised by the microprocessor whenever there is an attempt to access data out of its segment.

Note the specific case of anonymous exceptions [11.2(5)]. In this situation, the erroneous frame propagates an exception which is perceived by the calling frame but cannot be identified by this frame. Only the use of an 'others' choice allows a handling operation to be performed.

Implementation of the techniques

In the following sections we will describe the implementation of Fault Tolerance techniques in Ada. Remember that two classes of techniques exist:

- the **backward** techniques: some consist in restarting the execution with new data (Retry Mode); others consist in starting the execution of a new alternate with the previous data (Recovery Blocks);
- the **forward** techniques which consist in going to a new faultless state (N-version programming and exception monitor task).

For backward techniques, previously saved data must sometimes be recovered. This aspect will be dealt with in section 4.5.7.

Moreover, in this section, the most significant parts of the implementations are provided. Full examples will be given in appendix B.

Before describing fault tolerance technique implementations, the following question must be examined: 'are some features of the language, taken separately, fault tolerant by nature?'. Two features are to be highlighted:

- in Ada, **default values** can be associated with the subprogram 'in' and 'in out' mode parameters. Thus, absence of a precise value supplied on the call of a subprogram does not lead to the occurrence of an error. This point of view is however debatable as the numerous checks carried out by the compiler signal the omission of a parameter if default values are not used;
- the alternative 'when others =>' of the case statement handles the values not associated with other alternatives. It can therefore be considered as a device to tolerate the omission of these values. However, if the type of values is defined statically, it is preferable to list these values and not use the alternative 'when others =>' so that the compiler will detect and signal omissions.

In the following sections, we will propose only the implementations of the techniques described in section 2.4 of chapter 2. In particular, choice of techniques according to application characters will not be rediscussed.

4.5.2 Retry

The retry technique consists in executing the erroneous frame again after having corrected its input data. For this point, a problem is posed in Ada concerning the restoring of some global variables and the actual parameter values. This aspect will be developed in section 4.5.7.

Subprograms
In order to implement the retry technique after the detection of an error by the raising of an exception, we would like to consider the use of the **goto** statement:

```ada
BLOCK_NAME :
  declare
    -- declarative part
  begin
    NORMAL_FUNCTION;
  exception
    when EXCEPTION_X =>
      RECOVERY_ACTIONS;
      goto BLOCK_NAME;     -- not legal Ada
  end BLOCK_NAME;
```

This transfer of control is **forbidden** because BLOCK_NAME is not visible at the place of the **goto** statement. In addition, the transfer of control from the exception handler of a frame back to a statement of this frame is also forbidden [5.9(5)]. Lastly we have several times advised against the use of the goto statement.

The exception handler must therefore contain the whole code required to recover and perform the function provided by the frame.

```ada
procedure READ_INT_2_TRIAL(I: out INTEGER) is
begin
  GET(I);
exception
  when DATA_ERROR =>
    SKIP_LINE;   -- recovery action
    GET(I);
end READ_INT_2_TRIAL;
```

DATA_ERROR is raised when the input characters are not digits. Procedure SKIP_LINE allows the keyboard buffer to be flushed out (recovery action) before getting the integer value again.

Procedure READ_INT_2_TRIAL does not handle a second error. If another exception occurs in the exception handler, another frame must be nested in it. The following procedure must be written:

```ada
procedure READ_INT_3_TRIAL(I: out INTEGER) is
begin
  GET(I);
exception
  when DATA_ERROR =>
    begin
      SKIP_LINE;   -- recovery action
      GET(I);
    exception
      when DATA_ERROR =>
        SKIP_LINE; -- recovery action
        GET(I);
    end;
end READ_INT_3_TRIAL;
```

The same problem is posed for a third error, and so on. In order to provide a general solution, an extra frame must be introduced into the frame of the procedure:

```
procedure READ_INT_WITH_LOOP(I: out INTEGER) is
begin
  loop
    begin       -- extra frame
      GET(I);
      exit;     -- exit if GET is correct
    exception
      when DATA_ERROR => SKIP_LINE;  -- recovery action
    end;
  end loop;
end READ_INT_WITH_LOOP;
```

In this way a fault tolerant reading procedure is implemented using the retry technique (using **loop** and **exit** statements). In order to limit the number of trials, the **loop** statement should be preceded by a **while** clause.

The following procedure gives an example of another implementation of the retry technique using recursivity. The same fault tolerant reading procedure then becomes:

```
procedure RECURSIVE_READ_INT(I: out INTEGER) is
begin
  GET(I);
exception
  when DATA_ERROR =>
    SKIP_LINE;           -- recovery action
    RECURSIVE_READ_INT(I);
end RECURSIVE_READ_INT;
```

This implementation calls for some remarks: first, recursivity and exception mechanisms are not easily mastered together by the designer; also, it might cause errors due to a lack of memory space leading to the raising of exception STORAGE_ERROR (e.g. the 'stacking' of successive calls).

Tasks

In the case of tasks, the termination of exception handling provokes the completion of the task. To recreate a copy of the erroneous task the feature *'access on tasks'* must be used in order to dynamically create a new task which has the same type and the same name (clone).

The two following examples illustrate this method. In both cases, a main procedure (TEST_CLONE in the first example, and SELF_CORR in the second example) manages a SERVER task and a USER task. Assume that the SERVER task raises an exception **during** a rendezvous accepted on entry REQUEST then prematurely dies. In our example, exception DATA_ERROR is raised when a character which is not a digit is entered. The same exception is propagated to the caller (the USER task).

The following scenario takes place:

- the USER task will wait for the regeneration of the SERVER task,
- in the first example, the manager procedure (TEST_CLONE) will restart the SERVER task and generate an exact copy of it,
- in the second example, the SERVER task will recreate itself.

Of course it would be better to handle the exceptions raised during the rendezvous in the server task. This is obtained by adding a statement block such as:

```
accept REQUEST do
  begin
    ...
  exception
    ...
  end;
end REQUEST;
```

However, exceptions may not be handled locally and exceptions can be raised by the handler of the block.

First Example: the main procedure TEST_CLONE creates the SERVER and USER tasks. The USER calls the SERVER on entry REQUEST. If an integer is got by the IIO.GET(I) statement the tasks are TERMINATED (in a normal way) and then procedure TEST_CLONE ends. If a character different from a digit is provided, exception DATA_ERROR is raised in the SERVER task (which dies) and then in the USER task (due to the propagation). In this last task, the exception handling suspends the execution of the task during a delay (0.03 sec.) before a new request (SERVER.REQUEST) is made. This delay is used by procedure TEST_CLONE to recreate the SERVER task, etc.

```
with TEXT_IO; use TEXT_IO;
procedure TEST_CLONE is
  package IIO is new INTEGER_IO(INTEGER);

  task type T_TYPE_SERVER is
    entry REQUEST;
  end T_TYPE_SERVER;
  type ACC_T_TYPE_SERVER is access T_TYPE_SERVER;
  SERVER: ACC_T_TYPE_SERVER;
  task type T_TYPE_USER;
  type ACC_T_TYPE_USER is access T_TYPE_USER;
  USER: ACC_T_TYPE_USER;
```

```ada
task body T_TYPE_SERVER is
-- server task which can terminate in a failed status
  I: INTEGER;
begin
  accept REQUEST do
    PUT("Give an integer please :");
    IIO.GET(I);-- exception if an integer is not obtained
    NEW_LINE;
  end REQUEST;
exception
  when DATA_ERROR => SKIP_LINE;
                     -- to flush out keyboard buffer
                     -- (recovery action).
                     -- Then the task is completed
end T_TYPE_SERVER;

task body T_TYPE_USER is  -- task asking for a service
begin
  loop
    begin       -- nested block
      SERVER.REQUEST;
      exit;    -- RendezVous OK => USER task terminates
    exception
      when DATA_ERROR => -- propagated during rendezvous
        PUT_LINE
          ("Task USER is waiting for another SERVER");
        delay 0.03;  -- wait for the SERVER rescue
      when TASKING_ERROR => -- 2nd try fails
        PUT_LINE(" SERVER ended. Can't retry. ");
        exit;
    end;
  end loop;
end T_TYPE_USER;

begin    -- of procedure TEST_CLONE
  SERVER:= new T_TYPE_SERVER;   -- first elaboration
  USER:= new T_TYPE_USER;
  loop
    BLOCK:
      begin
        delay 0.01;
        if SERVER'TERMINATED then
          -- SERVER ended normally
          if USER'TERMINATED then
            exit; -- normal ending
```

```
              else
                 -- SERVER ended prematurely
                 -- SERVER is restarted
                SERVER:=new T_TYPE_SERVER;
                PUT_LINE
                  ("Controller restarts SERVER task");
              end if;
           end if;
        end BLOCK;
     end loop;
  end TEST_CLONE;
```

Wait for USER task can be implemented using an accept statement on a new entry (named for example RESUME) called by the main procedure (TEST_CLONE) instead of a delay statement whose parameter value is difficult to estimate.

Second Example: the main procedure SELF_CORR creates the SERVER and USER tasks. The USER task (respectively the normal operation of the SERVER task) is the same as the one defined in the first example. When exception DATA_ERROR is raised in the SERVER task, the exception handling of **this** task recreates the task by calling REGENERATE_SERVER. This is self-regeneration.

Remarks:

1. the first SERVER task (which raises the exception) still exists but becomes anonymous because the SERVER variable value is assigned when the second copy is created. In our example the anonymous task is terminated (no statement after the REGENERATE_SERVER call and the SERVER variable is declared outside the T_TYPE_SERVER body);

2. recreation cannot be done directly by the 'SERVER: = **new** T_TYPE_SERVER;' statement in the exception handler because we are in the body of T_TYPE_SERVER.

```
with TEXT_IO; use TEXT_IO;
procedure SELF_CORR is
   package IIO is new INTEGER_IO(INTEGER);

   ...
   -- the same as TEST_CLONE specification

   procedure REGENERATE_SERVER is
   begin
      SERVER := new T_TYPE_SERVER;
   end REGENERATE_SERVER;
```

```ada
task body T_TYPE_SERVER is
-- server task which can terminate in a failed status
   I:INTEGER;
begin
   accept REQUEST do
      PUT("Give an integer please :");
      IIO.GET(I);    -- exception if an integer is not given
      NEW_LINE;
   end REQUEST;
exception
   when DATA_ERROR =>
      SKIP_LINE;            -- to flush the wrong characters
      REGENERATE_SERVER;  -- Self-Regeneration
         -- it is impossible to regenerate directly with :
         -- SERVER := new T_TYPE_SERVER;
         -- because T_TYPE_SERVER is not visible here
end T_TYPE_SERVER;

task body T_TYPE_USER is -- task asking a service
begin
   -- ...
   -- the same as in TEST_CLONE
end T_TYPE_USER;
begin
   SERVER:=new T_TYPE_SERVER;
   USER:=new T_TYPE_USER;
end SELF_CORR;
```

However this implementation will create tasks dynamically. It can provoke new errors such as a STORAGE_ERROR if there is no garbage collector to reuse the free memory.

4.5.3 Recovery blocks

The Recovery Block technique consists in:

- having several alternate implementations of the same specification,
- having a dependable acceptance test,
- executing the alternates one by one, until we find one which is not erroneous.

This last criterion is valued by an acceptance test obtained from the invariant of the contract which defines dependability terms or from the specification. Time constraints (like delays) can be associated with this technique.

The implementation of this technique by means of procedures is proposed in (Burns, 1989). We propose an improved version which defines a generic monitor (RB_GEN generic package) of the blocks implemented as tasks. The proposed package menages three alternates referenced by access types (PT1, PT2, PT3). These types are generic parameters to be defined at instantiation-time for a specific application. A generic package is of interest for monitoring the 'task-blocks' because in a real application, it is then possible to have many uses of the recovery block implementation, that is many instantiations, in several locations. Moreover the types of the 'task-blocks' (PT1, PT2, PT3) can be different at different locations and specified by instantiation.

As the 'task-blocks' are generic, the type of the results is not unique. Moreover the check of the results depends on the invariant definition. For these reasons the acceptance test is also a generic parameter defined as a generic access type (PT_AC_T). The acceptance test execution is started by a generic procedure (RN_ACT) which must be provided at package instantiation.

The result of the acceptance test is communicated by means of a rendezvous on the RESULT entry of the RB_CONTROLLER task.

A last generic parameter is MAX_TIME which fixes a deadline for the computation of **one** alternate.

Let us give some comments on the implementation of the generic package. The RB_CONTROLLER task initializes the first alternate (N:=1;): procedure INIT creates the task associated with PT1 (for details see section B.3.2 of appendix B). Then this task waits for the end of this alternate execution with a watchdog (**select accept** END_PROC ... **or delay** CHRONO-CLOCK; ...).

If the result is not supplied before the delay is up, the process begins again (**loop** statement) and then the next alternate is chosen (N:=N+1;).

If the result is given in time, its value is checked by the acceptance test task: procedure RUN_ACT starts the task and the diagnosis is waited for (**accept** RESULT). If the result is not correct, the process begins again (**loop** statement) and then the next alternate is chosen.

If the result is obtained in time and is correct (i.e. is in accordance with the acceptance test), the iterative process is stopped by an exit from the loop.

```
-- this generic package RB allows a recovery block to be
-- implemented with 3 alternates and an acceptance test with
-- a watchdog for each of them
```
with TEXT_IO; **use** TEXT_IO;
with CALENDAR; **use** CALENDAR;
generic
   type PT1 **is private**;   -- access to alternate 1
   type PT2 **is private**;   -- access to alternate 2
   type PT3 **is private**;   -- access to alternate 3
   type PT_AC_T **is private**;   -- access to task
                           -- acceptance test

244 Chapter 4: Dependable Ada Software

```ada
      MAX_TIME : DURATION:=1.5; -- deadline to obtain a result
   with procedure INIT( NUM:in INTEGER; P1: in out PT1;
                        P2: in out PT2; P3: in out PT3);
      -- external procedure to be supplied which will
      -- generate one of the alternates
      -- according to NUM and to the tasks types
   with procedure RUN_ACT(P:out PT_AC_T);
      -- external procedure to be supplied which
      -- will start the acceptance test

package RB_GEN is
   NB_MAX : constant INTEGER :=3;
   subtype NO_TASK is INTEGER range 1..NB_MAX;
   task RB_CONTROLLER is
      entry START;
      entry END_PROC;
      entry RESULT(B: in BOOLEAN);
   end RB_CONTROLLER;
end;

with TEXT_IO, CALENDAR; use TEXT_IO, CALENDAR;
package body RB_GEN is
   ALTERNATE1 : PT1; ALTERNATE2 : PT2; ALTERNATE3 : PT3;
   T_AC_T : PT_AC_T;
   N : No_TASK;

   task body RB_CONTROLLER is
      CHRONO:TIME := CLOCK + MAX_TIME;
      CORRECT_TERMINATION: BOOLEAN;
   begin
      accept START;
      N:=1;
      loop
         INIT(N,ALTERNATE1,ALTERNATE2,ALTERNATE3);
         select
            accept END_PROC; -- the ALTERNATE N is terminated
               RUN_ACT(T_AC_T); -- run acceptance Test
               accept RESULT(B:in BOOLEAN) do
                  CORRECT_TERMINATION := B;
               end RESULT;
               if CORRECT_TERMINATION then
                  exit;
               end if;
```

```
        or
          delay CHRONO - CLOCK; -- alternate execution is
                                -- not terminated in time
                PUT_LINE("Time over");
        end select;
        if N < NB_MAX then
          -- the next alternate is chosen
          N := N + 1;
          CHRONO:= CHRONO + MAX_TIME;   -- timer is reset
        else exit;
        end if;
      end loop;
    end RB_CONTROLLER;
  end RB_GEN;
```

A complete example of an application which uses this package is given in section B.3.2 of appendix B.

As the Ada language does not authorize the definition of anonymous accesses (but only accesses to defined types), the programming of this example is cumbersome: see INIT procedure for instance. The use of tasks allows the successive alternates employed by the user of the block to be passed as parameters. However, the example proposed does not consider the case when an alternate is a communicating task. In this case the 'domino effect' must be taken into account (see section 2.4.3 of chapter 2). Moreover, the delay will be effectively respected if the run-time executive is pre-emptive and if the alternates have a lower priority than the RB_CONTROLLER task.

4.5.4 N-version programming

The Ada language was used by (Avizienis, 1988) (quoted in (Burns, 1990)) to write **one** version of a N-version program. The other versions were written in other languages.

We propose to use Ada tasking to implement a full Ada N-version program. Each version is executed by a task and a comparison task accepts (selective accept) the results produced by the different versions. The use of the **or delay** option of the selective accept allows the delayed versions to be detected. As in the previous section, the task manager must be pre-emptive and the priority of the comparison task higher than that of the versions.

The following program corresponds to the implementation of a generic package which monitors NB_TASK_MAX versions (in our example three). The interest of this package lies in the possibility of having several 'N-version' frames in an application. This is obtained by several instantiations at several locations in the program. Therefore the types of the tasks (versions and voter) can be different. They must be supplied during the instantiation of the generic package. In order to implement this, we have used the access to task type because it can be used for parameters (types PT1, PT2, PT3).

In the example, package NVP is provided:

- to start the VERSIONs (with an external procedure INIT which must be supplied during the instantiation because it depends on the type of tasks),
- to check that the versions are terminated before a specified deadline (TIME_OUT),
- to start the VOTER task (external procedure GO_VOTE) which determines the result which is supplied to the application.

Package SEPARATE_TYPES defines array types indexed by the number of versions (NB_TASK_MAX). This package is required to be able to use the same types in the monitoring package (NVP), in the voter procedure (GO_VOTE) and in the tasks associated with each version (PTi). For instance, common types such as these are required to share the data produced by the versions and used by the voter. In the application proposed as an example in section B.4.2 of appendix B, the result is composed of an integer and a character. Type TAB_BOOL_TASK is used to define array TAB_CONTROL storing the end of the running of the versions.

Package NVP contains the task NVP_CONTROLLER which:

- waits for a start from the user program (INIT),
- waits for the results of each version or for the deadline,
- calls the procedure GO_VOTE to start the voter task, passing the list of the tasks which are terminated.

```
-------------------------------------------------------------
--
-- This package which contains TYPES and constant
-- definitions is SEPARATEd because used at the same time
-- by the generic package NVP monitoring the versions and
-- the versions user program (NVP_USER: in section B.4.2)
--
-------------------------------------------------------------
package SEPARATE_TYPES is
   NB_TASK_MAX: constant INTEGER :=3;
   subtype NB_TASK is INTEGER range 1..NB_TASK_MAX;
   type TAB_BOOL_TASK is array(NB_TASK) of BOOLEAN;
   type TAB_INT is array(NB_TASK) of INTEGER;
   type TAB_CHAR is array(NB_TASK) of CHARACTER;
end SEPARATE_TYPES;
```

```ada
----------------------------------------------------------
---
-- generic package NVP
with TEXT_IO; use TEXT_IO;
with CALENDAR; use CALENDAR;
with SEPARATE_TYPES; use SEPARATE_TYPES;
generic
   type PT1 is private;     -- access to first task
   type PT2 is private;     -- access to second task
   type PT3 is private;     -- access to third task
   type PT_VOTER is private; -- access to voter task
   TIME_OUT : DURATION:=1.5; -- deadline to wait for results
   with procedure INIT( P1:out PT1; P2:out PT2;
                        P3:out PT3; T:out TAB_BOOL_TASK);
-- external procedure which must be supplied to start
-- the versions  (3 tasks) according to their types
   with procedure GO_VOTE( P:in out PT_VOTER;
                           T: in TAB_BOOL_TASK);
-- external procedure which will start the vote
package NVP is
   type T_NB_RESULT is range 0..NB_TASK_MAX;
   task NVP_CONTROLLER is
      entry START;
      entry PROC_END(N: in NB_TASK);
      entry RESULT(B: in BOOLEAN);
   end NVP_CONTROLLER;
end NVP;

package body NVP is
   package IIO is new INTEGER_IO(T_NB_RESULT);
   use IIO;
   VERSION1 : PT1; VERSION2 : PT2; VERSION3 : PT3;
   VOTER : PT_VOTER;
   N : NB_TASK;
   task body NVP_CONTROLLER is
      DEADLINE_TIME: TIME;
      NB_RESULT: T_NB_RESULT:=0;
      TAB_CONTROL: TAB_BOOL_TASK;
   begin
      accept START do
         DEADLINE_TIME:= CLOCK + TIME_OUT;
         INIT(VERSION1,VERSION2,VERSION3,TAB_CONTROL);
      end START; -- start the versions
```

248 Chapter 4: Dependable Ada Software

```
         loop
           select
             accept PROC_END(N: in NB_TASK) do
               -- the N version is ended
               TAB_CONTROL(N):=TRUE;
             end PROC_END;
             NB_RESULT:=NB_RESULT+1;
             if NB_RESULT=T_NB_RESULT'LAST then exit;
             -- if all the versions have terminated => exit
             end if;
           or
             delay DEADLINE_TIME - CLOCK;
               PUT_LINE("Timeout before the 3 results");
               exit;
           end select;
         end loop;
         PUT("Nb results: "); PUT(NB_RESULT); NEW_LINE;
         case NB_RESULT is
           when 0 => PUT_LINE("No result!");
           when others => GO_VOTE(VOTER,TAB_CONTROL);
                            -- start the vote
         end case;
       end NVP_CONTROLLER;
    end NVP;
```

A complete example of the use this program is given in section B.4 of appendix B.

4.5.5 Exception Monitor Task

We stated in the section 3.6.2 of the previous chapter and developed in section A.5.2 of appendix A the case of the Motorola RMS68K kernel which allows an 'exception monitor task' to be created. Such a task monitors the current task and takes control in case of an error. Each time the current task reaches a typical state (which is a normal or an exceptional state), the exception monitor task can take decisions concerning the progress of the monitored current task and also can change the state of this task. The exception monitor task can react differently therefore to a given exception according to the history of the erroneous task.

The programming of this technique in Ada would allow the exception handler to take the past of the monitored operation into account. For an exception raised by a given statement of the program, the exception handling would depend not only on the frame in which the statement is, but also on the history of the execution (the path that led to this situation). We think that this may be of interest to facilitate the design and read programs. As the exception feature allows the normal operation to be separated from the error handler (for a given frame), the principle of an exception monitor task provides the separation between a sequential application and its exceptional behaviour.

Consider the following example where P and V are 'access' and 'free' statements to the semaphore S:

```
begin
    -- ... 1
    -- ...
    P(S);
    -- ...
    -- ... 2    Critical section protected by S
    -- ...
    V(S);
    -- ... 3
exception
    -- ...
end;
```

If an exception is raised at location 2, the exception handler should free semaphore S, whereas this action must not be performed if the exception is raised at location 1 or 3. If the exception handler does not free S, then the raising of the exception in the critical part 2 will lead to the blocking of the resource and will undoubtedly involve a malfunction of the application. We must consider each part (1, 2, 3) as a frame with specific associated exception handlers.

In this example, we can see that the exception handling to be undertaken depends on the history of the execution process. In this example, a local variable could be used to note the part in which the exception is raised in order to inform the exception handler. This variable does not correspond to an entity of the 'normal' processing and, moreover, in more complex systems, the exceptional information mixed with the functional part (the body) would make the design more difficult and the software obtained less readable.

We will give an example in which the error handling does not depend on the state of the application at the time of the error occurring, but on the history of the application (sequence of events characterizing the execution of the application). We propose a design which separates the 'normal' behaviour from the 'exceptional' behaviour and then its implementation in Ada.

The system is a simplified cash dispenser taking user interaction errors into account. Figure 4.4 shows the normal operation.

250   *Chapter 4: Dependable Ada Software*

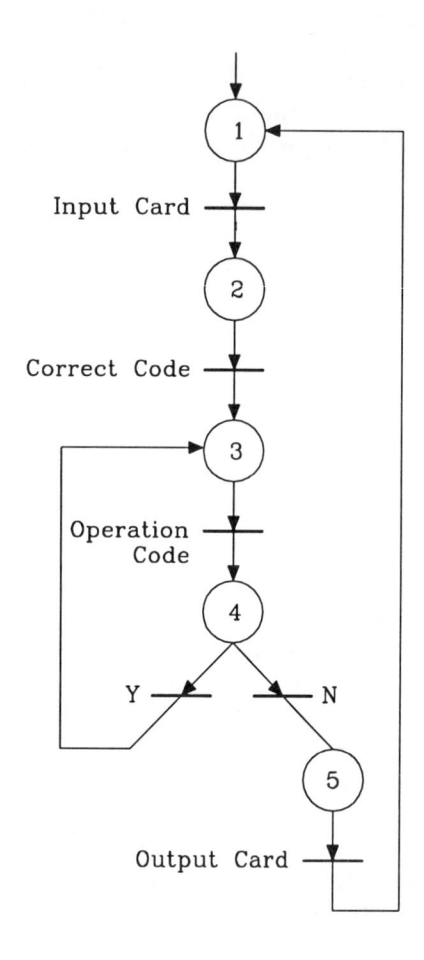

Figure 4.4: Normal processing of a cash dispenser

For each numbered state, the printed message is the following:

number:	state:	printed message
1	start	«Welcome. Insert your card»
2	check_point	«Enter your code»
3	menu	«1. account state»
		«2. withdraw money»
		«3. ...»
4	to_end_or_not_to_end	«Another operation?»
5	the_end	«Take your card back»

Fault Tolerance 251

We will consider two types of errors:

- incorrect input: incorrect code, operation already asked for,
- delay: the user does not give an order before a specified time is up.

The banker has specified the abnormal uses and the reactions required during the interactions between a client and the cash dispenser:

- if there are two incorrect inputs or one incorrect input and two time delays are exceeded, the cash dispenser 'eats' the card and waits for another client. The banker considers that incorrect use of this type is intolerable;
- if two consecutive time delays are exceeded, the card is returned. The banker considers that the client has involuntarily blocked the cash dispenser resource.

Figure 4.5 represents this specification: it describes the history of incorrect use and the reaction required by the error handling operation (the corrective action and the recovery state).

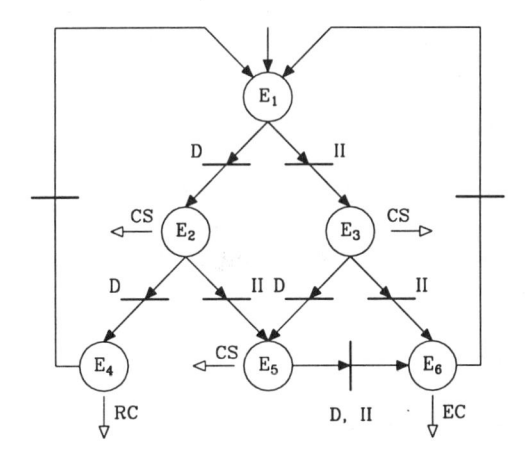

Figure 4.5: Error handling of a cash dispenser

Each state is associated with an opinion on the use of the cash dispenser. The transitions depends on two kinds of input data: incorrect input or time up. The recovery states are associated with states. This information is summarized by:

States:
E1: GOOD
E2: THINKING
E3: CLUMSY
E4: TOO_SLOW
E5: SUSPICIOUS
E6: INCAPABLE

Input:
II: Incorrect Input
D: Delay

Recovery States:
CS: Current State (the state is not modified)
EC: Eats Card and waits for an other client
RC: Returns Card to the client

252   *Chapter 4: Dependable Ada Software*

This design is easily translated in an Ada program:
```ada
procedure CASH_DISPENSER is
   INCORRECT_INPUT, DEADLINE: exception;
   type FUNCTIONAL_STATE is
         ( START, CHECK_POINT,   MENU,
            TO_END_OR_NOT_TO_END, THE_END);
   task  NORMAL_BEHAVIOUR;
   task  EVENTS_MANAGER is
      entry RESET;
      entry INCORRECT_INPUT(STATE: in out FUNCTIONAL_STATE);
      entry DEADLINE(STATE: in out FUNCTIONAL_STATE);
   end EVENTS_MANAGER;

   package EXTERNAL_OPERATIONS is
      task  PRODUCER;
      task  BUFFER is
         entry WRITE  (C: in     CHARACTER);
         entry READ   (C:    out CHARACTER);
         entry CLEAN;
      end BUFFER;
      procedure GET_CARD;
      procedure GET_AND_CHECK_CODE;
               -- raises INCORRECT_INPUT or DEADLINE
      procedure GET_AND_TREAT_OPERATION;
               -- raises INCORRECT_INPUT or DEADLINE
      procedure GET_RESPONSE(RESPONSE: out BOOLEAN);
      procedure RETURN_CARD;
      procedure EAT_CARD;
   end EXTERNAL_OPERATIONS;

   package body EXTERNAL_OPERATIONS is separate;
   use EXTERNAL_OPERATIONS;

   task body NORMAL_BEHAVIOUR is
      CURRENT_STATE : FUNCTIONAL_STATE := START;
      YES : BOOLEAN := TRUE;
   begin
      loop
         begin
            case CURRENT_STATE is
               when START       => EVENTS_MANAGER.RESET;
                                   GET_CARD;
                                   CURRENT_STATE := CHECK_POINT;
               when CHECK_POINT => GET_AND_CHECK_CODE;
                                   CURRENT_STATE := MENU;
```

```ada
            when MENU            =>GET_AND_TREAT_OPERATION;
                                  CURRENT_STATE :=
                                          TO_END_OR_NOT_TO_END;
            when TO_END_OR_NOT_TO_END
                                 =>GET_RESPONSE(YES);
                                   if YES then
                                           CURRENT_STATE:=MENU;
                                   else CURRENT_STATE:=THE_END;
                                   end if;
            when THE_END         =>RETURN_CARD;
                                   CURRENT_STATE := START;
       end case;
     exception
       when INCORRECT_INPUT =>
           EVENTS_MANAGER.INCORRECT_INPUT(CURRENT_STATE);
       when DEADLINE =>
           EVENTS_MANAGER.DEADLINE(CURRENT_STATE);
     end;
   end loop;
end NORMAL_BEHAVIOUR;

task body EVENTS_MANAGER is
  type USER_STATE is
      ( GOOD,    THINKING,    TOO_SLOW,
        CLUMSY,  SUSPICIOUS,  INCAPABLE);
  LOCAL_STATE: USER_STATE := GOOD;
begin
  loop
    select
    accept RESET;
      LOCAL_STATE:= GOOD;
    or
    accept DEADLINE(STATE: in out FUNCTIONAL_STATE) do
      case LOCAL_STATE is
        when GOOD          =>LOCAL_STATE:= THINKING;
                             -- STATE not modified
        when THINKING      =>LOCAL_STATE:= TOO_SLOW;
                             STATE:= THE_END;
        when CLUMSY        =>LOCAL_STATE:= SUSPICIOUS;
                             -- STATE not modified
        when SUSPICIOUS    =>LOCAL_STATE:= INCAPABLE;
                             EAT_CARD;
                             STATE:= START;
        when others        =>null;
      end case;
    end DEADLINE;
```

254 *Chapter 4: Dependable Ada Software*

```ada
          or
          accept INCORRECT_INPUT
                              (STATE: in out FUNCTIONAL_STATE) do
            case LOCAL_STATE is
              when GOOD             =>LOCAL_STATE:= CLUMSY;
                                    -- STATE not modified
              when THINKING         =>LOCAL_STATE:= SUSPICIOUS;
                                    -- STATE not modified
              when CLUMSY|SUSPICIOUS
                                    =>LOCAL_STATE:= INCAPABLE;
                                      EAT_CARD;
                                      STATE:= START;
              when others           =>null;
            end case;
          end INCORRECT_INPUT;
        end select;
      end loop;
    end EVENTS_MANAGER;
  begin
    null;
  end CASH_DISPENSER;
```

The complete program is given in section B.5 of appendix B. This example illustrates a design and implementation method allowing:

- the functional solution to be separated from the handling of exceptional events,
- errors as sequences of events to be handled.

The monitor task (EVENTS_MANAGER in our example) is an extension of the facilities offered by the Ada exception mechanism. With this task, the separation is better between the normal behaviour and the exceptional behaviour if sequencing is concerned.

4.5.6 Common operation

In many cases, the handling of an error needs an operation independent of the identity of the exception and an operation specific to each exception. This is programmed by using, one more time, the exception mechanism and more precisely the '**raise;**' statement which propagates the handled exception whatever its identity. The following example is proposed in (Rosen, 1989):

```
begin
   SEQUENCE_OF_STATEMENTS;
exception
   when others =>
      begin
         COMMON_HANDLING;
         raise;    -- the same exception
      exception
         when EXCEPTION_1 =>
            EXCEPTION_1_HANDLING;
         when EXCEPTION_2 =>
            EXCEPTION_2_HANDLING;
         -- ...
         when others =>
            OTHER_EXCEPTIONS_HANDLING;
      end;
end;
```

This structure can be used to program saving and/or restoring operations before and/or after correction operations. This will be used, for instance, during recovery operations and to log the occurrence of the exceptional situation. This structure seems cumbersome but is the best way to identify an exception by using the '**when**' clause of the exception handler.

The Ada implementation of the common parts of handlers were developed in section 3.6.2 of chapter 3 and therefore is not detailed again in this chapter.

4.5.7 Recovery

To correct an error, the program must be placed in a safe state. For this, there are two possibilities: either go back to a previous safe state (backward recovery) or go to a new safe state (forward recovery).

Going to a previous state requires a preliminary save operation. For instance, to go back to the execution of a procedure, it may be necessary to reinitialize the actual parameters and the global variables modified by the erroneous execution. Indeed in the case of the **out** or **in out** parameter modes, the actual parameters are updated either at the end of the normal (non erroneous) execution -in the case of passing by copy- or progressively during the execution -in the case of passing by reference- [6.2(7)]. In addition, as we do not know the place where the exception is raised, we do not know if the statements used modified any parameters. The parameters must therefore be reinitialized to retain the integrity of the operation.

In section 4.5.2, the use of the SKIP_LINE procedure (to flush out the keyboard buffer) places the program into a safe state before a new data acquisition.

256 Chapter 4: Dependable Ada Software

Let us consider the procedure specification below:
```
procedure GET_AND_ADD ( T     :    in out T_ARRAY;
                        INDEX :    in out T_ARRAY_RANGE;
                        ADD   :    in out T_ITEM) ;
```

which acquires the values of an array T and sums them (in ADD). The index of the last effective value of the array T is given in INDEX. A design may produce the following body:
```
procedure GET_AND_ADD ( T     :    in out T_ARRAY;
                        INDEX :    in out T_ARRAY_RANGE;
                        ADD   :    in out T_ITEM) is
    ITEM_NUL : constant T_ITEM := ... ;
    ITEM : T_ITEM;
begin
  loop
    GET(ITEM);
    exit when ITEM = ITEM_NUL;
    INDEX := T_ARRAY_RANGE'SUCC(INDEX);
    T(INDEX) := ITEM;
    ADD := ADD + ITEM;
    exit when INDEX = T'LAST;
  end loop;
end GET_AND_ADD;
```

If an exception is raised during a read operation (GET(ITEM)), the first actual parameter of the procedure is a partially completed array (reference passing), whereas the second and third actual parameters have their initial values (the ones before the procedure call: value passing). The global state of the variables is then incoherent. A way to reach a safe state consists in counting and accumulating the values which are already in the array (recovery). Then procedure GET_AND_ADD may be called again. This avoids rereading the values acquired before the error occurred. This programming method consists in implementing a *forward* technique. A complete example is given in section B.6.1 of appendix B.

The implementation of a *backward* technique consists in creating a local copy of the array before putting the elements in this copy. The assignment of the copy does not modify the original array which only receives its value at the end of execution. A second possibility consists in writing over the original variables and keeping the copy only to restore the array if an error occurs. An example is given in section B.6.2 of appendix B.

We propose a general implementation of a procedure using backward recovery. The principles of the proposed implementation can be applied in a systematic way to any application. They are illustrated by a fully written example in section B.6.3 of appendix B.

Fault Tolerance

In this section we will only give a skeleton of the example. In this extract of program, the elements added for the backward recovery implementation are in *italics*, the original procedure is written in **bold** and normal characters. Surrounded numbers (which are not Ada characters) are added to locate the parts of the example relevant to the comments and to make the principles easier to understand.

The recovered procedure (BACKPROC) has a parameter passed by value (PARAM_INT) and a parameter passed by reference (PARAM_STRING). This procedure uses and modifies these parameters and a global variable (GLOBAL_STRING). It is called by procedure SAVE_DEMO with the two actual parameters ZERO and REFERENCE_STRING.

The use of the proposed technique adopts the following process:

- In the declarative part of the procedure to be recovered, the global variables are saved in local variables with the same name (using the **renames** statement) ①. The SAVE_GLOBAL variable designates the GLOBAL_STRING variable, so all the statements of procedure BACKPROC which use the GLOBAL_STRING variable will work with this local copy;
- A block must be nested within the procedure body (NESTED_BLOCK) ②;
- In the declarative part of this block, the parameters passed by reference are copied on local variables of the same type ③;
- **Exactly the same** procedure **body** is kept as nested block body: modifications of the global variables will be made to the local copies which have the same name (①), and the parameters passed by reference will be really modified, because they were saved (③);
- An exception handler is added to the nested block ④. This handler restores the values of the variables passed by reference ⑤ and then propagates the same exception ⑥;
- This is done in order to keep **the same exception handler**. Be careful, you cannot access the current values of variables passed by reference but only their old values; if you want to access them, the handler can be 'mixed up' with the one previously added in order to avoid this modification;
- At the end of the procedure (that is to say outside the nested block), the values are assigned to the global variables ⑦, because, at this time, no exceptions have been raised.

```
procedure SAVE_DEMO is
  ...
  subtype DEMO_TYPE_STRING is STRING(1..8);
  GLOBAL_STRING, REFERENCE_STRING :
                  DEMO_TYPE_STRING:="INITIAL ";
  ZERO: INTEGER :=0;
  procedure BACKPROC(PARAM_INT:    in out INTEGER;
                     PARAM_STRING: in out STRING) is
    LOCAL_STRING: DEMO_TYPE_STRING := "MODIFIED";
```

```ada
        SAVE_GLOBAL: DEMO_TYPE_STRING renames
                     SAVE_DEMO.GLOBAL_STRING; -- ①
        GLOBAL_STRING : DEMO_TYPE_STRING := SAVE_GLOBAL; -- ①
           -- save the global variable into a local
           -- variable with the same name!
   begin
      NESTED_BLOCK :      -- ②
      declare             -- ②
         SAVE_PARAM_STRING: DEMO_TYPE_STRING:=
                  PARAM_STRING; -- ③
         -- (save the parameters passed by reference)
         begin     -- normal body of your procedure
            GLOBAL_STRING := LOCAL_STRING;
               -- all modifications are only on local copies
               -- of global variables
            PARAM_STRING := LOCAL_STRING;
            PARAM_INT:=100/PARAM_INT;
            -- raises an exception into the body when PARAM_INT=0
            ...
            --normal end of the body
         exception     -- ②
            when others =>   -- ④
              begin
                 ...
                 PARAM_STRING:= SAVE_PARAM_STRING; -- ⑤
              -- RESTORE in out REFERENCE PARAMETERS
              -- : backward recovery
                 raise;   -- ⑥ <= to go to your exception handler
                exception    -- => your exception handler...
                   when CONSTRAINT_ERROR => raise;
              -- ...
              end;-- exception_block
         end NESTED_BLOCK; -- ②
         -- real assignment of global variables :
         -- the execution was OK
         SAVE_GLOBAL:= GLOBAL_STRING; -- ⑦
      end BACKPROC;

   begin    -- SAVE_DEMO
      ...
      BACKPROC(ZERO,REFERENCE_STRING);
      ...
   end SAVE_DEMO;
```

This example shows how statements implementing backward recovery can be, systematically (and 'automatically') added in a transparent manner.

4.6 Conclusion

This chapter dealt with the design of dependable programs with Ada language. We presented numerous pieces of information, highlighting that dependability intervenes during each step of the Ada program creation.

At first the choice of the means used to express the program (that is the programming language) is important. We signalled in chapter 3 the capabilities of the **Ada exception mechanism** to define errors at programming time and to detect errors at run time. This feature is essential because it allows the error concept to be expressed and handled by the programmer. For other programming languages the absence of such a feature does not inhibit the presence of faults but makes the programmer unaware of their existence.

In this chapter we also described the extended **possibilities of other features to detect** design and programming **faults**. However the Ada language is a tool whose good or bad use depends on the programmers.

In section 4.2 of the present chapter **we warned** the Ada application designers **about the use of some features**. We successively approached:

- unsafe features: the use of these features is not recommended because it increases the risk of fault introduction independently to the program to be designed;
- hazardous features: these features may lead to unpredictable behaviours for the applications using them. We shared the set of these features considering their causes: erroneous execution, incorrect order dependencies, unportability. We did not forbid the use of such features but we said that the designer has to pay especially attention.

After such warnings the reader may have in mind the following question: 'is Ada a dangerous language?'. This question implicitly refers to a comparison with other languages. Firstly design and programming are dangerous activities according to the consequences of the presence of a fault in the produced software. We developed this aspect in chapters 1 and 2. Secondly complexity of software products needs complex tools (such as complex languages) the use of which requires more knowledge and more attention. However, we showed in section 4.3.1 that Ada language possesses features preventing fault introduction because they made comprehension of the programs easier or they are close to the design concepts making the translation of the design product into a program easier.

Moreover, we presented the capabilities of the Ada language features to detect errors in order to remove faults. We described the important role of the compiler (4.4.1), the interests of the exception mechanism to increase the test efficiency (section 4.4.2) and the possibilities to introduce expected properties in the programs. We conclude that **Ada language is intrinsically a dependable language** because it favours fault avoidance and removal.

In this chapter we also presented how general dependability techniques, which principles were described in chapter 2, may be implemented with Ada to avoid, to remove and to tolerate faults.

Finally, the dependability of a software depends on the dependability of the program and of the means used to execute this program. The **certification process** imposed on the Ada run-time **environments** (compilers and executives) justifies the reliance in these environments. However, even if the dependability of both main components (program and environment) are necessary, the interactions between these components must be mastered. As the Ada exception mechanism was frequently used, we will examine in chapter 5 the problems linked to its implementation and the interactions between this mechanism and various components of the Ada executive.

CHAPTER 5

Ada Exception Mechanism and Implementation

5.1 Introduction

In chapter 3, we presented the characteristics of the Ada exception mechanism. These characteristics were especially used in chapter 4 to implement dependability techniques. The description of the exception mechanism was based on information provided by the language standard. Constraints due to the implementation of the exception mechanism, that is the run-time environment, were not considered. However this knowledge is useful:

- the designers of hard-dependable applications (for instance plane control systems) must master of all the components of the executable application. In particular they must understand what happens when exceptions are used;
- knowledge of exception mechanism implementation is also necessary because the choice of an implementation can have an effect on the temporal behaviour of the application. We will present two techniques. The first technique is more efficient in the case of error-free operation but the second technique provides software tools which react quicker when an error occurs;
- we will show that the implementation of the exception mechanism is distributed between the code generated by the compiler from the Ada program of the application and the Executive System. The implementation must then be studied to standardize the interfaces between the application and the Run-Time System in order to facilitate the portability of the software tools and their maintainability.

An identical situation, which is no doubt more critical, exists concerning the Ada language tasking features. They can be used by designers who have no information on their implementation by a Real-Time Kernel. However, certain features require knowledge albeit superficial. For instance, pragma PRIORITY plays a role in the arbitration of the execution of several tasks as there is no real parallelism (on a computer equipped with a single processor). Also, certain phenomena can only be explained by more detailed knowledge: starvation of the low priority tasks, lateness in the resumption of the execution of a task using a `delay` statement, etc.

In addition, the dependability of a software tool depends on the dependability of the Ada program designed and also on the execution means supplied by the run-time environments. The designer of dependable Ada applications must therefore have a critical outlook towards these means. This is the viewpoint which is also discussed in this chapter.

Finally we will see that several new features offered by the package `Ada.Exceptions` of the new standard (Ada95) were influenced by characteristics of the exception mechanism implementations. This chapter justifies their presence but also explains the effects of their use.

In section 5.2 we will explain the entities (Application, Exception Management Function, Run-Time System, Hardware) that intervene during exception handling and their correlations. This study will allow us to define an architecture for the implementation of the Ada exception mechanisms.

In section 5.3 we will present the techniques used to implement the Exception Management Function. More precisely, we will successively describe how an error is detected, then how an exception is identified and raised, how the handler is selected, and how 'normal processing' is resumed. In the conclusion of this section we will examine the constraints added by an industrial real-time context and their consequences as far as the choices of implementation are concerned. This study was conducted taking the constraints imposed in the avionics field as examples; they are however of general interest.

5.2 Architecture of the Implementation

5.2.1 General view

Architecture
In previous chapters, the Ada exception mechanism was considered from a user's point of view. This viewpoint concerns the relationships between the exceptions and the other Ada features, examined at program level. It is also call the *horizontal view*.

In practice, the exception mechanism is implemented by the Execution Environment and uses some of its components. We are now going to present the *vertical view* that is related to the study of mechanism implementation.

Architecture of the Implementation 263

In order to specify the aim of such a study, let us consider the following situation. From the user's point of view, the raising of an exception during a rendezvous must cause the exception to be propagated to the calling task. From the implementation point of view, the identity of the calling task must be known and so communication with the Run-Time System (R.T.S.) is required. In addition the choice of the exception handler and the transfer of control to this exception handler must be treated by a special part called the **Exception Management Function** (E.M.F.). The Exception Management Function manages the propagation of the exception as long as it is established that there is no handler. This may require interactions with the application. If the server task does not have an exception handler, this task must be completed. The completion of the task requires calls for other functionalities of the Run-Time System which, in particular, is in charge of task management. We can see that the Run-Time System can use other mechanisms to honour this request. For instance, to release a completed task, the Dynamic Memory Management function may be called on to free the memory allocated to the task. These indirect consequences and therefore the links between other components induced by these consequences will not be studied in this chapter. More detailed information on this subject can be found in (Mrtsi, 1988). The vertical view and the horizontal view are presented on Figure 5.1

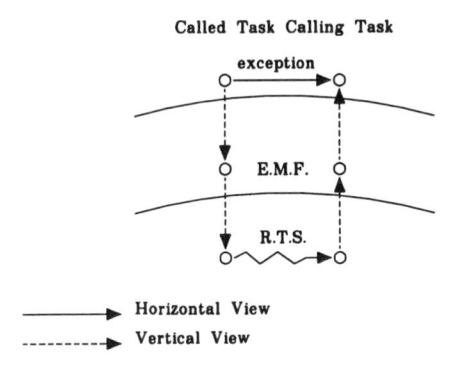

Figure 5.1: Horizontal and vertical views

In section 3.3.1 of chapter 3, an Ada executable application was presented as comprising:

- the **compiled program** obtained by compiling the source program written in Ada. As in the remainder of this chapter we will only concern ourselves with implementation, the compiled program will be called the application because it is the application executable by the Ada Abstract Machine;
- the **executive** implementing the Ada Abstract Machine. This executive consists of many components each with its own function: the Exception Manage-

ment Function managing that which is specific to the exceptions, the dynamic Memory Management Function, the Task Manager, etc. As we are more especially studying the implementation of the exception mechanism, we will divide the executive into the Exception Management Function (E.M.F.) and that we will call the Run-Time System (R.T.S.) which includes all the other functions. We admit to improperly use of the term as usually the Exception Management Function is a part of the Run-Time System.

Interactions exist between the three components: application, Exception Management Function and Run-Time System. Figure 5.2 symbolizes the vertical point of view studied in this chapter.

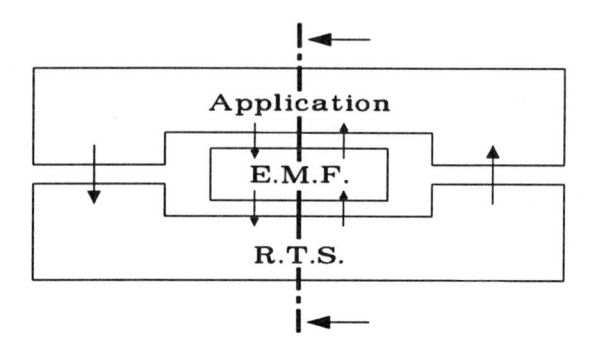

Figure 5.2: Components of the implementation

Role of each component
In this section we will discuss the role of each component: the **application**, the **Exception Management Function** (E.M.F.), the **Run-Time System** (R.T.S.) and the **hardware** support. The choice of separating the Exception Management Function from the other parts of the Run-Time System is based on a logical viewpoint, independent of the implementation possibilities. This separation is introduced for academic purposes, to make the implementation of the exception mechanism easier to understand. In practice, the separation between the different components (application, Exception Management Function, Run-Time System) is not well defined as the distribution of the functionalities of the operations between the application (compiled program) and the 'run-time routines' (E.M.F. + R.T.S.) depends on the possibilities and the limits of the target's configuration (Fdare, 1987) (Burns, 1989). For instance, we will explain later (section 5.2.2) the case of exception CONSTRAINT_ERROR (previously NUMERIC_ERROR) which can be detected by the Run-Time System (from the hardware) or the application, not only according to the microprocessor's possibilities, but also according to the implementation designer's choices.

Architecture of the Implementation 265

This is why we will study the logical entities in this chapter, without attempting to ascertain whether certain parts are nested in others or not. Figure 5.3 sums up and labels these parts and the links which will be commented on later.

```
                    ┌─────────────────┐
                    │   Application   │
                    │       ①         │
                    └─────────────────┘
                      ↓ L1      ↑ L2
                    ┌─────────────────┐
              L5    │     E.M.F.      │
                    │       ②         │
                    └─────────────────┘
                      ↓ L3      ↑ L4
                    ┌─────────────────┐
              └────→│ Runtime System  │
                    │       ③         │
                    └─────────────────┘
                             ↑ L6
                         Hardware
                            ④
```

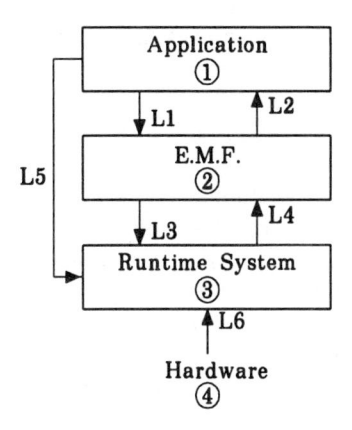

Figure 5.3: Links between implementation components

Before studying the links between the different parts, these parts must be specified from a general point of view (Fdare, 1987):

① **Application Software**: *Generated Program i.e. the set of instructions and data in a machine executable representation that is directly produced by the compiler from the application program.* Remember that in the following, the word 'application' does not define the Ada source.

② **Exception Mechanism** or **Exception Management Function (E.M.F.)**: *that part of the Ada run-time environment which implements Ada semantics for exceptions: that is, detection of an exception and selection of the appropriate handler if one exists; if there is no matching handler, it invokes the Task Termination function* (included in the R.T.S.) *to terminate the task at hand or the main program.*

③ *Run-Time System (R.T.S.): set of predefined routines in a machine executable representation that is selected by the Ada compilation system from a run-time library to support the functionality of the application program not supported in the generated program.* For instance, we consider that the task management functions (Rendezvous Management function, Task Termination function, etc.) are part of the Run-Time System.

④ **Hardware**: All the underlying computing resources available (microprocessor, memory, etc.).

Links between components

As illustrated by the example of the exception raised during a rendezvous at the start of this section, the raising of an exception leads not to a call for one component from another but to a sequence of information propagated between the components. This propagation creates information paths through the links. In the following sections we will look at the links (Figure 5.3), the information paths between the components, and the nature of the logical information sequences communicated through these links. This study is divided into several parts:

- in section 5.2.2 we will study the starting points for the sequences, that is to say, the locations where an error is detected;
- in section 5.2.3 we will show using examples, the interactions which exist between the components. In this presentation, all types of interactions will be studied even if all the causes of the interactions are not considered. A single illustrative example will be provided for each interaction;
- in section 5.2.4 we will present a synthesis of the possible paths (interaction sequences). Unlike the previous section, this synthesis will give all the possible configurations. It was made from a systematic analysis of all the cases whose causes were detailed in section 3.5.1 of chapter 3;
- the portability of the applications (executable programs) requires a standardized interface for the components. This is why we will present in section 5.2.5 a standardization for the interface between the applications, the Exception Management Function and the Run-Time System proposed by ARTEWG (Ada Run-Time Environment Working Group). We will limit our presentation to the aspects relevant to exceptions.

Before we start to describe the exception mechanism implementation viewpoint, we would like to point out that the lack of detailed papers from companies building Ada compilers has obliged us to extrapolate the implementations from the fragmented information available. Our studies are based on work performed by ARTEWG (Mrtsi, 1988) (Fdare, 1987) and on the information concerning the Ada language semantics outlined in the standard (ARM, 1983).

5.2.2 Exception detection

Before we study the different paths activated between exception detection and the recovery of 'normal' execution by the application, we can first of all define **which** part of the system detects the predefined exceptions. It is obvious that the origin of the detection of a user or predefined exception raised voluntary by a raise statement is in the application (① on Figure 5.3).

In this section we are not interested in the mechanism which performs detection (this aspect will be developed in section 5.3.2) but in the place where the error is detected, that is the component as defined in section 5.2.1 and schematized on Figure 5.3.

We must emphasize the fact that here we are only analysing the effective **origin** of the detection (Application, Exception Management Function, Run-Time System or Hardware) and not its logical location in the application: the application is considered as being one of the components (black box). For instance, an exception can be propagated in the calling task during a rendezvous in which an exception is raised. The raising of the exception within the calling task is only the **consequence** of the primary exception raising.

The study presented also lists the origins of the detections according to the nature of the predefined exceptions. The origins proposed are the ones that seem to be the most natural because of the exception semantics and the implementation that appears to be the most appropriate.

Let us now successively examine the predefined Ada exceptions.

CONSTRAINT_ERROR

The checks of the properties which cause the raising of exception CONSTRAINT_ERROR are contained in the **application** (code generated from an Ada source). In fact, this exception groups under the same identifier all the errors associated with constraints implicitly defined by the programmer. Section 3.5.1 of chapter 3 shows that all the cases in which exception CONSTRAINT_ERROR is raised correspond to an erroneous state of the application generated by the violation of a property given by the programmer.

NUMERIC_ERROR

The checks which caused the raising of exception NUMERIC_ERROR corresponded to validity checks on the mathematical data or results. We have already shown the ambiguity between this exception and CONSTRAINT_ERROR: data or results are considered as inaccurate if they do not belong to the specified domain of the operation. In fact, this differentiation seemed to be due more to implementation problems than to semantic reasons and so seems to be artificial. Besides, ISO has agreed that implementations should not raise NUMERIC_ERROR but CONSTRAINT_ERROR (AI-00387 in (Ada_comm, 1989) and new standard (Ada95, 1995)).

Location of the detection of a numeric errors depends on the microprocessor's capabilities and on the Ada Environment implementation choices. For instance, a division by zero can cause an hardware interrupt or can modify a flag of a state register of the microprocessor. In the first case, the interrupt activates the execution of an interrupt handler associated by the Run-Time System. In the second case, the register must be explicitly tested by the application. Even if the error is physically detected by the microprocessor, the logical error NUMERIC_ERROR is detected either by the **Run-Time System or** by the **application**. This example also shows that, for a given implementation, the place where the exception is raised can depend on the type of numeric error. For instance, an overflow can be detected by a flag test in an application and a division by zero can be detected by the Run-Time System after transfer of control by an interrupt.

STORAGE_ERROR

Exception STORAGE_ERROR is raised if the available memory space is not sufficient. The memory space is managed by the *'Dynamic Memory Management function'* ((Fdare, 1987)) which is *'that part of the run-time environment which concerns itself with the allocation and deallocation of storage at run-time. This function is also responsible for detecting when a request for storage cannot be fulfilled, and for raising the exception STORAGE_ERROR as appropriate'*.

This function is generally divided into two:

- the *Stack Management function is usually implemented via generated code sequences, rather than via run-time routines*. It manages the memory space requirements (local variables, subprogram calls, etc.);
- the *Heap Management function is usually implemented via run-time routines*. It manages the memory space requirements for objects created by allocator evaluations.

Note that this division is an implementation choice even if it is a conventional one. Usually exception STORAGE_ERROR is detected by the **application** if it occurs during a space request in the stack or by a part of the **Run-Time System** for a dynamic allocation request (heap).

TASKING_ERROR

In section 3.5.1 of chapter 3 we discussed the cases raising exception TASKING_ERROR. This exception is related to synchronization and communication errors. It therefore seems natural that the detection of an erroneous configuration, which involves the raising of TASKING_ERROR, should be made by the part of the **Run-Time System** which manages the task specific problems (Task Termination function, Rendezvous functions, etc. (Fdare, 1987)). For instance, the detection of an entry call of a completed task can be only made by the Run-Time System.

PROGRAM_ERROR

The checks concerning the situations in which PROGRAM_ERROR is raised depend on the application as far as the elaboration order constraints are concerned. The end of a function without any return statements and the closed alternative evaluations of a 'select statement' can also be detected by the application. In the same way, all the *erroneous execution* or *incorrect order dependence* cases that raise exception PROGRAM_ERROR would have been detected during the compilation and replaced by the compiler [1.6(10)]:

- either by the code that raises this exception (explicit detection by the application, like a raise statement),
- or during the execution by a generated check.

All cases raising exception PROGRAM_ERROR can therefore be detected by the **application**.

Detection Location	CONSTRAINT _ERROR	NUMERIC _ERROR	STORAGE _ERROR	TASKING _ERROR	PROGRAM _ERROR
Application	X	X	X		X
RTS		X	X	X	

Figure 5.4: Detection location

Conclusion
Figure 5.4 shows the exception detection locations according to the identity of the exception. This table corresponds to conventional solutions. The detection location (application or Run Time System) is effectively fuzzy. It depends on the definition of the Ada Abstract Machine. If this machine provides operations the specification of which includes the evaluation of the properties formulated by the standard, then detection will be made by the Run-Time System. If not, the checks must be incorporated into the application generated by the compiler. A part of the functionalities of the Run-Time System are fulfilled by the microprocessor which can then be at the origin of the detection.

The development of Ada technology should allow the check of the properties to be integrated into the definition of the Ada Abstract Machine and the machine to be implemented in the form of a microprocessor. This solution would reduce the volume of the application generated by the compiler and accelerate execution by integrating checks into the silicon chip.

5.2.3 Interactions with the R.T.S. involving the E.M.F.

Now that we have presented the functionality of each component (section 5.2.1) and specified the exception detection location (section 5.2.2), we will study the links between the different components. In this study we will successively discuss the causes of component activation then the activations caused by the components. We will analyse the inputs and outputs of the components during the managing of an exception. We will not describe the behaviour of the components (presented in section 5.3) but we will specify their interactions. The interactions will be considered separately; they are not correlated (paths of interaction sequences are examined in section 5.2.4).

The labels given in the text correspond to those used on Figure 5.3.

Sources of EMF and RTS activations
The Exception Management Function can be activated by:

- the application (link L1 on Figure 5.3): for instance the explicit raise statement or the implicit raising of exception CONSTRAINT_ERROR,
- the Run-Time System (link L4):
  (a) from the hardware (L6 and then L4): for instance NUMERIC_ERROR (now CONSTRAINT_ERROR) obtained by a microprocessor hardware interrupt,
  (b) from the application (L5 and then L4): for instance, the entry call of a completed task.

The Run-Time System can be activated and have consequences on the Exception Management Function by:

- a primitive (L5): entry call of a completed task,
- an exception detected by the hardware (L6): NUMERIC_ERROR,
- the Exception Management Function (L3): exception propagation to the calling task at the time when the exception is raised during a rendezvous.

The examples given were developed in section 5.2.2.

Activation destinations
In this part, we will analyse the activations caused by the Exception Management Function, then the Run-Time System. These activations correspond to the outgoing arrows on Figure 5.3.

The Exception Management Function calls:

- the application (link L2) to communicate a new execution context (such as a transfer of control to an exception handler),
- the Run-Time System (L3): to 'complete' a task in which an exception was raised.

The Run-Time System calls:

- the Exception Management Function (L4) to inform the application that an exception must be raised (such as the propagation of an exception raised during a rendezvous).

Before studying the functionalities ensured by the application, the Exception Management Function and the Run-Time System (section 5.3), we will study in section 5.2.4 the interaction paths taken on Figure 5.3 for the different exception raising cases (section 5.2.2).

5.2.4 Synthetic study of the paths

Selective criteria
In this section we will describe the paths representing the progress of the interactions between the components. The contents of this section are the result of a previous analysis where each situation raising an exception was considered individually. We will not present this analytic study here but the synthesis deduced from it, in the form of a table. We saw during the study that the path induced by raising an exception is different for each exception and depends on several criteria characterizing the exceptions. Thus, the identity of an exception does not define a selective criterion:

- we already pointed out in section 5.2.2 that, for instance, the handling path of exception CONSTRAINT_ERROR on numeric operations (formerly NUMERIC_ERROR) can start in the application or in the Run-Time System. The starting point and then the path may therefore vary for a single exception;
- the study also showed that the identity of the exception cannot be used to distinguish between the paths: different exceptions may lead to the same path.

Before we present the result of the study we would like to make the following remarks:

- the propagation of an exception is considered as a new raising of this exception [11.4.1(9)]. This will therefore be indicated, but the path induced must be followed by entering the summary table again. This point of view does not contradict the handler choice optimizations made by the *static analysis* (see section 5.3). Even if the Exception Management Function *directly* transfers control to the handler located several nesting levels above, previous interactions are however necessary at each nesting level in order to deallocate memory areas for example. So, if an exception is raised in a procedure A3 called by a procedure A2 called by a procedure A1 which contains the corresponding exception handler, the 'activation record stack' (context stored at each call) must be popped for each propagation.
- with tasks, the raising of an exception can cause exceptions to be propagated towards other tasks. The initial path will then continue while a second one is initialized in parallel; to be followed the summary table must be entered again.

Our study of the different possible paths between ① (application), ② (EMF), ③ (RTS) and ④ (hardware) showed that these paths depend on 4 characteristic criteria which can take the following values:

1. Exception raised during:

    (a) execution of statements or,
    (b) elaboration of declarations.
2. Nature of the frame in which the exception is raised:

    (a) block, subprogram (different from the main program), package (different from a library unit),
    (b) main program, package that is a library unit,
    (c) task (except during rendezvous),
    (d) accept statement to achieve a rendezvous.
3. Presence or not of a local handler in the frame. This criterion is only significant when the value of the first criterion (raising of an exception) is 'during the execution of statements'.

4. Origin of the detection, that is to say 'What detected the exception?': application or Run-Time System (studied in 5.2.2).

Synthetic table
The various paths are synthesized in Figure 5.5. The rows correspond to the first and third criteria; the columns correspond to the second criterion. Each cell is divided into a higher part and a lower part. This subdivision corresponds to the fourth criterion.

In order to be able to understand and use this table, we will successively give: (1) the notations, (2) an example, (3) comments on the table.

a. Definitions of the notations used
The cells contain a part of the path. Each part starts by an arrow coming from an exception transmitted by the application (higher part of the cell) or by the Run-Time System (lower part of the cell). The number 'i' associated with the arrow corresponds to the link 'Li' of Figure 5.3. Control is transferred to a component (application ①, EMF ② or RTS ③), which then transfers the control via a new link, etc., until:

- a current task termination request is made (⇧),
- a dependent tasks termination request is made (↑),
- a main program termination request is made (⇡),
- a new exception is raised (◆).

Architecture of the Implementation

The three crosses show the end of the current path whereas ◆, corresponding to the reraising of an exception, starts a new path.

b. Example of path
In order to illustrate the use of the table we will present a concrete example and follow the path until normal execution is resumed. Consider the following part of a program:

```
task body T1 is
   ...
begin
   ...
   begin
      ...
      accept E do
         ... TAB(I)... -- raising of CONSTRAINT_ERROR
      end E;
      ...
   end;
   ...
exception
   when CONSTRAINT_ERROR => ...
   ...
end T1;

...
task body T2 is
   ...
begin
   ...
   T1.E;
   ...
end T2;
```

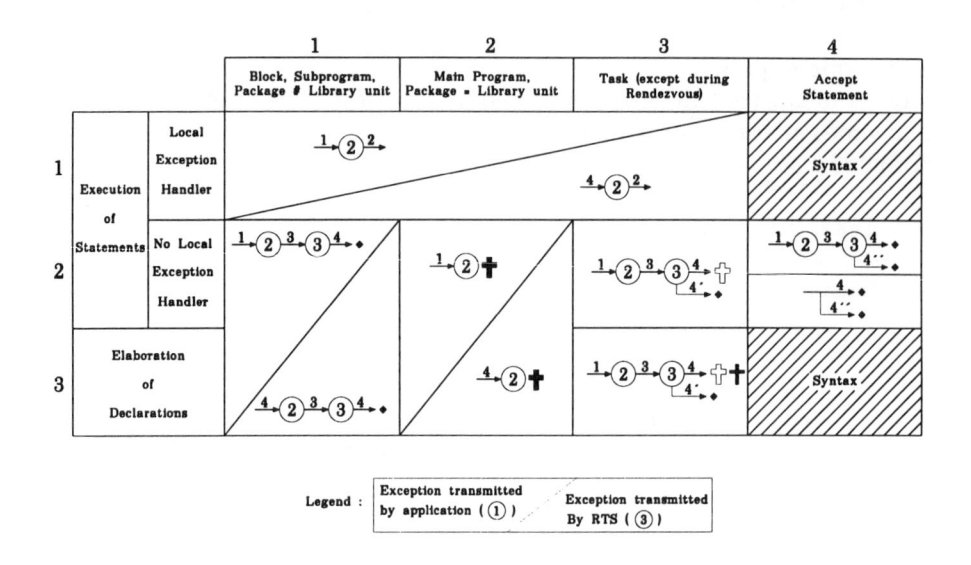

274 Chapter 5: Ada Exception Mechanism and Implementation

Figure 5.5: Paths to manage exceptions

Exception CONSTRAINT_ERROR is raised in the application that detected the overflow of the index of array TAB [4.1.1(4)]. This is the case of an exception raised by the execution of a statement with no local exception handler for the frame (accept) (row 2), detected by the application (higher part) for an accept statement (column 4). The path is composed of the following arcs:

1: from the application to the Exception Management function (②) to indicate the raising of the exception,

3: from the Exception Management Function (②) to the Run-Time System (③) to indicate an error during the execution of a rendezvous.

This initializes two subpaths that are executed in parallel:

4: the Run-Time System (③) calls the Exception Management Function in order to propagate the exception in task T1 and

4": the Run-Time System (③) calls the Exception Management Function in order to propagate the same exception to task T2.

Remember that a propagation is considered as the reraising (a new raising) of an exception and so induces a new entry point into the table. In our example, the first path can be continued by re-entering the table: 1st column, 2nd row, lower part; the second path can be continued in the same way: 3rd column, 2nd row, lower part, etc. Let us follow the two paths:

1. **Propagation in T1 out of the rendezvous**: row 2, column 1 of the table indicates that the Run-Time System calls the Exception Management Function (②) that calls the Run-Time System (③) back because the lack of an exception handler requires propagation and therefore exit from the block frame. Then, we go to column 3, row 1 of the table since task T1 has a local handler. Then we transfer control to this handler (arc 2).

2. **Raising in T2**: T2 does not have a local handler so the path to be followed is defined in column 3, row 2, lower part of the table (the cell is not divided because the behaviours are identical, that is independent of the fourth parameter). Since we are in a task with no local handler, the Run-Time System is called (arc 3) to complete this task (arc 4). If task T2 has an entry on which some calls are pending, the Run-Time System propagates exception TASKING_ERROR to the calling tasks (arc 4').

Several remarks:

1. After each call, the components react by performing operations which are proper to them that we will look at later on (section 5.3). For instance, the Run-Time System identifies the caller, frees the memory associated with a frame in case of propagation, etc.

2. In the case of an error detected by an interrupt that raises an exception via the Run-Time System (Link 6), as in the case of an exception raised by the Run-Time System subsequent to an application call (Link 5), the path is indicated in the 'lower parts' of the table because the exception is considered as transmitted by the Run-Time System.

c. **Comments on the table**

   Row 1: The Exception Management Function takes control (②). It stores the identity of the exception (possible propagation by a 'raise;' statement (Cifo, 1987)). Whatever the context, since the erroneous frame possesses a local handler (by an explicit alternative or by a default handler), the control is transferred to this handler. It is only later, in order to **terminate** the erroneous frame, that a communication to the Run-Time System (③) will be necessary (depending tasks, etc.).

   Row 2: The call to the Run-Time System (② $\to^3$ ③) is necessary:

   (a) to wait for the termination of the tasks which depend on the erroneous frame before terminating it [9.4(6)],

(b) in the case of a task, to indicate its completion which will involve the propagation of TASKING_ERROR in tasks possibly waiting at an entry of the erroneous task [9.5(16)] (see example developed previously),
(c) in case of a rendezvous, to identify the communicating task and to propagate the exception to it ($\rightarrow^4$") (see previous example).

Row 3: When an exception is raised by the elaboration of a declaration, a call to the Run-Time System is necessary:

(a) to terminate the tasks elaborated in this declarative part and not yet activated [9.3(4)],
(b) to wait for the termination of the activated tasks. This is only possible if they were created by an allocator; these aspects are not precisely defined by the standard [9.3(4),(6)&(8)].

In this study, we considered the **accept** statement as a 'frame' for it has a particular status regarding the exceptions and the paths taken (second criterion). This statement is not considered as a frame in the standard for it has neither a declarative part nor an exception handler. For these reasons, the cells of column 4, rows 1 and 3, cannot be reached. In order to avoid propagations, a block with an exception handler must be nested in **accept** statements. To avoid this, the presence of exception handlers within **accept** statements was proposed as an extension to the present standard ((Ada9X, 1990), RR0499, p.9_112).

5.2.5 Interface

We saw in the previous sections that the handling of exceptions requires interactions with the Run-Time System. The need to master the interactions, as well as the will to use 'multiple and interchangeable implementations of the Run-Time System' (portability), led (Baker, 1986a) and (Mrtsi, 1988) to specify a standardization of the Run-Time System interface. It would also provide the Ada program designers with access to certain functions of the Run-Time System through a standardized specification without assumptions on the implementation chosen.

The part of the interface specified by ARTEWG (Ada Run-Time Environment Working Group) that we will present is used for the exchanges between the Exception Management Function and the Run-Time System (links L3 and L4). It is expressed in the form of a package specification. It allows the Run-Time System and the compiler to be implemented independently. Because it logically separates the functionalities, each part does not access the implementation details of the others. This specification given in (Mrtsi, 1988) and seemingly based on the work of T.P. Baker (Baker, 1986a) is as follows:

```ada
with MACHINE_SPECIFICS;
-- non-executive portion of the RTS interface
-- which depends on target machine and that defines
-- in particular the hardware exceptions
package COMPILER_EXCEPTIONS is
  type EXCEPTION_ID is private;
  NULL_EXCEPTION: constant EXCEPTION_ID;
  CONSTRAINT_ERROR: constant EXCEPTION_ID;
  NUMERIC_ERROR: constant EXCEPTION_ID;
  PROGRAM_ERROR: constant EXCEPTION_ID;
  STORAGE_ERROR: constant EXCEPTION_ID;
  TASKING_ERROR: constant EXCEPTION_ID;
  INTERFACE_ERROR: constant EXCEPTION_ID;
  procedure RAISE_EXCEPTION(
    E: EXCEPTION_ID;
    MODIFIED_REGISTERS: MACHINE_SPECIFICS.PRE_CALL_STATE);
  procedure NOTIFY_EXCEPTION(
    WHICH: MACHINE_SPECIFICS.MACHINE_EXCEPTIONS;
    INFO: MACHINE_SPECIFICS.ERROR_INFORMATION;
    MODIFIED_REGISTERS: MACHINE_SPECIFICS.PRE_CALL_STATE);
private ... -- compiler-defined
end COMPILER_EXCEPTIONS;
```

Of course, the Ada program designers do not have today access to this package. It only provides an Ada specification of a component of the Ada Run-time Environment. However let us remark that certain subprograms of the package Ada.Exceptions given by the new standard (Ada95, 1995) are close to the ones of the package COMPILER_EXCEPTIONS. For instance:

```ada
procedure Raise_Exception( E: in Exception_Id;
                           Message: in String:="");
```

raises an exception defined by its identity and associates a message with it. This message is available calling

```ada
function Exception_Message( X: Exception_Occurrence)
                           return String;
```

which returns pieces of information specific to the implementation if the exception E was raised by the conventional 'raise E;' statement.

The functioning of procedures RAISE_EXCEPTION and NOTIFY_EXCEPTION is defined as follows: '*RAISE_EXCEPTION has the effect of raising the specified exception in the task executing the call. It is provided so that the Run-Time System can raise an exception in a task that may have been interrupted, suspended, or have called the Run-Time System (including when it needs to propagate an exception between tasks for EXCEPTIONAL_COMPLETE_RENDEZVOUS).*' Parameter MODIFIED_REGISTERS is required to pass register values. For instance, assume that a task T1 calls an entry of a server task ST, and that the value of the Instruction Pointer of the microprocessor (register) is IP1. Assume also that an exception occurs in task ST during the rendezvous and that the value of the Instruction Pointer is IPST. The exception must be propagated to task T1. This is done by the Run-Time System calling procedure RAISE_EXCEPTION. However it must communicate the original T1 context (MODIFIED_REGISTERS). For instance the Exception Management Function must know the Instruction Pointer of T1 (IP1) to select a handler (see section 5.3.5).

When an hardware exception occurs (L6 on Figure 5.3), the Run-Time System cannot establish the mapping between the hardware exception and the Ada exception. It therefore calls procedure NOTIFY_EXCEPTION passing WHICH hardware exception occurred and machine specifics information.

Procedure NOTIFY_EXCEPTION is thus called by the Run-Time System to signal a hardware exception to the Exception Management Function, whereas procedure RAISE_EXCEPTION is called by the Run-Time System to signal other exceptions to the Exception Management Function. Figure 5.3 is expanded in Figure 5.6. It shows that interactions exist between various components of the Run-Time System. These aspects will not be detailed further.

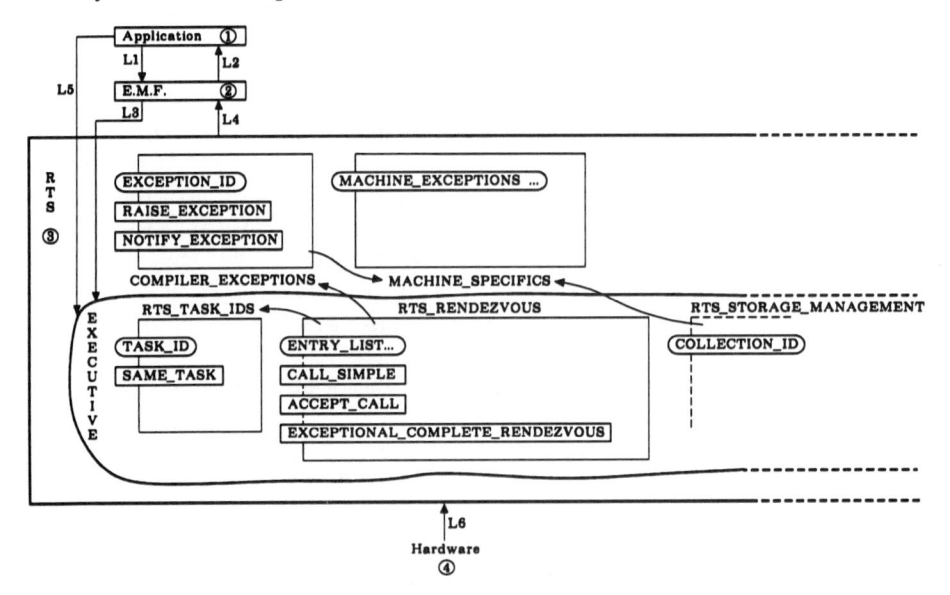

Figure 5.6: RTS architecture

In section 5.2, we introduced the components involved in the implementation of the exceptions. We only described the interdependencies of these components. We will present the techniques used to implement these components in the next section.

5.3 Implementation of Ada Exceptions

5.3.1 Introduction

The content of this section is based on papers (Baker, 1986b) (Rationale, 1986) and on reports and discussions relative to the work done with other partners of the European BRITE-EURAM project, called IMAGES (Integrated Modular Avionics General Executive Software) (AS_1b, 1990) (Cri_ddc, 1990) (Cap_alsys, 1990) (Cap_tld, 1990) (Als_doc, 1989). We will describe the techniques used to implement the components presented in the previous section.

The Ada exception mechanism is composed of four functions:

- error **detection** (section 5.3.2) whose role is to perceive the occurrence of an error at run time,
- **raising** of an exception (section 5.3.3) whose aim is to signal the detected error to the mechanism which decides what reaction is to be undertaken,
- **exception identification** (section 5.3.4) that gives the identity of the exception,
- **selection of the handler** (section 5.3.5) that makes the choice and transfers the control to the exception handler,

In section 5.2 we showed that the four functions listed above are not centralized, but are distributed among the components of the software tool. For instance, an error can be detected by the hardware, the Run-Time System or the application.

Although the presentation of these four functions is split up in the following subsections to facilitate its comprehension, in reality they are tightly bound together. We can quote three examples to illustrate such relationships:

1. When an application raises an exception in a procedure that does not have an exception handler, the exception mechanism detects and raises the same exception in the calling procedure.

2. When an exception is raised during a rendezvous, it is propagated in the called task out of the frame accept (previous example). The same exception is communicated to the Run-Time System to be propagated to the calling task and is raised there by the exception mechanism.

3. For a **raise** statement, the detection, raising and even identification functions (if the name of the exception is specified) are located in the application.

Logical information on implementation will be given in the presentation. More details will be furnished in section 5.3.6 on the implementation of the Exception Management Function. The industrial application constraints (in time or memory) will be considered in the section 5.3.7. However we will only provide information at the design level, no information on detailed design or the coding will be given.

5.3.2 Error detection

In this section we will describe the notion of detection, the place where it can be made, then the way it is implemented. Distinction must be made between the notions of occurrence and detection of an error because an error can occur which is not perceived by the system. For example this situation corresponds to the suppression of the detections, dealt with in the conclusion of this section.

An error can be detected by:

- the **application** by means of check instructions generated by the compiler; for instance the errors associated with exception CONSTRAINT_ERROR,
- the **hardware**: for instance the errors that, most of the time, raise exception CONSTRAINT_ERROR for arithmetic operations (formerly NUMERIC_ERROR),
- the **Run-Time System**: for instance, in case of an entry call to a completed task (exception TASKING_ERROR),
- the **Exception Management Function** in the case of propagation in nested frames.

We pointed out in section 5.2 that the detection location (application, hardware, Run-Time System, Exception Management Function) has consequences on the progress of the interactions between the components (notions of paths). However, it has no effect on the behaviour of each component because the components do not know the path that led to their calls. For instance, when we look at the functioning of the Exception Management Function in detail (section 5.3.5) we will see that it is independent of the detection mechanism.

The **detection** of an error can be **implicit or explicit**. We say detection is implicit if the *means* allowing detection are inside a function and therefore are not perceptible outside. If these means are external, detection is said to be explicit.

These notions (implicit or explicit) depend on the abstract level considered. For example, the '**raise** E;' statement is an explicit detection. However, when writing 'X:=TAB(I)', detection of constraint violations on the I index or the TAB(I) value are implicit at the Ada level. These detections are probably made by checks generated by the compiler (except if some '**pragma** SUPPRESS' were applied). These checks are explicit at Executive level. We wish to point out that, for this example, the checks could have been made by explicit tests written into the Ada program (**if** statements).

There are also implicit detections at Executive level; this is often the case for stack overflows. This situation may correspond to the violation of segments which is explicitly detected by the microprocessor. We can use as another example the case of division by zero. Detection of this kind of error can be made explicitly by:

- the Ada program (test of the divisor by an **if** statement),
- the code generated of the application by the compiler, before the division instruction (test of the divisor by a test instruction),

- the code of the application generated by the compiler, after the division instruction (test of a microprocessor flag).

It can also be implicitly detected by the Run-Time System after an interrupt generated by the microprocessor.

Error detection can be suppressed by suppressing the check instructions in the generated code of the application in the case of implicit detections.

We emphasize the fact that this is a suppression of checks. It was verified on compilers studied (Cap_alsys, 1990) (Cri_ddc, 1990). However, the standard does not guarantee that the use of '**pragma** SUPPRESS' effectively eliminates these checks [11.7(20)]. For instance, this fact was encountered in the study of the TLD compiler (Cap_tld, 1990): exception NUMERIC_ERROR might be raised in spite of the use of '**pragma** SUPPRESS' with an OVERFLOW_CHECK parameter because an error provokes an hardware interrupt.

5.3.3 Raising

An error can be detected by the application, the hardware, the Run-Time System or the Exception Management Function. Therefore a single representation of the Ada exceptions must exist (see section 5.3.4) even if each component has its own check mechanisms (Mrtsi, 1988). A raising technique must then be standardized for instance by means of a software interrupt call (such as a TRAP instruction on the 68000 microprocessor) (Als_doc, 1989). The same raising technique is used by each component, whether the error is detected by the software or by the hardware. The Run-Time System must also know the raising procedure. For example, when an exception occurs during a rendezvous, the Run-Time System is in charge of raising the same exception in the calling task. The aim of this technique is to implement means to call the Exception Management Function in order to warm it of the detection of an exceptional state. To do this, we gave, in section 5.2.5, the procedure RAISE_EXCEPTION proposed by ARTEWG. This allows the specification of the Exception Management Function call to be standardized.

However, it does not provide a specification on the way used from the detection to the Exception Management Function call. For instance, if an exception is raised during a rendezvous, the need to raise the same exception in the calling task is detected by the Run-Time System. Two techniques are available to implement the call to the Exception Management Function.

In the first solution (see Figure 5.7), the Exception Management Function (E.M.F. on figure) is immediately called by the application (link 1). Then the Exception Management Function calls the Run-Time System (link 3) to signal an abnormal completion of the rendezvous. The Run-Time System is the only component which knows the identity of the calling task. The Run-Time System then calls the Exception Management Function twice, one to cause the exception

282 Chapter 5: Ada Exception Mechanism and Implementation

to be raised outside the accept frame (4) then again to propagate this exception to the calling task (4").

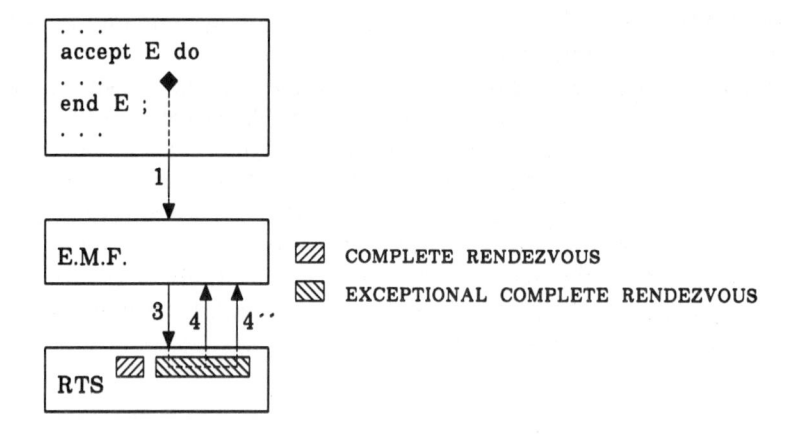

Figure 5.7: First solution for propagation between tasks

A second implementation architecture is given in (Baker, 1986b) and shown on Figure 5.8. In this solution, the application calls a single rendezvous completion primitive of the Run-Time System (link 5). If an exceptional state was detected during the execution of an **accept** statement, the application calls this primitive with a parameter that indicates this fact. Then the Run-Time System calls the Exception Management Function twice (4 and 4") to raise the exception in the called task and in the calling task.

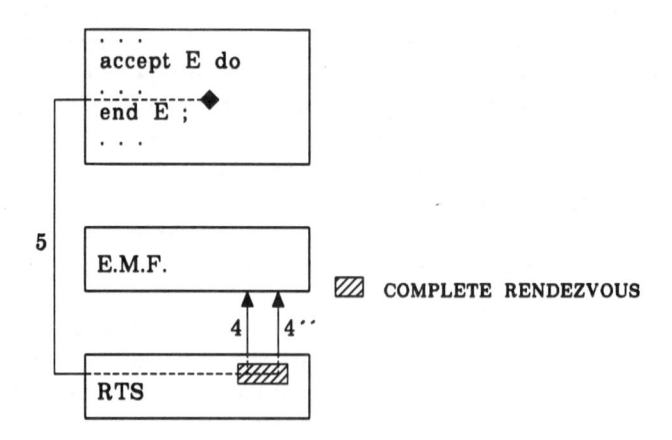

Figure 5.8: Second solution for propagation between tasks

The advantage of the second implementation technique is that it requires a single (but parametrized) rendezvous completion primitive. The drawback is the need for the Run-Time System to test the value of this parameter at the beginning of the execution of this primitive: this generates overheads in the case of faultless execution. This drawback is avoided with the first solution because correct execution of the rendezvous is concluded by a normal completion primitive call. However the implementation is heavier if an exception occurs.

5.3.4 Identification

In the previous section we showed the need to have a single representation of the exceptions, in particular to communicate parameters to or from the Exception Management Function. A process giving a non-ambiguous identification must be defined (Carid, 1988).

One solution consists in defining an identifier by the complete name of the exception. The 'complete' qualifier expresses the fact that we must add the list of prefixes (frame names) to the current name to distinguish between identical exception names declared in different frames. The names of frames can be explicit in the program (identifiers of packages, procedures or tasks) or must be created (anonymous blocks).

This solution is coded identifying each exception by the pointer on the string that expresses the complete name and not by the string itself. Two different names are placed at two different addresses. This will accelerate the manipulation of the exception identifiers. For instance, the comparison between two exceptions will consist in comparing two addresses. This process of coding is used in the TLD environment (Cap_tld, 1990). Note that the string which represents the exception is only useful for debugging or for writing in ASCII files. Certain compilers therefore offer an option allowing the mnemonics to be suppressed.

Another way of coding would be to identify the exceptions by numbers (Baker, 1986b). This method is used, for example, in the Alsys environment. Whatever the coding choice made, two problems arise:

- a **predefined** exception must be coded in the same way irrespective of the frame in which it occurs for a single name in various frames represents a single exception. Consequently, a predefined exception that appears in two packages must be coded by the same identifier although the packages are compiled separately (Mrtsi, 1988).
- by contrast, two **user** exceptions declared in different frames with the same identifier are distinct and therefore must be coded differently. This case arises when a given exception name appears in two packages. The same problem is encountered with an exception specified in a generic package: each instantiation of this package must create a new identification of the exception.

The case of predefined exceptions is in fact not specific: a predefined exception is one declared in the STANDARD package.

If exceptions are identified by their complete names then this identification is sufficient. Unfortunately, in practice, this type of coding is not suitable. We proposed two alternatives: string addresses or numbers. The complete identification cannot be resolved at compile time. However, two identifiers placed in different compilation units may have been coded by the same address (the strings may be placed at the same address in each compilation unit) or by the same number (for instance, if the code corresponds to the order number in the declarations).

This problem is the same as the one concerning subprogram identifier coding. The identification (address of the subprogram) defined at compile time is relative. It is only at link time that a definitive identification will be made (Rationale, 1986). In the case of coding by address, the absolute addresses are obtained at link time (Sherman, 1980). The coding problems associated with the exceptions come from the fact that **an exception is an entity global to the application** because a propagated exception must keep its identity. This aspect was already illustrated by an example from (Rationale, 1986) and commented on in section 3.3.2 of chapter 3. It shows that an exception propagated out of its scope can come back into it.

We would like to mention an additional problem for generic packages. If, to minimize the memory size of the code, a single sample of the code is shared by all the instances of the generic package, then the addresses (of the strings of the exception names) are identical for all the instances whereas they represent different exceptions. Since it is necessary to have different identifiers, the addresses must be different for each instantiation. To obtain such a result, the exceptions must be considered in the same way as the local variables for which each instance creates a memory place (Baker, 1986b).

The coding technique must allow the **'others'** alternative of the exception handler to be coded too. In particular, it must handle exceptions which become anonymous.

We stated that an anonymous exception may come back into its scope and must be handled taking its original identifier into account. The Exception Management Function must therefore store the identifier of the current exception. The identification of an exception must also be stored even when it has been handled (Cifo, 1988) because the current exception can be raised again by means of the **'raise;'** statement in the handler. Moreover, the allocation of a single memory storage in the Exception Management Function is not sufficient because another exception can be raised and handled in an exception handling operation, as shown in the following example.

```
   begin
     ...
   exception
     when E1 =>           -- handling of E1
       ...
       begin
         ...              -- E2 is raised!
       exception
         when E2 =>       -- handling of E2
           ...
       end;
       ...
       raise;             -- must raise E1
   end;
```

If the handling of the first exception E1 raises a second exception E2, E2 will become the current exception to be handled. When its handling is concluded, E1 again becomes the current exception identifier. Therefore, a stack mechanism is required to manage the identities of the current handled exceptions.

An implementation must possess an interface mechanism in order to change a hardware interrupt which signals the detection of an error into an Ada exception. This change generates a loss of information as far as the error identification is concerned. For example, the UNDERFLOW and OVERFLOW errors are grouped under the same Ada identifier NUMERIC_ERROR (now CONSTRAINT_ERROR). By contrast, when several errors are signalled by a single interrupt (e.g. TRAP instruction of the 68000 microprocessor) -see section 5.3.3-, the identification of the particular Ada exception requires the examination of the part of the program that generated the interrupt, in order to identify the cause (Als_doc, 1989).

The implementation of the exception mechanism then requires the management of identification means and of the names of the exceptions. This two aspects are also found in the package Ada.Exceptions provided by the new standard:

```
   type Exception_Id is private;
   ...
   function Exception_Name(Id: Exception_Id) return String;
   ...
   function Exception_Identity(X: Exception_Occurrence)
              return Exception_Id;
   ...
   function Exception_Name(X: Exception_Occurrence)
              return String;
```

We saw why these features are available and we gave pieces of information on their implementations.

5.3.5 Selection of the handler

We will now assume that an exception was raised after the detection of an error and that it generated a call to the Exception Management Function communicating the identity of the exception raised. In this section we will study the mechanisms used by the Exception Management Function to find the handler of the exception raised. We will successively describe:

   a. the information required by the mechanism,

   b. the selection techniques of the first *exception handler case structure* (that is the first '**exception** exception_handler {exception_handler} **end**' part) with regard to the frame where the exception is raised,

   c. the means useful to know if this structure has an exception_handler associated with the raised exception. If not, the exception must be propagated,

   d. the mechanism searching for the following structure in case of propagation.

a. Information communicated to the EMF
The Exception Management Function must receive:

   • the identification of the exception to be handled. Since this information is not always given when the exception is raised (propagation or '**raise**;' statement), the default value of this parameter is the identifier of the exception which was previously communicated;
   • the address of the program instruction which caused (directly or not) the exception to be raised because the choice of the handler for this exception depends on the location where the exception is raised. This dependence was described in section 5.2. For instance, the search for the handler must take the nesting and the nature of the frames into account and must also distinguish between the declarative part and the body. This information is essential because the Exception Management Function can be called directly by the application (the Exception Management Function can then easily find the address in the stack) or indirectly by means of the Run-Time System. For example, an exception raised during a rendezvous is propagated to the calling task; the Exception Management Function is not able to find the address of the call statement in the calling task context. Therefore this address must be supplied by the Run-Time System when it calls the Exception Management Function (see the example in section 5.2.4). In (Baker, 1986b) the call to the Exception Management Function is specified by:

```
HANDLE ( E: in EXCEPTION_ID := PREVIOUS;
         L: in out ADDRESS:= location where called);
```

However, this is not a procedure specification because the call to the Exception Management Function is not necessarily terminated by returning the control to the caller. In any case, the execution never comes back to the statement following the erroneous statement but possibly to an exception handler statement. This is due to the *Termination* mode chosen by Ada.

b. Selection of the exception handler case structure
An *exception handler case structure* is a part of the program which defines exception handlers:
```
exception
    exception_handler
    {exception_handler}
end
```

The Exception Management Function must initially determine the first exception handler case structure in which the handler of the identified exception is **likely** to be found. Whether the handler associated with the exception is in this structure or not will be studied in the next subsection.

A sequence of statements with which an exception handler case structure is associated is called an *exception handler context*. Its syntax is as follows [11.2(4)]:
```
begin
    sequence_of_statements
exception
    exception_handler
    {exception_handler}
end
```

The start of the execution of an exception handler context is called *the entering into the context*; the end of the execution of an exception handler context is called *the leaving of the context*.

We will present two techniques to select the exception handler case structure ('dynamic tracking' and 'static mapping'). They are differentiated by the way the exception handler contexts are taken into account.

In the **'dynamic tracking'** technique, the application pushes the address of the exception handler case structure onto a stack when, at run time, it enters into a new exception handler context. This address is popped from the stack each time the context is left. The Exception Management Function then has immediate access (at the top of the stack) to the address of the first exception handler case structure. In addition, the implementation of this technique is relatively easy. However it introduces overheads during execution without the raising of exceptions because any change of context adds a pushing or popping action. For instance, the 'dynamic tracking' technique is used by the Alsys 386 compiler (Cap_alsys, 1990) and the TLD 386 compiler (Cap_tld, 1990). A programming trick is given in (Baker, 1986b). Baker and Riccardi propose to save the current exception handler case structure address in the current stack used to manage nested blocks and subprograms calls (which contain local variables, return pointers, etc.) at an address fixed relative to the Base Pointer in order to find it immediately and to avoid the management of a supplementary stack.

While in the 'dynamic tracking' technique the current exception handler context is only known during execution by stacking, the '**static mapping**' technique establishes the relations between the context and the handler case structure at compile time. The compiler generates a *map* which specifies, for each context, the `beginning_address..ending_address` range that delimits the executable code with which the exception handler case structure address is associated. So, if, and only if, an exception is raised during the execution, the Exception Management Function compares the address where the exception is raised with the ranges defined in the map. It then deduces the address of the handler case structure searched for. Because of the nested blocks, the map can be a tree. The determination of this map requires cooperation between the compiler, the binder and the translator because the map must be modified when the addresses of the code are modified. This technique has the advantage of not adding execution overheads when no exceptions are raised. The drawbacks are:

- the implementation is more difficult,
- the run time overheads are greater when an exception occurs: the determination of the range and, therefore, of the address of the handler are not immediate,
- extra storage is needed: memorization of the map may require extensive data space.

This technique is used, for example, by the DDC/286 (Cri_ddc, 1990) and ALSYS/68000 (Als_doc, 1989) compilers.

c. Selection of the alternative
The Exception Management Function selected the first handler case structure using one of the two techniques presented above. Now it must determine if a handler (an alternative **when** ... =>) associated with the exception raised exists in this handler case structure. For this we can:

- either test the exceptions handled by the alternatives one by one, by means of successive tests until we find the correct one (if it exists),
- or directly access the handler by means of an array indexed by the means used to code the exception identifiers.

Implementation of the Ada Exceptions   289

d. Propagation cases

To manage the voluntary propagations when handling an exception, or when the handler case structure selected does not have a handler matching the exception raised, the Exception Management Function must integrate a propagation mechanism. This is done in two stages:

1. calls to functions of the Run-Time System (Dynamic Memory Management function, Rendezvous Management function, etc.) in order to complete the current context, then

2. the exception is raised again by a call to the application.

The first point concerns the additional actions to be performed by the Exception Management Function, which will be discussed in section 5.3.6.

Raising the exception again by the call to the application (second point) will cause a new call to be made to the Exception Management Function that will begin the stages we saw in this subsection again.

To simultaneously solve the selection of the alternative problem and the possible propagation problem, a question may be considered: 'is it possible to get, at compile time, the address of the exception handler to be executed?'. This address can be obtained in the case of nested blocks. The **static nesting of the blocks** allows the chaining of the contexts to be analysed at compile time. Unfortunately, it cannot be done for subprograms since a subprogram can be called by several other subprograms. The caller is unknown at compile time when the called subprogram is compiled (Burns, 1989) (Baker, 1986b).

However, maps of the exception handler to be executed could be obtained at compile time for static blocks. These arrays are then used at run time to update the current access array. We did not find an Ada Environment using such a solution probably because the copies of the array would increase the overheads of the 'dynamic tracking' technique during exception-free execution.

To conclude this section let us a remark that the coding of the Exception Management Function requires the use of *static variables* (defined at compile time) since the Exception Management Function must maintain in memory a part of its execution state (handler arrays, current exception, etc.) (Fdare, 1987). For instance, the current exception identifier must be stored because the propagation phenomenon or the use of the 'raise;' statement does not give the identity again.

5.3.6 Implementation of recovery

Let us assume that an exception E is raised at a location (address) L in a frame. The Exception Management Function must determine the new value of the L address where the application will resume its processing and restore the context for resumption. A specification of the Exception Management Function is (Baker, 1986b):

```
HANDLE ( E: in EXCEPTION_ID := PREVIOUS;
         L: in out ADDRESS:= location where called);
```

The new value of L is the address of the exception handler which will process the exception. The routine uses the handler selection mechanisms: selection of the first exception handler case structure, search for the presence of an alternative and propagation, if necessary. The implementation of each of the mechanisms was presented in the previous section. We saw that, in addition to the selection of the handler, certain actions must be done. For instance, if a propagation occurs (rendezvous, no handler, exception raised during the elaboration of a declarative part), the mechanism must ensure correct termination of the abandoned frame: wait for the termination of the dependent tasks, possible release of the memory that was allocated to this frame, etc.

Two approaches of the Exception Management Function implementation are: the interpretive approach and the compiled approach. The distinction between the aims of these two implementations is similar to the one presented for the handler selection (dynamic tracking and static mapping). In the first case, the routine solves the problems at run time. In the second case, the main actions are done at compile time.

a. Interpretive approach
With the interpretive approach, the various actions required are put together in a single routine which at run time does the work to be done.

In order to achieve the propagation of the exception until the handler is found, we use a loop statement: each iteration performs the actions to find the handler and, if not found, correctly terminates the frame before propagation is made. These actions depend on the nature of the frame.

We give below an algorithm derived from (Baker, 1986b) for the implementation of this routine. Note that in the algorithm, the term 'L is immediately within an X' means that X is the most nested structure which contains location L.

```
HANDLE( E: in EXCEPTION_ID:=PREVIOUS;
        L: in out ADDRESS:=location where called) is
begin
  loop
    if L is immediately within an accept statement
        then call a RTS function to end the rendezvous and
            propagate the exception E to the calling task;  ①
        elsif L is immediately within the sequence of
            statements of a frame which possesses a handler
            for E  ②
        then    L:=address of E_handler;
            return to L;  ③
```

```
          else      -- no handler for E
          if L is immediately within a master of tasks
               then  call a RTS function for completion
                     of master of tasks; ④
       end if;
       if L is immediately within a task body
          then request a RTS function to complete the task; ⑤
          elsif L is immediately within a main program
               or library package
               then request a RTS function to complete the
                  main program; ⑥
          end if;
       end if;
    ⑦ Do work for exit from this unit (accept statement
       or frame), possibly including deallocating storage
       and restoring the environment to that of the
       immediately enclosing unit (propagation);
       L:= normal transfer location on exit from this unit;
    end loop;
 end HANDLE;
```

Some comments:

- When an exception is raised during a rendezvous (①), the Run-Time System 'EXCEPTIONAL_COMPLETE_RENDEZVOUS' function (see Figure 5.6) is called to propagate the exception to the calling task. The same exception is also handled outside the **accept** statement (⑦+**loop**).
- When an exception is raised in a frame which has a local handler for E (②), the address of the handler is obtained using the selection mechanism (section 5.3.5) and the application is resumed at this address (③). To select the exception handler case structure, dynamic tracking or static mapping can be used indifferently.
- When the frame does not have a handler for E but is a master of tasks, it must wait for the completion of the dependent tasks (④). Then, if the frame is a task, it must be completed by the Run-Time System (⑤); otherwise, if the frame is a main program or a library package, then the main program must be completed (⑥). ⑤ and ⑥ are 'requests' and not 'subprogram calls' because there is no return: the actions relative to the propagation (⑦) are not executed.

The originality of this algorithm is that it only hands back the control to the application when an appropriate handler has been found or after completion of the task or the main program. Hence, in this solution, the work done by the Exception Management Function is centralized in the Executive.

b. Compiled approach

In this second approach, the major part of the work required to achieve the handler recovery is to be done by the code of the application. So the compiler must analyse the program to generate the required actions. The code must especially deal with the exception propagations, the transfers of control between frames, etc. This is therefore an Exception Management Function implementation solution centralized in the application. However dialogue with the Run-Time System is still necessary. For instance, the Run-Time System is the only component which can provide information to propagate an exception raised during a rendezvous.

c. Hybrid approach

The two approaches presented above are centralized solutions. In particular, the executive (interpretive approach) or the application (compiled approach) must completely manage the propagation problems. In the solution proposed in section 5.2.4, a propagation creates interactions between the Exception Management Function, the Run-Time System and the application including a retroaction phenomenon between the application and the Exception Management Function. A propagation is considered in the Exception Management Function as the new raising of an exception in the application which causes a new call to the Exception Management Function (with a new context) etc. This approach corresponds to a hybrid strategy distributing the work among the components.

To conclude, we would like to point out that when the exception handling is completed, the system must do more than just call (as for normal completion of execution) the 'Call-Return function' to obtain return to the caller of the frame. In fact, cooperation must be established between this function and the Exception Management Function for the completion of the exception handling operation (Fdare, 1987). The Exception Management Function must know for example that the current exception was handled in order to pop information associated with its identifier from the stack (see 5.3.4).

5.3.7 Implementation in industrial context

We described in the previous sections the principles of the techniques used to implement the exception mechanisms. In this section, we will examine the constraints added by the industrial context and their consequences as far as the implementation choices are concerned. Our application domain is avionics but the purpose and the interest of this section are more general.

We will successively examine the following criteria:

a. portability,

b. maintainability,

c. performance,

d. dependability.

Different implementations are suitable to separately take these criteria into account. The implementation chosen will therefore be a compromise allowing for the relative importance of each constraint. We will discuss the implementation when performance and dependability criteria are jointly considered.

a. Portability

In section 5.2, we proposed an architecture which introduced several components (subsection 5.2.1), the operations and the implementations of which were described in the other subsections. We will show how this architecture meets the portability constraints imposed by the industrial context.

The proposed architecture allows **the distribution of the functions** in the various components (application, Exception Management Function, Run-Time System) and their interactions to be **clearly expressed**. This distribution also facilitates the **standardization of the interfaces** between the components. This approach will:

1. **allow separate developments** for each component (particularly the Exception Management Function) in order to reduce costs. For example, this is explicitly expressed in the ARINC 651 report (Arinc651, 1990): '*The primary goal of a modular avionics design is to contribute to reducing the cost of ownership through lower acquisition cost and an increase in flexibility to accommodate variations.*' ... '*In an IMA* (Note: IMA = Integrated Modular Avionics) *design, a particular function may be divided into even smaller pieces resulting in the potential for more suppliers to contribute to the complete function.*'.

2. **increase the adaptability** of an application. This meets the demands described in the ARINC 651 report: '*Avionics development costs will also be reduced since standard interchangeable modules can be used in a variety of aircraft types without modifications... Ideally, interchangeability can be applied to any manufacturer's components and between any two aircraft types and models.*'.

3. **facilitate the relationships with the subcontractors** and allow the implementation of certain parts to be masked: '*In the software area, the basic IMA concepts allow application software to be implemented via a standard interface to the executive software. This enables suppliers to competitively supply software to implement different avionics applications. It is expected that users, hardware suppliers and software suppliers will establish closer relationships as a result.*'.

A problem posed by the portability of the Ada applications comes from the **semantic fuzziness** of certain features (see section 4.2.2 of chapter 4). We will give an extreme example related to the domain of exceptions and show the drawbacks in the industrial context. The standard does not specify what happens at the termination of an application after an unhandled exception ((Carid, 1988) p.99). This makes it impossible to envisage an application reconfiguration mechanism acceptable for every implementation.

Moreover, an architecture **can be suitable for the portability criterion** but not for **performance point of views**. For instance, we described three kinds of implementations (interpretive, compiled or hybrid approaches) in section 5.3.6. Each of them imposes specific interactions between the application, the Exception Management Function and the Run-Time System. Consequently, the choice of a specific interface for the components of a given architecture imposes an implementation technique which may not be the most suitable one from a performance point of view.

b. Maintainability
Maintainability means that the system is easy to modify and faults are easy to detect.

The architecture and the specification of the component interfaces that we described allow changes to be easily incorporated. It will be possible to **modify** (improve, correct, etc.) **one of the components** (Exception Management Function, Run-Time System or application) independently of the others.

When we studied the interactions between the components in the second section, we saw that the paths necessarily went through the Exception Management Function. Thus, if maintenance information must be stored, it must be written by the Exception Management Function. This solution answers the following remark made in the Arinc 651 report: '... *to provide a completely accurate status report of its own health and therefore allows users to achieve the maintenance goals that were previously unattainable. Therefore, it is a goal to ... notify the maintenance crew, and allow maintenance to be deferred until a convenient time.*'.

c. Performance
Industrial systems frequently require that the **time constraints** be taken into account. This requirement is still true when an error occurs: '*The system reaction time to detect a fault and accomplish reconfiguration needs to be defined*' (Arinc651, 1990). In this section, we will study the impact of the exception mechanism implementation on performance. We will describe the influence of **pragma** SUPPRESS and then the time-related consequences of the theoretical implementation choices. We will conclude with effective performance from measures obtained from the ALSYS and DDC compilers on target machines 80286. The examples chosen are limited. Also, as Ada Environment implementors are permanently preoccupied with optimizing implementations, the values given are probably no longer valid for current products. Our aim is only to highlight and comment on a certain number of situations so that the Ada software tool designer using the exception mechanisms

has a critical attitude towards the Execution Environment that he or she uses or must choose.

The **use of pragma SUPPRESS** logically allows time to be saved since it is supposed to suppress the generated code checks. This assertion is proved by the results of (Ada_perf, 1990) (page 219): a study made on a dozen current compilers (hosts or targets) shows, using pragma SUPPRESS (ALL), that the checks take up on average 20 to 25% of the CPU time. Note that this number represents an average over the checks as a whole: if the checks are suppressed separately the gains obtained are lower.

Certain checks are not physically suppressed in spite of the use of pragma SUPPRESS in accordance with the standard: *'For certain implementations, it may be impossible or too costly to suppress certain checks... The occurrence of such a pragma within a given unit does not guarantee that the corresponding exception will not arise...'* [11.7(20)]. This is justified by the fact that the **suppression** of certain checks would **involve a loss of time** (Rationale, 1986). This loss is due to the hardware that makes these checks inside itself. In order to prevent it from doing so, calls for masking instructions must be added. The deactivation then the activation (reactivation) instructions must be placed therefore around the instruction blocks using an entity which must not be checked. Imagine the overheads induced for instance in the case of arithmetical expressions that handle variables which are checked and others which are not.

We can **theoretically assess the performance** of the various techniques used to implement the exception mechanisms and presented in sections 5.3.5 and 5.3.6. This time aspect has already been quoted. For instance, the choice of the handler can be achieved by two techniques:

- static mapping: this technique does not add any overheads for exception-free execution, but it is slower when an exception is raised. It requires additional memory space to store the *map*;
- dynamic tracking: this technique introduces overheads during exception-free execution and in addition requires an increase in the stack space where the information added for the implementation of this technique is stored. However it is quicker than the static mapping technique if an exception is raised.

As far as propagation is concerned, we pointed out in section 5.3.5 that time can be optimized to immediately obtain the handler associated with the exception raised in the case of nested frames. However we indicated that the memory space overheads for an exception-free execution are in this case increased.

We wish to point out in this section that the desire to standardize for maintainability and portability purposes can be contrary to the performance criterion. For instance, the use of interrupts to unify the implementation of the raising of an exception (see section 5.3.3) makes development easier and more maintainable but is probably not time-optimized in all circumstances because the interrupt mecha-

296 Chapter 5: Ada Exception Mechanism and Implementation

nism requires time overheads to save and restore the microprocessor context at interrupt raising time and at interrupt return time.

The expectations estimated in the principles of the techniques that we have just studied must be tempered by the **reality of the implementations** as shown by the study of two compilers on target 80286: the ALSYS compiler that uses the dynamic tracking technique and the DDC compiler that uses the static mapping technique. The results given in (Ada_perf, 1990) lead to some surprises:

1. To raise and to handle an exception (tests E000001 to E000004, p.177), the code generated by the ALSYS compiler is on average 20% quicker than the one obtained from the DDC compiler (which is logical).

2. For the Dhrystone test (p.166), which is a combination of various Ada statements, the code generated by the ALSYS compiler is 3 times slower. The reduction in speed is theoretically normal but we do not know if it is only due to exception management.

3. For the P_test that analyses the calls for procedures (p.190), the code generated by the ALSYS compiler is 2 or 3 times quicker. This contradicts the theory (the dynamic tracking technique needs pushing and popping of the exception context) summarized in the conclusion given (p.76) in the presentation of the tests relative to the exception mechanisms: '*However faster is not necessarily better since quick exception handling may be achieved at the expense of a slower procedure call.*'.

What can we conclude? The results given tend to show that the choice of the exception implementation techniques does not greatly affect overall performance. An effort made in the code optimization domain seems to be more rewarding for the other features of the language than an effort made on exceptions.

d. Dependability
Dependability is one of the main concerns of embedded avionics systems. '*A basic goal of IMA is to develop an architecture which meets the regulatory requirements for certification. Depending upon the architecture, integration candidates, and number of aircraft systems to be integrated, some level of fault tolerance is necessary to meet these regulatory demands.*' A whole chapter (the fourth) of the Arinc report is dedicated to this subject. We have already given a general approach to the problems and the associated solutions in chapter 2. We highlighted in several sections of chapter 4 the advantages and the limits of Ada language. In this section we will study only the domain concerning exception mechanism implementation. We will describe the problems (from the dependability point of view) of the architecture presented above.

An embedded application consists of the application code generated by the compiler and by the implementation of the Ada Abstract Machine (Exception Management Function, Run-Time System, hardware).

One problem concerns the reliance we can place on the compilation product: is the generated code semantically equivalent to the source code? If the answer is no, this may be due to an erroneous compiler (bugs) or to various interpretations of the standard by the compiler implementer and the program designer. Concerning the code generation problem, we can quote the studies conducted by Wichman (Wichman, 1989) on the general problem of *'Insecurities in the Ada Programming Language'*. This report says that *'Unfortunately, most Ada compilers lack 'maturity' and one sometimes gets the impression that they have learnt to pass ACVC (Ada Compiler Validation Capability) but little else!'*. This problem is developed later on: *'CWI in the Netherlands had a 200 line program which no compiler handled correctly (many have now been rectified to handle this test)'*. Even if dependability requires a critical attitude to the execution means, languages other than Ada are generally worse because public validation procedures do not exist. The dependability of the language implementation is therefore only based on the dependability of the company which produces the Execution Environment which cannot be measured by the client.

Concerning the Ada Abstract Machine implementation, the proposed architecture (separation of the application, the Exception Management Function and the Run-Time System) and the component interface specification has two advantages:

1. the specified interfaces and the behaviour of each component lead to a more dependable design for the implementation;

2. the architecture introduced and the fences obtained from the interface specification, limit the risks of contamination between the components.

Furthermore, this architecture leads to the isolation of the Exception Management Function. This solution therefore allows an Exception Management Function to be associated with each application or each functionality (see Figure 5.9) supported by the hardware, which is interesting in many industrial systems and in particular the IMA (Integrated Modular Avionics) context used as an example.

298   *Chapter 5: Ada Exception Mechanism and Implementation*

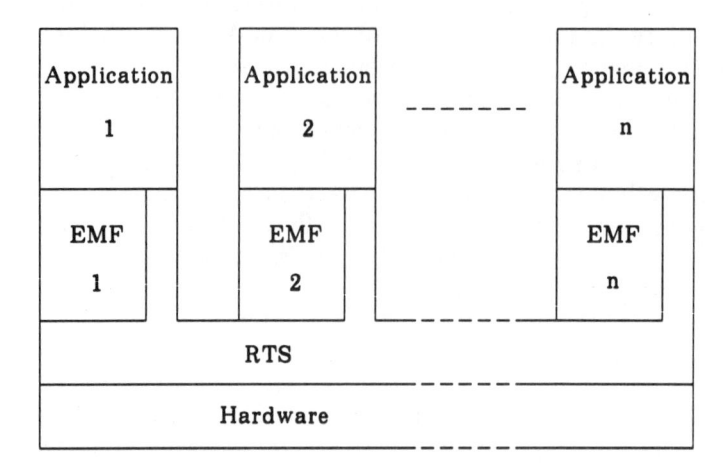

```
┌─────────────┬─────────────┬──────┬─────────────┐
│ Application │ Application │      │ Application │
│      1      │      2      │ ---- │      n      │
├─────────────┼─────────────┤      ├─────────────┤
│    EMF      │    EMF      │      │    EMF      │
│     1       │     2       │      │     n       │
├─────────────┴─────────────┴──────┴─────────────┤
│                    RTS                         │
├────────────────────────────────────────────────┤
│                  Hardware                      │
└────────────────────────────────────────────────┘
```

Figure 5.9: Multiple applications

This architecture has three advantages specific to exception handling:

1. having established that the Exception Management Function is the central node of the exception handling, the solution proposed avoids the communications between Exception Management Functions associated with various applications and so reduces the risk of error propagation between applications;

2. this solution allows several applications to handle exceptions at the same time (search for the exception handler by the Exception Management Function, etc.). The presence of a single non re-entrant Exception Management Function would prohibit the pre-emptive execution of the exception handling operation of an application;

3. it seems easier to implement the Exception Management Functions with the compiled approach. An Exception Management Function is centralized in an application, the Run-Time System manages several applications. With an interpretive implementation the cooperation between the Run-Time System and several Exception Management Functions would be more complex.

e. Performance / Dependability
In an industrial real-time context, the various criteria listed in the introduction of this section must be jointly taken into account. We will particularly study here the influences of the performance and dependability criteria on the implementation of the exception mechanism. This study is illustrated on IMA applications.

The proposed architecture presents obvious advantages for portability, maintainability and dependability. However it imposes additional operations due to the presence of interfaces such as subprogram calls.

This architecture and the association of an Exception Management Function with every application increase both dependability (see preceding part) and performance. Different implementation techniques can be used for different Exception Management Functions associated with different applications taking the application characteristics into account. For applications where the main criterion is rapidity in 'normal' execution, the static mapping technique is more suitable; whereas, for applications where the execution time constraints are less critical but which must react quickly when an error occurs, the dynamic tracking technique will be used. However the joint use of both techniques in one system can generate overheads in memory space.

Unfortunately, this attractive implementation cannot be achieved because each technique requires a different type of interface with the Run-Time System and we only have a single Run-Time System for several applications.

Most of the fault-tolerance techniques need to resume the system in a safe state (backward or forward techniques). To use such techniques to obtain fault-tolerant Run-Time Systems, the state of the Run-Time System must be handled.

One solution is to make the application ask for its execution context to be saved (processor registers, memory area of the application and the Run-Time System) either periodically or at specified points (recovery points). This solution would allow quick recovery of the execution of all the applications in a similar context if the save operations are made frequently. This solution has three drawbacks:

- the time required to perform the save operations is not negligible and will increase with their frequency,
- the physical environment will probably change between the last save operation and current time and this will require a correction in addition to the restoration,
- a single Run-Time System imposes the saving of certain pieces of information associated with all the applications because the Run-Time System is shared by all the applications.

Another solution consists in resuming the complete execution of the application from its initial state. This state will have to be corrected to take the change of the physical environment into account. Moreover, in Ada the elaboration of the initial state is lengthy (creation of tasks, allocation and initialization of variables, etc.) when the application is initialized. To avoid this drawback, the system would have to store in a ROM an image of the application context after the elaboration phase but before the execution phase. Recovery would consist therefore in copying the application context from the ROM to the RAM. This possibility is the technical solution corresponding to the extension (**pragma** PRE_ELABORATE) proposed by (Cifo, 1987). The IMA (Integrated Modular Avionics) concept makes the imple-

300 Chapter 5: Ada Exception Mechanism and Implementation

mentation of this technique more difficult. The context of the application to be saved is broadly speaking the application context, that is the application context developed to perform the function, plus the context of the kernel that monitors this application (stack state, rendezvous queues, etc.). In this case, the solution which consists in having a single Run-Time System would make the reconfiguration complex whereas only the context of the reconfigured application needs to be reinitialized.

Two solutions can be considered:

- having one Run-Time System where the data structures are well partitioned for each application,
- having several Run-Time Systems and a *hyper-scheduler* which dispatches the CPU time and manages the other hardware features (see Figure 5.10).

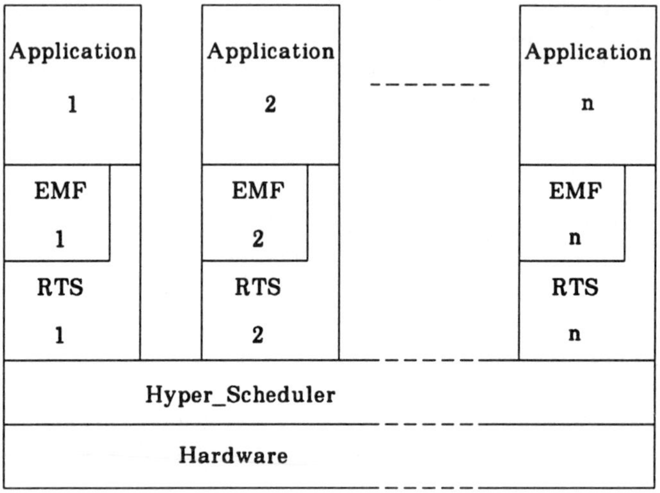

Figure 5.10: Multiple Run-Time Systems

This new architecture also allows various types of Exception Management Function to be implemented as was desired previously in this section.

f. Conclusion

In this section we showed how the industrial software requirements (illustrated by the Integrated Modular Avionics applications) influence the implementation of the exception mechanism. We highlighted that the structuring (application, Exception Management Function, Run-Time System, hardware) favours the important criteria which are portability, maintainability, dependability. We gave the performance intrinsic (that is which may be expected from a theoretical point of view) to each usable technique but tempered them by studying the results of effective implementations.

CHAPTER 6

Dependability Consequences on Ada Exceptions

6.1 Introduction

In this book, we presented how Ada language allows dependable applications to be developed. We saw that the Ada standard features generally make easy the use of dependability techniques to avoid, remove and tolerate faults. In particular we highlighted the great interests of the exception mechanism provided by Ada. However we mentioned throughout the chapters that some techniques cannot be used or that their use is cumbersome. In this chapter, we will reverse the situation and look at the consequences of dependability requirements on the Ada exception mechanism definition. We will show what this mechanism should be, to easily meet all the dependability needs. The specific problems encountered for the implementation of dependability techniques are grouped according to three general requirements: the hierarchical structuring of the errors, the specification of the errors, the expression of more complex relations between the erroneous program and error handling.

The set of these requirements should eventually allow extensions to the Ada language to be contemplated. We will point out the benefits obtained on the dependability of the applications as we go along. The new standard of the language (Ada95) gives extensions whose interests were mainly discussed in chapter 3. However we hope that the language will have a long life and that new releases will appear in the future.

Actual Ada users' interests are not to obtain modifications of the standard. Today, the knowledge given in this chapter is useful for these designers to know the main difficulties concerning the fault handling which will be encountered to produce dependable Ada software. The aim of this chapter is thus not to enumerate criticisms on the Ada language but to provide information so that the Ada program designers can be aware of some difficulties. This warning constitutes a normal attitude with the dependability viewpoint.

302 Chapter 6: Dependability Consequences on Ada Exceptions

The content of this chapter uses the results carried out in the previous chapters relevant to the general needs of dependability (chapter 2) and the capabilities of Ada language to take these needs into account (chapters 3 and 4). Our main interest will concern the Ada exception mechanism. However this chapter does not propose a global solution (a new mechanism) but partial replies to the requirements: expression of hierarchies of errors (section 6.2), association of errors with specification of components (section 6.3) and relations between an erroneous component and an associated handler (section 6.4).

6.2 Hierarchy of errors

6.2.1 Requirements

Hierarchy of components
We gave in section 1.4.1 of chapter 1 the definition of fault, error and failure. We said that these notions are relative to a component. Then we explained that, because of the functional hierarchy of the components of a program (a subprogram calls other ones, etc.), dynamic relations exist at run time between these notions: an error caused by a fault of a subcomponent may then provoke the failure of this subcomponent. This failure may lead the implementation of the component using the subcomponent to an error (erroneous implementation state), etc. Thus the propagation phenomenon associated with the errors provokes at run time a bottom-up breaking of the execution control for error handling.

The main difficulty of mastering errors at design time comes from the opposition existing between the **control** mode used in conventional situations (normal processing) and the control mode obtained from an exception handling. The top-down hierarchical processes used to design sequential systems means that the higher level components control the lower level components: a component at level I is implemented defining the sequence and the execution conditions of the subcomponents that it uses at the lower level I+1. In parallel systems, control relations mainly concern those existing between components on the same level, for instance, synchronization by rendezvous. On the contrary, an exception state reached by a component requires a bottom-up modification of the control of the higher level components.

This situation is especially true if Ada exception mechanism is used. An unhandled exception causes a 'jump' to the exception handler of the calling frame. In a sequential program, the **propagation** of an exception then breaks the control in the higher level components (Figure 6.1).

The techniques proposed in chapter 2 and implemented with Ada in chapter 4 are mainly associated with one level (one implementation level or one specification level). However, in practice, detection and correction may be partially done at a level and completed by the higher level components. New problems occur to allow the mastering of this bottom-up phenomenon. The problems brought up here related to obtaining dependable software are due in the main to this aspect.

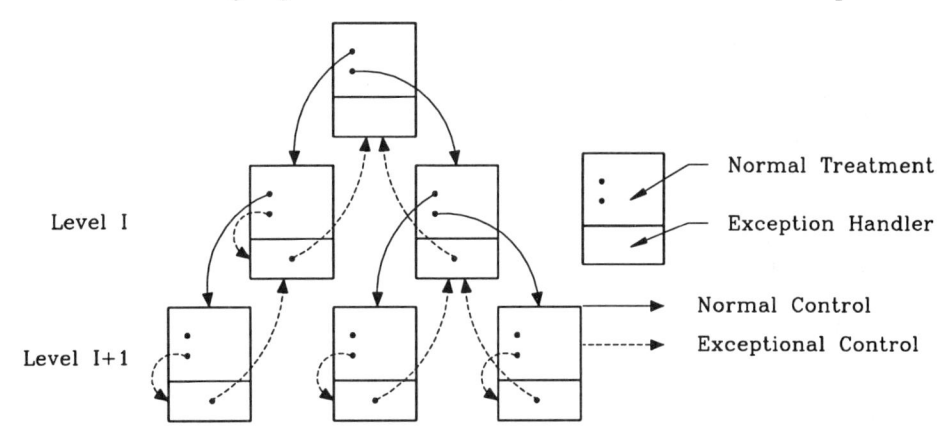

Figure 6.1: Normal and exceptional controls

Hierarchy of exception

The first requirement concerns the need to identify the propagation phenomenon at each level by a specific name because it is necessary to identify each error on the abstraction level where it is considered. We point out the large choice of predefined exceptions available in programming languages (section A.2.1 of appendix A). These range from hardware exceptions such as 'privilege violation' to very general ones such as TASKING_ERROR. However hierarchical relationships exist between the exception names. For example, the old Ada exception NUMERIC_ERROR was considered as a CONSTRAINT_ERROR (more vague) because we do not wish to take its 'arithmetic' origin into account. The NUMERIC_ERROR exception situations are therefore handled by:
    when CONSTRAINT_ERROR =>....

By contrast, distinction may be necessary between the OVERFLOW and UNDER-FLOW cases in order to design an appropriate correction. For instance, if a function returning a positive float raises a CONSTRAINT_ERROR exception, we would like to write:

```
    ...
    exception
      when OVERFLOW  => return FLOAT'LAST;
      when UNDERFLOW => return 0.0;
    end;
```

Chapter 6: Dependability Consequences on Ada Exceptions

This need for accuracy relevant to the predefined exceptions is felt on reading the standard when suppressions of checks are defined [11.7]: the CONSTRAINT_ERROR exception is raised when ACCESS_CHECK, DISCRIMINANT_CHECK, INDEX_CHECK, LENGTH_CHECK, RANGE_CHECK do not give satisfactory results.

What we would like to be able to do is to specify an error identifier hierarchy expressing the '...is a kind of...' relation. For instance, OVERFLOW is a kind of NUMERIC_ERROR which is a kind of CONSTRAINT_ERROR; INDEX_ERROR is a kind of CONSTRAINT_ERROR, etc. Figure 6.2 shows an example of an exception hierarchy.

```
                    CONSTRAINT_ERROR
              /            |           \
     NUMERIC_ERROR    INDEX_ERROR      ...
      /      |     \
OVERFLOW  UNDERFLOW  ...
```

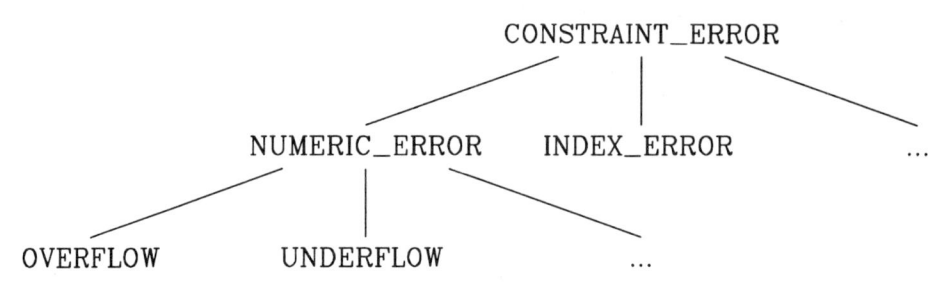

Figure 6.2: Hierarchy of exceptions

The need of such a hierarchy was illustrated with predefined exceptions and also exist for user-defined exceptions. Thus, a CONSTRAINT_ERROR exception raised in a STACK package could be propagated with the STACK_OVERFLOW identifier if it is due to a PUSH procedure called on a full stack or with the STACK_UNDERFLOW identifier if it is due to a POP procedure called on an empty stack. These two exceptions can be considered as an ERROR_ON_STACK if the user does not require more accuracy. This example shows that the desired hierarchy is not only defined by the identifiers (case of CONSTRAINT_ERROR in our example) as a single identifier can cover multiple causes depending on the location where it appears.

In the following sub-sections we will discuss the solutions.

6.2.2 Use of the re-raising technique

The Ada language allows the hierarchy of errors to be expressed by using the re-raising technique as shown in the example below. The STACK_OVERFLOW and STACK_UNDERFLOW exceptions are propagated as an ERROR_ON_STACK exception.

```
procedure MAIN is
  ERROR_ON_STACK: exception;
  procedure NESTED is
    STACK_OVERFLOW, STACK_UNDERFLOW: exception;
  begin
    ...
  exception
    when STACK_OVERFLOW =>
      ...
      raise ERROR_ON_STACK;  -- explicit renaming
    when STACK_UNDERFLOW =>
      ...
      raise ERROR_ON_STACK;  -- explicit renaming
  end NESTED;
begin
  ...
exception
  when ERROR_ON_STACK =>
    ...
end MAIN;
```

This kind of programming prevents an anonymous exception from occurring and adapts the error identifier to the abstraction level where it is considered. However, this solution has four drawbacks:

1. It is bulky as it requires that the higher level exception be raised explicitly in the case of voluntary propagation by the exception handler of the lower levels.

2. As the proposed technique is used manually, its use might be forgotten: the designer does not re-raise the appropriate exception. In the case of involuntary propagation (no handler or the re-raising of an exception that is not visible at a higher level), the exception becomes anonymous. We therefore lose control of the identified error and a part of the benefits of exception handling.

3. In the case of separate compilation of a NESTED procedure, the raising of the exception defined at the highest level is impossible. This comes from the fact that this exception cannot appear in the specification of the procedure.

4. The exception ERROR_ON_STACK may be defined in the specification of a package which exports the NESTED procedure. However the solution which consists of renaming exception does not allow the 'is a kind of' link to be retained because the original identity of the exception is lost by 'when

STACK_UNDERFLOW => raise ERROR_ON_STACK;'. This means that in ERROR_ON_STACK handling, we cannot distinguish between the STACK_OVERFLOW case and the STACK_UNDERFLOW case as required previously.

To meet the requirements expressed, we can consider the use of the renaming statement supplied by the Ada language. For instance, this technique is used in the Input/Output packages:

```
package TEXT_IO is
   ...
   -- Exceptions
   ...
   DATA_ERROR: exception renames IO_EXCEPTIONS.DATA_ERROR;
   ...
end TEXT_IO;
```

This technique may be used to avoid anonymous propagation.

```
procedure MAIN is
   ERROR_ON_STACK: exception;
   procedure NESTED is
      STACK_OVERFLOW  : exception renames ERROR_ON_STACK;
      STACK_UNDERFLOW : exception renames ERROR_ON_STACK;
   begin
      ... raise STACK_OVERFLOW;
      ... raise STACK_UNDERFLOW;
   end NESTED;
begin
   ...
exception
   when ERROR_ON_STACK =>
      ...
end MAIN;
```

In the procedure NESTED the two statements raise the unique exception ERROR_ON_STACK with two names. Then the absence of handlers provokes the propagation of the exception ERROR_ON_STACK.

Using the **renames** statement does not define new exceptions. Then the extract from the following program is not legal because in an exception handler case structure the 'exception choices [...] must all be distinct' [11.2(5)]:

```
procedure MAIN is
  ERROR_ON_STACK: exception;
  procedure NESTED is
    STACK_OVERFLOW  : exception renames ERROR_ON_STACK;
    STACK_UNDERFLOW : exception renames ERROR_ON_STACK;
  begin
    ...
  exception
    when STACK_OVERFLOW  =>   ...
    when STACK_UNDERFLOW =>   -- not legal Ada
  end NESTED;
begin
  ...
exception
  when ERROR_ON_STACK =>
    ...
end MAIN;
```

In this case, on account of the **renames** statement, STACK_OVERFLOW and STACK_UNDERFLOW are two identifiers of the single ERROR_ON_STACK exception and this prohibits two handlers from being associated with them.

6.2.3 Type Exception

Type
In section 3.6.2 of chapter 3 we saw that it is useful to express common handling operations, that is, handlers which are not associated with one exception but with a set of exceptions. This can be achieved in Ada by means of the **others** alternative which, however, groups all the exceptions unhandled by the previous alternatives. Another solution consists in enumerating the exceptions for which a common handling operation is required:

   when E1 | E2 | E3 | E4 => ...

The presence of a handler common to several exceptions expresses the fact that the exceptions correspond to a given class of errors. The listed errors are considered as a 'kind of' new error the identity of which is not explicitly expressed. A solution to this problem consists in defining an 'exception' type. This was proposed for the new Ada95 standard ((Ada9x, 1990) RR0036, p.3-16 and RR0101, p.11-5). This would allow us to write:

```ada
type ERROR is exception;  -- not Ada
E1, E2, E3, E4: ERROR;
...
exception
   when in ERROR =>  ...  -- handler for E1, E2, E3, E4
```

The 'exception handler choice' semantics of the current Ada language version is near to that of cascade test (**if...then...elsif...**). The extension proposed is closer to the **case** construction whose **when** clauses can specify discrete expressions grouping sets of values. If we consider the stack example again, this can be written:

```ada
procedure MAIN is
   type ERROR_ON_STACK is exception;  -- not Ada
   procedure NESTED is
      STACK_OVERFLOW, STACK_UNDERFLOW: ERROR_ON_STACK;
   begin
      ...
   exception
      when STACK_OVERFLOW =>
         ...
         raise;
   end NESTED;
begin
   ...
exception
   when in ERROR_ON_STACK =>  -- not Ada
      ...
end MAIN;
```

This example illustrates that the proposed extension allows two problems to be solved:

- the omission of the STACK_UNDERFLOW handler in the NESTED procedure is corrected at the highest level. The NESTED procedure propagates the same exception that becomes anonymous because of the scope of the STACK_UNDERFLOW declaration; however, as this exception is declared as being of the ERROR_ON_STACK type, it will be handled by the corresponding alternative in the MAIN procedure.
- the case of **raise** explicit propagation in the STACK_OVERFLOW handler corresponds to the previous situation.

Subtype

The subtype notion would allow the case where the number of levels is higher than two to be solved. The following program illustrates such an example.

```
procedure MAIN is
   type ERROR_ON_STACK is exception;   -- not Ada
   procedure NESTED is
      subtype STACK_OVERFLOW  is ERROR_ON_STACK;
      subtype STACK_UNDERFLOW is ERROR_ON_STACK;
   begin
      ...
   exception
      when in STACK_OVERFLOW =>    -- not Ada
         ...
         raise;
   end NESTED;
begin
   ...
exception
   when in ERROR_ON_STACK =>   -- not Ada
      ...
end MAIN;
```

This example calls for several remarks:

1. the keyword **in** of the **when** clause seems to be pointless with regards to our analysis of the problem: we want to handle an error without knowing the accuracy and the cause (type, subtype or variable).

2. we should be able to write:
   raise EXCEPTION_TYPE;
   because of the previous remark: we want to raise an error.

3. the presence of types, subtypes and variables in the clauses poses a problem that should be studied. Consider for instance:

```
E1: STACK_OVERFLOW;
...
exception   -- not Ada
   when in STACK_OVERFLOW => ...
   when in ERROR_ON_STACK => ...
   when E1 => ...
   -- E1 is an exception of type STACK_OVERFLOW
```

Exception handler
The previous example shows that the construction proposed must not be interpreted in the same way as a case statement. The aim of the case statement is to list all the possible situations without recovering (test order not determined) and without omissions (others option). However, here the subtype notion is associated with the inclusion notion (total recovering) and the property sought is not limited to a membership check but is closer to the object-language 'property overload' notion. In the example, the occurrence of exception E1 must lead to a reaction by the statements associated with the '**when** E1 => ...' clause and not the statements associated with the '**when in** STACK_OVERFLOW' clause in spite of the fact that E1 belongs to the STACK_OVERFLOW type.

Dynamic association
However, this solution does not allow the nested procedure to be compiled separately because the definition of the STACK_OVERFLOW and STACK_UNDERFLOW **subtype**(s) references the ERROR_ON_STACK type which is defined by the higher level frame. This is its principle and for us its drawback. To solve it, we should consider ERROR_ON_STACK as a formal parameter of the NESTED procedure. It is not yet a conventional formal parameter as ERROR_ON_STACK is considered in the NESTED procedure as a type and not as a variable. This notion of type of raised exception is close to the one of the type of value returned by a function. We can therefore consider the following specification:
    procedure NESTED **raises** ERROR_ON_STACK; -- not Ada

The similarity with the types returned by the functions is limited. It should, in fact, impose the definition of the ERROR_ON_STACK type before the NESTED procedure instead of considering it as a 'formal type', subtype of a generic exception type. With this aim in view, it should be necessary to specify an 'actual type' (subtype of the exception type) on procedure call. For instance, the NESTED procedure is called as follows.
    NESTED **raising** MY_ERROR_ON_STACK; -- not Ada

Thus a procedure should specify the list of exception types likely to be propagated. The previous proposal would allow different error names to be specified during the various procedure calls and therefore distinction between the handling of these errors in accordance with their context (procedure call condition). Thus we could write:
    begin
    ...
    NESTED **raising** ERROR_STACK1; -- not Ada
    ...
    NESTED **raising** ERROR_STACK2;
    ...
    exception
      when ERROR_STACK1 => ...
      when ERROR_STACK2 => ...
    end;

Hierarchy of errors 311

With Ada

At present, to obtain this result, frames must be added around the calls. We criticized this solution on account of the cumbersome syntax.

This kind of dynamic association which associates an actual exception name with a formal exception name can at present be implemented in the case of packages by instantiation and/or renaming. The technique is shown in the example below which defines a stack as an object.

```
generic
   type ITEM is private;
package STACK is
   ERROR_STACK: exception;
   ... -- without specification of stack type
end STACK;
...
package INTEGER_STACK1 is new STACK(ITEM=>INTEGER);
package INTEGER_STACK2 is new STACK(ITEM=>INTEGER);
```

The creation of two stacks (INTEGER_STACK1 and INTEGER_STACK2) gives rise to two exceptions which are identified by INTEGER_STACK1.ERROR_STACK and INTEGER_STACK2.ERROR_STACK. Renaming can then be used to lighten or to specify the identifiers as follows.

```
ERROR_STACK1: exception renames INTEGER_STACK1.ERROR_STACK;
```

Consider the example above where the package specification explicitly includes the STACK type, inspired from that provided in the standard [12.4(5)]:

```
generic
   type ITEM is private;
package STACK is
   type STACK(SIZE: POSITIVE) is limited private;
   ERROR_STACK: exception;
private
   ...
end STACK;
```

Then a single instantiation is in general performed:

```
package INTEGER_STACK is new STACK(INTEGER);
```

Two stacks are defined as follows:

```
INTEGER_STACK1, INTEGER_STACK2: INTEGER_STACK.STACK(10);
```

However, for this programming, the raising of the ERROR_STACK exception does not allow the cause, that is the erroneous stack, to be distinguished.

Conclusion

The handling of errors involves the identifier hierarchy notion to take the functional hierarchy introduced at design time and the propagation of errors into account. We saw the difficulties involved to implement this hierarchy in the Ada programming. The current possibilities of the exception mechanism may be improved. The exception type and subtype could be used as a means to express this hierarchy. However, this would require studies reconsidering the language as a whole. In the current version of the Ada language, the use of packages as abstract objects, renaming and raising statements provides means allowing the notion of error identifier hierarchy to be partially implemented.

6.3 Specification of errors

Exception specification

We have established in section 3.6 of chapter 3 that the definition of an adapted exception handler requires knowledge of two pieces of information: the causes of the raised exception and the consequences of raising that exception. These allow a diagnosis to be made on the status of the program. The definition of user-exceptions must therefore specify this information. In section 3.3.2 of chapter 3, we pointed out that in Ada it is frequently impossible to specify explicitly the relations between entities (such as frames) and exceptions (except for the exception definition in the package specification). For instance the knowledge of these relations would make the use of F.M.E.A. (Failure Modes and Effect Analysis, presented in chapter 2) easier at each step in the development. Such a specification would allow the consequences of the raising of an exception to be systematically analysed. This is facilitated by the splitting of the specification and the body of Ada entities. A construction of the following form

```
procedure X(A ...; B ...) raises ERROR;  -- not Ada
```

would be interesting. A solution of this type was rejected during the design of the language on account of the heaviness of implementation (*this would require extra run-time code* (Rationale, 1986)). The predefined exceptions create another major difficulty: there potentiality may be unpredictable during design as it depends on the environment (compiler, executive kernel, hardware) (Gauthier, 1989). For example, for a procedure call, a compiler can use the stack (parameter passing) which then may generate a STORAGE_ERROR exception. The raising of this exception is impossible concerning the call if the procedure body code 'inline' insertion technique is used and parameters passed by the registers of the microprocessor. Consequently the standard could not specify exceptions associated with predefined operations.

Specification of errors

Exception causes

The specification of an entity can be considered as the definition of a contract for the user and the implementer of the entity. An error can come either from incorrect use or from incorrect implementation or both. The specification must be able to express the circumstances of correct utilization or the exception raising conditions. We would thus like to specify:

procedure X(A: **in** ...; B: **in** ...) **raises** ERROR **when** A<B;
-- not Ada

This introduces a precondition which would be automatically evaluated on each call for procedure X which delivers a diagnosis (A<B) if the exception is raised.

Adding specifications relevant to the causes of an error will facilitate the use of the Fault-Tree Method, presented in chapter 2. Remember that this technique is used to demonstrate that an error can never occur or to determine a logic combination of its causes. This result is especially interesting to help in designing exception handlers. For instance, if the type of A and B parameters is INTEGER, the ERROR exception will never be raised by the following call:
     X(U+3, U);
because the first parameter value will be always greater than the second one.

Exception consequences

The design of the exception handlers must also take into account the state of the program at the time when the exception is raised. In particular, for subprograms, the specification must define the information relevant to the state of the output parameter values ('out' mode) during the propagation of an exception. For this, it is essential to add assertions. For example:

procedure P(X: **in out** ...; Y: **out** ...) **raises** ERROR
                    => (X = **in** X) **and** (X < Y); -- not Ada

This specification of P procedure expresses that, if the ERROR exception is propagated by procedure P, the value of X ('in out' mode) has not been modified and that the value Y is higher than that of X. We wish to insist on the fact that this specification provides information for the user of the procedure P and constraints for its implementer. This information is however indispensable to design a handler and allow procedure implementation interchangeability.

The previous extension proposals can be enlarged to allow for an invariant definition. Example:

    X, Y: ...
    ERROR **when** X<3*Y: **exception**; -- not Ada

314 Chapter 6: Dependability Consequences on Ada Exceptions

This specification associates an exception error identifier with its cause. The advantages inherent to invariants are obtained: avoid the introduction (and possibly the omission) of multiple tests in the body which thus only defines the normal behaviour, detect errors at earliest possible stage for fault-tolerant mechanisms, etc. The previous example defines a constraint between two variables (X and Y). The error specification could be associated with various constructions of the language as in the following example:

```
type PORTRAIT is
  record
  HEIGHT: POSITIVE;
  WIDTH:  POSITIVE;
  ERROR_PORTRAIT when HEIGHT<WIDTH: exception;  -- not Ada
  end PORTRAIT;
```

Other exception raising specification modes (and the associated causes and effects) can be considered. We will not try to list them here because it would need a complete book which would be based on (Luckham, 1990) concerning sequential programming and (Helmbold, 1985) concerning parallel programming.

6.4 Relations between an erroneous program and an error handler

In this section, we will study the consequences of the requirements relevant to the relations between an erroneous program and an error handler on the Ada language. These requirements cover the relations when an exception is raised (control transfer), during the execution of the correction handler and when normal execution is resumed.

Control transfer
We pointed out certain impossibilities or difficulties concerning the implementation in Ada of control transfer modes different from the one defined by the exception mechanism (termination mode). Remember that when an exception is raised, this mechanism imposes an immediate branch to exception_handler which replaces the erroneous function and then resumes normal execution considering the erroneous function as terminated.

Concerning the transfer of control from the erroneous frame, we may wish to defer or inhibit this transfer. This last requirement can be achieved by using the pragma SUPPRESS. Currently, it is not possible to defer easily the handling of an exception. One solution may consist in introducing a pragma MASK(EXCEPTION_NAME) associated with a frame, pragma which would defer the raising of the exception until the end of the execution of the frame concerned.

An error detected in a frame during the execution of a program, and in particular for a multi-task program, can be both due to the frame and its context (all the frames of the application). For example, the raising of a STORAGE_ERROR exception may not only be due to the procedure where it is raised but also to many push coming from earlier multiple calls for procedures. The contextual and non-local aspect is also found in the processing of corrections. We saw in section 2.4.3 of chapter 2 that a backward recovery performed in a task may impose backward recovery in the other tasks with which synchronizations were made (domino effect). The Ada exception mechanism only allows the raising of an exception to be taken into account at a local level. Tasks only perceive that an error has occurred in another task later through secondary effects. For example, during a rendezvous, the call may cause a TASKING_ERROR exception to be raised in the calling task, if an error previously let the called task to become abnormal. In order to be able to inform the other tasks of the occurrence of an error, it would be nice to have the following statement

raise E **in** T; -- not Ada

raising an exception E in the target task T. This extension has been proposed many times: the 1980 version allowed the **raise** T' FAILURE statement (Ledgard, 1981) raising the predefined FAILURE exception in task T. The proposed extension was rejected first of all for semantic reasons as for example the visibility of E by T -hence the proposal in the first version of the predefined FAILURE exception (Rationale, 1986). The extension proposal was also rejected for implementation reasons: in effect, for this statement, asynchronous events must be managed. This heaviness in the management can be reduced by limiting the taking into account of exception E by task T only to simply the *synchronisation points* as for the abort statement [9.10(6)].

Correction
In addition, the exception handler may not act on the sequence of statements of the erroneous frame but only on its data. This therefore does not allow for easy implementation of an 'exception monitor task', the interest of which we pointed out in chapters 2 and 4. The presence of an exception raising statement directed to a target task, as proposed previously, would facilitate the implementation of this kind of task.

Also, as the exception notion is mainly related to that of error, it may assume a notion of urgency (of importance) close to that encountered for interrupts. For this reason, it may be possible to consider the handling of an exception as being more important than that of other current operations even if the operation in which the error occurs is secondary. This requirement comes from the fact, previously mentioned, that the presence of an error in a task of a multi-task application can generate problems in other tasks and therefore must be urgently handled. For this, we would like to be able to associate a priority different than that of the erroneous task with an exception handler. Note that the priority change problem has already been solved in the rendezvous case: the statements executed by a server task during a rendezvous take the higher priority value, either that of the calling task (client) or their own (server) [9.8(5)].

Resuming
The last point concerns the transfer of control after the handling of the exception. We have seen the possible heaviness of implementing modes other than the 'termination mode' offered by the Ada exception mechanism. A syntactic solution would consist in adding **retry** and **resume** statements respectively allowing the complete execution of the same frame to be restarted or its execution to be resumed in sequence. Thus, by associating the **retry** keyword with the **end** one, a DEPENDABLE_GET procedure could have the following form:

```
procedure DEPENDABLE_GET(I: out INTEGER) is
begin
  GET(I);
exception
  when DATA_ERROR =>
    SKIP_LINE;   -- flush the buffer
    PUT("Give the number again");
end retry DEPENDABLE_GET;   -- not Ada
```

The resumption mode is generally applied in the case of errors occurring on data: the data are corrected, then normal processing is resumed in sequence. This case arises, for example, if a stack has been under-sized. In this situation, it would be interesting to be able to associate the correction handler with the error linked to a data. Q. Cui and J. Gannon (Cui, 1990) propose the correlation of exceptions to types and correction handlings. Example:

```
type STACK is limited private;
# exception OVERFLOW(S: in out STACK) => EXPAND(S, 10);
```

where the EXPAND(S, 10) procedure call increments the size of the stack S by 10 places when an OVERFLOW exception associated with S is raised.

If local resumption cannot be considered, the application must be completely restarted. However, this solution requires a lot of time due to the elaboration of the initial execution context (allocation and initialisation of variables, elaboration of tasks, etc.). For this reason, **pragma** PRE_ELABORATE is interesting to primarily make the initial elaborations and to store them in order to reload the initial context (rapid action) during a request. This extension has been requested by the CIFO group (Cifo, 1991). Finer resumption could be achieved if a statement allowing the global execution context or the context associated to an identity at a given point (and not only initially) to be saved. For example, this would allow 'recovery points' to be implemented to manage the 'backward recovery' (see section 2.4.2 of chapter 2).

Lastly, we pointed out in section 4.5.3 of chapter 4 dealing with the implementation of 'recovery blocks' (and also 'N-versions'), the difficulties encountered due to the fact that in Ada there is no pointer to an anonymous task. The introduction of this possibility goes however against the strong typing which comprises one of the advantages of the language. Another solution to solve the problem would consist in being able to define several separate bodies (several versions) of the task for a given task type specification and to select the effective body on creation of a task. This amounts to defining the task types by their specifications and considering the different bodies as specific values.

CHAPTER 7
Conclusion

We introduced in chapter 2 the definitions of the notions relevant to dependability and the associated techniques. These principles allowed us, in chapter 3, to present and to characterize the exception mechanism proposed by the Ada language. In chapter 4, we developed the use and the implementation of the dependability techniques by means of the Ada language. This chapter gave concrete examples of the implementation of the principles in Ada and allowed the adequacy of the language to be judged in this field. An industrial application requires knowledge on the concepts, their uses and also their implementations. For the last reason, we described in chapter 5 the exception mechanism implementation principles.

Design of dependable Ada programs
The aim of this book was to present the use of the Ada language for designing dependable software and also to define the capabilities of the Ada language in this field. We established in chapters 3 and 4 that the features of Ada facilitate the writing of dependable software. The following five main characteristics were highlighted:

- the strong typing (types and subtypes) allowing the constraints obtained from the specification to be expressed and at the same time allowing static checks (fault avoidance) or dynamic checks (fault removal (test) and fault tolerance (detection means)) to be obtained;
- packages facilitating the reuse of already improved components;
- genericity extending the utilization range of the components by the definition of models, that is solutions independent of the data structures (generic type parameters) and by underscoring only the subprograms whose expression depends on the structures (generic subprogram parameters);
- task management which, integrated into the language, facilitates the translation of a parallel design (and thus avoids errors) and allows checks at compile-time and at run-time;

- and the last but not the least, the exception handling mechanism which facilitates the application of the dependability techniques.

The exception mechanism is often only used to a small extent as its possibilities are not well known. One of the aims of this book was to bring these possibilities to the fore. We underscored the potentialities of the Ada mechanism by comparison with the dependability requirements (chapter 3) and with the exception mechanisms offered by other languages (appendix A). However the exception mechanism must be considered as a primitive tool (in the 'basic building block' sense). It can be used to build other mechanisms expressing more complex dependability functions such as those presented in chapter 4.

Dependability of the design method
We established, at the start of this chapter, that the raising of an exception leads to a break in the control of the current execution to remain at a given location (the exception handler of the frame) or to go to higher frames by breaking their sequencing (propagation). However, conventional design methods basically define control by the upper level frames on the lower level frames presuming a perfect execution in the lower frames. Unfortunately faults exist and associated errors must be handled or propagated by means of exception. This makes difficult the design of tools to control the bottom-up phenomenon caused by exceptions. The use of the exception mechanisms therefore requires the previous use of a design approach integrating this characteristic. In particular, this method must allow the exceptional states and the associated information (causes, context after the raising, reaction, etc.) to be specified for each component.

The breaking of the control which follows the raising of an exception calls into question the sequential relations which exist between the components and implies that a new type of relation be established between these components. We brought to the fore an approach named 'exception monitoring' (see section 4.5.5) whose role is to manage the sequencing of each component and the relation between them. In particular, we pointed out that this notion would take into consideration the domino effect where the processing of an error which occurs in one task influences other tasks (Figure 7.1).

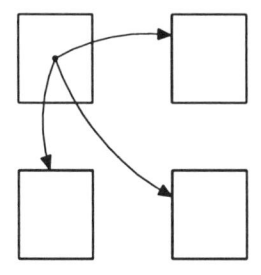

Figure 7.1: Influence on the environment

320 Chapter 7: Conclusion

One of the objectives assigned to this approach is also to be able to express errors which are not local but contextual: each component has a representation of the status of the outside world which must be coherent with its own status (Figure 7.2). An error is defined as a violation of this invariant.

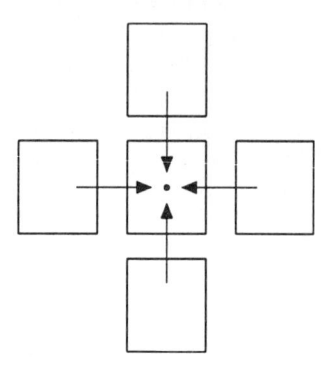

Figure 7.2: Influence of the environment

We therefore require a mechanism which takes into account the hypotheses formulated by the components and the assertions made by others.

The considerations above lead us to conclude that the algorithmic (expressing a program from sequence, test and loop statements), and the conventional top-down design methods expressing a strong functional hierarchy (a component defines the sequencing of the subcomponents) are unsuitable for obtaining dependable software. This is not due to the manner the methods are used but the undependability is intrinsically associated with the method principles. These methods produce software where the operation established in a 'very stringent' way may seem dependable. Such software systems do not behave well when an error occurs.

We described techniques to avoid, remove and tolerate faults in the programs and we gave advice concerning the use of the design approaches. The future works to be done concern design method studies themselves: evaluation of the methods taking dependability criteria into account, proposal of a design method preventing or tolerating fault introduction, study of the design process, that is the intellectual process used to design, in order to obtain dependable software.

APPENDIX A

Comparison of exception mechanisms

A.1 Aim and contents

Aim

In chapter 3, we defined the notion of exception as a concept then presented the characteristics of the Ada exception mechanism. This chapter assumed knowledge of the syntactic and semantic aspects of the features offered by the Ada exception mechanism in order to characterize, that is describe, their fundamental natures. However, many other languages or real-time kernels provide means to handle exceptions during program design. A comparison of the exception mechanisms of these programming tools is interesting in order to:

- improve comprehension of the Ada exception mechanism by positioning this mechanism with regards to those offered by other tools. This comparison is especially useful if the reader knows and has possibly already used some of these tools. This knowledge will make good command over the exception mechanism offered by the Ada language easier for the development of a new application. This knowledge is also useful if the reader needs to reprogram in Ada an application designed with another tool.
- provide a comparative study to see if the features offered by the Ada language on the exception mechanism are more suitable for the programming of an application under design than those provided by other tools. This study justifies the interest of choosing Ada in preference to other programming means.

Our aim is not to give an exhaustive study as the volume of text required would be abnormally large compared to its interest in this book. Also, it would suppose that the reader has in-depth knowledge of all the tools studied. We prefer rather to highlight the characteristic situations showing the possibilities and the limits of the Ada exception mechanism.

Tools studied

We assume here that chapter 3 has already been read as the information specific to Ada will not be repeated. Also, our aim is not to describe the exception mechanisms of the various programming tools in detail but to point out their main interesting characteristics.

The writing of this appendix is based on the following tools and references: Ada (ARM, 1983) and (Ada95, 1995), Chill (Branquart, 1982), Clu (Liskov, 1979), Eiffel (Meyer, 1988), LTR3 (LTR3, 1984), PL/I (Veillon, 1971) and (PL/I, 1976), RMK386 (RMK386, 1988), RMS68K (RMS68K, 1980), RMX286 (RMX286-2/User, 1988) and (RMX286-3/System, 1988), Unix System 3 (Bourne, 1982), Unix System 5 (System5, 1988). For specific remarks, other references will be quoted in the text. Proposals to introduce exception mechanisms exist in other languages. Note for example the case of C++.

Comparison criteria

The studied programming tools are compared considering seven characteristics highlighted in chapter 3: exception declaration, handler association, exception handling, relations between the exception handling and the erroneous program, raising of an exception, exception propagation, case of concurrent programming.

Contents

This appendix contains seven main sections describing the basic items for comparison taking each of the seven characteristics into account one at a time.

In **section A.2** we will examine the exception declaration capabilities. The study deals with the predefined exceptions and the possibility of declaring new exceptions.

The different kinds of associations between exceptions and handlers available for the various tools will be analysed in **section A.3**. We will study the element of the language to which an exception handler is associated. Then the case of two association modes will be discussed: static (defined at compile-time) and dynamic (evolving during the execution). We will conclude this section by examining the scope of the exceptions and the actions performed by default (that is if no handler exists).

In **section A.4** the various possibilities offered for expressing the exception handler will be presented: statements allowed, parametrization and, access to the objects (as data) of the application. The common handling notion and exception priority will also be dealt with. Finally, the case of exceptions raised during exception handling will be considered.

When the handler has been designed, several strategies may be considered to resume the application processing (simple sequential return, retry attempt, etc.). In **section A.5** we will present the strategies adopted by the tools.

In **section A.6** we will discuss with the problems related to the raising of exceptions: automatic (implicit, such as exceptions detected by the Executive System) or voluntary (explicit, such as for declared exceptions).

The problem of propagating exceptions between several levels of an application will be studied in **section A.7**.

In **section A.8** features of concurrent programming interacting with the use of exceptions will be described. The question of the propagation of exceptions between concurrent tasks will be tackled.

In **section A.9** we will not deal with the comparison of the programming tools but discuss the various ways of using the exceptions offered by such tools.

A.2 Declaration

The present topic deals with the comparison of various tools with their capabilities to declare exceptions. Only the expression of an error is considered, not its raising or its handling. The following aspects are successively examined: the predefined exceptions, the possibility of declaring user exceptions, the introduction of exceptions in the specification of application objects (procedures, etc.), and the scope and the visibility of the declarations.

A.2.1 Predefined exceptions

Most of the languages or kernels studied possess predefined exceptions which are implicitly raised by the run-time executive. The word *implicitly* expresses the fact that the detection of the error is not written in the application statements. Presence of an error is checked directly by a test performed in the application code produced by the compiler or in the kernel, or indirectly as a reaction to an interrupt raised by the hardware (mainly by the microprocessor) as described in section 5.2.2 of chapter 5.

The study of the lists of predefined exceptions is interesting as shown in the following sub-sections. The interest does not concern the enumeration but the comparison of the predefined exceptions chosen by the tool designers. Indeed our goal is not to provide extensive knowledge of each tool but to highlight the characteristics of each of them. The comparison criteria are the number and the abstraction level. The reader who wants an exhaustive list of the exceptions must refer to the programmer's manuals given in the references.

The number
The number of predefined exceptions widely depends on the tool used. The predefined exceptions of the RMK386 kernel, of the Ada and LTR languages, of the System 3 and System 5 versions of Unix, of the PL/I language, of the RMS68K and RMX286 kernels and of the Chill and Eiffel languages are examined because they correspond to various choices.

The RMK386 Intel kernel performs very few checks at run-time. It supposes that design faults have been extracted during the design and programming phases. So this kernel raises only three exceptions (send_unit, suspend_task, resume_task). The first two correspond to the overflow of constrained variables of the kernel caused by:

- incrementing a semaphore counter which has the maximum value 65535 (primitive send_unit);
- incrementing the suspension depth level of a task which has reached the maximum depth (255) (primitive suspend_task).

These exceptions only concern the errors associated with implementation constraints which prevent the kernel from working correctly. The last one detects one design error: the awakening of a non-suspended task (primitive resume_task). No checks are made on errors corresponding to the misuse of other primitives. Moreover the errors relative to sequential aspects (such as constraint errors associated with the use of arrays) must be managed by the sequential language (C-language for instance) used to call the kernel primitives.

The Ada language possesses four predefined exceptions: CONSTRAINT_ERROR, (and formerly NUMERIC_ERROR), PROGRAM_ERROR, STORAGE_ERROR and TASKING_ERROR [11.1] whose causes were detailed in section 3.5.1 of chapter 3. In this chapter we pointed out that a high number of errors are grouped under a few identifiers.

In Unix System 3, the notion of exception is a specific case of the general notion of events. Fifteen events are divided into external events (example: SIGINT = pressing of the 'break' key), internal events (example: SIGTERM = end of a process) or exceptional events. Six events of the latter type exist: SIGILL (illegal instruction), SIGFPE (floating point error), SIGBUS (error on the bus), SIGSEGV (segment violation), SIGSYS (inaccurate argument during the call of a system function) and SIGPIPE (writing in a pipe without consumer). In the System 5 version of Unix, exception SIGCLD, signalling the end of a child process to the father process, was added. The number of exceptions is close to that of Ada. However the comparison of this list with the one defined in Ada shows that exceptions in Unix are very close to hardware faults. They are generally detected by hardware devices and handled by low level software means which implement fault tolerance techniques at hardware level. Therefore they are not propagated to application level. Exception SIGSYS groups the main misuses of the Unix executive primitives.

The LTR language has eight predefined exceptions: index_error (accessing of an array with an index out of bounds), overflow (arithmetic), range_error (assignment of a value out of the declared range to a discrete variable), ref_error (using a reference to nil value or undefined value), size_error (assignment or comparison of two objects of different dimensions), storage_error (not enough space available for dynamic allocation), variant_error (access to an ineffective variant), length_error (access to a string out of the 'useful part'). An approach rather similar to the original Ada (Ichbiah, 1979) one led to this list. Now Ada offers more abstraction: for instance, index_error, range_error, size_error and length_error are grouped under the single identifier CONSTRAINT_ERROR. No errors derived from task management are provided in LTR3 whereas the language offers features to use tasks.

In PL/I, nine predefined exceptions are subdivided into six exceptions tied to numeric computation (UNDERFLOW, OVERFLOW, ZERODIVIDE, FIXEDOVERFLOW, CONVERSION, SIZE) and three are said to be useful for debugging (STRINGRANGE, SUBSCRIPTRANGE, CHECK). It is obvious that the designers of this language wanted constraint errors to be detected by the tests during the debugging and not during the execution of the embedded software. Hardware errors are absent and we do not know for instance the effect of a memory overflow. Moreover, no details are provided on the software behaviour if errors concerning the control (a 'program error') occurs. However, the errors induced by a numeric computation are very detailed. In Ada, they were grouped under a single identifier NUMERIC_ERROR and now CONSTRAINT_ERROR.

The RMS68K kernel only offers the exceptions of the MC68000 microprocessor including nine predefined exceptions: bus error, address error, illegal instruction, zero divide, check instruction, trapV, violation privilege, line 1010 emulator, line 1111 emulator. Even if the number of exceptions is close to those of the previous tools, the exception semantics is very far from the application semantics.

The RMX286 kernel is an interesting case. It offers about 120 exceptions. They only concern errors occurring during the call of primitives of the kernel. This high number is due to the following three facts:

- the kernel is very complete (e.g. including file management),
- it detects many logical errors far from hardware (for instance 'time out'),
- no errors concerning the use of the kernel are detected during the compilation of the application using a sequential language such as C for example.

RMX286 and RMK386 are both INTEL products. The number of predefined exceptions is very different because the first one emphasizes the detection of errors and the second one favours run-time performance.

Some extreme cases were presented here. The other languages studied also have predefined exceptions: for example, CHILL (OVERFLOW, TAGFAIL, etc.), or Eiffel which has a class (called EXCEPTION) of predefined exceptions, similar to those encountered in Ada.

Abstraction levels of exceptions
A first approach to introduce a classification of predefined exceptions would tend to distinguish the ones close to hardware means (e.g. error on the bus, illegal instruction, etc.) from the ones close to software concepts (e.g. error in the

communication between tasks). The main idea of such a classification is to highlight the difference between two concepts: the cause (that is the fault) and the perception (that is the error). The first concept is used to specify the Exception Domain states associated with the implementation whereas the second one concerns the specification of the statements used. In fact, the analysis must be refined as this classification depends on the abstraction level selected by the designer of the language or the kernel.

The first choice consists in associating **an exception with the specification of each feature**. Such exceptions are, for instance, zero divide for division, range error for array access, length error for string use, size error for assignment, subprogram error for subprogram call, declaration elaboration error for variable declaration, entry call error, function return error.

This list may turn out to be long on account of the high number of features offered by the languages or kernels, a single exception is generally **associated with the specifications of several features**. For instance, NUMERIC_ERROR was raised by all the arithmetic operations of Ada programs. It especially includes divide error. Another example is CONSTRAINT_ERROR which includes now NUMERIC_ERROR causes and range error, length error, size error, etc. The groups chosen differ according to the tools. For instance in case of LTR3, one of the eight predefined exceptions, called ref_error, is raised if a statement uses as input a pointer type variable having a nil value or an undefined value. Ada program execution generates an exception called CONSTRAINT_ERROR in case of a pointer with a null value [11.1(5)], whereas the presence of an non-initialized variable causes an *erroneous execution* [1.6(7)] or raises exception PROGRAM_ERROR.

In addition to the fact that the statements which can raise a given exception are multiple (example CONSTRAINT_ERROR), for a given statement the erroneous states associated with the specification can be multiple (for example overflow or underflow for arithmetic operations).

On the contrary, exceptions can be distinguished even if the fault which is at its origin is unique. For example, memory overflow is the cause of a subprogram call error and a declaration elaboration error.

This last example allows us to make an interesting remark. If we observe the chronological evolution of languages, we can see that the exceptions proposed tend to move away from the low implementation levels to provide exceptions associated with **abstract points of view associated with the specification** of one or a set of operations offered by the languages. In Ada, integrating NUMERIC_ERROR into CONSTRAINT_ERROR is a good example.

However, certain exceptions are not related to the specifications and cannot be derived from them. They correspond to *abnormal terminations* which are the result of faults caused by the implementation constraints. For instance, the Ada exception STORAGE_ERROR which integrates the subprogram call error and declaration elaboration error notions does not express the negation of an invariant of the specification but that of an implementation constraint. Such an exception therefore cannot be designated by an identifier whose semantics corresponds to those of the language. The multitude of possible implementations (hardware and software) leads to different implementation errors. If the exceptions chosen for a given tool are close to the characteristics of its first implementation, portability problems will occur. On the contrary, an abstract definition of the exceptions requires the conversion of specific implementation errors.

Several distinct implementation errors must raise the same exception in order to be in compliance with the standards of the languages used. This leads to a loss of information. We will give two examples with the BSD4.2 Unix kernel for the SUN-3 systems (BSD4.2, 1988). The hardware exceptions 'privilege violation', 'coprocessor protocol error' and 'TRAP#n' (1<=n<=14) of the 680X0 microprocessor raise the same Unix logical exception SIGILL (illegal instruction). An identical phenomenon is encountered for exceptions 'integer division by zero', 'IEEE floating point underflow', 'IEEE floating point overflow' and 'IEEE floating point operand error' that raise the same logical exception SIGFPE (floating point error). In case of the implementation of an Ada executive on the 680X0 microprocessor and Unix operating system, exceptions 'bus error' and 'illegal instruction' would probably be handled by the Ada run-time environment or would raise exception PROGRAM_ERROR.

The choice of the list of predefined exceptions shows the difficulties encountered by the designers in choosing between the increasing number of exceptions or the generality of each of them (if in particular they do not have to make their choices on simple hardware implementation criteria). A tool offering a high number of exceptions does not guarantee more checks than a tool providing a small number as an exception can include numerous error cases. Also, a small number of exceptions does not mean that only a few faults are possible with this tool. The tool may not carry out the check, which does not mean that faults are absent. In the extreme case of RMK386, the only three exceptions introduced suppose either a good application test or the use of exception mechanisms offered by the 80386 microprocessor. However, this small number enables a minimization of both the memory size and the execution time of the kernel.

A.2.2 User exception declaration

The possibility for the designer to declare exceptions called *user exceptions* is not offered by all programming tools. For instance, Unix System 3 and RMS68K, RMX286 and RMK386 do not offer such possibilities. Their designers considered that it was not the role of these kernels to manage the notion of exceptions and that this must be performed by the language used to call the primitives of these kernels.

In case of Unix System 5, two user exceptions whose identifiers are predefined (SIGUSR1 and SIGUSR2) were introduced. Then 16 software events were added. These events can be used as user exceptions, but their number is limited.

The languages studied allow user exceptions, expressing error situations proper to the application operation, to be defined and managed. In the case of Ada or LTR3, these exceptions are identifiers which could be seen as constants of a pseudo predefined type 'exception', but they are not. Their declarations introduce new error identifiers without specifying their cause, which will never be expressed since the raising of these errors will be explicitly requested (Ada's statement raise for instance). This approach is opposed to the technique of invariants that predefines normal conditions of good operation (that is the contract) and so it implicitly provokes the raising of an exception when these conditions are not fulfilled. This point of view is particularly developed in Eiffel (Meyer, 1988) and it will be detailed in section A.6 dealing with exception raising.

For Ada and LTR3, a type 'exception' does not exist. For instance it should allow:

- definition of formal exceptions as subprogram parameters or generic unit parameters,
- building of types (record, array, etc.) integrating some exception types in order to put together in one component data structures and exceptions associated with them,
- definition of subtypes in order to create an exception and handling hierarchy.

The object-oriented approach allows user exceptions to be created by instantiation of an 'exception class' (Dony, 1989). The use of an inheritance technique offered by the object-oriented languages will be above all interesting for the association of exception handlers. Thus, exception ZERO_DIVIDE can be seen as a specialization of exception NUMERIC_ERROR and then CONSTRAINT_ERROR and therefore inherit its handling.

A.2.3 Specification

In this section, the exception specification will be approached. It concerns the declaration of exceptions in the interfaces of the features of the tools, whose raising is possible during the execution of the instructions associated with these features. The association of the reaction will be dealt with in section A.3.

No information on the potentially raised exceptions is given in the specification of the primitives of the kernels studied. This is due to the fact that kernel primitives are called by a language that does not know this notion (for instance C-language).

By contrast, in LTR3 (de Bondelli, 1984), two levels of declaration are present. The exceptions raised by subprograms exported by a module (an equivalent to an Ada package) must be declared in the module interface (level 1) and they must appear later in the interface of the procedure that raises the exception (level 2).

Example:

```
interface of MATRIX_MONITOR ;
  type ...
  exception SINGULAR;
  ...
end interface ;
body of MATRIX_MONITOR ;
  procedure INVERSE(...) signals SINGULAR ;
  begin
    ...
    signal SINGULAR ;
    ...
  end;
end body;
```

Due to the double declaration of the SINGULAR exception, the process (the task in Ada terminology) which uses the procedure INVERSE is informed of the possible raising of this exception by the execution of this procedure. This declaration seems to be essential in case of LTR3 for, as we will see later, the handling of an exception (other than the suppression of the calling task) is never done in the erroneous procedure but in the calling procedure.

A rather similar situation is encountered in the Chill language for which a declaration of exceptions in the specification is compulsory for propagated exceptions. Such a declaration must not be done if the exception is handled locally by the procedure.

The obligation to list the exceptions that can be raised by a procedure in its specification is also present in Clu language, including the ones obtained from the propagation (except the predefined exception failure). For example, the following declaration gives the specification of subprogram divide which may raise (that is signal) exception zero divide.

divide=proc(x,y:int) returns(int) **signals(zero_divide)**

A similar feature was described in (Booch, 1991) for the C++ language. A different proposal was made in (Adamo, 1991) in which a supplementary type intervenes. It specifies the type to be returned by the correction handling (this aspect will be developed in section A.5).

Unanimity seems to be established in the obligation to declare, in the specifications, the exceptions not handled locally and propagated to the caller. The aim of this is to avoid the omission of an exception handler in the caller frame. We said in section 3.3.2 of chapter 3 that Ada features have limited capabilities in this domain. Some authors (Gauthier, 1989) stress the fact that the list must be complete and so must also include the potential predefined exceptions. They point out that it can pose problems for the exceptions associated with implementation faults such as STORAGE_ERROR. In effect, for a given feature, the potentiality of the raising of an exception such as STORAGE_ERROR cannot be established by simply reading the standard. In practice, this potentiality depends on the choices of the 'Ada Execution Environment' designers. For instance, if a 'Stack Machine' model is chosen to manage the memory (no register, all data is stored in a stack), then execution of an addition may cause the raising of exception STORAGE_ERROR.

Also, in Ada language, we showed in section 3.3.2 of chapter 3 the dynamic aspect of the exceptions raised, due to the propagation mechanism. The coherence between specified and propagated exceptions cannot be established at compile-time, this check would be performed during run-time. The heaviness of the checks to be conducted by the executive has been judged as unacceptable (Rationale, 1986).

No specifications are mandatory imposed in PL/I. The presence of an exception detection prefix may indicate the possibility of the occurrence of this exception. Detection is then authorized.

```
(ZERODIVIDE): div: procedure;
```

If the exception identifier is prefixed by 'NO', then the error will not be detected (and the exception will not be propagated) unless it is explicitly specified when the procedure is called (see next section). Therefore, masking can be specified.

```
(NOZERODIVIDE): div: procedure;
```

For C-language, the absence of library management by the compiler (unlike Ada packages) implies that the separated compilation of a function requires two specifications for this function. The first is associated with the definition of the function and the second with its use (extern specification). For C++ it is proposed (Adamo, 1991) to use this necessity to offer the renaming capability for the exceptions propagated by the functions.

```
char *convert(int *code, char *result) raises char badcode (int)
{...}
...
extern char *convert(int *, char *) raises char codeerror (int);
```

Therefore the name of the exception is adapted to the context where the function is used. A similar effect can be obtained using the renames capability of Ada.

```
    package P is
      E: exception;
      ...
    end P;
    with P;
      ...
      MY_ERROR: exception renames P.E;
      ...
```

A.2.4 Scope and Visibility

Two different approaches are again present concerning scope and visibility notions whether we are dealing with a language (such as Ada or LTR) or a kernel.

Languages

In the case of languages, exceptions are identifiers declared in modules (LTR3 feature) or in subprograms or blocks (Ada features). The scope and the visibility of exceptions follow the conventional laws defined for the identifiers. The characteristics of Ada are more general since exceptions may be defined locally in a statement block whereas they are associated with procedures in LTR3.

However, user exceptions differ from conventional variables. Variables have the same life as the frame in which they are declared whereas the raising of an exception can cause its propagation out of the frame to the other objects of the program. For this reason, the declaration of the exception, in the header of the procedure that can raise it, is an interesting feature of LTR3, even if the propagation is limited to one level (the caller). In Ada, the lack of exception declarations in the specification of a subprogram and the dynamic propagation of exceptions can cause an exception to go out of its scope and then to come back possibly as presented in section 3.3.2 of chapter 3.

Kernels

In case of kernels, the exceptions raised from calling primitives offered by these kernels must be distinguished from the exceptions raised by the application.

As far as calling primitives of the kernel is concerned, the problems of scope or visibility are not posed since these exceptions are proper to the primitives, they are not associated with syntactical frames and so are valid in the whole unit (e.g. in the task for RMX286 and in the application for RMK386). This situation is the same as that of language predefined exceptions.

For kernels with a user exception handling mechanism, the notions of scope and visibility are not managed as rigorously as they are for languages. This requires careful attention on behalf of the designer. In effect, the designer must handle two tools (a kernel and a sequential language) designed separately and for which no relations exist, other than check of kernel primitive call syntax correctness in a program written in the sequential language. Thus the call for a primitive raising an exception is considered by the language compiler as a call for any external function for which it possibly checks the conformity of the type of parameter defining the raised exception. The compiler cannot establish if the value of the parameter (that is if the identity of the exception) is acceptable for the analysed frame.

Also, kernels do not generally offer exception declaration primitives but only a list of pre-established user exceptions; these exceptions being used or not. These are, for instance, numbers 64 to 255 for RMS68K, constant identifiers SIGUSR1 and SIGUSR2 for the initial version of Unix System 5, etc. In this case, the notion of scope does not exist as it encompasses the complete program. No checks are possible at compile-time or at run-time. Thus, programs such as the one given below will not be considered as erroneous by the compiler or the executive.

```
f()
/* raises exception number 12 */
   { ...
      if C { raise(21) }
      ... }
```

Masking and kernels
As the primitives dealing with the exceptions offered by the kernels are not features of the language used to call them, the scope of the exceptions is not verified. This makes the masking concept difficult to program.

The kernels generally present primitives for masking or unmasking exceptions. A masked exception will be ignored, that is to say that no detection will be done or no handling will be done when it is raised. This use of masking and unmasking primitives supposes a special attention from the designer since no control can be made at compile-time or at run-time. In this way programs can be obtained, for which the detection of an exception in a certain frame depends on the program path used at run-time before the execution of the frame and not on the structure (nested frames) of the program. The program below shows an example of this (in pseudo-code):

```
EXCEPTION_DECLARATION;
...
if CONDITION
   { MASK_EXCEPTION;
     ...
   } /* UNMASK_EXCEPTION statement omitted (design fault) */
   else { ... }
... /* <= according to the used path (CONDITION true */
    /* or false) the exception is masked or not  */
```

In the case of Unix, an exception (my_exception) can be masked associating a predefined (SIG_IGN) handler (signal(my_exception, SIG_IGN)). Note that, for this kernel, masking does not consist in inhibiting the detection of an error but in associating a null reaction (without effect) with it. Unmasking is achieved by reassociating the handler replaced beforehand. This handler must be saved at masking-time as shown in the following example:

```
...
old_handler = signal(my_exception, SIG_IGN);
   /* masking: my_exception ignored and */
   /* previous handler is saved in old_handler */
...
signal(my_exception, old_handler);
   /* re-establishes the detection and the handler */
```

Masking and languages
Most of the languages studied (except Clu) allow predefined exceptions to be masked by features taken into account at compile-time (like: pragma SUPPRESS in Ada [11.7], check option in Eiffel, (NO ...) in PL/I) whereas for the kernels primitives are considered at run-time (signal(x, SIG_IGN) in Unix). Ada, Eiffel and PL/I require further explanation.

In the case of Ada, the pragma SUPPRESS is not applied to the predefined exceptions but to some of their causes which allows more precise selectivity. For instance, exception CONSTRAINT_ERROR can be masked on specific checks, (ACCESS_CHECK, DISCRIMINANT_CHECK, INDEX_CHECK, LENGTH_CHECK and RANGE_CHECK) and even for specific variables or types [11.7(5)].

The Ada standard clearly defines [11.1(3)] that an exception is a static entity. This was illustrated in section 3.3.2 of chapter 3 by recursive calls of a procedure: the compiler only creates one exception propagated along the procedure call chain though the declaration of the exception is within the procedure. The exceptions therefore cannot be masked and unmasked dynamically using the basic mechanism. Also, concerning user exceptions, no masking mechanism is available especially as the Ada language does not allow invariants defining user errors to be expressed. We did however propose the implementation of such a mechanism in section 3.5.2.

On the contrary, in Eiffel, it is possible to suppress the valuation of assertions for a list of classes or for all the object classes. Predefined exceptions of the class EXCEPTIONS can be masked as a whole or not.

Language PL/I offers an intermediary mechanism between those provided by high level languages such as Ada or LTR3 and those provided by kernels. The nine predefined exceptions can be detectable or not. This turning on or off of the detection mechanism is associated with a frame such as a statement, a block or a procedure.

Example:

```
(SUBSCRIPTRANGE): IF A(I)=0
    THEN (NOSUBSCRIPTRANGE): A(I/2)=B/C;
    ELSE : I=I+1;
```

At run time, the evaluation of the condition of the IF statement can generate the exception SUBSCRIPTRANGE if I is not in the range of the index of array A. The same check is disabled when assigning A(I/2).

Even if the masking is syntactically associated with a frame, the absence of information allows dynamic masking to be obtained. For instance the statement A(I/2)=B/C can generate exception ZERODIVIDE, if the above program extract is syntactically inside a frame checked by (ZERODIVIDE). However this exception is masked if the extract is the body of the subprogram called by another one which uses the disabling option (NOZERODIVIDE).

Masking and performance
Masking of exceptions is frequently used for optimization reasons and more precisely to avoid executing the implicit check instructions (for instance divisor different from zero, array index or stack pointer in a given range). This possibility is more suitable for languages than for kernels. When, in a program, primitives of kernels are called to mask exceptions in a part of the program, the check instructions are compulsorily present in the code because the program is compiled without knowing this demand. This is because the semantics of the primitives is not taken into account by the compiler. So no memory size benefits are obtained. Moreover the check instructions are either executed but the control is not transferred to the exception handler, or a preliminary test must be done to detect the masking or unmasking request in order to check or not the invariant associated with the exception. So temporal benefits are low.

A.3 Association

Raising an exception provokes a reaction from program execution to handle the exception if a handler is associated. In this section will look at this association, comparing the Ada language capabilities with those of other programming tools.

In the first section we will examine the syntactical element in which the association is defined. The following question will be examined: 'with what is the exception handler associated?'. In the second section we will study the syntactic element which makes the association. The following question will be examined: 'by what is the exception handler associated?'. In the third section we will explain when an exception handler is associated with an exception. The static mode (at compile-time) and the dynamic mode (changing during execution) will be successively explored. The scope of the association will be described in the fourth section. In the last section we will consider handling by default.

A.3.1 With what?

The following types of associations will be presented successively: a handler can be associated with an exception either globally (for the whole application) or for a given frame and, in the latter case, permanently or during a period when the given frame is used.

Associating a handler with an exception
In the first case, an exception is associated with a handler which is always the same whenever the exception is raised. For instance, this possibility is attractive for returning the biggest float value offered by the implementation if exception ZERO_DIVIDE is raised. This answer is independent of the subprogram in which a positive float number division is computed.

RMK386 only offers this kind of association. For this kernel an exception handler is associated during its initialization (KN_initialize). Moreover only one handler can be defined, so the association is always the same whatever the exception raised.

This kind of association also concerns cases of associations by inheritance. We can quote for instance:

- the objects of Eiffel that inherit handlers from their instantiated classes,
- the tasks of RMX286 that have the same exception handlers as the *job* they depend on,
- the children tasks of Unix created as a clone of a mother task (fork statement).

Associating a handler with an exception in a given frame
The second case concerns the association of a handler with an exception determined by the frame in which the exception is raised. The word frame is general for it can represent a task, a procedure, a package, a block of statements, etc., depending on the tool considered. In such a case the same exception raised in two different frames might not provoke the same reaction. The reaction is the same wherever the exception is raised inside a given frame.

Note that the single frame case (the application) is the one studied in the previous paragraph.

This kind of association is available in most of the programming tools studied. However the natures of the frames are extremely variable. For instance a frame is a task for RMS68K, a procedure for Eiffel and different structures (task, subprogram, block, package, generic unit) for Ada [11.2(3)] or for Chill.

Associating a handler with a frame in a using frame
In the third case, the association of a handler with an exception does not depend on the frame in which the exception is raised but on the calling frame. The term 'calling frame' indicates the frame in which the potentially erroneous frame is used (caller of a procedure, user of a package, etc.).

Associating a handler in the calling frame may be interesting. For example, if a subprogram is called at several locations in a real-time program and if it raises an exception, the correction handling can be different (fine or coarse) according to the call locations which impose various time constraints.

This kind of association exists in Ada for instance if exceptions are raised in the declarative parts [11.4.2] or if exceptions are propagated [11.4.1(9)]. This technique is the only one used in the case of LTR3 procedures.

(Goodenough, 1975) proposes to extend this kind of association to all levels (procedure calls, arithmetic operations, etc.).

```
G(A) {except1: action1}
```
———
———
———

```
G(A) {except1: action2}
```

We can have therefore two different handlings for an exception (except1) depending on the location of a procedure call (G(A)).

The implementation of such a proposal in Ada was studied in section 3.4 of chapter 3.

A.3.2 Where?

In this section we will present various solutions adopted by the programming tools studied to locate the exception handlers. This study presents the syntactical aspects separating the cases where the handlers are inside and outside the erroneous frames.

Within

In the first case, an exception handler can be placed within the frame where an exception can be raised. The choice of this location allows the occurrence of the exception to be masked for the user frame.

For example, procedure READ_DATA can, if erroneous data is given, raise exception CONSTRAINT_ERROR. An **internal exception handler** may consist in asking for the value again in the exception handler associated with this procedure.

This kind of 'internal association' is found in Ada [11.2(4)] [11.2(6)], RMS68K, Chill and Eiffel.

Outside

In the second case, the exception handler is outside the frame where an exception can be raised. Here we speak of **external handling**. The relations with the calling frame can be subdivided in two classes: global association with the calling frame or specific association depending on the call location.

a) Global

A global association with the calling frame expresses the fact that the handling of an exception occurring in the called frame is not linked with the particular call location but with the calling frame considered globally.

For example procedure READ_DATA can, if erroneous data is given, raise exception CONSTRAINT_ERROR where the external exception handling consists in supplying the last value given without error by this procedure.

This mechanism is the one adopted in LTR3. The exception handlers are not part of the procedure that raises the exception but of the calling procedure.

The association mechanisms of exception handlers with an object inherited from a class can be said to belong to this category.

The association of the propagated exceptions in Ada has the same characteristics. This case concerns exceptions unhandled inside or raised in the declarative part [11.4.2].

As the exception handling is global, it does not know the circumstances of the particular raising (which remains internal) or the circumstances of the calling of the erroneous frame.

b) Local

An association depending on the location where the erroneous frame is used is necessary if error handling must depend on the circumstances of the erroneous frame use.

For example procedure READ_DATA can, if erroneous data is given, raise exception CONSTRAINT_ERROR whose external handling consists in:

- supplying the previous value returned or,
- attempting a second reading or,
- calling another procedure on stand-by, etc.

(Goodenough, 1975) proposes the most precise static association. For instance, in the case of the following assignment statement

    X:=A* (B+C) ;

an OVERFLOW can be detected by the execution of the addition or the multiplication and we may want to associate a different handler depending on the case. This association leads to the following syntactic notation proposal:

    X:=(A*(B+C) [OVERFLOW:handle_+_overflow]) [OVERFLOW:handle_*_overflow];

Another example that illustrates this association mode for procedures was presented in third part of section A.3.1.

Even if this association makes for very precise handlings, it leads to unreadable programs where the syntactic elements (expressions, statements, etc.) are burst by exception handlers (Liskov, 1979) (Gauthier, 1989) whereas one of the forecast interests of the exception mechanism is to facilitate the distinction between the normal and the exceptional behaviour of a program.

The availability of the single association technique 'outside' can be criticized, because it does not allow a frame to correct itself (as in the case of handling within the frame) and so be autonomous and fault tolerant with regard to its use.

From inside to outside
In practice, the two situations shown in the preceding sub-sections can complement each other. An exception raised in a frame is **partially corrected** by an exception handler inside this frame and the correction is **completed** by an exception handler of the external frame.

Ada allows this solution to be expressed by authorizing the raising of an exception within an exception handler.

A.3.3 When?

An exception handler can be associated with an exception at two different times:

- either at compile-time: in this case we talk about *static association*,
- or at run-time: in this case we talk about *dynamic association*.

The association is **static** for Ada, LTR3, Clu and Chill. However, the propagation phenomenon provides a dynamic effect (Leverrand, 1982) since the exception handler is the one of the calling frame. On the contrary, in the case of RMK386, though the association is made during execution, it can be likened to a static association for it is established once and for all when the execution of the application is initialized.

The association is **dynamic** for kernels since no semantic analysis of the primitives used by the program is made at compile-time (RMS68K, RMX286, Unix). In addition, we will explain in what way the association is considered as dynamic in the case of PL/I.

Unix, RMX286 and RMS68K allow a handler to be associated with any task by means of a primitive. This association can be changed during the execution by calling the association primitive once again. We will now briefly describe the characteristics of the association techniques.

The first version of Unix provides function `signal` which associates a function (`func`) with an exception (`event`) and returns the handler function previously considered.

```
void(*signal(event,func))()
int event;
void (*func)();
```

The BSD (BSD4.2, 1988) version offers an equivalent primitive (`sigvec`).

The System V version possesses a similar function (`sigset`) that has an interesting extra possibility. An exception associated with the predefined symbol `SIG_HOLD` allows the raising of this exception to be stored without starting any handling. The normal execution is continued until a new association specifies an exception handler. This handler is executed if an occurrence of the exception was stored. This function allows critical sections of the code to be protected by delaying the association and therefore the execution of an exception handler.

In RMX286, an exception handler is associated with a job at time of creation (create$job), or with a task during its execution (set$exception$handler) by passing the function of the handler.

Kernel RMS68K can either make a conventional association (EXPVCT, TRPVCT) or associate an *exception monitor task* with one or more application tasks (EXMON). This monitor task is executed in parallel with the application tasks which are monitored. This association can be modified (DEXMON) and/or masked (ignored) (ERMMSK).

As previously highlighted for PL/I, the association (ON) of an exception with a handler is purely dynamic (though the language is compiled) and presents an original characteristic. At the time of a procedure call, the association is propagated until a called procedure specifies a new association. The previous process is iterative. A disassociation statement (REVERT) restores the previous association (stack phenomenon). Note that the stack is not managed automatically taking the nested frames of the program into account at compile-time but explicitly by the programmer (association and disassociation statements). For instance if a called procedure establishes an association and does not execute a disassociation statement, then this association is maintained when the calling procedure is resumed.

A.3.4 Up to where?

In this section we will address the association scope problem. Let us briefly list the cases encountered and classified by scope width:

- in Chill, the scope of an association declaration is either a declarative part or a statement or a procedure or a task,
- in Ada, the scope of an association declaration is a frame [11.2(3)],
- for the LTR3 and Eiffel languages, the scope of an association declaration is a whole procedure,
- in the RMS68K, RMX286 and Unix kernels, the scope of an association declaration is a whole task. This association remains valid as long as a new association is not explicitly requested,
- for the RMK386 kernel, the scope of an association declaration is the application taken as a whole.

The definition of the scope can be challenged for certain tools because of the disassociation statements (as in PL/I) or the introduction of masks (PL/I, RMS68K, Unix, pragma SUPPRESS Ada). Refer to section A.2.

A.3.5 And otherwise?

The programmer might forget (deliberately in certain cases) to associate a handler with a given exception. This section specifies the association performed in these situations called association by default.

In Ada, the default handling of an exception corresponds to a propagation of the exception to the calling frame. This propagation mechanism will be discussed in section A.7. Let us point out that the language specifies what happens when an exception is not handled at main program level: the main program is abandoned [11.4.1(5)]. But the action after the main program has been abandoned is not defined [11.4.1(20)]. Such information may be useful for embedded programs. A mechanism similar to the one presented for Ada (propagation) is encountered in Chill.

In Clu, a unhandled exception is changed into a predefined exception called failure. We mentioned in section 3.3.2 of chapter 3 the interest of such a solution to avoid anonymous exceptions.

In the RMK386 kernel, an exception that is not associated with a handler involves an interrupt (INT3) when raised.

In the case of Eiffel and PL/I, the default handling corresponds to the printing of a message and the termination of the application. For instance, in Eiffel, it occurs if the class of the instantiated object did not specify any exception handler. This notion of inheritance also exists in RMX286 although it is less developed. A task which does not have any exception handlers inherits the one of the job, or by default the one of the kernel.

Remember that in LTR3 the erroneous procedure does not handle an exception. This is done by the caller. If the caller did not specify any exception handlers, the task which involved the call of this procedure is killed even if there are several intermediate levels of nested procedures in which handlers are provided.

This also applies to the handling by default for Unix and RMS68K kernels. For Ada tasks, this solution is also used for handling by default.

A.4 Exception handling

The handler of an exception is the part of the program which is performed to react to the raising of this exception. It may receive information by parameters and may itself access certain information on objects (visibility) to try to understand what has happened (diagnosis) and therefore take appropriate action which can be:

- a precise correction, if the location and the cause of the raising of the exception and the means to handle it are known,
- an emergency measure, if the above mentioned information is not known, to limit the consequences and avoid the occurrence of others errors,
- an attempt to retry the erroneous action, hoping that it will work better,
- a masking, to ignore the exception, continuing as if nothing had happened.

The error correction or compensation techniques were presented in section 2.4 of chapter 2 and implemented with Ada in section 4.5 of chapter 4. Their principles are general but the language used to implement them makes this implementation more or less easy. A comparison of the programming tools concerning the exception handler's writing capabilities is interesting.

The association between an exception and its handler was presented in the previous section. We stated that raising an exception involves transferring the control to the associated handler. Another control transfer must be done at the end of the handling. The various (handling) starting and leaving strategies will be studied in section A.5.

In this section we will address only the features of the exception handling itself. In the first subsection (A.4.1) we will present the statements authorized for handling and the possibility for the handler to access the variables of the application. In the second subsection (A.4.2), we will look at the parametrizing of the exception handlers, then the possibility of using common handling for several exceptions (subsection A.4.3). The execution conditions will be analysed in subsection A.4.4 (memory allocation for the stack, priority and access to the processor). Finally, subsection A.4.5 will conclude this section giving the behaviour of the tools studied when an exception occurs during exception handling.

A.4.1 Visibility of the objects, authorized statements

In all the high level languages that we studied, the exception handling visibility (or object accessibility) rules are those relevant to the place where the handler is located. In Ada (or Eiffel), for instance, the visibility rules are those of the exception handler frame.

For **local** handling (within the frame, see section A.3.2), the statements of the handler have the same access rights to the variables and objects as the statement that raised the exception.

The authorized statements in an exception handler in Ada are the same as those allowed in the frame [11.2(8)]. The only limit prevents use of the goto statement which cannot transfer control back to the erroneous frame or to another exception handler [5.9(5)]. For the Eiffel and Clu languages, the authorized statements are also those used in the frame.

An exception handler in Unix is a function that has a formal parameter. The actual parameter is the identifier of the exception which caused transfer of control to this exception handler.

```
void handle_exception (event)
  int event;
  ...
```

As no function nesting exists in C (the language generally used for software programming using Unix primitives), the local variables of the erroneous function cannot be used by the exception handling function unless all variables are placed as global variables.

This problem can be solved as follows. It is possible to retry the execution of a program (longjmp) at a point in a function where the state of the context was previously saved (setjmp). The handling may only consist in returning to the erroneous function (longjmp) at the saved location (setjmp). A value is communicated when returning by longjmp function and then a different treatment (the exception handling) can be considered in the erroneous function. As this treatment is included in this function, all the variables usable by this function can be accessed by the handler. This programming mode is illustrated by the following example which is commented below.

Example:

```
#include <signal.h>
#include <setjmp.h>
jmpbuf save_context;
void handle_exception (event)
  int event;
  {
  signal(event, handle_exception);/*(4) reinitialization*/
  longjmp(save_context,1);/*(5) jump to the saved context*/
  printf("never executed");
  }
main ()
  {
  float dividend, result;
  dividend = 6.0;
  signal (SIGFPE, handle_exception );  /*(1) association */
  if ( setjmp(save_context) == 0) /* (2) context saving */
       divisor = 0.0;               /* the first time */
  else divisor = 3.0;   /*(6) after restoration of context*/
  result = dividend/divisor;   /* (3) */
  printf("%d", result);
  }
```

The signal function (1) associates the handle_exception function as the exception handler of the exception SIGFPE (Floating Point Error).

The setjmp function (2) saves the execution context in the global variable save_context and returns the integer value 0. Exception SIGFPE raised by the division by zero (3) involves transfer of control to the handle_exception function that handles this exception.

This handler re-establishes the association (4) destroyed by the transfer. Then the `longjmp` function (5) restores the context saved in `save_context` by a `setjmp` primitive and communicates the value 1.

The execution of the `main` function is therefore resumed at the `setjmp` statement (2) which then returns the integer value 1 (supplied as output parameter in `longjmp`). The correction process is specified in the `else` part of the `if` statement (6) of the main procedure.

Thus in the proposed solution, the correction process can use the local variables of the erroneous function because this process is included in this function. However this process cannot be distinguished from the normal behaviour since the `setjmp` statement which locates the resuming point must be executed by the normal processing to save the actual context.

The AT&T version of Unix introduced two new features. First, it became possible to avoid reinitialization of the exception handler by the default handling (which would kill the task) using the `sigset` primitive instead of the `signal` primitive. Moreover, the `ptrace` statement allows the data and the code of the erroneous task to be changed by the handler. We have therefore total access to the information of this task, plus the possibility of completely modifying its behaviour by having access to its executable code! This freedom is the best or the worst thing depending on the designer. The dependability of the software tool will therefore depend on the dependability of the designer.

The same problem concerns RMS68K kernel which allows one or more tasks to be associated with an exception monitor task. This task can, by means of 2 primitives, read *the state of a target task* (RSTATE) and modify it (PSTATE). The state of a task is its execution context: data registers, address registers, stack pointer, program counter, etc. Therefore the exception monitor task can completely master the controlled task. This controllability is made easier by passing parameters to the monitoring task as we will show in the following section. However the execution context concerns low level information as register values.

A.4.2 Parametrizing of exception handlers

The possibility of passing information to an exception handler is mentioned in the proposal made by (Goodenough, 1975) although it is not developed there. This is not provided for PL/I and Ada because they suppose local handling of exceptions (the local objects are visible). In section 3.6.1 of chapter 3 we mentioned the possibility of communicating a string value with Ada95. However these languages, through the propagation notion, allow external handlers to be defined which have no information other than the identification of the exception. This problem is particularly serious for the LTR3 language for which external handlings are the only ones permitted.

With parametrizing an exception handler can acquire information on values used in the erroneous module at raising time. The Clu language includes this possibility. The operation of such a parametrization is illustrated by the following example (Liskov, 1979):

```
sign=proc(x:int)returns(int)signals(zero,neg(int))
   if x<0 then signal neg(x)
      elseif x=0 then signal zero
      else return(x)
   end
end sign


nonzero=proc(x:int)returns(int)
   return(sign(x))
      except
         when neg(y:int):return(y)
      end
end nonzero
```

Procedure sign specifies that it can raise two exceptions zero and neg. Raising neg (by the statement signal neg(x)) communicates a parameter value which is caught by the exception handling (when **neg(y:int)**) of the calling procedure (nonzero).

Unix only allows the identifier of the exception to be passed (number of the exception) to the exception handler (see example in the preceding section).

In the RMX286 kernel, the exception handler is only executed because of errors detected in the calls to the primitives of the kernel. It has four parameters which are: the identifier of the exception (allowing the erroneous primitive to be identified), the number of the parameter of the primitive that causes the error, a reserved parameter and the state of the NPX (Numeric Processor eXtension), which is only useful when the error is numeric (ENDPERROR)). Detailed information is therefore available to write a precise handler.

The exception monitor task of the RMS68K kernel receives, as information, the identifier of the erroneous task (or of the task to be monitored), the cause of the transfer of control to the exception task (a task may ask for an association or a disassociation with the handler, or may raise an exception) and, if an exception is raised, its identifier.

A.4.3 Common parts of handling

In Ada and Clu, all the non-explicitly handled exceptions can be treated in common by using an exception choice others [11.2(5)]. We showed in section 3.6.2 of chapter 3 that this particularity can be useful for writing common handlers.

Clu language authorizes the passing of parameters. Therefore we can pass the name of the exception (e_name) as a parameter of others:

    others(e_name:string):body

Then the common exception handler which contains parts particular to certain exceptions can be written:

    if E_name = ERROR_ON_STACK then ...

In Eiffel the exception handling part does not involve the choice of an exception to be done statically as in Ada or in Clu by a when clause. Handling is common for all exceptions unless distinction is made by the use of test statements (if exception=Numerical_Error then ...etc.).

We stated that Ada95 permits such a design on account of the exception occurrence notion. However the when clauses are always available. They are useful for providing a clearly-marked structure of the handler if the different exceptions require different handlings.

The kernels studied authorize the association of an exception with any handler function. The same function can therefore be attached to several exceptions. Specific handlings can be performed by means of explicit tests (as in Eiffel language) using parameters communicated to the handler to specify the actual exception.

A.4.4 Execution conditions

In this section we will discuss two exception handling aspects relative to implementation constraints. The first aspect concerns stack allocation required to execute the exception handler. The second aspect concerns the introduction of the priority notion required when a single processor is used to execute several tasks and exception handlings.

Stack
As for the processing of the program, the execution of an exception handler generally requires the use of a stack associated with the program execution environment. For instance, it is required to save the erroneous task context, which will be used at the end of the handling, to allocate the local variables declared in the handler, etc. Usually this is not a problem as we suppose that this memory area

is transparently allocated in the stack of the erroneous program and managed by the Run Time Environment. However, stack overflow can occur if a program does not allow enough space allocation or if memory space is wasted in normal execution (without previously raising an exception). Note that another stack, different from the one allocated to the current program, can be used with RMX286, the Berkeley version of Unix (BSD4.2, 1988), and RMK386.

For BSD4.2, the stack of an exception handler can be specified at the time when the exception handler is associated (sigvec). The definition of this association primitive is given in the following subsection. The stack associated with an exception handler can also be changed dynamically with the sigstack primitive.

Exception priority

In the case of a multitask application or if several applications are executed simultaneously, the processor's time is shared. The notion of priority has been introduced to make sharing management easier. As the exception concept is associated with the error concept, this may imply the need to execute correction handlers with an urgency greater than that of the erroneous function.

This section deals with the primitives of the BSD4.2 version of Unix and the RMS68K kernel which allow relative priorities to be introduced between the exceptions and therefore favour the execution of certain exception handlers with respect to others.

In BSD4.2, a handler is associated with an exception by means of the statement sigvec(sig,&vec,&oldvec). This statement associates a context (vec) with an exception (sig) and returns the previous context (oldvec). The context parameter type is tsigvec. It defines:

- the function used as handler (sv_handler),
- a mask (sv_mask) to assign a relative priority to the exception,
- a parameter (sv_onstack) allowing a special stack to be defined for the execution of the exception handler different from the current stack.

Its declaration in C-language is as follows:

```
        struct tsigvec {
                int (*sv_handler)();
                int sv_mask;
                int sv_onstack;
            } vec, oldvec; /* new & old contexts */
        int sig;      /* signal number*/
        ...
```

The sv_mask parameter allows the handling of certain exceptions to be delayed during the execution of other exception handlers. The notion of priority (of hierarchy) can then be introduced into the reaction to the exceptions. For instance, if we assume that exception EXC1 has a higher priority than EXC2 which has priority over EXC3, the mask of EXC1 must delay EXC2 and EXC3, the mask of EXC2 must delay EXC3, and the mask of EXC3 must not delay any events. This mechanism is fairly close to the one used for hardware interrupts.

For RMS68K, when an exception is raised, the exception handler is not instantaneously executed but the exceptional event is placed in a queue called ASQ (Asynchronous Service Queue) which is associated with the exception task. It handles the events one at a time. As the handler of an exception is a task, it possesses a priority that can be used to favour one exception or another. The exceptions which are not handled immediately are not lost for they are buffered in the ASQ.

A.4.5 Exceptions occurring during exception handling

An exception handler may itself raise an exception during its execution (this is not a voluntary propagation like the raise statement in Ada). In Eiffel, it can have serious consequences for detection is not performed during the handling of an exception. In LTR3, the raising of exception during an exception handling involves the suppression of the task which called the erroneous subprogram. In Clu, PL/I, Chill or Ada this detection generates propagation to the calling frames.

In Ada the frames can be nested. This characteristic, used in an exception handler, increases dependability by handling the exception raised in an exception handler. This hides the double faults from the caller of the frame. An example of nesting exception handlers was given in section 3.6.2.

A.5 Relations between exception handling and erroneous treatment

This section presents the capabilities of the programming tools to implement the relations existing between the program where an exception occurs and the associated handling. We will successively present:

- the control transfer mode between the erroneous program (that is, which leads to an error) and the exception handling at raising time (section A.5.1),
- the relations established during the execution of the exception handler (section A.5.2),
- the control transfer mode and the information exchanged between the exception handler and the erroneous program at end of handling (section A.5.3).

These three aspects are symbolized on Figure A.1 already presented in section 3.6 of chapter 3 to detail the Ada exception mechanism capabilities.

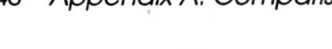

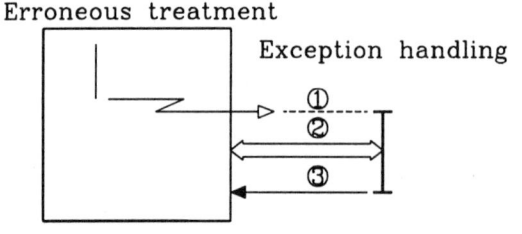

348 *Appendix A: Comparison of Exception Mechanism*

Figure A.1: Relations between exception handling and erroneous treatment

A.5.1 Control transfer at raising time

In this section we will describe the control transfer mode between the erroneous treatment, in which an exception was raised, and the associated exception handler. In most of the programming tools studied, the raising of an exception provokes the immediate suspension of the erroneous treatment. However, remember that among the tools we looked at, several allow exceptions to be masked in an imperative way: for instance the SIG_IGN option of the Unix signal primitive developed in section A.2.4. Non-transfer of control can also be context dependent: for the RMX286 kernel, transfer depends on the *type of the exception* raised (programmer's error or environmental error) and on the *mode of the task* where the exception occurred (programmers only, environment condition only, all conditions or no conditions). The starting of the execution of the exception handler can then be filtered. If type of exception is compatible with the mode of the task, control is transferred immediately; otherwise, the erroneous primitive simply returns an error code. Less drastic transfer conditions can be considered with other tools.

In the System V version of Unix, the suspension of the erroneous treatment and therefore the initialization of the exception handling can be delayed (see section A.3).

The RMS68K and Real Time Unix (RTU, 1986) kernels allow exception handling to be delayed by the introduction of exceptional event buffers respectively called ASQ (Asynchronous Service Queue) and AST (Asynchronous System Trap). Each exception handler is associated therefore with a buffer which stores the exceptions which occurred. These exceptions will be taken into account by this handler later on. As the exception handlers are tasks which possess a priority, the processor is assigned to them according to the other tasks managed on the computer. We can point out that for the RTU kernel, the exceptions themselves have priorities which overload the current priority of the exception task during its execution. So, a notion of relative importance can be introduced between exceptions and not simply between exception handlers. The technique introduced by RMS68K and RTU is much more general than the one offered by Unix SystemV for it considers an exception handler as a task and not as a function.

A.5.2 Relations during exception handling

This section deals with the relations which exist between the erroneous treatment and the exception handler during the execution of this handler. The relations that exist at the time when the exception is raised have just been described; the parameters that may be passed at this time were dealt with in section A.4. The transfer of control and the information transferred at end of exception handling to normal execution will be approached in the following section.

Two cases must be distinguished:

- a *local exception handler* is a subprogram called when an exception is raised, involving the resumption of the execution of the normal treatment when the subprogram has been executed,
- an *exception monitor task* is a task that is executed in parallel with the erroneous task in order to control it even if no exceptions occur.

Whereas a local exception handler acts on data and goes back to the execution of the application at a specified point, an exception monitor task can control the processing of the erroneous task and therefore act on its behaviour.

Possible actions on the data were mentioned in section A.4. We will only develop here the statements that can influence the sequencing.

Considering the RMS68K kernel (which is the most original in this domain), the occurrence of an exception or the modification of an exception association involves the suspension of the current treatment and the transmission of a message to the ASQ buffer (defined in the previous section) of the associated exception monitor task. Then the exception monitor task can return control to the erroneous task:

- which can be resumed anywhere (REXMON) since it is possible to modify the state of the task (see section A.4);
- to execute a single (or a certain number of) MC68000 instruction(s) of the erroneous task before taking back control;
- to execute the erroneous task until the value of a word at a given address changes;
- possibly until a new exception occurs in the erroneous task.

This last case does not correspond to a conventional return to the erroneous treatment because, when a new exception is raised in this treatment, the execution of the exception handler will not be restarted at the beginning. The exception monitor task will be resumed at the instruction following the one that returned the control to the erroneous task. The application task therefore remains under control. This solution allows sharp sequential relations to be considered between an application task and its exception monitor task. For instance, if we want to make two trials before considering another type of correction (if they are unsuccessful), this will be handled by the exception task and not by the application.

350 Appendix A: Comparison of Exception Mechanism

The System V version of Unix also provides a primitive called ptrace. It is interesting to describe its principle. Let us consider a child process C created by a father process F (fork) which is waiting (wait). The father F becomes the supervisor (controller) of the child process C which then asks for monitoring by its father (ptrace(0,.,.,.)). When an exception occurs in the child task, this task is suspended and the father starts its execution again. It can read or write the code or the data of the child task by means of the same ptrace(N, child_pid, addr, data) statement (where N is between 1 and 6 depending on the action performed) in order to correct it. This statement (ptrace(N, child_pid, 1, data) where N is between 7 and 9) also allows the child process to be stopped or resumed.

A.5.3 Control transfer at end of exception handling

In this section we will study the capabilities of the programming tools to implement control modes and information transfers between the exception handler and the erroneous frame on completion of the exception handling.

Control
In section 2.4 of chapter 2 we distinguished between three modes:

- the *termination mode*, in which the erroneous frame is left after the execution of the exception handler (the frame is terminated),
- the *retry mode* and the *resumption mode*, in which the exception handler goes back to the execution of the erroneous frame. The *retry mode* is adopted to retry the execution of the entire frame (from the beginning) whereas the *resumption mode* is used to continue the execution at the statement following the erroneous statement.

The term *erroneous frame* is very general, it can cover a basic operation, a block of statements, a procedure, a task, etc., depending on the tool considered (see section A.3).

The three modes are shown on Figure A.2.

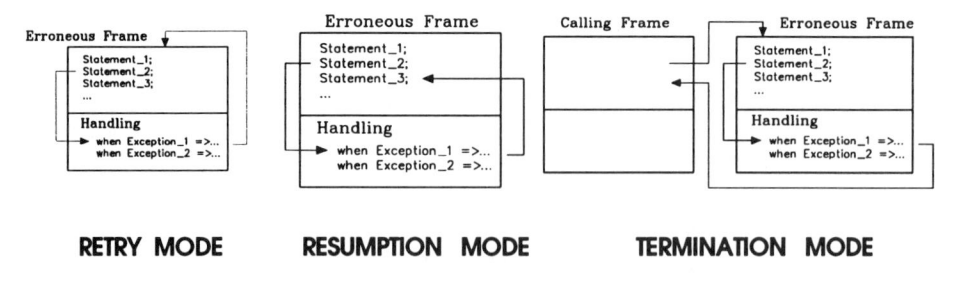

Figure A.2: Control transfer at end of handling

Relations between exception handling and erroneous treatment

We will specify the mode chosen by each tool. This choice is the one made by the basic exception mechanism. It can be used to implement the other modes (easily or not, efficiently or not). For instance, we presented the capabilities of Ada to do this in section 4.5 of chapter 4.

The **termination mode** is chosen by the Ada [11.4(1)], LTR and Clu languages, and by the Unix kernels for exceptions raised by primitive calls (i.e. for all the primitives of the System 3 and System V kernels and most of the BSD primitives (BSD4.2, 1988)). The local exception handlers of RMS68K adopt the same principle. The Eiffel language offers both termination and retry modes. In the termination mode, an exception is automatically raised in the procedure which called the erroneous one because in Eiffel a procedure must either fail (and indicate this to the caller) or succeed (and therefore if an exception occurs, it must try again (retry mode)).

The erroneous frame can be resumed at the statement following the erroneous statement (**resumption mode**). This occurs in the case of predefined exceptions raised by certain primitives of Unix BSD4.2 and for all the user exceptions that are raised in the application. A particularity of Unix is that it is possible to go back to any point in the erroneous frame (see setjmp and longjmp statements in section A.4.1) and not necessarily to the following statement. The resumption mode is also chosen for RMX286.

There can also be a pure **retry** of the complete frame. This situation is encountered in the Eiffel language where the retry statement provokes return to the beginning of the procedure. However, this complete retry often involves bulky programming to account for the fact that this is a retry and not a first execution. For instance, this is the reason for which a supplementary variable (division_tried) is incorporated into the example below (Meyer, 1988):

```
quasi_inverse(x : real) : real is
   -- 1/x if possible; otherwise 0
local
   division_tried : BOOLEAN := false
do
   if not division_tried then
      -- test if it's a retry execution
      Result := 1/x
   else
      Result :=  0
   end
rescue          -- exception handler
   division_tried := true;
   retry
end
```

We would like to point out that it is possible to introduce the retry statement in a procedure called by the exception handler. This however poses some readability problems. It is mainly for comprehension reasons that the retry model

352 Appendix A: Comparison of Exception Mechanism

is criticized (Liskov, 1979). In particular it does not highlight the normal and exceptional parts of the subprograms (for instance division_tried variable in the previous example).

The exception handling mechanism proposed in (Adamo, 1991) for C++ offers three control transfer possibilities at the end of exception handling:

- in the first case, the conventional return statement allows a resumption model to be implemented. The erroneous function is resumed assigning the value returned by the handler as the result of the function which raises the exception. Figure A.3 gives an example. Function f calls the function convert (P=convert(...)) which raises an exception. The convert specification expresses the name of the function which is the handler (Code_Error) (see first line of the figure). In the case considered, the convert function is resumed after handling (① in figure);
- in the second case, handling is concluded by a terminate statement implementing the termination model. As the handling replaces the erroneous function, it must return the value expected by the calling function. On Figure A.3 function Code_Error handles the exception concluding the work which would be done by the erroneous function convert and then goes back to function f (② on figure);
- the third case consists of a propagation. On Figure A.3 the Not_Solved exception is propagated (③ on figure) and then raised at the call location of function f.

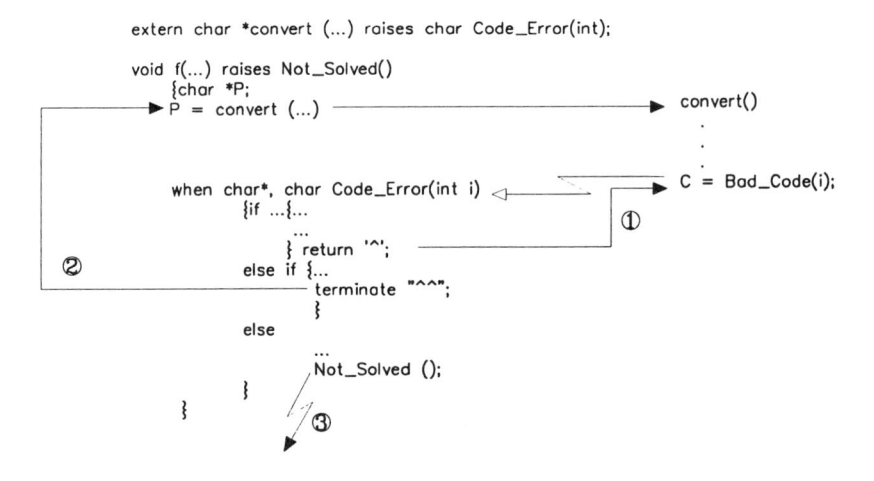

```
extern char *convert (...) raises char Code_Error(int);

void f(...) raises Not_Solved()
    {char *P;
    P = convert (...)                              convert()

            when char*, char Code_Error(int i)
                {if ...{...                        C = Bad_Code(i);
                                                       ①
                } return '^';
            else if {...
                    terminate "^^";
                }
            else
                ...
                Not_Solved ();
            }
    }
                   ③
```

Figure A.3: Control transfer proposal for C++

We can see that the type of information returned depends on the control transfer mode.

Returned information
In some of the tools studied resumption of normal treatment is completed by information passing from the exception handling to the caller of the erroneous frame (termination mode) or to the erroneous frame itself (retry or resumption modes).

For instance, for primitives calls of the Unix kernels, an error code is returned by the exception handler (errno==EINTR). It can be checked to get to know the handler processing conclusions.

The System V version of Unix allows *software exceptions local for a process* to be raised by using the gsignal (event) statement, where event is the number of the exceptional event. The exception handler returns an integer value which may be considered as information on handler processing. This is illustrated in the following example:

```
int f(event)
   {
   ...
   return(17);
   }
void g()
   {
   ...
   ssignal(3,f); /* associates event 3 to the function f*/
   ...
   i=gsignal(3); /* raises explicitly 3 */
   /* when come back, i has the value 17 */
   }
```

A.6 Raising of an exception

In this section we will discuss the means offered by the programming tools studied for raising predefined and user exceptions. We shall distinguish between implicit raising (not requested in the program by a specific statement) and explicit raising. These two aspects will be presented in sections A.6.1 and A.6.2 respectively.

A.6.1 Implicit raising

Predefined exceptions are naturally raised in an implicit way. They are detected and raised by the Abstract Machine associated with the programming tool semantics. The Ada Abstract Machine notion was discussed in section 3.3.1 of chapter 3. Such detections are made by software components by checks:

- on state variables of the executive environment: for instance, this kind of check is made for an entry call to a terminated task in Ada programs on variables of the task manager;
- done by the instructions generated by the compiler: for instance, checks on the variable associated with the constrained subtype in Ada.

Detection can also be signalled by a hardware exception which triggers the execution of an interrupt handler. In general this interrupt handler changes the hardware event into an exception processed by the software.

The variety in the semantics of the programming tools available implies a high variety of predefined exceptions. This was shown in section A.2.1. It means that a design fault can either lead to an error detected by a predefined exception for an application programmed with a given language or must be expressed explicitly as a user exception if the application is programmed with another tool.

Studying the predefined exceptions also showed the wide diversity of abstraction levels considered. However, even if a single language is used, components (e.g. Ada packages) are often used in programming an application which can implicitly raise exceptions which must then be considered as predefined by the user application. In Ada, exceptions raised by the file handling subprograms are examples of this (i.e. text_io, etc.).

The existence of predefined exceptions is of major interest: the abstract machine executing the statements offered by the language can be used (by the program) without imposing that the user (the program designer) place checks in this program to verify if the statements are correctly used. This verification is performed implicitly. We would like to have such a mechanism for all the new components designed using the language. For this, the language must allow invariants to be expressed. Even if we showed in chapter 4 how a special way of designing components in Ada makes the implementation of certain checks easier, the difficulty in expressing invariants is a weak point of the language. A language such as Eiffel makes the writing of contracts easy and even incites the designer to do this. Thanks to this possibility, components can be used without adding checks which would make the programming cumbersome whilst guaranteeing that these checks are effectively (implicitly) performed.

A.6.2 Explicit raising

Eiffel is the only language studied which does not offer the possibility of explicitly raising an exception. We stated in section A.5 that an Eiffel routine must succeed (maybe after several retries) or fail. If it fails an exception is implicitly propagated. An Eiffel routine does not therefore need to reraise an exception during exception handling to signal an error to the caller since it will be done automatically. The voluntary raising of an exception which could be useful within the routine body is not allowed. B. Meyer (the designer of the Eiffel language) argues that a lot of programmers use the raise statement as a goto statement, that the use of this control transfer is dangerous and that the programmers misuse the mechanism. We hope that after reading this book, Ada designers will never be the subject of such criticism.

All the other languages and kernels studied have a specific explicit (i.e. voluntary) exception raising statement. The consequences of executing this statement vary with each language and its handling and propagation rules.

The Clu, LTR3 and PL/I languages possess a signal statement which allows an exception, predefined or not, to be voluntarily raised. An example written in Clu was presented in section A.4.2 to illustrate that an exception can be parametrized in this language.

The Clu language has an additional raising statement called exit which allows local transfer of control. It is similar to the signal statement, except for the fact that a signal statement signals the exception to the calling procedure (propagation) whereas the exit statement raises the exception which can be handled in the same procedure.

We have already seen that in LTR3, an exception is handled by the caller and must be specified in the interface of the erroneous procedure. Therefore exceptions which do not appear in this interface cannot be raised. Consequently, certain design errors can be avoided. Firstly, the interface specifies the exception potentially raised by a procedure then incites the designer to provide a handler. It avoids involuntary omission of this exception handler in the units which call such a subprogram (de Bondelli, 1984). Secondly, only the specified exception can be raised in the body. It is checked at compile-time. Anonymous exceptions therefore cannot exist.

The voluntary raising of exceptions in Chill language is made similarly by the CAUSE statement. This language also possesses an assertion check statement (ASSERT B, where B is a Boolean assertion). This statement would be really interesting if assertion B could be checked during the complete execution of a subprogram (but, of course, not during the execution of the subprograms called, which must be considered as critical sections) and if an exception could be raised as soon as B is no longer true. Unfortunately this is not the case and, in fact, ASSERT B, which raises the predefined exception ASSERTFAIL if B is false, is strictly equivalent to the statement:

    IF NOT B **THEN** CAUSE ASSERTFAIL **FI**

The different versions of Unix have a kill(pid, event) statement which provokes the raising of an exception (event) in a process identified by pid or is propagated through all the processes of the application if pid=0. Local raising is achieved using the identifier of the task which processes the kill statement. In Ada, this asynchronous communication, by means of exceptions between processes, is not present.

A.7 Propagation

If the exception handling cannot lead the erroneous component into a state of its Standard Domain, it must signal the exceptional situation by propagating a new exception. The interest of such a propagation comes from the possibility given to the handler to signal its inability to solve the problem alone. The user component now is responsible for deciding which solution must be taken to solve the problem. According to the various languages and kernels studied, this propagation may be done:

- by an implicit or automatic mechanism. This approach will be dealt with in the following section (A.7.1),
- by the explicit raising of a new exception (section A.7.2).

In section A.7.3 we will make some comments on the two approaches.

A.7.1 Automatic propagation

Automatic propagation characterizes a mechanism allowing propagation without using specific statements.

This mechanism is available in Ada. If an exception is raised in a frame which has no handler for this exception, or if an exception is raised in an exception handler, the same exception is raised again out of the frame (in the calling block or subprogram) [11.4.1(4)&(10)]. A drawback of such a mechanism is the risk of anonymous exception propagation.

In Clu language an identified exception raised by a procedure must be handled by the immediate caller of this procedure. However the exception handler of the calling procedure may explicitly raise a new exception (with a new identity). If an exception is not handled by the calling procedure, the predefined exception `failure` is propagated from procedure to procedure until it is handled. The principle is close to the one of Ada, apart from two variants: one, in Clu an exception is directly and automatically propagated to a higher level and thus not handled locally as in Ada; and two, it only keeps its name in the calling procedure before it becomes some kind of anonymous exception explicitly indicated as such (`failure`) in the higher levels.

Eiffel also propagates exceptions automatically to the user of a routine which fails.

A.7.2 Explicit propagation

In section A.6.2, we presented the notion of explicit raising. The notion of explicit propagation differs in the sense that it is the explicit raising of an exception during the handling of an exception (and not during normal execution). An interest of such a propagation is to modify the identity of the exception which will be passed to the calling frame. It allows a significant error identifier to be given to this frame.

The explicit propagation mode is chosen by all the kernels studied. Thus the `kill` statement of the Unix versions provokes voluntary transmission of an exception to another task or to all tasks (as seen in section A.6.2).

Explicit propagation is also possible in Ada (`raise`), but does not allow an exception to be propagated to another task. This make it difficult to broadcast the occurrence of an exceptional situation to other tasks in a voluntary and asynchronous way except by killing them (`abort`). However the `abort` statement cannot be considered as a sending event (as in Unix) because the aborted task cannot have a reaction. Moreover the `abort` statement does not formally have an asynchronous effect [9.10(6)]. The possibility of targeted raising (`raise E in T;`) was voluntarily abandoned when the Ada language was designed (Rationale, 1986) in order to maintain a certain consistency in the semantics of the language, especially in the case of distributed implementation.

A.7.3 Comments

The choice of automatic propagation corresponds to the following 'philosophy': if a block is unable to handle an error, it may be considered that this is because the solution can only be found by the caller. This concerns for instance misuse of the component. However, this point of view is only valid if the programming is correct and the use of the propagation technique is voluntary, controlled and not induced by the omission of an exception handler. Some languages do not want to take this risk and consider that the software designer cannot make up for this; LTR3 is an example.

Automatic propagation induces the following problem (Goodenough, 1975). If a statement is added likely to raise an exception in a module of a lower level, then the whole hierarchy of the user modules must be revised. The possible consequences of this exception must be determined if it is not handled in this module. In particular, the sequence of exceptions raised must be studied. To avoid such a study Goodenough proposes to directly propagate an exception to a desired higher level. In any case, a hierarchical structure which defines a top-down control on the components must take into account the bottom-up control due to the propagation of the exceptions (Marpinard, 1993).

The omission of an exception handler can lead to the interception of a propagated exception on an unexpected level. It will then be handled badly because the handler is designed for different exceptions with the same name. Therefore, the designer must pay special attention to predefined exceptions. For P. de Bondelli (de Bondelli, 1984), the propagation of an Ada exception moves the exception away from its causes. He considers this phenomenon to be pernicious, because information is lost.

As mentioned, explicit propagation allows another name to be given to an exception before its propagation. The main interest of this is that it takes the notion of abstraction levels into account: when an exception occurs in a low-level frame, the meaning of this exception is different in the high-level frames to which it is propagated. For example what is the meaning of a `CONSTRAINT_ERROR` propagated by a `STACK` package? The user of this package would certainly prefer to receive information such as `STACK_OVERFLOW` or `STACK_UNDERFLOW`.

A.8 Concurrent programming

In this section we will discuss exceptions in concurrent programming. We will comment on the features offered by the programming tools used for the specific field of multi-tasking applications.

Some of the languages studied have no multi-tasking features. Others integrate this facility but do not provide any special features concerning exceptions. The tasks are considered as sequential units in which the raising of an exception only has consequences on the erroneous task and does not directly influence the behaviour of the other tasks. For example, a task waiting for an event produced by an other task which has been stopped because of the occurrence of an exception is not directly informed of this exceptional state of the application and might wait indefinitely. This is the case of applications programmed with LTR3 and OCCAM2 (Shepherd, 1987). When an exception occurs in OCCAM2 programs, one of the following behaviours is possible:

- no handling is performed: execution continues and could be uncertain,
- the task is killed,
- the whole application is stopped.

Obviously this language has very limited capabilities in this field.

The case of Ada was studied in detail in section 3.7 of chapter 3. Other languages offers similar possibilities. For instance Chill has a feature to send a message to another task:

```
SEND S (V1,V2,.....,Vn) PRIORITY p [ TO D]
```

where S identifies a *signal*, (V1,V2,......,Vn) is a list of values composing a message, P a priority and D an optional consumer identifier.

This sending statement can cause a certain number of exceptions:

- EMPTY if D is NULL (for example undefined consumer),
- EXTINCT if the D consumer process is finished,
- MODEFAIL if there is an incompatibility between consumer D and the signal definition,
- an assignment exception if one of the Vi values is not conformable with the definition of the signal (exception equivalent to the Ada CONSTRAINT_ERROR).

By comparison with the Ada language, exceptions related to the communication between tasks are more detailed.

The kill statement of Unix allows a task to transmit events towards a target task. Therefore a task can raise an exception (exceptional event) in another task. This is the way in which the *horizontal propagation* of an exceptional situation is expressed. We also presented in section A.5.1 the capabilities of the RMS68K and RTU (RTU, 1986) kernels to monitor buffers of exceptional events (classified by priority in case of RTU). This monitoring allows exceptional events to be exchanged between tasks and dynamic modifications of the priority of exception handler tasks to be implemented.

The RMS68K and SYSTEM V kernels introduce the definition of an *exception monitor task*. An exception handler is then no longer considered as a subprogram, called when an exception is raised, but as a task controlling the processing of the task in which an error can occur. The interest of this was developed in section A.5. This section also contains the presentation of the statements enabling the dialogue between the erroneous task and the monitor task (ptrace of SYSTEM V, REXMON of RMS68K).

A.9 Use

In this section we will not look at the capabilities of programming tools to manage exceptions but discuss the use of the exceptions offered by such tools. We do not want to conclude the debate concerning this subject but to give and to compare some arguments.

According to the exception mechanisms of the software tools mentioned up until now, we can ask ourselves two questions:

- 'what use can these mechanisms be put to?', and
- 'what results can be expected?'.

The use of the exception mechanism considered in this book is the handling of errors detected during the execution of a program. It was intentionally created for this purpose to increase the dependability of the applications. The handling of errors by means of the exception handling mechanism allows an application to keep control during execution in spite of the detection of an abnormal condition. Therefore this mechanism is, in the first place, suitable for critical applications which require continuous and permanent operation. We described in chapter 4 how the Ada mechanism can be used practically to implement the techniques presented in chapter 2 in order to obtain dependable software.

Note that Clu and PL/I consider that this mechanism is particularly adapted to debugging as it allows variables or labels to be monitored. Besides, some available exceptions are forbidden in the final application. This is also the case with RMK386 where exception handling by default is an interruption (number 3) used by the debugger.

Use of exception mechanism characteristics

The exception mechanism can also be used for other purposes. (Goodenough, 1975) presents three possible uses of the exception mechanism as extra tools for functional programming:

1. **Exit from a loop** is the first use proposed. This possibility actually corresponds to the **exit** statement of the Ada language. The proposal is illustrated by the following syntax:

```
begin
  while ... loop
    while ... loop
      ...
      if ... then raise X;
      ...
    end loop;
  end loop;
exception
  when X => null; -- or any other treatment
end;
```

Obviously such use in Ada would be excessive as this language also possesses the **exit** statement which does not have the consequences induced by a propagation. We can consider this use of the exception mechanism as a **goto** statement.

In our opinion, this boils down to diverting the exception mechanism from the use for which it was designed, that is for which a theoretical basis and utilization principles (discussed in this book) exist. Indeed, this proposal consists in using a characteristic of the exception mechanism (the branch to a handler) to design disorderly functional branches.

2. The exception mechanism also allows **the domain** of certain operations **to be extended**. For instance, we can add the number zero to the domain of the division operator. This use permits generalization of the operations supplied.

```
function "/" (DIVIDEND,DIVISOR: in FLOAT) return FLOAT is
begin
  return (DIVIDEND/DIVISOR);
exception
  when CONSTRAINT_ERROR =>
    if DIVIDEND>0.0 then
      return(FLOAT'LAST);
    else return(FLOAT'FIRST);
    end if;
end "/";
```

In this approach, a zero value for the divisor is not considered as an error but as a possible but rare input (exceptional). The introduction of tests due to this particular case would make the writing of the program cumbersome. The use of exception handling is preferable because:

- the test of the divisor is implicit;
- the processing of the *particular* case is separate from the *normal* treatment.

This use is based on a characteristic of the exception mechanism, that is the syntactic separation of the treatments based on the state notion (Standard Domain and Exception Domain). In our opinion, this solution is only just acceptable as it is in fact a division of the Standard Domain into Current Domain and Rare Domain, the Exception Domain not being considered.

3. The **validity of a result** or the **circumstances to obtain the result**, provide supplementary information given by using exception mechanisms. We can take as an example two file reading procedures: first, if an 'end of file' is found, the procedure returns as a result the previous record read and raises an exception (END_OF_FILE) to indicate the state reached. In a second procedure, when the last record is read its value is returned and an exception LAST_RECORD is raised to indicate this exceptional but non-erroneous situation (circumstance).

Exception mechanisms can be put to another interesting use: a handler can monitor an operation. It is used to measure the evolution of a program and to obtain extra information on it. Raising an exception in the application would correspond in this case to asking for control by a 'monitor task'. For instance, the raising of an exception, meaning that the component looked for in a tree by a recursive procedure has been found, would allow return to the first caller without having to work back through the recursion.

For this use, a specific characteristic of the exception mechanism is once more employed. Conventionally, subprograms communicate information on their execution state by using parameters. However, the caller must check the values of these parameters to undertake one treatment or another. The propagation of an exception by the called subprogram avoids this check on account of the branch provoked implicitly by the exception mechanism.

The aim of the uses presented is to employ one of the characteristics of the exception mechanism and not the basic principles of the mechanism itself. For this, we should not criticize the mechanism but rather its users.

Advantages and limitations

Certain **advantages** linked to the use of exception mechanisms have to be highlighted.

For a syntactic association between an exception handler and a frame, the syntactic partitioning makes **the frame bodies easier to write and read**. The program can be structured better and more easily than it would be without this mechanism, for we would often need to conduct many auxiliary checks to obtain same program behaviour.

When an error is detected in an application, the different types of possible reactions to this error (abandon the execution of the frame, try the operation again, use a different method, repair the cause of the error, etc.) can be formulated with the help of the exception handling mechanism.

The exception propagation mechanism allows information (such as exception identifier) significant for this abstraction level to be passed to a higher level frame (or on the same level for tasks). For example, the propagation of exception STACK_OVERFLOW by procedure PUSH has a meaning for the caller which does not necessarily know the implementation of the procedure.

Exception mechanisms allow the **definition of the location** where the control is transferred to be separated from the location where this transfer is started when an exception is raised.

However some **difficulties** can be expected.

The use of the exception mechanism in embedded critical applications generates some **overheads** which can be unacceptable for real-time applications. In chapter 5, dealing with Ada exception mechanism implementation, we gave some information on this subject.

The raising of an exception voluntarily considered as an **implicit transfer of control** can correspond to excessive use of the mechanism. B. Meyer (Meyer, 1988) considers that most of the applications that integrate this mechanism must only use it to deal with cases difficult to handle by a structured algorithm.

Attention must be paid during the writing of applications using exception mechanisms because the design phase can **generate errors** such as:

- forgetting that a statement can raise an exception,
- bad positioning of the exception handler,
- associating a handler with an exception that cannot occur.

In conclusion we recommend the designer to use exceptions to solve the problems for which they were introduced: the mastering of the errors. Other uses are frequently odd jobs, employed not to solve general problems but to use a particular aspect of the mechanism (such as the control breaking).

APPENDIX B

Complete examples

In chapter 4 few extracts of programs, sufficient to explain the principles of fault tolerance techniques and to illustrate them, were presented. This appendix contains the complete programs. Moreover it provides concrete examples for using these techniques.

B.1 Generic package for stack implementation

The generic package ON_STACKS is used in section 4.3.2.

```
generic
  type ITEM is private;
package ON_STACKS is
  type STACK(SIZE : POSITIVE) is limited private;
  procedure PUSH(S : in out STACK; E : in ITEM);
    -- raises OVERFLOW
  procedure POP(S : in out STACK; E : out ITEM);
    -- raises UNDERFLOW
  OVERFLOW, UNDERFLOW : exception;
private
  type TABLE is array (POSITIVE range <>) of ITEM;
  type STACK(SIZE : POSITIVE) is
    record
      SPACE : TABLE(1..SIZE);
      THE_TOP : NATURAL := 0;
    end record;
end ON_STACKS;
```

364 Appendix B: Complete Examples

```ada
package body ON_STACKS is
  procedure PUSH(S : in out STACK; E : in ITEM) is
  begin
     S.SPACE(S.THE_TOP + 1):= E;
     S.THE_TOP:= S.THE_TOP + 1;
  exception
     when CONSTRAINT_ERROR =>
        raise OVERFLOW;
  end PUSH;
  procedure POP(S : in out STACK; E : out ITEM) is
  begin
     E:= S.SPACE(S.THE_TOP);
     S.THE_TOP:= S.THE_TOP -1;
  exception
     when CONSTRAINT_ERROR =>
        raise UNDERFLOW;
  end POP;
end ON_STACKS;
```

B.2 Invariant implementation

The following programs are used in section 4.4.3.

B.2.1 Resource package

```ada
-----------------------------------------------------------
-- generic package RESOURCE: buffer with only one place
--  -> buffering an ITEM (entry WRITE)
--  -> giving the last ITEM buffered (entry READ)
-- constraints: must be initialized: an ITEM must be written
--   before the first READ
-----------------------------------------------------------
generic
   type ITEM is private;
package RESOURCE is
   task type BUFFER is
      entry READ(X: out ITEM);
      entry WRITE(X: in ITEM);
   end BUFFER;
end RESOURCE;
```

```ada
package body RESOURCE is
  task body BUFFER is
    LOCAL:ITEM;
  begin
    accept WRITE(X: in ITEM) do
      LOCAL:=X;
    end WRITE;
    loop
      select
        accept WRITE(X: in ITEM) do
          LOCAL:=X;
        end WRITE;
      or
        accept READ(X: out ITEM) do
          X:=LOCAL;
        end READ;
      or
        terminate;
      end select;
    end loop;
  end BUFFER;
end RESOURCE;
```

B.2.2 Assertion definition packages

```
-----------------------------------------------------------
-- package ASSERTION: contains the procedure ASSERT which
-- -> evaluates a PROPERTY
-- -> propagates the exception ASSERT_ERROR if the
--PROPERTY is not true (defined in section 4.4.3)
-----------------------------------------------------------
```

```ada
package ASSERTION is
  procedure ASSERT(PROPERTY: in BOOLEAN);
  ASSERT_ERROR: exception; -- raised by ASSERT
end ASSERTION;
```

```ada
package body ASSERTION is
  procedure ASSERT(PROPERTY: in BOOLEAN) is
  begin
    if (not PROPERTY) then
       raise ASSERT_ERROR;
    end if;
  end ASSERT;
end ASSERTION;

-----------------------------------------------------------
-- package A_LESS_THAN_B: implements the means allowing the
-- checks of the validity of the assertion A<B where A and B
-- are two characters, to be automatically done each time
-- A or B are assigned
-----------------------------------------------------------
with ASSERTION; use ASSERTION;
with RESOURCE;
package A_LESS_THAN_B is

  package CHARTASK is new RESOURCE(ITEM=>CHARACTER);
  INIT_ERROR: exception;
  A_GREATER_THAN_OR_EQUAL_TO_B: exception renames
                              ASSERTION.ASSERT_ERROR;
  A_INIT, B_INIT :BOOLEAN :=FALSE;
  procedure ASSERT(B: in BOOLEAN) renames ASSERTION.ASSERT;
  package CONTROL_ASSERT is
    A,B:CHARTASK.BUFFER;
  end CONTROL_ASSERT;

  -- these functions return value of the variable
  -- using the same name
  function A return CHARACTER;
  function B return CHARACTER;

  -- these procedures assign parameter value to
  -- the variable using the same name
  procedure A(X: in CHARACTER);
  procedure B(X: in CHARACTER);

end A_LESS_THAN_B;  -- specification
```

```ada
package body A_LESS_THAN_B is
  package body CONTROL_ASSERT is
  begin
    null; -- to start the two tasks
  end CONTROL_ASSERT;
  function A return CHARACTER is
    X: CHARACTER;
  begin
    if A_INIT then
      CONTROL_ASSERT.A.READ(X);
      return X;
    else
      raise INIT_ERROR;
    end if;
  end A;

  function B return CHARACTER is
    X: CHARACTER;
  begin
    if B_INIT then
      CONTROL_ASSERT.B.READ(X);
      return X;
    else
      raise INIT_ERROR;
    end if;
  end B;

  procedure A(X: in CHARACTER) is
  begin
    -- check of the assertion A<B
    ASSERT(not(B_INIT) or else X<B);
    CONTROL_ASSERT.A.WRITE(X);
    A_INIT:=TRUE;
  end A;

  procedure B(X: in CHARACTER) is
  begin
    -- check of the assertion A<B
    ASSERT(not(A_INIT) or else A<X);
    CONTROL_ASSERT.B.WRITE(X);
    B_INIT:=TRUE;
  end B;
end A_LESS_THAN_B;
```

368 Appendix B: Complete Examples

B.2.3 Example of invariant use

```
----------------------------------------------------------
-- procedure TEST_INV uses A and B and shows the
-- efficiency of the automatic check of the invariant (A<B)
----------------------------------------------------------
with TEXT_IO; use TEXT_IO;
with A_LESS_THAN_B; use A_LESS_THAN_B;
procedure TEST_INV is
-- INIT_ERROR:exception; can be raised using A_LESS_THAN_B
-- functions. A_INIT, B_INIT: BOOLEAN:= FALSE;
-- visible variables from package A_LESS_THAN_B

  function GET return CHARACTER is -- overload
     C: CHARACTER;
  begin
     TEXT_IO.GET(C);
     return(C);
  end GET;


begin
  -- A and B are initialized
  A('a');
  B('b');

  loop
     PUT("Give a new A:"); A(GET);
     NEW_LINE;
  -- why this statement to get a value and not GET(A)?
  -- because get parameter is in mode OUT!
  -- what can you do if you want to have call(a) if the call
  -- specification is: procedure CALL(X: in out CHARACTER);?
  -- if you don't want to modify CALL => you can add:
  -- function CALL(X: in CHARACTER) return CHARACTER;
  --LOCAL: CHARACTER :=X;
  -- begin
  --CALL(LOCAL); return(LOCAL);
  -- end CALL;
  -- and you make A VERY NICE call:  A(CALL(A))
  -- but your variable will be really modified only after
  -- the call to CALL...
```

```
      PUT("Give a new B:"); B(GET);
      NEW_LINE;
   end loop;
exception
   when A_GREATER_OR_EQUAL_TO_B =>
      PUT_LINE("You were warned!");
      PUT_LINE("The assertion became false!");
end TEST_INV;
```

B.3 Recovery blocks implementation

The following programs are used in section 4.5.3.

B.3.1 Generic blocks monitor task

```
-----------------------------------------------------------------
-- this generic package RB allows a recovery block to be
-- implemented with 3 alternates and an acceptance test
-- with a watchdog for each of them
-----------------------------------------------------------------
with TEXT_IO; use TEXT_IO;
with CALENDAR; use CALENDAR;
generic

   type PT1 is private;      -- access to task 1
   type PT2 is private;      -- access to task 2
   type PT3 is private;      -- access to task 3
   type PT_AC_T is private;  -- access to Task Acceptance Test
   MAX_TIME: DURATION:= 1.5; -- time to obtain a result

   with procedure INIT(NUM: in INTEGER; P1: in out PT1;
                       P2: in out PT2; P3: in out PT3);
-- external procedure to be supplied which will generate
-- one of the alternates
-- according to NUM and to the tasks types

   with procedure RUN_ACT(P: out PT_AC_T);
-- external procedure to be supplied which will start the
-- acceptance test
```

```ada
package RB_GEN is
  NB_MAX: constant INTEGER:= 3;
  subtype No_TASK is INTEGER range 1..NB_MAX;
  task RB_CONTROLLER is
    entry START;
    entry END_PROC;
    entry RESULT(B: in BOOLEAN);
  end RB_CONTROLLER;
end RB_GEN;

with TEXT_IO, CALENDAR; use TEXT_IO, CALENDAR;
package body RB_GEN is
  ALTERNATE1: PT1; ALTERNATE2: PT2; ALTERNATE3: PT3;
  T_AC_T: PT_AC_T;
  N: No_TASK;

  task body RB_CONTROLLER is
    CHRONO: TIME := CLOCK + MAX_TIME;
    CORRECT_TERMINATION: BOOLEAN;
  begin
    accept START;
    N:=1;
    loop
      INIT(N,ALTERNATE1,ALTERNATE2,ALTERNATE3);
      select
        accept END_PROC; -- the ALTERNATE N is terminated
        RUN_ACT(T_AC_T);  -- RUN ACceptance Test
        accept RESULT(B: in BOOLEAN) do
          CORRECT_TERMINATION:= B;
        end RESULT;
        if CORRECT_TERMINATION then exit;
        end if;
      or
        delay CHRONO - CLOCK; -- ALTERNATE N blocked
        PUT_LINE("Time overhead");
      end select;

      if N<NB_MAX then -- the next alternate is chosen
        N:= N + 1;
        CHRONO:= CHRONO + MAX_TIME; --reset timer
      else exit;
      end if;
    end loop;
  end RB_CONTROLLER;
end RB_GEN;
```

B.3.2 User program

```ada
------------------------------------------------------------
--User program of recovery blocks (package RB)
--The three alternates are TP1, TP2, TP3: separate tasks
--The common variables (I and C) for these tasks are declared
--The task initialization procedures are always the sames, but
--   cannot be into the generic package, because they are
--   dependent on the tasks types
------------------------------------------------------------
with RB_GEN; -- the generic package containing RB_CONTROLLER
with TEXT_IO; use TEXT_IO;

procedure RB_USER is
   package IIO is new INTEGER_IO(INTEGER);
   task type TP1; task type TP2; task type TP3;
   task type TPACT;

   type POINT1 is access TP1;
   type POINT2 is access TP2;
   type POINT3 is access TP3;
   type POINT4 is access TPACT;

   subtype No_TASK is INTEGER range 1..3;

   ------- GLOBAL VARIABLES
   I: INTEGER:= 4; C: CHARACTER:= 'x';

   procedure GO_ACT(P: out POINT4) is
   begin
      P:= new TPACT;
   exception
      when STORAGE_ERROR =>
         PUT_LINE("Storage error! AcT Task not generated");
   end GO_ACT;

   procedure INIT_ALTERNATES(NUM: in No_TASK:= 1;
      P1: in out POINT1; P2: in out POINT2; P3: in out POINT3) is
   begin
      case NUM is
         when 1 => P1:= new TP1;
         when 2 => P2:= new TP2; P1:= null;
         when 3 => P3:= new TP3; P2:= null;
      end case;
```

```
   exception
     when STORAGE_ERROR =>
       PUT_LINE("Storage error! Alternate not generated");
   end INIT_ALTERNATES;

   package RB_TEST is new RB_GEN( PT1 => POINT1,
                 PT2 => POINT2,
                 PT3 => POINT3,
                 PT_AC_T => POINT4,
                 MAX_TIME => 5.0,
                    -- max time for every alternate
                 INIT => INIT_ALTERNATES,
                 RUN_ACT => GO_ACT);

   task body TPACT is separate;
   task body TP1 is separate;
   task body TP2 is separate;
   task body TP3 is separate;
begin
   RB_TEST.RB_CONTROLLER.START;
end RB_USER;
```

B.3.3 User blocks

The provided alternates do not solve any specific problems. They were only chosen to have three alternates which can become erroneous depending on the value given by the program user.

```
separate (RB_USER)
task body TP1 is
   -- I: INTEGER; C:CHARACTER; of RB_USER
begin
   PUT_LINE("Give an INTEGER:");
   IIO.GET(I);
   PUT_LINE("Give a CHARACTER");
   GET(C);
   RB_TEST.RB_CONTROLLER.END_PROC; -- (1)
exception
   when DATA_ERROR => -- CHARACTER different from a digit
      skip_line;
end TP1;
-------------------------------------------------------------
```

```ada
separate (RB_USER)
task body TP2 is
   -- I:INTEGER;C:CHARACTER; of RB_USER
begin
   PUT_LINE("Give the INTEGER to divide");
   IIO.GET(I);
   I:=10/I; -- to provoke the task termination if I=0 (exception)
   C:='a';
   NEW_LINE;
   RB_TEST.RB_CONTROLLER.END_PROC;  -- (2)
end TP2;

separate (RB_USER)
task body TP3 is
begin
   PUT_LINE("Task 3 _ Last possibility!");
   PUT_LINE("Give an INTEGER:");
   IIO.GET(I);
   PUT_LINE("Give a CHARACTER");
   GET(C);
   C:=CHARACTER'PRED(C);
   RB_TEST.RB_CONTROLLER.END_PROC;  -- (3)
end TP3;
```

B.3.4 User Acceptance Test

```ada
separate (RB_USER)
task body TPACT is
   B: BOOLEAN;
begin
   B:= ((I<=3) and (C in 'a'..'l'));
   if B then PUT_LINE("Acceptance test OK");
      else PUT_LINE("Acceptance test failed");
   end if;
   RB_TEST.RB_CONTROLLER.RESULT(B);
exception
   when others =>
      PUT_LINE("Error in Acceptance test");
end TPACT;
```

B.4 N-Version Programming implementation

The programs provided in this section are used in section 4.5.4

B.4.1 Generic versions monitor task

```ada
----------------------------------------------------------------
-- This package which contains TYPES and constant definitions,
-- is SEPARATEd because it is used at the same time by the
-- generic package NVP monitoring the versions and the versions
-- user program
----------------------------------------------------------------
package SEPARATE_TYPES is
   NB_TASK_MAX: constant INTEGER :=3;
   subtype NBTASK is INTEGER range 1..NB_TASK_MAX;
   type TABBOOLTASK is array(NBTASK) of BOOLEAN;
   type TAB_INT is array(NBTASK) of INTEGER;
   type TAB_CHAR is array(NBTASK) of CHARACTER;
end SEPARATE_TYPES;


----------------------------------------------------------
-- generic package NVP

with TEXT_IO; use TEXT_IO;
with CALENDAR; use CALENDAR;
with SEPARATE_TYPES; use SEPARATE_TYPES;

generic

   type PT1 is private;     -- access to first task
   type PT2 is private;     -- access to second task
   type PT3 is private;     -- access to third task
   type PT_VOTER is private; -- access to voter task
   TIME_OUT: DURATION:=1.5; -- deadline to wait for the results

   with procedure INIT(P1: out PT1; P2: out PT2; P3: out PT3;
                       T: out TABBOOLTASK);
-- external procedure to supply. It will start the three
-- versions (tasks) according to their types

   with procedure GO_VOTE(P: in out PT_VOTER;
                          T: in TABBOOLTASK);
-- external procedure which will start the vote
```

```ada
package NVP is
  type T_NBRESULT is range 0..NB_TASK_MAX;
  task NVP_CONTROLLER is
    entry START;
    entry PROC_END(N: in NBTASK);
    entry RESULT(B: in BOOLEAN);
  end NVP_CONTROLLER;
end NVP;

package body NVP is
  package IIO is new INTEGER_IO(T_NBRESULT);
    use IIO;
  VERSION1: PT1; VERSION2: PT2; VERSION3: PT3;
  VOTER : PT_VOTER;
  N: NBTASK;

  task body NVP_CONTROLLER is
    DEADLINE_TIME: TIME;
    NBRESULT: T_NBRESULT:= 0;
    TAB_CONTROL: TABBOOLTASK;
  begin
    accept START do
      DEADLINE_TIME:= CLOCK + TIME_OUT;
      INIT(VERSION1,VERSION2,VERSION3,TAB_CONTROL);
    end START; -- start the versions
    loop
      select
        accept PROC_END(N: in NBTASK) do -- N version is ended
          TAB_CONTROL(N):= TRUE;
        end PROC_END;
        NBRESULT:=NBRESULT+1;
        if NBRESULT=T_NBRESULT'LAST then exit;
        end if;
        -- if all the versions are terminated => exit
      or
        delay DEADLINE_TIME - CLOCK;
        PUT_LINE("Time out before the 3 results");
        exit;
      end select;
    end loop;
```

```
      PUT("Nb results: "); PUT(NBRESULT); NEW_LINE;
      case NBRESULT is
        when 0 => PUT_LINE("No result!");
        when others=> GO_VOTE(VOTER,TAB_CONTROL);--start the vote
      end case;
    end NVP_CONTROLLER;
end NVP;
```

B.4.2 User program

```
--------------------------------------------------------
-- NVP_USER : user program of the N_versions
--------------------------------------------------------
with NVP; -- the generic package containing NVP_CONTROLLER
with TEXT_IO; use TEXT_IO;
with SEPARATE_TYPES; use SEPARATE_TYPES;

procedure NVP_USER is
  package IIO is new INTEGER_IO(INTEGER);

-- NB_TASK_MAX : constant INTEGER :=3; defined in SEPARATE_TYPES
-- subtype NBTASK is INTEGER range 1..NB_TASK_MAX;
-- type TABBOOLTASK is array(NBTASK) of BOOLEAN;

  task type TP1; task type TP2; task type TP3;
  task type TPVOTE is
    entry RUN( T: in TABBOOLTASK; C: in CHARACTER;
               TI: in TAB_INT; TC: in TAB_CHAR);
  end TPVOTE;

  type POINT1 is access TP1;
  type POINT2 is access TP2;
  type POINT3 is access TP3;
  type POINTV is access TPVOTE;
  type STRATEGY is (FIRST_VERSION, COMPARISON, MAJORITY);

  STRAT: STRATEGY:= FIRST_VERSION;
  CHOICE_STRAT: CHARACTER;

  ------- GLOBAL VARIABLES
  I: INTEGER:= 4; C: CHARACTER:= 'x';
```

```ada
TAB_VAR_I: TAB_INT;
TAB_VAR_C: TAB_CHAR;
TAB_CONTROL: TABBOOLTASK:= (others =>FALSE);

procedure RUN_VOTE(P: in out POINTV; T: in TABBOOLTASK) is
begin
  loop
    PUT("Give the strategy: f -> FIRST_VERSION, ");
    PUT_LINE("c -> COMPARISON, m -> MAJORITY");
    GET(CHOICE_STRAT);
    case CHOICE_STRAT is
      when 'f' => STRAT:= FIRST_VERSION;
      when 'c' => STRAT:= COMPARISON;
      when 'm' => STRAT:= MAJORITY;
      when others => exit;
    end case;
    P:= new TPVOTE;
    P.RUN(T, CHOICE_STRAT, TAB_VAR_I, TAB_VAR_C);
  end loop;
exception
  when STORAGE_ERROR =>
    PUT_LINE("Storage error! Voter Task not generated");
end RUN_VOTE;

procedure INIT_ALTERNATES(P1: out POINT1; P2: out POINT2;
              P3: out POINT3; T: out TABBOOLTASK) is
begin
  P1:= new TP1;
  P2:= new TP2;
  P3:= new TP3;
  T:= TAB_CONTROL; -- initialized in its declaration
exception
  when STORAGE_ERROR =>
    PUT_LINE("Storage error! Not all alternates generated");
end INIT_ALTERNATES;

package NVP_TEST is new NVP(PT1 => POINT1, PT2 => POINT2,
  PT3 => POINT3, PT_VOTER => POINTV, TIME_OUT => 5.0,
  INIT => INIT_ALTERNATES, GO_VOTE => RUN_VOTE);
```

```
    task body TP1 is separate;
    task body TP2 is separate;
    task body TP3 is separate;
    task body TPVOTE is separate;

begin
    NVP_TEST.NVP_CONTROLLER.START;
end NVP_USER;
```

B.4.3 User versions

```
separate(NVP_USER)
task body TP1 is
    I: INTEGER renames TAB_VAR_I(1);
    C: CHARACTER renames TAB_VAR_C(1);
begin
    PUT_LINE("Hello! I am the first version");
    I:= 1; C:= 'a';
    PUT_LINE("   results => I=1, C='a'");
    NVP_TEST.NVP_CONTROLLER.PROC_END(1);
end TP1;

separate(NVP_USER)
task body TP2 is
    I: INTEGER renames TAB_VAR_I(2);
    C: CHARACTER renames TAB_VAR_C(2);
begin
    PUT_LINE("Hello! I am the second version");
    I:= 1; C:='c';
    PUT_LINE("   results => I=1, C='c'");
    NVP_TEST.NVP_CONTROLLER.PROC_END(2);
end TP2;

separate(NVP_USER)
task body TP3 is
    I: INTEGER renames TAB_VAR_I(3);
    C: CHARACTER renames TAB_VAR_C(3);
begin
    PUT_LINE("Hello! I am the third version");
    I:= 1; C:='c';
    PUT_LINE("   results => I=1, C='c'");
    NVP_TEST.NVP_CONTROLLER.PROC_END(3);
end TP3;
```

B.4.4 User voter

```ada
separate(NVP_USER)
task body TPVOTE is
  package IIO is new INTEGER_IO(INTEGER);
    use IIO;
  type TASK_CPT is range 0..NB_TASK_MAX;

  TAB: TABBOOLTASK;
  CPT: NBTASK:= 1;
  CPT2, CPT_END: NBTASK:= NBTASK'LAST;
        -- used in comparison strategy
  OK: BOOLEAN:= FALSE;
  TAB_VAR_i: TAB_INT;
  TAB_VAR_C: TAB_CHAR;
  STRAT: CHARACTER;

begin
  accept RUN(T: in TABBOOLTASK; C: in CHARACTER;
      TI: in TAB_INT; TC: in TAB_CHAR) do
    TAB:= T;
    TAB_VAR_I:= TI;
    TAB_VAR_C:= TC;
    STRAT:= C;
  end RUN;
  PUT_LINE("Hello! I am the voter");
  case STRAT is
    when 'f' =>     -- FIRST_VERSION
      PUT_LINE("and the chosen strategy is: FIRST_VERSION");
      loop
        if TAB(CPT) then
          OK:=TRUE;
          exit;
        else if CPT<NBTASK'LAST then
            CPT:=CPT+1;
          else
          -- OK:=FALSE;
            exit;
          -- when no task
          end if;
        end if;
      end loop;
```

```ada
      when 'c' =>   -- COMPARISON, we have 2 counters CPT, CPT2
        PUT_LINE("and the chosen strategy is: COMPARISON");
        while not(TAB(CPT_END)) and then CPT<CPT_END loop
          CPT_END:= CPT_END-1;
        end loop;   -- finding the last task
        while not(TAB(CPT)) and then CPT<CPT_END loop
          CPT:= CPT+1;
        end loop;   -- finding the first task

        CPT2:= CPT+1;

        while CPT2<=CPT_END loop
          while not(TAB(CPT2)) and then CPT2<=CPT_END loop
            CPT2:= CPT2+1;
          end loop;   -- finding a second task to compare
          PUT("I compare"); PUT(CPT); PUT(" and");
          PUT(CPT2); NEW_LINE;
          OK:= ((TAB_VAR_I(CPT) = TAB_VAR_I(CPT2)) and
            (TAB_VAR_C(CPT) = TAB_VAR_C(CPT2)));
          exit when OK;   -- 2 sames values
          if CPT2=CPT_END then   -- the next
            CPT := CPT + 1;
            while not(TAB(CPT)) and then CPT<CPT_END loop
              CPT:=CPT+1;
            end loop;
            exit when CPT=CPT_END;
            CPT2:= CPT + 1;
          else
            CPT2:=CPT2+1;
          end if;
        end loop;

      when 'm' =>   -- MAJORITY
        PUT_LINE("and the chosen strategy is: MAJORITY");
      MAJ:
        declare
          CANDIDATE1, CANDIDATE2, CANDIDATE3: TASK_CPT :=0;
        begin
          null;   -- etc.
        end MAJ;
      when others => null;   -- for the case statement
    end case;
```

```
   if OK then I:= TAB_VAR_I(CPT); -- we have the result
      C:= TAB_VAR_c(CPT);
      PUT("Chosen Task :"); PUT(CPT); NEW_LINE;
      PUT("i:"); PUT(I); PUT(", c:"); PUT(C); NEW_LINE;
   end if;
end TPVOTE;
```

B.5 Exception Monitor Task

The programs provided in this section are used in section 4.5.5.

```
procedure CASH_DISPENSER is
   INCORRECT_INPUT, DEADLINE: exception;
   type FUNCTIONAL_STATE is
         ( START, CHECK_POINT,   MENU,
            TO_END_OR_NOT_TO_END, THE_END);
   task NORMAL_BEHAVIOUR;
   task EVENTS_MANAGER is
      entry RESET;
      entry INCORRECT_INPUT(STATE: in out FUNCTIONAL_STATE);
      entry DEADLINE(STATE: in out FUNCTIONAL_STATE);
   end EVENTS_MANAGER;
   package EXTERNAL_OPERATIONS is
      task PRODUCER;
      task BUFFER is
         entry WRITE(C: in CHARACTER);
         entry READ(C: out CHARACTER);
         entry CLEAN;
      end BUFFER;
      procedure GET_CARD;
      procedure GET_AND_CHECK_CODE;
               -- raises INCORRECT_INPUT or DEADLINE
      procedure GET_AND_TREAT_OPERATION;
               -- raises INCORRECT_INPUT or DEADLINE
      procedure GET_RESPONSE(RESPONSE: out BOOLEAN);
      procedure RETURN_CARD;
      procedure EAT_CARD;
   end EXTERNAL_OPERATIONS;
```

382 Appendix B: Complete Examples

```ada
package body EXTERNAL_OPERATIONS is separate;
use EXTERNAL_OPERATIONS;

task body NORMAL_BEHAVIOUR is
  CURRENT_STATE : FUNCTIONAL_STATE := START;
  YES : BOOLEAN := TRUE;
begin
  loop
    begin
      case CURRENT_STATE is
        when START           => EVENTS_MANAGER.RESET;
                                GET_CARD;
                                CURRENT_STATE := CHECK_POINT;
        when CHECK_POINT     => GET_AND_CHECK_CODE;
                                CURRENT_STATE := MENU;
        when MENU            => GET_AND_TREAT_OPERATION;
                                CURRENT_STATE:=TO_END_OR_NOT_TO_END;
        when TO_END_OR_NOT_TO_END => GET_RESPONSE(YES);
                                if YES then
                                     CURRENT_STATE := MENU;
                                 else CURRENT_STATE := THE_END;
                                end if;
        when THE_END         => RETURN_CARD;
                                CURRENT_STATE := START;
      end case;
    exception
      when INCORRECT_INPUT =>
              EVENTS_MANAGER.INCORRECT_INPUT(CURRENT_STATE);
      when DEADLINE =>
              EVENTS_MANAGER.DEADLINE(CURRENT_STATE);
    end;
  end loop;
end NORMAL_BEHAVIOUR;

task body EVENTS_MANAGER is
  type USER_STATE is
      ( GOOD,    THINKING,   TOO_SLOW,
        CLUMSY,  SUSPICIOUS, INCAPABLE);
  LOCAL_STATE: USER_STATE := GOOD;
begin
  loop
    select
    accept RESET;
      LOCAL_STATE:= GOOD;
```

```
       or
       accept DEADLINE(STATE: in out FUNCTIONAL_STATE) do
         case LOCAL_STATE is
           when GOOD          =>LOCAL_STATE:= THINKING;
                                -- STATE not modified
           when THINKING      =>LOCAL_STATE:= TOO_SLOW;
                                STATE:= THE_END;
           when CLUMSY        =>LOCAL_STATE:= SUSPICIOUS;
                                -- STATE not modified
           when SUSPICIOUS    =>LOCAL_STATE:= INCAPABLE;
                                EAT_CARD;
                                STATE:= START;
           when others        =>null;
         end case;
       end DEADLINE;
       or
       accept INCORRECT_INPUT(STATE: in out FUNCTIONAL_STATE) do
         case LOCAL_STATE is
           when GOOD                  =>LOCAL_STATE:= CLUMSY;
                                        -- STATE not modified
           when THINKING              =>LOCAL_STATE:= SUSPICIOUS;
                                        -- STATE not modified
           when CLUMSY|SUSPICIOUS     =>LOCAL_STATE:= INCAPABLE;
                                        EAT_CARD;
                                        STATE:= START;
           when others                =>null;
         end case;
       end INCORRECT_INPUT;
       end select;
     end loop;
   end EVENTS_MANAGER;
begin
   null;
end CASH_DISPENSER;

with TEXT_IO; use TEXT_IO;
separate(CASH_DISPENSER)

package body EXTERNAL_OPERATIONS is
   task body PRODUCER is
      C: CHARACTER;
   begin
      loop
```

```
      if END_OF_LINE(STANDARD_INPUT) then
         BUFFER.WRITE(ASCII.LF);
      end if;
      GET(C);
      BUFFER.WRITE(C);
   end loop;
end PRODUCER;


task body BUFFER is       -- derived from N.GEHANI
   N: constant INTEGER := 51;
   Q: array(1..N) of CHARACTER; -- buffer size = N-1
   INB, OUTB: INTEGER range 1..N := 1;
      --INB mod N + 1: next free space in Q
      --OUTB mod N + 1: first element in Q, if any
      --INB = OUTB: Q is empty; initially true
      --INB mod N + 1 = OUTB: Q is full
begin
   loop
      select
         when INB mod N + 1 /= OUTB => -- Q not full
            accept WRITE(C: in CHARACTER) do
                Q(INB mod N + 1) := C;
            end WRITE;
            INB := INB mod N + 1;
      or when INB /= OUTB => --Q not empty
            accept READ(C: out CHARACTER) do
                C := Q(OUTB mod N + 1);
            end READ;
            OUTB := OUTB mod N + 1;
      or
            accept CLEAN do
               INB := 1;
               OUTB := 1;
            end CLEAN;
      or
            terminate;
      end select;
   end loop;
end BUFFER;
```

```ada
procedure GET_CARD is
  X: CHARACTER;
begin
  PUT_LINE("Welcome: insert your card");
  BUFFER.CLEAN;
  BUFFER.READ(X);
  if X = ASCII.LF then NEW_LINE;
  end if;
end GET_CARD;

procedure GET_AND_CHECK_CODE is
  DEMO_CODE: constant CHARACTER := 'I';
  ENTERED_CODE: CHARACTER := 'B';
begin
  PUT_LINE("Enter your code:");
  BUFFER.CLEAN;
  loop
    select
      BUFFER.READ(ENTERED_CODE);
      if ENTERED_CODE = ASCII.LF then NEW_LINE;
      else exit; -- Code entered
      end if;
    or
      delay 10.0;
      raise DEADLINE; --=> exit of the loop
    end select;
  end loop;
  if ENTERED_CODE /= DEMO_CODE then
    raise INCORRECT_INPUT;
  end if;
exception
  when CONSTRAINT_ERROR|INCORRECT_INPUT =>
    raise INCORRECT_INPUT;
--when DEADLINE => raise;
end GET_AND_CHECK_CODE;

procedure GET_AND_TREAT_OPERATION is
  subtype CHOICES is CHARACTER range '1'..'4';
  OPERATION: CHOICES;
begin
  PUT_LINE("1. Account state");
  PUT_LINE("2. Withdraw money");
  PUT_LINE("3. Deposit money");
```

```
   PUT_LINE("4. Last operations");
   PUT_LINE("Enter your operation:");
   BUFFER.CLEAN;
   loop
     select
       BUFFER.READ(OPERATION);
       if OPERATION = ASCII.LF then NEW_LINE;
       else exit; -- Operation entered
       end if;
     or
       delay 10.0;
       raise DEADLINE; --=> exit of the loop
     end select;
   end loop;
exception
   when CONSTRAINT_ERROR|INCORRECT_INPUT =>
     raise INCORRECT_INPUT;
--when DEADLINE => raise;
end GET_AND_TREAT_OPERATION;

procedure GET_RESPONSE(RESPONSE: out BOOLEAN) is
   R: CHARACTER;
begin
   PUT_LINE("Another operation (Y/N)?");
   BUFFER.CLEAN;
   loop
     BUFFER.READ(R);
     if R = ASCII.LF then NEW_LINE;
     else exit;
     end if;
   end loop;
   RESPONSE:= (R='Y') or (R='y');
end GET_RESPONSE;

procedure RETURN_CARD is
   X: CHARACTER;
begin
   PUT_LINE("Take your card back");
   BUFFER.CLEAN;
   BUFFER.READ(X);
   if X = ASCII.LF then NEW_LINE; end if;
end RETURN_CARD;
```

```
procedure EAT_CARD is
begin
  PUT_LINE("I eat your card...");
end EAT_CARD;
end EXTERNAL_OPERATIONS;
```

B.6 Data Recovery

The programs provided in this section are used in section 4.5.7.

```
-- procedure used as example in section 4.5.7
-- here, raises DATA_ERROR when the ITEM readed is not
-- an integer
procedure GET_AND_ADD( T: in out T_ARRAY;
         INDEX: in out T_ARRAY_RANGE; ADD: in out T_ITEM) is
  ITEM: T_ITEM;
begin
  loop
    GET(ITEM);
    exit when ITEM = ITEM_NUL;
    INDEX:= T_ARRAY_RANGE'SUCC(INDEX);
    T(INDEX):= ITEM;
    ADD:= ADD + ITEM;
    exit when INDEX = T'LENGTH-1;
  end loop;
end GET_AND_ADD;
```

B.6.1 Forward technique

```
with TEXT_IO; use TEXT_IO;
procedure FORWARD_DEMO is
  package IIO is new INTEGER_IO(INTEGER); use IIO;

  subtype T_ITEM is INTEGER;
  ITEM_NUL: T_ITEM:= 0;
  subtype T_ARRAY_RANGE is INTEGER range 0..20;
  type T_ARRAY is array(T_ARRAY_RANGE) of T_ITEM;
  T: T_ARRAY:= (others => 0);
  CUMULATION: T_ITEM := 0;
  TOP: T_ARRAY_RANGE := T_ARRAY_RANGE'FIRST;

  procedure GET_AND_ADD( T: in out T_ARRAY;
```

                  INDEX: **in out** T_ARRAY_RANGE;
                  ADD: **in out** T_ITEM) **is**
    ...

begin
   GET_AND_ADD(T,TOP,CUMULATION);
-- normal termination of GET_AND_ADD
-- ...
exception
   when DATA_ERROR =>
   -- CUMULATION which is an INTEGER parameter passed by copy
   -- was not modified!
      for I **in** T_ARRAY_RANGE'SUCC(T_ARRAY_RANGE'FIRST)
                                    ..T_ARRAY_RANGE'LAST **loop**
         exit when T(I) = ITEM_NUL;
         TOP:= I;
         CUMULATION:= CUMULATION + T(I);
      end loop;
   -- here CUMULATION is restored by a new cumulation...
end FORWARD_DEMO;

B.6.2 Backward technique
with TEXT_IO; **use** TEXT_IO;
procedure BACKWARD_DEMO **is**

   -- same definitions as in FORWARD_DEMO

begin
   GET_AND_ADD(T,TOP,CUMULATION);
-- normal termination of GET_AND_ADD
-- ...
exception
   when DATA_ERROR =>
      -- CUMULATION which is an INTEGER parameter passed by copy
      -- was not modified but array T was modified
      -- (passed by reference)!
      T:= (**others** =>0);
      -- here T is reseted
      -- the procedure can be recalled
end BACKWARD_DEMO;

B.6.3 Systematic backward implementation

```ada
with TEXT_IO; use TEXT_IO;
procedure SYSTEMATIC_BACKWARD_DEMO is
  -- same definitions as in FORWARD_DEMO
  procedure GET_AND_ADD( T: in out T_ARRAY;
        INDEX: in out T_ARRAY_RANGE; ADD: in out T_ITEM) is
    ITEM: T_ITEM;
    -- no global variables used => no difference
  begin
    NESTED_BLOCK:       -- ②
      declare           -- ②
        SAVED_T:T_ARRAY:=T; -- ③ parameter passed by reference
      begin
        loop-- same body

        end loop;
      exception         -- ②
        when others => -- ④
          begin
            T:= SAVED_T;  -- ⑤
            raise; -- ⑥
          end;
      end NESTED_BLOCK;   -- ②
    -- no exception handler in the first version of GET_AND_ADD
  end GET_AND_ADD;
begin
  GET_AND_ADD(T,TOP,CUMULATION);
-- normal termination of GET_AND_ADD
-- ...
exception
  when DATA_ERROR =>
  -- T, CUMULATION and TOP were already reseted
  -- the procedure can be recalled
end SYSTEMATIC_BACKWARD_DEMO;
```

Bibliography

References used for chapter 1

(ARM, 1983) *Reference Manual for the Ada programming language*, (ANSI/MIL-STD-1815A), US government, Ada Joint Program Office, (1983)

(Ada95, 1995) Intermetrics, *Ada Reference Manual, version 6.0*, ISO/IEC 8652:1995(E), US government, Ada Joint Program Office, (1995)

(Barnes, 1984) Barnes J., *Programming in Ada*, Addison-Wesley, (1984)

(Béounes, 1993) Béounes C., Aguéra M., Arlat J., Bachman S., Bourdeau C., Doucet J.-E., Kanoun K., Laprie J.-C., Metge S., Moreira de Souza J., Powell D., Spiesser P., "SURF-2: a Program for Dependability Evaluation of Complex Hardware and Software Systems", in *Proceedings of the Twenty-Third International Symposium on Fault-Tolerance Computing*, IEEE publisher, (June 22-23, 1993), pp. 668-673

(Booch, 1986) Booch G., *Software Engineering with Ada*, Benjamin Cummings, (1986)

(Booch, 1991) Booch G., *Object Oriented Design with Applications*, Benjamin Cummings, (1991)

(Brian, 1990) Brian D., Mendal G., *Exploring Ada*, Prentice Hall, (1990)

(Burns, 1985) Burns A., *Concurrent Programming in Ada*, Ada Companion Series, Cambridge University Press, (1985)

(Burns, 1990) Burns A., Wellings A., Davies G., "Asynchronous Transfer of Control", *Ada Letters*, vol. X, no. 9, (Fall 1990), pp. 75-84

(Carter, 1987) Carter W.C., "Experiences in Fault Tolerant Computing, 1947 - 1971", in *The Evolution of Fault-Tolerant Computing*, Avizienis, Kopetz, Laprie (eds.), Springer-Verlag, (1987), pp.1-36

(Corbato, 1991) Corbato F., "On building systems that will fail", *Communications of the ACM*, vol. 34, no. 9, ACM publisher, (Sep. 1991)

(Costes, 1981) Costes A., Doucet J.-E., Landrault C., Laprie J.-C., "SURF: A Program for Dependability Evaluation of Complex Fault-Tolerant Computing Systems", in *Proceedings of the 11th Int. Symp. Fault-Tolerant Computing*, Portland, Maine, (June 1981), pp. 72-78

(Emerson, 1990) Emerson E., "Temporal and Modal Logic", in *Handbook of Theoretical Computer Science*, Elsevier, (1990), pp. 996-1072

(Gauthier, 1993) Gauthier M., *Ada, a top-down course*, McGraw-Hill, (1993)

(Goldsack, 1985) *Ada for Specification: possibilities and limitations*, edited by S. Golsack, The Ada Companion Series, Cambridge University Press, (1985)

(Helmbold, 1985) Helmbold D., Luckham D., "TSL: Task Sequencing Language", in *Proceedings of the Ada International Conference*, Cambridge University Press, (1985), pp. 255-274

(Kruchten, 1990) Kruchten P., "Error Handling in Large, Object-Based Ada Systems", *SIGAda Letters*, vol. X, no. 7, ACM publisher, (Sept.-Oct. 1990), pp. 91-103
   In French: (Kruchten, 1989) Kruchten P., "Traitement des Erreurs Ada dans les Grands Systèmes Utilisant la Conception par Objet", *Génie Logiciel et Systèmes Experts*, no. 17, EC2 Editeur, (Dec. 1989), pp. 12-18

(Laprie, 1989a) Laprie J.-C., "Dependability evaluation: hardware and software", in *Dependability of Resilient Computers*, Blackwell Scientific Publications, T. Anderson editor, (1989)

(Laprie, 1989b) Laprie J.-C., "A Unifying Concept for Reliable Computing and Fault-Tolerance", in *Dependability of Resilient Computers*, Blackwell Scientific Publications, T. Anderson editor, (1989)

(Laprie, 1992) Laprie J.-C.(Ed.), "Dependability: Basic Concepts and Terminology", *IFIP WG 10.4 Dependable Computing and Fault Tolerance*, vol. 5, Springer-Verlag, (1992)

(Littlewood, 1975) Littlewood B., "A Reliability Model for Markov structured software", in *Proceedings of Int. Conf. on Reliable Software*, Los Angeles, CA, (April 1975), pp. 204-207

(Liskov, 1974) Liskov B.H., Zilles S.N., "Programming with Abstract Data Types", *SIGPLAN Notices*, vol. 9, no. 4, ACM publisher, (April 1974), pp. 50-59

(Luckham, 1990) Luckham D., *Programming with Specifications. An Introduction to Anna a Language for Specifying Programs*, Springer-Verlag, (1990)

(Milner, 1989) Milner R., *Communication and Concurrency*, Prentice Hall International Series in Computer Science, (1989)

(Motet, 1995) Motet G., Kubek J.-M., "Dependability Problem of Ada Components Available via Information Superhighways", in *Proceedings of 13th Annual National Conference on Ada Technology*, Valley Forge (PA), 13-16 March 95, Rosenberg & Risinger Publisher, Culver City (CA), (1995), pp. 8-18

(Murata, 1989) Murata T., Shenker B., Shatz S.M., "Detection of Ada Static Deadlocks Using Petri Net Invariants", in *Transactions on Software Engineering*, vol. 15, no. 3, (March 1989), pp. 314-326

(Musa, 1987) Musa J.D., Ianino A., Okumoto K., *Software Reliability: Measurement, Prediction, Application*, McGraw-Hill, Singapore, (1987)

(Villemeur, 1991) Villemeur A., *Reliability, Availability, Maintenability and Safety Assessment: Methods and techniques*, vol. 1 and 2, Wiley, (1991)
   In French: (Villemeur, 1988) Villemeur A., *Sûreté de Fonctionnement des Systèmes Industriels*, Collection DER/EDF, Eyrolles, (1988)

(Viswanadham, 1987) Viswanadham N., Sarma V., Sigh M., *Reliability of Computer and Control Systems*, Systems and Control Series, vol. 8, North-Holland, (1987)

(Wichman, 1990) Wichman B.A., "Insecurities in Ada", in *Proceedings of the Ada-Europe Conference*, The Ada Companion Series, Cambridge University Press, (1990)

(Wing, 1990) Wing J., "A specifier's Introduction to Formal Methods", *IEEE Computer*, IEEE publisher, (Sep. 1990)

References used for chapter 2

(Abid, 1989a) Abid M., (in French) "Test sequence validation of complex integrated circuits", Ph.D. Thesis of Institut National des Sciences Appliquées, Complexe Scientifique de Rangueil, 31077 Toulouse Cedex, France, (March 1989)

(Abid, 1989b) Abid M., Geffroy J.C., Motet G., "State Machine Identification for Test Evaluation", in *Proceedings of IASTED Conference on Simulation*, Lugano, Switzerland, (July 1989)

(Albin, 1982) Albin J.-L., Ferreol R., "Collection and Analyze of Software measurements", (in French), *Technique et Science Informatique*, vol. 1, no. 4, (1982), pp. 297-313

Bibliography

(Anderson, 1979) Anderson T., Lee P.A., Shrivastava S.K., "System Fault Tolerance", *2nd Advanced Course on Computing Systems Reliability*, Toulouse, (Sept. 1979)

(Anderson, 1981) Anderson T., Lee P.A., *Fault Tolerance: Principles and Practice*, Prentice Hall International, (1981)

(Annaratone, 1982) Annaratone M.A., Sami M.G., "An approach to functional testing of microprocessors", in *Proceedings of 1982 Fault-Tolerant Computing Symposium*, Santa Monica, CA, USA, (June 1982), pp. 158-164

(ANSI, 1984) American National Standard Institute, *IEEE Guide to Software Requirements Specification*, STD-830-1984, IEEE publisher, (1984)

(Appelbe, 1988) Appelbe W.F., DeMillo R.A., Guindi D.S., King K.N., McCracken W.M., "Using mutation analysis for testing Ada programs", in *Proceedings of Ada-Europe International Conference*, Munich, (June 1988)

(Arlat, 1990) Arlat J., Kanoun K., Laprie J.C., "Dependability Modeling and Evaluation of Software Fault-Tolerant Systems", *IEEE Transactions on Computer*, vol. 39, no. 4, IEEE publisher, (April 1990), pp. 504-513

(Avizienis, 1984) Avizienis A., Kelly J., "Fault tolerance by design diversity: concepts and experiments", *Computer*, vol. 14, no. 8, IEEE publisher, (Aug. 1984), pp. 67-80

(Banâtre, 1981) Banâtre, J.P., Gamatie, B., Ployette, F., "Exceptions and residual faults handling in programming languages" (in French), *RAIRO Informatique/Computer Science*, vol. 15, no. 1, (1981), pp. 3-38

(Bellon, 1985) Bellon C., Kolokithas E., Velazco R., "The GAPT system: a test line for microprocessors" (in French), *L'onde électrique*, vol. 65, no. 6/99, (Nov. 1985)

(Berthomieu, 1991) Berthomieu B., Diaz M., "Modelling and Verification on Time Dependent Systems Using Time Petri Nets", *Transactions on Software Engineering*, vol. 17, no. 3, IEEE publisher, (March 1991), pp. 259-273

(Bhandari, 1993) Bhandari I.S., Halliday M.J., Traver E., Brown D., Chaar J.K., Chillarege R., "A Case Study of Software Process Improvement During Development", *Transactions on Software Engineering*, vol. 19, no. 12, IEEE publisher, (1993), pp. 1157-1170

(Bidoit, 1987) Bidoit M., Capy F., Choppy C., Choquet N., Gresse G., Kaplan S., Schlienger F., Voisin F., "ASSPRO: an integrated and interactive programming environment" (in French), *T.S.I.*, vol. 6, no. 1, (1987)

(Boehm, 1984) Boehm B.W., "Verifying and Validating Software Requirements and Design Specifications", *IEEE Software*, IEEE publisher, (January 1984), pp. 75-88
    also in *System and Software Requirements Engineering*, R.H. Tayer, M. Dorfman editors, IEEE Computer Society Press Tutorial, (1990), pp. 471-484

(Boehm, 1989) Boehm B.W., "Introduction and Overview", in *Software Risk Management*, B. W. Boehm editor, IEEE Computer Society Press, (1989), pp. 1-16

(Booch, 1991) Booch G., *Object Oriented Design with Applications*, Benjamin Cummings, (1991)

(Bouge, 1986) Bouge L., Choquet N., Fribourg L., Gaudel M.-C., "Test Set Generation from Algebraic Specifications using Logic Programming", *Journal of Systems and Software*, (Nov. 1986)

(Brahme, 1984) Brahme D., Abraham J.A., "Functional Testing of microprocessors", *IEEE Transactions on Computer*, vol. C-33, no. 6, IEEE publisher, (June 1984)

(Briere, 1990) Briere D., Traverse P.-J., "Airbus A320 flight controls_ A fault tolerant system" (in French), in *Proceedings of 7th International Conference on reliability and maintainability*, Brest, France, (June 1990)

(Brindle, 1989) Brindle A.F., Taylor R.N., Martin D.F., "A Debugger for Ada Tasking", *IEEE Transactions on Software Engineering*, vol. 15, no. 3, IEEE publisher, (March 1989), pp. 293-304

(Cha, 1988) Cha S.S., Leveson N.G., Shiweall T.J., "Safety Verification in Murphy Using Fault Tree Analysis", in *Proceedings of 10th International Conference on Software Engineering*, IEEE publisher, (1988)

Bibliography 393

(Chandra, 1987) Chandra S.J., Palel J.H., "A hierarchical approach to test vector generation", in *Proceedings of 24th Conference on Design Automation of ACM*, IEEE, Miami, USA, (1987)

(Chen, 1978) Chen L., Avizienis A., "N-version programming: a fault-tolerance approach to reliability of software operation", in *Proceedings of 8th International Symposium on Fault-Tolerant Computing* (FTCS 8), Toulouse, (1978), pp. 3-9

(Cheng, 1989) Cheng J., Ushijima K., "Partial order transparency: a minimum requirement for monitoring concurrent systems", in *Proceedings of 2nd Workshop on Software Engineering & its Applications*, vol. 2, EC2 Paris, Toulouse, (Dec. 1989), pp. 827-839

(Chillarege, 1992) Chillarege R., Bhandari I.S., Chaar J.K., Halliday M.J., Moebus D.S., Ray B.K., Wong M.Y., "Orthogonal Defect Classification. A Concept for In-Process Measurements", *Transactions on Software Engineering*, vol. 18, no. 11, IEEE publisher, (1992)

(Courtois, 1987) Courtois B., Gaudel M.-C., Laprie J.-C., Powell D., "Dependable computing for critical space systems" (in French), *LAAS-CNRS research report no. 87.176*, (Nov. 1987)

(David, 1980) David R., Thevenod-Fosse P., "Minimal detecting transition sequences: application to random testing", *IEEE Trans. on Comp.*, vol. C-29, no. 6, IEEE publisher, (June 1980)

(Davis, 1990) Davis A.M., "The Analysis and Specification of Systems and Software Requirements", *in Systems and Software Requirements Engineering*, IEEE Computer Society Press Tutorial, (1990), pp. 119-144

(DeMillo, 1987) DeMillo R.A., McCracken W.M., Martin R.J., Passafiume J.F., *Software Testing and Evaluation*, Benjamin/Cummings, (1987)

(Dillon, 1990) Dillon L.K., "Verifying General Safety Properties of Ada Tasking Programs", *IEEE Transactions on Software Engineering*, vol. 16, no. 1, IEEE publisher, (Jan. 1990), pp. 51-63

(Drake, 1993) Drake J.M., Xie W.W., Tsai W.T., Zaulkernan I.A., "Approach and Case Study of Requirement Analysis Where End Users Take an Active Role", in *Proceedings of the 15th International Conference on Software Engineering*, IEEE publisher, (1993), pp. 177-186

(Eckhardt, 1991) Eckhardt D.E., Caglayan A.K., Knight J.C., Lee L.D., McAllister D.F., Vouk M.A., Kelly J.P., "An Experimental Evaluation of Software Redundancy as a Strategy for Improving Reliability", *Transactions on Software Engineering*, vol. 17, no. 7, IEEE publisher, (1991), pp. 692-702

(El Maadani, 1991) El Maadani K., Geffroy J.-C., "Identification of Structured Automata", in *Proceedings of the 5th IEEE VLSI Test Symposium, Atlanta-City, USA*, IEEE publisher, (April 91)

(Feldman, 1989) Feldman M.B., Moran M.L., "Validating a Demonstration Tool for Graphics-Assisted Debugging of Ada Concurrent Programs", *IEEE Transactions on Software Engineering*, vol. 15, no. 3, IEEE publisher, (March 1989), pp. 305-313

(Gaudel, 1991) Gaudel M.-C., "Advantages and Limits of Formal Approaches for Ultra-High Dependability", in *Proceedings of the 6th International Workshop on Software Specification and Design*, IEEE publisher, (1991), pp. 237-241

(Ghezzi, 1991) Ghezzi C., Mandrioli D., Morasca S., Pezze M., "A Unified High Level Petri Net Formalism for Time Critical Systems", *IEEE Transactions on Software Engineering*, vol. 17, no. 2, IEEE publisher, (Feb. 1991), pp. 160-172

(Hecht, 1986) Hecht H., Hecht M., "Fault-Tolerant Software" in *Fault-Tolerant Computing: Theory and Techniques*, vol. 11, D.K. Pradhan editor, (1986), pp. 658-695

(Hollocker, 1990) Hollocker C., "A review process mix", in *System and Software Requirements Engineering*, R.H. Tayer, M. Dorfman editors, IEEE Computer Society Press Tutorial, (1990), pp. 485-491

(Hourtolle, 1987) Hourtolle C., "Design of dependable software: software safety analysis; decision mechanisms for N-version programming" (in French), Ph.D. Thesis, *LAAS-CNRS report no. 87.267*, (Oct. 1987)

(Howden, 1990) Howden W., "Comments Analysis and Programming Errors", *IEEE Transactions on Software Engineering*, vol. 16, no. 1, IEEE publisher, (Jan. 1990), pp. 72-81

(IEEE, 1983) IEEE Std. 729-1983, "IEEE Standard Glossary of Software Engineering Technology", *IEEE-CS*, order no. 729, Los Alamitos, California, (1983)

(Kanoun, 1987) Kanoun K., "Software Dependability by Fault Tolerance" (in French), in *Proceedings of 9ème Séminaire Tuniso-Français d'Informatique*, Tunis, (Apr. 1987)

(Kelly, 1986) Kelly J.P.J, Avizienis A., Ulery B.T., Swain B.J., Lyu R.-T., Tai A., Tso K.S., "Multiversion Software Development", in *Proceedings of 5th International Workshop on Safety of Computer Control Systems* (SAFECOMP'86), Sarlat (France), (Oct. 1986), pp. 43-49

(Knight, 1993) Knight J., Myers E., "An Improved Inspection Technique", *Communications of the ACM*, vol. 36, no. 11, ACM Publisher, (Nov. 1993), pp. 51-61

(Kubek, 1995) Kubek J.-M., Motet G., "Application of Temporal Constrained Predicate Nets to Production Systems", in *Proceedings of the INRIA/IEEE Conference on Emerging Technologies and Factory Automation*, Paris, (October 1995)

(Lano, 1990) Lano R.J., "A Structured Approach for Operational Concept Formulation", in *Systems and Software Requirements Engineering*, IEEE Computer Society Press Tutorial, (1990), pp. 48-59

(Laprie, 1987) Laprie J.-C., Arlat J., Beounes C., Kanoun K., Hourtolle C., "Hardware and software fault tolerance: definition and analysis of architectural solutions", in *Proceedings of 17th Int. Symp. on Fault Tolerant Computing* (FTCS 17), Pittsburg, PA, (July 1987), pp. 116-121

(Leveson, 1983) Leveson N.G., Stolzy J.L., "Safety Analysis of Ada Programs Using Fault Trees", *IEEE Transactions on Reliability*, vol. R-32, no. 5, IEEE publisher, (Dec. 1983), pp. 479-484

(Leveson, 1987) Leveson N.G., Stolzy J.L., "Safety Analysis Using Petri Nets", *IEEE Transactions on Software Engineering*, vol. SE-13, no. 3, IEEE publisher, (March 1987), pp. 386-397

(Leveson, 1991) Leveson N., "Software Safety in Embedded Computer Systems", *Communications of the ACM*, vol. 34, no. 2, ACM publisher, (Feb. 1991), pp. 34-46

(Liskov, 1974) Liskov B.H., Zilles S.N., "Programming with Abstract Data Types", *SIGPLAN Notices*, vol. 9, no. 4, ACM publisher, (April 1974), pp. 50-59

(Martinolle, 1990) Martinolle F., "Commandability and observability analysis of hierarchical systems. Study and implementation of the PHOEBUS tool" (in French), Ph. D. Thesis, INSAT, Complexe Scientifique de Rangueil 31077 Toulouse Cedex, France, (Nov. 1990)

(Martinolle, 1991) Martinolle F., Geffroy J.-C., Soulas B., "Testability Analysis of Hierarchical Finite-State Machines", in *Proceedings of the IEEE European Design Automation Conference*, Amsterdam, Holland, (Feb. 1991)

(Meyer, 1988) Meyer B., *Object-Oriented Software Construction*, Prentice Hall, (1988)

(Meyer, 1991) Meyer B., "Design by Contract", in *Advances in Object-Oriented Software Engineering*, Prentice Hall, (1991)

(Meyer, 1992) Meyer B., "Applying Design by Contract", *Computer*, vol. 25, no. 10, IEEE publisher, (Oct. 1992), pp. 40-51

(Motet, 1995) Motet G., Kubek J.-M., "Dependability Problem of Ada Components Available via Information Superhighways", *Proc. of 13th Annual National Conference on Ada Technology*, Valley Forge (PA), 13-16 March 95, Rosenberg & Risinger Publisher, Culver City (CA), (1995), pp. 8-18

(Muenier, 1989) Muenier M., "Software testing and validating. Panorama of techniques and tools" (in French), *BIGRE+GLOBULE*, no. 60, IRISA, Rennes, France, (Jan. 1989), pp. 3-12

(Murata, 1989a) Murata T., "Petri Nets: Properties, Analysis and Applications", in *Proceedings of the IEEE*, vol. 77, no. 4, IEEE publisher, (April 1989), pp. 541-580

(Murata, 1989b) Murata T., Shenker B., Shatz S.M., "Detection of Ada Static Deadlocks Using Petri Net Invariants", *IEEE Transactions on Software Engineering*, vol. 15, no. 3, IEEE publisher, (March 1989), pp. 314-326

(Myers, 1979) Myers G.J., *The Art of Software Testing*, Wiley - Interscience, (1979)

(Nakajo, 1993) Nakajo T., Kume H., "A Case History Analysis of Software Error Cause-Effect Relationships", *IEEE Transactions on Software Engineering*, vol. 17, no. 8, IEEE publisher, (1993), pp. 830-838

(Nelsen, 1990) Nelsen E.D., "System Engineering and Requirement Allocation", in *Systems and Software Requirements Engineering*, IEEE Computer Society Press Tutorial, IEEE publisher, (1990), pp. 60-76

(Neumann, 1986) Neumann P.G., "On hierarchical Design of Computer Systems for Critical Applications", *IEEE Transactions on Software Engineering*, vol. SE-12, no. 9, IEEE publisher, (September 1986), pp. 905-920

(O'Connor, 1991) O'Connor P.D.T., *Practical Reliability Engineering*, John Wiley & Sons, (1991)

(Parnas, 1972) Parnas D., "On the criteria to be used in decomposing systems into modules", *Communications of ACM*, vol. 5, no. 12, ACM publisher, (Dec. 1972), pp. 1053-1058

(Peterson, 1981) Peterson J.L., *Petri Net Theory and the Modelling of Systems*, Prentice Hall, (1981)

(PhamVan, 1989) Pham Van N., Amar B., "The techniques of structural test" (in French), *BIGRE+GLOBULE*, no. 60, IRISA, Rennes, France, (Jan. 1989), pp. 24-31

(Pyle, 1991) Pyle I., *Developing Safety Systems. A guide using Ada*, Prentice Hall, (1991)

(Randell, 1975) Randell B., "System Structure for Software Fault Tolerance", *IEEE Transactions on Software Engineering*, vol. SE-1, no. 2, IEEE publisher, (June 1975), pp. 220-232

(RMX286, 1988) *Extended IRMX II.3, System Calls*, vol. 3, Intel Corporation, (1988)

(Roman, 1985) Roman G.C., "A Taxonomy of Current Issues in Requirements Engineering", *Computer*, IEEE publisher, (April 1985), pp. 14-22

(Rouquet, 1986) Rouquet J.C., Traverse P.J., "Safe and Reliable Computing on Board the Airbus and ATR aircraft", in *Proceedings of 5th International Workshop on Safety of Computer Control Systems* (SAFECOMP'86), Sarlat, France, (Oct. 1986), pp. 93-97

(Saucier, 1981) Saucier G., Robach C.H., "Test of systems and microprocessors: state of the art and prospect" (in French), *L'onde électronique*, vol. 61, no. 3, (1981)

(Sharer, 1981) Sharer L., *Pinpointing Requirements*, Datamation, Cahners Publishing Company, (April 1981), pp. 139-154

(SPC, 1991) Software Productivity Consortium, *Ada Quality and Style: Guidelines for Professional Programmers*, SPC-91061-N, Version 02.00.02, Herndon, Virginia, (1991)

(Su, 1982) Su S.H., Hsieh YU-I, "Testing Functional Faults in Digital Systems Described by Register Transfert Language", *Journal of Digital Systems*, (1982)

(Sullivan, 1991) Sullivan M., Chillarege R., "Software Defects and their Impact on System Avaiblability. A Study of Field Failures in Operating Systems", in *Proceedings of 21th IEEE Fault-Tolerant Computing Symposium (FTCS 21)*, (1991), pp. 2-9

(Tamai, 1993) Tamai T., Itou A., "Requirements and Design Change in Large-Scale Software Development: Analysis from the Viewpoint of Process Backtracking", in *Proceedings of the 15th International Conference on Software Engineering*, IEEE publisher, (1993), pp. 167-176

(Thayer, 1990) Thayer R.H., Royce W.W., "Software System Engineering", in *Systems and Software Requirements Engineering*, IEEE Computer Society Press Tutorial, IEEE publisher, (1990), pp. 77-116

(Thatte, 1980) Thatte C., Abraham J., "Test generation for microprocessor architectures", *IEEE Transactions on Computer*, vol. C-29, no. 6, IEEE publisher, (June 1980)

(Thevenod-Fosse, 1981) Thevenod-Fosse P., David R., "Random testing of the data processing section of a microprocessor", in *Proceedings of 11th IEEE Fault-Tolerant Computing Symposium* (FTCS 11), Portland, (June 1981), pp. 275-280

(Thevenod-Fosse, 1983) Thevenod-Fosse P., David R., "Random testing of the control section of a microprocessor", in *Proceedings of 13th IEEE Fault-Tolerant Computing Symposium (FTCS 13)*, Milan, (June 1983), pp. 366-373

(Thevenod-Fosse, 1991) Thevenod-Fosse P., Waeselynck H., "An Investigation of Statistical Software Testing", *The Journal of Software Testing, Verification and Reliability*, vol. 1, no. 2, Sigma Press, (July 1991), pp. 5-25

(Tokuda, 1988) Tokuda H., Kotera M., Mercer C.W., "A Real-Time Monitor for a Distributed Real-Time Operating System", in *Proceedings of Workshop on Parallel and Distributed Debugging*, May 5-6, 1988, published in ACM Sigplan Notices, vol. 24, no. 1, ACM publisher, (Jan. 1989), pp. 68-77

(Tso, 1986) Tso K.S., Avizienis A., Kelly J.P.J., "Error recovery in Multi-version Software", in *Proceedings of 5th International Workshop on Safety of Computer Control Systems* (SAFECOMP'86), Sarlat, France, (Oct. 1986), pp. 35-41

(Villemeur, 1991) Villemeur A., *Reliability, Availability, Maintenability and Safety Assessment: Methods and techniques*, vol. 1 and 2, Wiley, 1991.
    In French: (Villemeur, 1988) Villemeur A., *Sûreté de Fonctionnement des Systèmes Industriels*, Collection DER/EDF, Eyrolles, 1988.

(Wise, 1993) Wise J., Wise M., "Basic Considerations in Verification and Validation", in *Verification and Validation of Complex Systems: Human Factors Issues*, edited by J. Wise, V. Hopkin, P. Stager, Nato ASI Series, Computer and System Sciences, vol. 110, Springer-Verlag, (1993), pp. 87-95

(Wolff, 1989) Wolff J.G., "The Management of the Risk in System Development: 'Project SP' and the 'New Spiral Model'", *IEEE Software Engineering Journal*, IEEE publisher, (May 1989)

References used for chapter 3

(Ada95, 1995) Intermetrics, *Ada Reference Manual, version 6.0*, ISO/IEC 8652:1995(E), US government, Ada Joint Program Office, (1995)

(ARM, 1983) *Reference Manual for Ada Programming Language*, (ANSI/MIL-STD-1815A), US Government Ada Joint Program Office, (1983)

(ARTEWG, 1988) Ada Run-Time Working Group, *A Model of Run-Time System Interface for Ada*, release 2.3, ACM, (Oct. 1988)

(ARTEWG, 1991) Ada Run-Time Working Group, "Catalogue of Interface Features and Options for the Ada Runtime Environment", Release 3.0, proposed by ARTEWG of SIGAda, in *SIGAda Letters*, vol. XI, no. 8, ACM publisher, (Fall 1991)

(Bert, 1982) Bert D., (in French) *Les Exceptions dans le langage Ada*. In *Le langage Ada: Manuel d'Evaluation*, Dunod Informatique, (1982), pp. 124-136. Translated by J. Howlett, *Evaluating Ada*, North Oxford Academic, (1985)

(Booch, 1987) Booch G., *Software Components with Ada*, Benjamin Cummings, (1987)

(Bron, 1976) Bron C., Fokkinga M., De Haas A., "A proposal for Dealing with Abnormal Termination of Programs", *Report no. 150*, Technische Hogeschool Twente, P.O. Box 217, Enschlede, The Netherlands, (Nov. 1976)

(Bundy, 1993) Bundy G., Mularz D., "Common Defects in the Exception Handling of Large Ada Systems", in *Proceedings of the Ada Europe'93 Conference*, Lectures Notes in Computer Sciences no. 688, M. Gauthier Editor, Springer-Verlag, (June 1993), pp. 153-170

(Burns, 1985) Burns A., *Concurrent Programming in Ada*, Ada Companion Series, Cambridge University Press, (1985)

(Burns, 1990) Burns A., Wellings A., Davies G., "Asynchronous Transfer of Control", *Ada Letters*, vol. X, no. 9, ACM publisher, (Fall 1990), pp. 75-84

(Changes, 1995) Intermetrics, *Changes to Ada, version 6.0*, ISO/IEC 8652:1995(E), US government, Ada Joint Program Office, (1995)

(Cheriton, 1986) Cheriton D., "Making Exceptions Simplify the Rule (and Justify their Handling)", in *Proceedings of IFIP'86*, H.J. Kugler Editor, Elsevier Sciences Publisher (North Holland), (1986), pp. 27-33

(Cristian, 1982) Cristian F., "Exception Handling and Software Fault Tolerance", *IEEE Transactions on Computer*, vol. C-31, no. 6, IEEE publisher, (June 1982), pp. 531-539

(Cui, 1990) Cui Q., Gannon J., "Data-Oriented Exception Handling in Ada", in *Proceedings of the International Conference on Computer Languages*, IEEE publisher, (March 12-15, 1990), pp. 98-106. Also in *IEEE Transactions on Software Engineering*, (May 1992)

(de Bondelli, 1984) de Bondelli P., "Comparaison des Concepts des Langages Ada et LTR3", (in French) *Actes des Journées Ada*, Bigre+Globule, no. 42, éditeur AFCET, (Dec. 1984), pp113-135

(Gauthier, 1989) Gauthier M., (in French) "Les Règles Confirment les Exceptions", *Génie Logiciel et Systèmes Experts*, no. 17, EC2 éditeur, (Dec. 1989), pp. 20-34

(Gauthier, 1993) Gauthier M., *Ada, a top-down course*, McGraw-Hill, (1993)

(Goodenough, 1975) Goudenough J.B., "Exception Handling: Issues and Proposed Notations", *Communications of the ACM*, vol. 18, no. 12, ACM publisher, (Dec. 1975), pp. 683-696.

(Helmbold, 1984) Helmbold D., Luckham D., "Debugging Ada Tasking Programs", *Program Analysis and Verification Group report no. 25, Technical report no. 84-262*, Stanford University, California, (1984)

(Helmbold, 1985) Helmbold D., Luckham D., "TSL: Task Sequencing Language", in *Proceedings of the Ada International Conference*, Cambridge University Press, (1985), pp. 255-274. Also in *Ada Letters*, vol. V, Issue 2, ACM publisher, (Sept.-Oct. 1985)

(Holzapfel, 1987) Holzapfel R., Winterstein G., *Safe Ada, Language Study*, Systeam KG report, (Aug. 1987)

(Ichbiah, 1979) Ichbiah J.D. et al., "Rationale for the Design of the Ada Programming Language", *SIGPLAN Notices*, vol. 14, no.6, ACM publisher, (June 1979)

(Kruchten, 1990) Kruchten P., "Error Handling in Large, Object-Based Ada Systems", *SIGAda Letters*, vol. X, no. 7, ACM publisher, (Sept.-Oct. 1990), pp. 91-103
  In French: (Kruchten, 1989) Kruchten P., "Traitement des Erreurs Ada dans les Grands Systèmes Utilisant la Conception par Objet", *Génie Logiciel et Systèmes Experts*, no. 17, EC2 Editeur, (Dec. 1989), pp. 12-18

(Ledgard, 1981) Ledgard H., *Ada: an Introduction and Ada Reference Manual*, Springer-Verlag, (1981)

(Leverrand, 1982) *Le Langage Ada : Manuel d'Evaluation* (in French), Dunod Informatique, Bordas, (1982). Translated by J. Howlett, *Evaluating Ada*, North Oxford Academic, (1985)

(Liskov, 1979) Liskov B., Snyder A., "Exception Handling in Clu", *IEEE Transactions on Software*, vol. SE-5, no. 6, IEEE publisher, (Nov. 1979), pp. 546-558

(Luckham, 1987) Luckham D., Helmbold D., Meldal S., Bryan D., Haberler M., "Task Sequencing Language for Specifying Distributed Ada System", TSL-1, in *Proceedings of the CRAI Worshop on Software Factories and Ada*, Lecture Notes in Computer Sciences no. 275, Springer-Verlag, (1987), pp. 249-305

(Luckham, 1990) Luckham D., *Programming with Specifications. An Introduction to Anna a Language for Specifying Programs*, Springer-Verlag, (1990)

(Mendal, 1992) Mendal G., Bryan D., *Exploring Ada*, vol. 2, Prentice Hall, (1992)

(Meyer, 1990) Meyer B., *Conception et Programmation par Objet* (in French), InterEditions, (1990)
  in English: (Meyer, 1988) Meyer, B., *Object-Oriented Software Construction*, Prentice Hall, (1988)

(Motet, 1994) Motet G., Kubek J.-M., "Hazards in Real-Time Ada Features", *Report of the Laboratoire d'Etude des Systèmes Informatique et Automatique, no. 94-4*, Institut National des Sciences Appliquées, 31077 Toulouse cedex, France (1994)

(Motet, 1995) Motet G., Kubek J.-M., "Dependability Problem of Ada Components Available via Information Superhighways", in *Proceedings of 13th Annual National Conference on Ada Technology*, Valley Forge (PA), 13-16 March 95, Rosenberg & Risinger Publisher, Culver City (CA), (1995), pp. 8-18

(Parnas, 1972) Parnas D., "On the criteria to be used in decomposing systems into modules", *Communications of ACM*, vol. 5, no. 12, ACM publisher, (Dec. 1972), pp. 1053-1058

(Pyle, 1991) Pyle I., *Developing Safety Systems. A guide using Ada*, Prentice Hall, (1991)

(Rationale, 1986) Ichbiah J., Barnes J., Firth R., Woodger M., *Rationale for the Design of the Ada Programming Language*, Honeywell System and Research Center & Alsys, Alsys Editor, Paris, 1986.
(Rosen, 1986) Rosen J.-P., "Chère Comtesse...", (in French) *AdaTech*, no. 10, Aix-en-Provence, (Nov.-Dec. 1986)
(Schwille, 1993) Schwille J., "Use and Abuse of Exceptions for Proper Exception Handling", in *Proceedings of the Ada-Europe'93 conference*, M. Gauthier editor, Springer-Verlag, (1993), pp. 142-152
(SPC, 1991) Software Productivity Consortium, *Ada Quality and Style: Guidelines for Professional Programmers*, SPC-91061-N, Version 02.00.02, Herndon, Virginia, (1991)
(Veillon, 1971) Veillon F., Cagnat J.-M., *Cours de Programmation en Langage PL/I*, (in French) Collection U, Tome I, Armand Colin, (1971)
(Watt, 1987) Watt, Wichmann B., Findlay W., *Ada Language and Methodology*, Prentice Hall, (1987)
(Welz, 1992) Welz A., "Ada in Safety Critical Applications", in *Proceedings of the Ada-Europe conference*, Springer-Verlag, (1992)
(Winkler, 1981) Winkler J., "Differences Between Preliminary and Final Ada", *Sigplan Notices*, vol. 16, no. 11, ACM publisher, (Nov. 1981), pp. 35-48
(Yemini, 1985) Yemini S., Berry D., "A Modular Verifiable Exception Handling Mechanism", *ACM Transactions on Programming Languages and Systems*, vol. 7, no. 2, ACM publisher, (April 1985), pp. 214-243

References used for chapter 4

(Ada_com, 1989) "Approved Ada Language Commentaries", *SIGAda Letters Special Edition*, vol. IX, no. 3, ACM publisher, (Spring 1989)
(Avizienis, 1988) Avizienis A., Lyu M., Schutz W., "Multi-Version Software Development: A UCLA/Honeywell Joint Project for Fault-Tolerant Flight Control Systems", *CSD-880034*, Department of Computer Science, University of California, Los Angeles, (April 1988)
(Booch, 1986) Booch G., *Software Engineering with Ada*, Benjamin Cummings, (1986)
(Bundy, 1993) Bundy G., Murlaz D., "Error-Prone Exception Handling in Large Ada Systems", in *Proceedings of the Ada-Europe'93 conference*, M. Gauthier editor, Springer-Verlag, (1993), pp. 153-170
(Burns, 1989) Burns A., Wellings, A., *Real-Time Systems and their Programming Languages*, Addison-Wesley, (1989)
(Burns, 1990) Burns A., "Real-Time Ada Outstanding Problem Areas", in *Proceedings of the 3rd Int. Workshop on Real-Time Ada Issues*, June 1989, in ACM SIGAda Letters, vol. 10, no. 4, (Spring 1990)
(Carid, 1988) "Catalogue of Ada Runtime Implementation Dependencies", Labtek Corporation for U.S.Army, *ARTEWG*, Oct. 1988
(Cheng, 1989) Cheng J., Ushijima K., "Partial order transparency: a minimum requirement for monitoring concurrent systems", in *Proceedings of 2nd Workshop on Software Engineering & its Applications*, vol. 2, EC2 Paris, Toulouse, (Dec. 1989), pp. 827-839
(de Bondelli, 1983) de Bondelli P., "Models for the Control of Concurrency in Ada based on Predicate-Transition Petri Nets", in *Proceedings of the Adatec-Ada/Europe Joint Conference on Ada*, edited by the C.E.C., Brussels, (March 1983)
(Goldsack, 1985) *Ada for Specification: possibilities and limitations*, edited by S. Goldsack, The Ada Companion Series, Cambridge University Press, (1985)
(Helmbold, 1985) Helmbold D., Luckham D., "Debugging Ada Tasking Programs", *IEEE Software*, vol. 2, no. 2, IEEE publisher, (March 1985), pp. 47-57

(Holzapfel, 1988) Holzapfel R., Winterstein G., "Ada in Safety Critical Applications", in *Proceedings of the Ada-Europe conference*, The Ada Companion Series, Cambridge University Press, (1988)
(Lai, 1990) Lai M., "Why not combine HOOD and Ada?", Ada: Experiences and prospects, in *Proceedings of the Ada-Europe International Conference*, Dublin 12-14 June 1990, The Ada Companion Series, Cambridge University Press, (June 1990), pp. 235-249
(Leveson, 1983) Leveson N.G., Stolzy J.L., "Safety Analysis of Ada Programs Using Fault Trees", *IEEE Transactions on Reliability*, vol. R-32, no. 5, IEEE publisher, (Dec. 1983), pp. 479-484
(Luckham, 1990) Luckham D., *Programming with Specifications. An Introduction to ANNA, a language for Specifying Ada Programs*, Springer-Verlag, (1990)
(Motet, 1994) Motet G., Kubek J.-M., "Hazards in Real-Time Ada Features", *Report of the Laboratoire d'Etude des Systèmes Informatique et Automatique, no. 94-4*, Institut National des Sciences Appliquées, 31077 Toulouse cedex, France (1994)
(Motet, 1995) Motet G., Kubek J.-M., "Dependability Problem of Ada Components Available via Information Superhighways", in *Proceedings of 13th Annual National Conference on Ada Technology*, Valley Forge (PA), 13-16 March 95, Rosenberg & Risinger Publisher, Culver City (CA), (1995), pp. 8-18
(Murata, 1989) Murata T., Shenker B., Shatz S.M., "Detection of Ada Static Deadlocks Using Petri Net Invariants", *IEEE Transactions on Software Engineering*, vol. 15, no. 3, IEEE publisher, (March 1989), pp. 314-326
(Peterson, 1981) Peterson J.L., *Petri Net Theory and the Modelling of Systems*, Prentice Hall, (1981)
(Pyle, 1991) Pyle I., *Developing Safety Systems. A guide using Ada*, Prentice Hall, (1991)
(Rosen, 1989) Rosen J.-P., "Dear Countess..." (in French), *ADATECH*, no. 10, Aix-en-Provence, (Nov.-Dec. 1989)
(SPC, 1992) Software Productivity Consortium, *Ada Quality and Style: Guidelines for Professional Programmers*, SPC-91061-CMC, Version 02.01.01, 2214 Rock Hill Road, Herndon, Virginia 22070, (1992)
(Wichman, 1989) Wichman B.A., "Insecurities in the Ada programming language", *NPL report DITC 137/89*, Teddington, U.K., (Jan. 1989)
(Wichman, 1990) Wichman B.A., "Insecurities in Ada", in *Proceedings of the Ada-Europe Conference*, The Ada Companion Series, Cambridge University Press, (1990)

References used for Chapter 5

(Ada9x, 1990) *Ada 9X Project Revision Request Report* and *Supplement 1*, Office of the Under Secretary of Defense for Acquisition, Washington, D.C. 20301, (January 1990)
(Ada95, 1995) Intermetrics, *Ada Reference Manual, version 6.0*, ISO/IEC 8652:1995(E), US government, Ada Joint Program Office, (1995)
(Ada_com, 1989) "Approved Ada Language Commentaries", *SIGAda Letters Special Edition*, vol. IX, no. 3, ACM publisher, (Spring 1989)
(Ada_perf, 1990) "Ada Performance Issues", *SIGAda Letters Special Edition*, vol. X, no. 3, ACM publisher, (Winter 1990)
(Als_doc, 1989) "Design Specifications: Exception Handling" and "Module Implementation Specification: Exception Handling", *ALSYS*, (Dec. 1989)
(Arinc651, 1990) "Design guidance for Integrated Modular Avionics", Draft 5 of Project Paper 651, *Aeronautical Radio Inc.*, (Aug. 1990)
(ARM, 1983) *Reference Manual for the Ada programming language*, (ANSI/MIL-STD-1815A), US government, Ada Joint Program Office, (1983)

400 Bibliography

(As_1.b, 1990) "Executive Software Functional Requirements", *IMAGES Project report AS_003_OD_1.b*, Edition 1.0, (July 90)
(Baker, 1986a) Baker T.P., "An Improved Ada Runtime System Interface", *Report TR 86_07_05*, Computer Science Department, University of Washington, Seattle, (September 2, 1986)
(Baker, 1986b) Baker T.P., Riccardi, G.A., "Implementing Ada Exceptions", *IEEE Software*, IEEE publisher, (Sept. 1986), pp. 42-51
(Burns, 1989) Burns A., Wellings A., *Real-Time Systems and their Programming Languages*, Addison-Wesley, (1989)
(Cap_Alsys, 1990) Kermode J.P., Cleere J.F., "Catalogue of RTS Supported Features", CAPTEC, *IMAGES Project report CAP_001_WD_3.a*, Edition 2.0, (Nov. 1990)
(Cap_tld, 1990) Kermode J.P., "Catalogue of RTS Supported Features", CAPTEC, *IMAGES Project report CAP_001_WD_3.a*, Edition 1.0, (June 1990)
(Carid, 1988) *Catalogue of Ada Runtime Implementation Dependencies*, Labtek Corporation for U.S.Army, Woodbridge, CT 06525, (Oct. 1988)
(Cifo, 1987) "A Catalogue of Interface Features and Options for the Ada Runtime Environment", Release 2.0, proposed by *ARTEWG of SIGAda* (ACM), (Dec. 1987)
(Cri_ddc, 1990) Jorgensen C., "An Evaluation of the DDC_I DACS_80286 Ada Runtime System", CRI, *IMAGES Project report CRI_001_OD_3.a*, Edition 1.0E, (July 1990)
(Fdare, 1987) "A Framework for Describing Ada Runtime Environment", proposed by *ARTEWG of SIGAda* (ACM), (Oct. 1987)
(Mrtsi, 1988) "A Model Runtime System Interface for Ada", Version 2.3, *ARTEWG of SIGAda* (ACM), (Oct. 1988)
(Rationale, 1986) Ichbiah J.D., Barnes J.G.P., Firth R.J., Woodger M., "Rationale for the Design of the Ada Programming Language", *Alsys Editor*, 78170 La Celle Saint Cloud, France, (1986)
(Sherman, 1980) Sherman M., "An Ada Code Generator for VAX 11/780 with Unix", in *Proceedings of ACM SIGPLAN Symposium on Ada*, ACM publisher, (Nov. 1980), pp. 91-100
(Wichman, 1989) Wichman B.A., "Insecurities in the Ada programming language", *NPL report DITC 137/89, Teddington, U.K.*, (Jan. 1989)

References used for chapter 6

(Ada9x, 1990) *Ada 9X Project Revision Request Report* and *Supplement 1*, Office of the Under Secretary of Defense for Acquisition, Washington, D.C. 20301, (Jan. 1990)
(Cifo, 1991) "Catalogue of Interface Features and Options for the Ada Runtime Environment", Release 3.0, proposed by ARTEWG of SIGAda, in *SIGAda Letters*, vol. XI, no. 8, ACM publisher, (Fall 1991)
(Cui, 1990) Cui Q., Gannon J., "Data-Oriented Exception Handling in Ada", in *Proceedings of 1990 International Conference on Computer Languages*, IEEE publisher, (March 12-15, 1990), pp. 98-106
(Gauthier, 1989) Gauthier M., "The rules confirm the exception (especially in Ada)" (in French), *Génie Logiciel et Systèmes Experts*, no.17, EC2, (December 1989), pp. 20-34
(Helmbold, 1985) Helmbold D., Luckham D., "Debugging Ada Tasking Programs", *IEEE Software*, vol. 2, no. 2, IEEE publisher, (March 1985), pp. 47-57
(Ledgard, 1981) Ledgard H., *Ada; an introduction*, Springer-Verlag, (1981)
(Luckham, 1990) Luckham D., *Programming with Specifications. An Introduction to ANNA, a language for Specifying Ada Programs*, Springer-Verlag, (1990)
(Rationale, 1986) Ichbiah J.D., Barnes J.G.P., Firth R.J., Woodger M., "Rationale for the Design of the Ada Programming Language", *Alsys Editor*, 78170 La Celle Saint Cloud, France, (1986)

References used for appendix A

(Ada95, 1995) Intermetrics, *Ada Reference Manual, version 6.0*, ISO/IEC 8652:1995(E), US government, Ada Joint Program Office, (1995)
(Adamo, 1991) Adamo J.M., "Exception handling for a communicating-sequential-processes-based extension of C++", *Concurrency: Practice and Experience*, vol. 3, no. 1, (May 1991), pp. 15-41
(ARM, 1983) *Reference Manual for the Ada programming language*, (ANSI/MIL-STD-1815A), US government, Ada Joint Program Office, (1983)
(Booch, 1991) Booch G., Vilot M., "Designing with exceptions", *The C++ Report*, vol. 3, no. 5, (May 1991), pp. 11-14
(Bourne, 1982) Bourne S., *The Unix System*, Addison-Wesley, (1982)
(Branquart, 1982) Branquart P., Louis G., Wodon P., "Aspects of Chill, the CCITT language" (in French), *T.S.I.*, vol. 1, no. 1, (1982), pp. 43-52
(BSD4.2, 1988) *Sun OS Reference Manual*, Release 4.0, Sun Microsystem, (1988)
(de Bondelli, 1984) de Bondelli P., "Comparison between Ada & LTR3 languages concepts" (in French), in *Actes des journées Ada du 11 & 12 Décembre 1984*, BIGRE+GLOBULE, no. 42, AFCET, ISSN 0221_5225, (Dec. 1984), pp. 113-135
(Dony, 1989) Dony C., "The Benefits of object formalism to problems of exceptions management", in *Proceedings of the 2nd International Workshop on Software Engineering and its Applications*, Toulouse, vol. 1, EC2, (Dec. 1989), pp. 401-416
(Gauthier, 1989) Gauthier M., "The rules confirm the exception (especially in Ada)" (in French), *Génie Logiciel et Systèmes Experts*, no. 17, EC2, (Dec. 1989), pp. 20-34
(Goodenough, 1975) Goodenough J., "Exception Handling : Issues and a Proposed Notation", *Communications of the ACM*, vol. 18, no. 12, ACM publisher, (Dec. 1975), pp. 683-696
(Ichbiah, 1979) Ichbiah J.D. et al., "Rationale for the Design of the Ada Programming Language", *SIGPLAN Notices*, vol. 14, no.6, ACM publisher, (June 1979)
(Leverrand, 1982) *Le Langage Ada : Manuel d'Evaluation* (in French), Dunod Informatique, Bordas, (1982). Translated by J. Howlett, *Evaluating Ada*, North Oxford Academic, (1985)
(Liskov, 1979) Liskov B., Snyder A., "Exception handling in CLU", *IEEE Transactions on Software Engineering*, vol. SE-5, no. 6, IEEE publisher, (Nov. 1979), pp. 546-558
(LTR3, 1984) *LTR3 Reference Manual*, Centre Electronique de l'Armement, vol. 1: *The language* (in French), no. ICEV 2.84/41421, (Jan. 1984)
(Marpinard, 1993) Marpinard A., "Effets des Mécanismes d'Exception sur la Structure des Logiciels. Application aux Systèmes Ada Sûrs de Fonctionnement", (in French) Ph. D. Thesis, no. 232, INSA, Complexe Scientifique de Rangueil, 31077 Toulouse Cedex, France, (1993)
(Meyer, 1988) Meyer B., *Object-Oriented Software Construction*, Prentice Hall, (1988)
(PL/I, 1976) *OS PL/I Checkout and Optimizing Compilers : Language Reference Manual*, IBM GC33_0009-4, 5th edition, (1976)
(Rationale, 1986) Ichbiah J.D., Barnes J.G.P., Firth R.J., Woodger M., "Rationale for the Design of the Ada Programming Language", *Alsys Editor*, 78170 La Celle Saint Cloud, France, (1986)
(RMK386, 1988) *IRMK I.2 Real Time Kernel Reference Manual*, Intel Corporation, (1988)
(RMS68K, 1980) *M68000 Real-Time Multitasking Software User's Guide*, Motorola, (1980)
(RMX286-2/User, 1988) *Extended IRMX II.3, User Guides*, vol. 2, Intel Corporation, (1988)
(RMX286-3/System, 1988) *Extended IRMX II.3, System Calls*, vol. 3, Intel Corporation, (1988)
(RTU, 1986) Talbott S., *RTU Programming Manual*, MASCOMP, (1986)
(Shepherd, 1987) Shepherd R., "Security aspects of OCCAM2", *7th OCCAM Users Group and International Workshop on Parallel Programming on Transputer based Machines*, Grenoble, (Sep. 14-16, 1987), pp. 1-10
(System5, 1988) *Unix System V Programmer Reference Manual*, Prentice Hall, (1988)
(Veillon, 1971) Veillon F., Cagnat J., *PL/I Language Programming Tutorial* (in French), Collection U, Armand Colin, (1971)

Index

abnormal task   170
abnormal termination   135, 144, 148, 180
abort statement   170, 186
abstract data type   148
abstract formal state   127
abstract state   127
abstraction   9, 34, 97, 116, 127, 325
accept statement   170, 186, 198, 202, 208, 224, 272, 276, 282
acceptance test   103, 105, 121, 242
access   171
access on task   238
ACCESS_CHECK   168
ACCESS_ERROR   140
activation of task   170, 186
Ada   14, 122, 223, 322
Ada Abstract Machine   141, 166, 263
Ada features   76, 129, 142, 194, 203
Ada.Exceptions   137, 262, 277, 285
adaptive vote   111
address clause   196
aggregate   169, 217
allocator   170
alternate   103, 104, 242
ANNA   144, 180, 230
anonymous exception   148, 155, 164, 208
anticipate   133
application   27, 265
arc   61
array   142, 169, 206
ASSERT procedure   225
assertion   24, 46
ASSERTION package   226

assignment statement   169, 200, 207
association of a handler   138, 144, 155, 334
assumption   25, 46
Assumptions of Failures   88
automata   82
availability   4
avoidance   14, 32, 202

backup   98
backward recovery   99, 101, 255, 316
basic operation   142, 222
basis paths   85
behaviour   1, 78, 86, 127
black box testing   78, 119
block   202, 204, 206, 207, 272
branch   85
break down   35

cache   101
CALENDAR   172
CALLABLE   191
case statement   85, 207, 217, 225, 236
cause   60, 86, 139, 207, 209, 233
cause tree   57
Chill   322
choice_parameter_specification   182
circumstance   50
client   24, 35
Clu   322
code   141
comments   195, 205
common handling   181, 345

communication 106
compensate 98, 110, 111
compilation 140, 141, 206, 215, 263, 305
compiled approach 292
compiler 76, 91, 197, 201, 223
completion of task 170
complex 35
component 34, 46, 116, 127, 222
concatenation 169
connection to the exception handler 176
constant 204, 206, 216
constrained type 132
CONSTRAINT_ERROR 140, 142, 168, 267, 304, 324
constructor 142, 223
contract 23, 26, 36, 44, 64, 89, 90, 105, 128, 188
control 97, 138, 302, 314, 348
control graph 83
control path 85
control structure 206
controllability 118, 220
conversion 169, 171
correction 32, 97, 178, 315
correctness 2, 85
COUNT 191, 199
coverage rate 83, 119
creation process 5
cure 14

data structure 45, 223
deadlock 61, 71
debugging 86
declaration 159, 168, 202, 204, 272, 323
declare statement 156
default values 236
defensive programming 232
deferred constant 206
delay statement 224
dependability 2, 143, 193, 203
dependability of exception implementation 296
derived subprogram 217
derived type 217, 223
design model 64
design process 66
design review 65, 214
designer 25, 35
detection 32, 95, 232, 280
detection of predefined exception 167, 266

detection of user exception 172
diagnosis 97, 110, 178, 232
discrete type 223
discriminant 168, 171, 196, 225
DISCRIMINANT_CHECK 168
DISCRIMINANT_ERROR 140
DIVIDE_ERROR 140
division 169
DIVISION_CHECK 169
domino effect 107
dynamic analysis 70
dynamic life of exception 149
Dynamic Memory Management 268
dynamic object 170
dynamic properties 46
dynamic tracking 287, 295

E.M.F. 265
effect 60, 86, 140
Eiffel 322
elaboration 168, 170, 202, 272, 316
ELABORATION_CHECK 168, 170
embedded 95
end 206
entry 170, 188, 202, 204, 224
enumeration type 216
environment 171, 196, 197, 261, 295
erroneous execution 126, 187, 196, 268
erroneous situation 171
error definition 7, 132
error identity 100
evaluation 4, 82, 168, 200
Event Tree Method 57, 117
exception 16, 136, 207, 231, 321
exception associated by ... 160, 336
exception associated with ... 156, 334
exception detection 266
Exception Domain 131, 184, 187
Exception Domain of the implementation 135
exception handler 138, 340
exception handler case structure 287
exception handler context 287
exception handler: connection 176
exception handler: parameter 179, 343
exception handler: return 183
exception handler: visible variable 179, 341
Exception Management Function 265
exception mechanism 122, 177
exception monitor task 183, 248

exception number   139, 323
exception raising   220, 353
exception specification   143, 312, 328
Exception_Id   137, 285
Exception_Identity   138, 285
Exception_Message   179, 219, 277
Exception_Name   137, 183, 285
Exception_Occurrence   138, 182
exceptional state   132, 221
exceptions for testing   219
execution environment   91, 295
executive   141, 166, 197, 223, 263
exit statement   48, 77, 195, 204, 206
explicit detection   280
explicit vote   111
exponentiation   169
expression evaluation   168
external association of exception   158

F.M.E.A.   51, 117, 207
F.M.E.C.A.   54
F.T.M.   56, 71, 89, 209
failure   7
failure mode   52, 208
Failure Modes and Effects Analysis   51, 117, 207
family of entries   170
fault   6, 132, 139
fault analysis   117
fault avoidance   34, 202
fault detection   88
fault injection   120
fault location   89
fault removal   69, 215
fault tolerance   95, 117, 232
Fault Tree Method   56, 71, 89, 209
features of Ada   194, 203
features unsafe   195
float   198
formal methods   9
formal object   170
formal review   66
formal state   128, 185
format   204
forward recovery   99, 255
frame   97
function   1, 46, 86, 143, 170, 195
functional equivalence   78
functional testing   78, 93, 119

G.F.C.M.   54
genericity   150, 152, 161, 170, 205
global variable   195
goto statement   48, 138, 176, 195, 236
guarantee   24
guideline   37

handler: association   138, 144, 334
handler: common part   181, 345
handler: interaction with the erroneous frame 183, 348
handler: test   220
handling   95, 110, 178, 181, 340
handling by default   165, 340
hardware   91, 141
hazard   62
hazardous features   196, 218
Heap Management function   268
hidden clauses   48, 77
hierarchy of abstractions   35, 99, 116, 302
hierarchy of errors   302
homology rule   170

identification of exception   283
identification technique   82
identifier   204
identifier evaluation   168
Identity   137
if statement   48, 71, 85
implementation   34, 127, 130, 142, 145, 187, 197, 209, 296
implementation abstraction   134, 144, 173
implementation dependent feature   171
implementation exceptional state   185
implementation formal state   134
implementation invariant   135, 173
implementation of Ada exception mechanism   261
implementation Standard Domain   185
implementation state   189, 221
implementer   35
implicit detection   280
in mode parameter   76, 129, 142, 171, 204, 217, 224, 236
in out mode parameter   132, 180
incorrect order dependence   171, 187, 196, 268
index   142, 168
INDEX_CHECK   168

INDEX_ERROR 140
inhibit 97
initialized object 168, 196
INLINE 214
input 76
inspection 66
instantiation 170, 205
integer type 169, 197
integration 115
interface 276
internal association of exception 156
internal state 28, 134
interpretation 12
interpretive approach 290
interrupt 196
invariant 28, 44, 70, 75, 88, 90, 105, 127, 144, 189, 227
invariant of implementation 135, 173

kernel 116, 321

language features 76, 129, 143, 321
LENGTH_CHECK 169
level of abstraction 35, 46, 97, 116
library unit 202, 272
limited private type 206, 217
location of an error 97, 232
loop statement 48, 85, 88, 204, 206, 217
LTR3 322

main program 202, 272
maintainability 4, 294
maintenance 104
marking 61
masking 110, 167, 235, 332
masking of user exception 173
master 6
MDT 5
measurement 4, 120
memory size 142, 268
microprocessor 116
misunderstanding 12
mod operation 169
mode of parameters 142, 171, 180, 201, 204, 217, 224, 236, 255, 313
module 127
monitor task 188, 248
MTBF 5
MTTF 4

MTTR 4
MUT 5
mutation 88, 120

N-Self-Checking 112
N-version programming 110, 245
name of identifiers 204
new statement 170
non-adaptive vote 111
non-association of a handler 164
normal termination 135
numbers 197
numeric type 169
NUMERIC_ERROR 142, 169, 267, 324
nurse 14

obligation 25
observability 88, 118, 133, 221
occurrence of an error 280
occurrence of an exception 138
Omega Strategy 174
operation 95
operation evaluation 168
optimization 142, 201
or operation 201
oracle 81, 90
order of evaluation 201
others 150
out mode parameter 76, 129, 142, 171, 180, 201, 204, 217, 224, 255, 313
output 76
OVERFLOW 140
OVERFLOW_CHECK 169

package 45, 143, 202, 205, 206, 216, 231, 272
parameter 45, 76, 129, 142, 170, 181, 204, 217, 224, 231, 236
parameter mode 217, 255, 313
parameter passing mechanism 171, 196
path 85
perception 96, 164, 232
performance 104, 114, 120, 167, 214, 294, 334
permanent fault 98
Petri net 61, 71, 212
PL/I 322
place 61
portability 197, 293
pragma INLINE 214

pragma PRE_ELABORATE 299, 316
pragma SUPPRESS 126, 167, 171, 196, 281, 294
pre-emption 187
PRE_ELABORATE 299, 316
PRED 168
predefined exception 139, 141, 166, 186, 207, 212, 213, 222, 266, 303, 323
predefined type 222
prefix 168
prevent 14
priority 346
private type 206, 217
probability 4, 81
PROGRAM_ERROR 143, 168, 170, 187, 268, 324
programmer's work 214
programming language 129
propagation 8, 99, 138, 158, 164, 178, 180, 184, 289, 302, 356
property 75, 90, 180, 188, 222
pseudo-random testing 81

qualified expression 169
quality 6, 66, 85, 93

R.T.S. 265
raise statement 172, 220
Raise_Exception 179, 219, 277
raising 138, 166, 220, 353
raising delayed 174
random testing 81
range 168, 206, 207, 223
RANGE_CHECK 168
RANGE_ERROR 140
rare situation 136, 145, 220
readability 203, 233
real 169
record 168, 196, 217
recovery 99, 101, 108, 255, 289
recovery blocks 103, 242
recovery cache 101, 121
recovery point 101, 255, 316
recursivity 238
reliability 4
reliance 2, 23, 44, 120, 124, 128, 189
rem operation 169
removal 14, 32, 69, 215
renames 100, 152, 204, 306

rendezvous 106, 170, 186, 198, 208, 238
replication 98
representation clause 171
requirement 27, 65
Reraise_Occurrence 183
resume mode 184
resumption mode 99, 184, 316, 351
retry mode 107, 184, 236, 351
return statement 77, 143, 169, 170, 177, 195
reuse 193, 206
review 64, 214
risks associated with Ada features 194
RMK386 322
RMS68K 322
RMX286 322
robustness 120
role 64
rule 27, 45, 52
rule book 37
run-time environment 91, 166, 181, 196, 197, 218, 223, 261
Run-Time System 265

safe state 99
SAFE-ADA 124
safety 4
scope 148, 207, 331
select statement 170, 187, 198, 224
self-checked 106
separate 216
service 2
shared variable 171, 196
side effect 195
size of arrays 169
spare frame 98
SPARK 124
specialization 205
specification 1, 27, 127, 140, 142, 207
specification abstraction 144
specification formal state 134
specification invariant 130, 136, 140
specification of exception 143, 312, 328
specification of subprogram 205, 216, 224
specification of task 188
specification state 222
Stack Management function 268
Standard Domain 184
Standard Domain of the implementation 135
Standard Domain: task 187

starvation 121
state 44, 63, 128, 138
statement testing 84
statement: abort 170, 186
statement: accept 170, 186, 208, 224, 272, 276, 282
statement: assignement 169, 200, 207
statement: case 85, 207, 217, 225, 236
statement: declare 156
statement: delay 224
statement: exit 48, 77, 195, 204, 206
statement: goto 48, 176, 195, 236
statement: if 48, 71, 85
statement: loop 48, 85, 88, 204, 206, 217
statement: new 170
statement: raise 172, 220
statement: return 77, 143, 169, 170, 177, 195
statement: select 170, 187, 198, 224
statement: while 72, 88, 195
static analysis 69, 70
static definition of exception 148
static mapping 288, 295
static properties 46
step 35, 46
STORAGE_CHECK 170
STORAGE_ERROR 140, 142, 171, 268, 324
strong propagation 145
structural testing 83, 93, 119
structure 34, 83, 86
structured design 48, 177
structured functional analysis 86
structured programming 176
style of programming 218
subprogram 48, 129, 143, 170, 202, 204, 214, 231, 272
subprogram specification 205, 216, 224
subtype 142, 168, 196, 205, 223
SUCC 168
SUPPRESS 126, 167, 171, 196, 281, 294
synchronization 106

task 71, 106, 121, 170, 186, 196, 202, 204, 208, 214, 224, 231, 238, 272, 358
task activation 170, 186
task completion 170
task management 198
task specification 188
task: predefined exception 186
task: user exception 187
TASKING_ERROR 170, 186, 191, 202, 268, 324

termination mode 109, 176, 183, 351
termination state 135
test of exception handlers 220
test sequence 70, 79
test sequence evaluation 93
test sequence validation 87
testing 70, 118
time 64, 90, 105, 106, 112, 120
time replication 98
TIME_ERROR 172
TIME_OF 172
token 61
tolerance 14, 32, 95, 115, 232
transient fault 98
transition 61
translation 12
trial set 83
TSL 189, 230
type 45, 76, 142, 168, 205, 206, 214, 216, 217, 223, 225, 230
typing errors 206

UNCHECKED_CONVERSION 196
UNCHECKED_DEALLOCATION 196
unconstrained record 171, 196
UNDERFLOW 140
unit test 221
Unix 322
unportable features 197
unsafe features 195
user exception 143, 172, 187, 208, 213, 304, 327

VAL 168
validation 37, 56, 93
VALUE 168
var 76
variant component 168
verification 36, 93
visibility 148, 331, 341
vote 111

walkthrough 66
weak exception annotation 180
while statement 72, 88, 195
white box testing 83, 119

Zero-Exception technique 161